The Gallup Poll

Public Opinion 1978

GEORGE H. GALLUP, founder and chairman of the
American Institute of Public Opinion (The Gallup Poll)
received a Ph.D. in psychology from the University of
Iowa in 1928. From his undergraduate days he has had
three prime interests: survey research, public opinion,
and politics.
Dr. Gallup is the author of many articles on public
opinion and advertising research and he has published
the following books: *The Pulse of Democracy* (1940);
A Guide Book to Public Opinion Polls (1944); *The Gallup
Political Almanac* (1952); *Secrets of Long Life* (1960);
The Miracle Ahead (1964); *The Sophisticated Poll
Watcher's Guide* (Rev. 1976); *The Gallup Poll,
1935–1971* (1972); and *The Gallup Poll: Public Opinion, 1972–1977* (1978).

The
Gallup
Poll.

Public Opinion 1978

Dr. George H. Gallup
Founder and Chairman
American Institute of Public Opinion

  Scholarly Resources Inc.
Wilmington, Delaware

ACKNOWLEDGMENTS

I have incurred many agreeable debts of gratitude in the preparation of this volume. I particularly wish to acknowledge the assistance of: George Gallup, Jr., president of the Gallup Poll; Alec M. Gallup, vice president, The Gallup Organization, Inc.; Tom Reinken, editor of the Gallup Poll; James Shriver, associate editor of the Gallup Poll; and Professor Fred. L. Israel, City College of New York.

Scholarly Resources Inc.
104 Greenhill Avenue
Wilmington, Delaware 19805

Distributed in the United Kingdom and Commonwealth
by George Prior Associated Publishers, Ltd.
37-41 Bedford Row, London WC1R 4JH, England

Library of Congress Cataloging in Publication Data
Main entry under title:

The Gallup poll: public opinion, 1978.

    Includes index.
    1. Public opinion polls—United States.
2. Public opinion—United States.   I. Gallup,
George Horace, 1901–
HN90.P8G34   301.15′4′0973   79-11610
ISBN 0-8420-2159-0

CONTENTS

Preface vii
Design of the Sample xxxix
Record of Gallup
    Poll Accuracy xliii
Chronology xlv
Polls 1
Index. 277

PREFACE

[This introductory essay by Dr. George Gallup is excerpted from a section entitled "How Polls Operate" from his book *The Sophisticated Poll Watcher's Guide.*]

THE CROSS-SECTION

The most puzzling aspect of modern polls to the layman is the cross-section or sample. How, for example, is it possible to interview 1,000 or 2,000 persons out of a present electorate of about 150 million and be sure that the relatively few selected will reflect accurately the attitudes, interests, and behavior of the entire population of voting age?

Unless the poll watcher understands the nature of sampling and the steps that must be taken to assure its representativeness, the whole operation of scientific polling is likely to have little meaning, and even less significance, to him.

With the goal in mind of making the process understandable, and at the risk of being too elementary, I have decided to start with some simple facts about the nature of sampling—a procedure, I might add, that is as old as man himself.

When a housewife wants to test the quality of the soup she is making, she tastes only a teaspoonful or two. She knows that if the soup is thoroughly stirred, one teaspoonful is enough to tell her whether she has the right mixture of ingredients.

In somewhat the same manner, a bacteriologist tests the quality of water in a reservoir by taking a few samples, maybe not more than a few drops from a half-dozen different points. He knows that pollutants of a chemical or bacteriological nature will disperse widely and evenly throughout a body of water. He can be certain that his tiny sample will accurately reflect the presence of harmful bacteria or other pollutants in the whole body of water.

Perhaps a more dramatic example is to be found in the blood tests given routinely in clinics and hospitals. The medical technician requires only a few drops of blood to discover abnormal conditions. He does not have to draw a quart of blood to be sure that his sample is representative.

These examples, of course, deal with the physical world. People are not as much alike as drops of water, or of blood. If they were, then the world of individuals could be sampled by selecting only a half-dozen persons anywhere. People are widely different because their experiences are widely different.

Interestingly, this in itself comes about largely through a sampling process. Every human being gathers his views about people and about life by his own sampling. And, it should be added, he almost invariably ends with a distorted picture because his experience is unique. For example, he draws conclusions about "California" by looking out of his car or airplane window, by observing the people he meets at the airport or on the streets, and by his treatment in restaurants, hotels, and other places. This individual has no hesitancy in telling his friends back home what California is really like—although his views, obviously, are based upon very limited sampling.

The Black man, living his life in the ghetto, working under conditions that are often unpleasant and for wages that are likely to be less than those of the white man who lives in the suburban community, arrives at his own views about racial equality. His sample, likewise, is unrepresentative even though it may be typical of fellow Blacks living under the same conditions. By the same token, well-to-do whites living in the suburbs with the advantages of a college education and travel have equally distorted views of equality. These distortions come about because their sampling, likewise, is based upon atypical experiences.

Although every individual on the face of the earth is completely unique, in the mass he does conform to certain patterns of behavior. No one has expressed this better than A. Conan Doyle, author of the Sherlock Holmes series. He has one of his characters make this observation:

> While the individual man is an insoluble puzzle, in the aggregate he becomes a mathematical certainty. You can never foretell what any one man will do, but you can say with precision what an average number will be up to. Individuals vary, but averages remain constant.

Whenever the range of differences is great—either in nature or man—the sampling process must be conducted with great care to make certain that all major variations or departures from the norm are embraced.

Since some differences that exist may be unknown to the researcher, his best procedure to be sure of representativeness is to select samples from the population by a chance or random process. Only if he follows this procedure can he be reasonably certain that he has covered all major variations that exist.

This principle can be illustrated in the following manner. Suppose that a government agency, such as the Bureau of the Census, maintained an up-to-date alphabetical list of the names of all persons living in the United States eighteen years of age and older. Such a file, at the present time, would include approximately 148 million names.

Now suppose that a survey organization wished to draw a representative sample of this entire group, a sample, say of 10,000 persons. Such a representative sample could be selected by dividing 150,000,000 by 10,000—which produces a figure of 15,000. If the researcher goes systematically through the entire file and records the name of every 15,000th listed, he can be sure that his sample is representative.

The researcher will find that this chance selection, in the manner described, has produced almost the right percentage of Catholics and Protestants, the proper proportion of persons in each age and educational level. The distribution of persons by occupation, sex, race, and income should be broadly representative and consistent with the best available census data. It is important, however, to emphasize the words "broadly representative." The sample—even of 10,000— most likely would not include a single person belonging to the Fox Indian tribe or a single resident of Magnolia, Arkansas. It might not include a single citizen of Afghanistan heritage or a single Zoroastrian.

For the purposes served by polls, a sample normally needs to be only broadly representative. A study could be designed to discover the attitudes of American Indians, in which case the Fox Indians should be properly represented. And a specially designed study of Arkansas would likely embrace interviews with residents of Magnolia.

But for all practical purposes, individuals making up these groups constitute such a small part of the whole population of the United States that their inclusion, or exclusion, makes virtually no difference in reaching conclusions about the total population or even of important segments of the population.

Unfortunately, there is no master file in the United States of persons over the age of eighteen that is available to the researcher. Moreover, even a few weeks after the decennial census such a file would be out of date. Some citizens would have died, some would have moved, and still others would have reached the age of eighteen.

Unlike some European countries, no attempt is made in the United States to keep voter registration lists complete and up to date. Because of this failure to maintain accurate lists of citizens and of registered voters, survey organizations are forced to devise their own systems to select samples that are representative of the population to be surveyed.

Any number of sampling systems can be invented so long as one all-important goal is kept in mind. Whatever the system, the end result of its use must be to give every individual an equal opportunity of being selected. Actually, not every individual will have an equal chance, since some persons will be hospitalized, some in mental or penal institutions, and some in the armed forces in foreign lands. But while these individuals help make up the total United States citizenry, most are disenfranchised by the voting laws of the various states or find difficulty in implementing their opinions at election time. Typically, therefore, they are not included in survey cross-sections.

The Gallup Poll has designed its sample by choosing at random not individuals as described previously, but small districts such as census tracts, census enumeration districts, and townships. A random selection of these small geographical areas provides a good starting point for building a national sample.

The United States population is first arranged by states in geographical order and then within the individual states by districts, also in geographical order. A sampling interval number is determined by dividing the total population of the nation by the number of interviewing locations deemed adequate for a general purpose sample of the population eighteen years of age and older. In the case of the Gallup Poll sample, the number of locations, so selected, is approximately 300.

At the time of this writing, the population of the United States eighteen years and older is approximately 150,000,000. Dividing 150,000,000 by 300 yields a sampling interval of 500,000. A random starting number is then chosen between 1 and 500,000 in order to select the first location. The remaining 299 locations are determined by the simple process of adding 500,000 successively until all 300 locations are chosen throughout the nation.

A geographical sampling unit having been designated, the process of selection is continued by choosing at random a given number of individuals within each unit. Suppose that the sampling unit is a census tract in Scranton, Pennsylvania. Using block statistics, published by the Census Bureau for cities of this size, a block, or a group of blocks, within the tract is chosen by a random method analogous to the procedure used to select the location.

Within a block or groups of blocks so selected, the interviewer is given a random starting point. Proceeding from this point, the interviewer meets his assignment by taking every successive occupied dwelling. Or, as an alternative procedure, he can be instructed to take every third or every fifth or every tenth dwelling unit and to conduct interviews in these designated homes.

In this systematic selection plan, the choice of the dwelling is taken out of the hands of the interviewer. As a reminder to the reader, it should be pointed out that the area or district has been selected by a random procedure; next, the dwelling within the district has been chosen at random. All that now remains is to select, at random, the individual to be interviewed within the household.

This can be done in several ways. A list can be compiled by the interviewer of all persons of voting age residing within each home. From such a household list, he can then select individuals to be interviewed by a random method. Ingenious methods are employed to accomplish this end. One survey organization in Europe, for example, instructs the interviewer to talk to the person in the household whose birthday falls on the nearest date.

Now the process is complete. The district has been selected at random; the dwelling unit within the district has been selected at random; and the individual within the dwelling unit has been selected at random. The end result is that every individual in the nation of voting age has had an equal chance of being selected.

This is the theory. In actual practice, problems arise, particularly in respect to the last stage of the process. The dwelling unit chosen may be vacant, the individual selected within a household may not be at home when the interviewer calls. Of course, the interviewer can return the next day; in fact, he or she can make a half-dozen call backs without finding the person. Each call back adds that much to the cost of the survey and adds, likewise, to the time required to complete the study.

Even with a dozen call backs, some individuals are never found and are never interviewed. They may be in the hospital, visiting relatives, on vacation, on a business trip, not at home except at very late hours, too old or too ill to be interviewed—and a few may even refuse to be interviewed.

Since no nationwide survey has ever reached every person designated by any random selection procedure, special measures must be employed to deal with this situation. In the early 1950s, the Gallup Poll introduced a system called Time-Place interviewing. After an intensive study of the time of day when different members of a household are at home, an interviewing plan was devised that enabled interviewers to reach the highest proportion of persons at the time of their first call.

Since most persons are employed outside the home, interviewing normally must be done in the late afternoon and evening hours, and on weekends. These are the times when men, and especially younger men, are likely to be at home and therefore available to be interviewed.

In various nations, survey organizations are working out new ways to meet this problem of the individual selected for the sample who is not at home. These new procedures may meet more perfectly the ideal requirements of random sampling.

Many ardent advocates of the procedure described as "quota sampling" are still to be found. This, it should be pointed out, was the system generally employed by the leading survey organizations in the pre-1948 era.

The quota system is simplicity itself. If the state of New York has 10% of the total population of the United States, then 10% of all interviews must come from this state. In the case of a national sample of 10,000, this would mean 1,000 interviews.

Going one step further, since New York City contains roughly 40% of the population of the state, then 40% of the 1,000 interviews must be allocated to New York City, or 400. And since Brooklyn has roughly a third of the total population of New York City, a third of the 400 interviews, or 133, must be made in this borough. In similar fashion, all of the 1,000 interviews made in the state of New York can be distributed among the various cities, towns, and rural areas. Other states are dealt with in similar fashion.

Making still further use of census data, the interviews to be made in each city, town, or rural areas can be assigned on an occupational basis: so many white-collar workers, so many blue-collar workers, so many farmers, so many business and professional people, so many retired persons, and so many on the welfare rolls. The allocation can also be made on the basis of rents paid. The interviewer, for example, may be given a "quota" of calls to be made in residential areas with the highest rental values, in areas with medium priced rentals, and in low rental areas.

Typically, in the quota sampling system, the survey organization predetermines the number of men and women and the age, the income, the occupation, and the race of the individuals assigned to each interviewer.

In setting such quotas, however, important factors may be overlooked. In 1960, for example, a quota sample that failed to assign the right proportion of Catholic voters would have miscalculated John Kennedy's political strength. An individual's religious beliefs, obviously, cannot be ascertained by his appearance or by the place where he dwells; this applies to other factors as well.

Not only do theoretical considerations fault the quota system but so do the problems that face the interviewer. When the selection of individuals is left to him, he tends to seek out the easiest-to-interview respondents. He is prone to avoid the worst slum areas, and consequently he turns up with interviews that are likely to be skewed on the high income and educational side. Typically, a quick look at the results of quota sampling will reveal too many persons with a college education, too many persons with average and above average incomes, and in political polls, too many Republicans. Therefore, one of the many advantages of the random procedure is that the selection of respondents is taken out of the hands of the interviewer. In the random method, the interviewer is told exactly where to go and when to go.

Another consideration with cross-sections is keeping them up to date. Although America's population is highly mobile, fortunately for polltakers the basic structure of society changes little. Perhaps the greatest change in America in recent years has been the rising level of education. In 1935, when the Gallup Poll first published poll results, only 7.2% of the adult population had attended college for one year or more. Today that figure is 27%.

How does a research organization know that the sample it has designed meets proper standards? Normally, examination of the socioeconomic data gathered by the interviewer at the end of each interview provides the answer. As the completed interview forms are returned from the field to the Princeton office of the Gallup Poll, the facts from each are punched into IBM cards. In addition to the questions that have dealt with issues and other matters of interest, the interviewer has asked each person to state his occupation, age, how far he went in school, his religious preference, whether he owns or rents his dwelling, and many other questions of a factual nature.

Since the Census Bureau Current Population Surveys provide data on each one of these factors, even a hasty examination will tell whether the cross-section is fairly accurate—that is, whether the important factors line up properly with the known facts, specifically:
—the educational level of those interviewed
—the age level
—the income level
—the proportion of males to females
—the distribution by occupations

—the proportion of whites to nonwhites
—the geographical distribution of cases
—the city-size distribution.

Typically, when the educational level is correct (that is, when the sample has included the right proportion of those who have attended college, high school, grade school, or no school), when the geographical distribution is right and all areas of the nation have been covered in the correct proportion, when the right proportion of those in each income level has been reached, and the right percentages of whites and nonwhites and of men and women are included—then usually other factors tend to fall in line. These include such factors as religious preference, political party preference, and most other factors that bear upon voting behavior, buying behavior, tastes, interests, and the like.

After checking all of the above "controls," it would be unusual to find that every group making up the total population is represented in the sample in the exact percentage that it should be. Some groups may be slightly larger or smaller than they should be. The nonwhite population eighteen years and older, which makes up 11% of the total population, may be found to be less, or more, than this percentage of the returned interviews. Those who have attended high school in the obtained interviews may number 58%, when actually the true figure should be 54%.

Ways have been developed to correct situations such as these that arise out of the over-representation or under-representation of given groups. The sample can be balanced, that is, corrected so that each group is included in the proportion it represents in the total population. When this procedure is followed, the assumption is made that persons within each group who are interviewed are representative of the group in question. But there are obvious limitations to this. If only a few persons are found in a given category, then the danger is always present that they may not be typical or representative of the people who make up this particular group or cell.

On the whole, experience has shown that this process of weighting by the computer actually does produce more accurate samples. Normally, results are changed by only negligible amounts—seldom by more than 1 or 2 percentage points.

A persistent misconception about polling procedures is that a new sample must be designed for measuring each major issue. Actually, Gallup Poll cross-sections are always based upon samples of the entire voting age population. Every citizen has a right to voice his opinion on every issue and to have it recorded. For this reason, all surveys of public opinion seek to reach a representative cross-section of the entire population of voting age.

Some people ask if we go back to the same persons with different polls. The answer, in the case of the Gallup Poll, is "no"; the same person is not interviewed again. Some survey research is based upon fixed cross-sections or "panels." The same persons are reinterviewed from time to time to measure shifts in opinion.

There are certain advantages to this system—it is possible to determine to what extent overall changes cloak individual changes. But a practical disadvantage is that the size of the sample remains fixed. Unless the panel is very large, reliable information cannot be produced for smaller subgroups. In the case of the Gallup Poll, the same question can be placed on any number of surveys and the total sample expanded accordingly, since the same persons are not reinterviewed.

Panels have other limitations. One has to do with determining the level of knowledge. Having asked a citizen what he knows about a certain issue in the first interview, he may very well take the trouble to read about it when he sees an article later in his newspaper or magazine. There is, moreover, a widespread feeling among researchers that the repeated interviewing of the same person tends to make him a "pro" and to render him atypical for this reason. But the evidence is not clear-cut on this point. The greatest weakness, perhaps, is that panels tend to fall apart; persons change their place of residence and cannot be found for a second or subsequent measurement; some refuse to participate more than once and must be replaced by substitutes.

THE SIZE OF SAMPLES

When the subject of public-opinion polls comes up, many people are quick to say that they do not know of anyone who has ever been polled.

The likelihood of any single individual, eighteen years of age or older, being polled in a sample of 1,500 persons is about one chance in 90,000. With samples of this size, and with the frequency that surveys are scheduled by the Gallup Poll, the chance that any single individual will be interviewed—even during a period of two decades—is less than one in 200.

An early experience of mine illustrates dramatically the relative unimportance of numbers in achieving accuracy in polls and the vital importance of reaching a true cross-section of the population sampled.

In the decade preceding the 1936 presidential election, the *Literary Digest* conducted straw polls during elections, with a fair measure of success. The *Literary Digest*'s polling procedure consisted of mailing out millions of postcard ballots to persons whose names were found in telephone directories or on lists of automobile owners.

The system worked so long as voters in average and above-average income groups were as likely to vote Democratic as Republican; and conversely, those in the lower income brackets—the have-nots—were as likely to vote for either party's candidate for the presidency.

With the advent of the New Deal, however, the American electorate became sharply stratified, with many persons in the above average income groups who had been Democrats shifting to the Republican banner, and those below average to the Democratic.

Obviously, a polling system that reached telephone subscribers and automobile owners—the perquisites of the better-off in this era—was certain to overestimate Republican strength in the 1936 election. And that is precisely what did happen. The *Literary Digest*'s final preelection poll showed Landon winning by 57% and Franklin D. Roosevelt losing with 43% of the two-party popular vote.

Landon did not win, as everyone knows. In fact, Roosevelt won by a whopping majority—62.5% to Landon's 37.5%. The error, more than 19 percentage points, was one of the greatest in polling history.

The outcome of the election spelled disaster for the *Literary Digest*'s method of polling, and was a boon to the new type of scientific sampling that was introduced for the first time in that presidential election by my organization, Elmo Roper's, and Archibald Crossley's.

The *Literary Digest* had mailed out 10,000,000 postcard ballots—enough to reach approximately one family in every three at that point in history. A total of 2,376,523 persons took the trouble to mark their postcard ballots and return them.

Experiments with new sampling techniques had been undertaken by my organization as early as 1933. By 1935 the evidence was clear-cut that an important change had come about in the party orientation of voters—that the process of polarization had shifted higher income voters to the right, lower income voters to the left.

When the presidential campaign opened in 1936, it was apparent that the *Literary Digest*'s polling method would produce an inaccurate figure. Tests indicated that a large majority of individuals who were telephone subscribers preferred Landon to FDR, while only 18% of those persons on relief rolls favored Landon.

To warn the public of the likely failure of the *Literary Digest*, I prepared a special newspaper article that was widely printed on July 12, 1936—at the beginning of the campaign. The article stated that the *Literary Digest* would be wrong in its predictions and that it would probably show Landon winning with 56% of the popular vote to 44% for Roosevelt. The reasons why the poll would go wrong were spelled out in detail.

Outraged, the *Literary Digest* editor wrote: "Never before has anyone foretold what our poll was going to show even before it started . . . Our fine statistical friend (George Gallup) should be advised that the Digest would carry on with those old fashioned methods that have produced correct forecasts exactly one hundred percent of the time."

When the election had taken place, our early assessment of what the *Literary Digest* poll would find proved to be almost a perfect prediction of the *Digest*'s final results—actually within 1 percentage point. While this may seem to have been a foolhardy stunt, actually there was little risk. A sample of only 3,000 postcard ballots had been mailed by my office to the same lists of persons who received the

Literary Digest ballot. Because of the workings of the laws of probability, that 3,000 sample should have provided virtually the same result as the *Literary Digest*'s 2,376,523 which, in fact, it did.

Through its own polling, based upon modern sampling procedures, the Gallup Poll, in the 1936 election, reported that the only sure states for Landon were Maine, Vermont, and New Hampshire. The final results showed Roosevelt with 56% of the popular vote to 44% for Landon. The error was 6.8 percentage points, the largest ever made by the Gallup Poll. But because it was on the "right" side, the public gave us full credit, actually more than we deserved.

The *Literary Digest* is not the only poll that has found itself to be on the "wrong" side. All polls, at one time or another, find themselves in this awkward position, including the Gallup Poll in the election of 1948. Ironically, the error in 1936—a deviation of 6.8 percentage points from the true figure—was greater than the error in 1948—5.4 percentage points. But the public's reaction was vastly different.

The failure of polls to have the winning candidate ahead in final results is seldom due to the failure of the poll to include enough persons in its sample. Other factors are likely to prove to be far more important, as will be pointed out later.

Examination of probability tables quickly reveals why polling organizations can use relatively small samples. But first the reader should be reminded that sampling human beings can never produce findings that are *absolutely* accurate except by mere chance, or luck. The aim of the researcher is to come as close as possible to absolute accuracy.

Since money and time are always important considerations in survey operations, the goal is to arrive at sample sizes that will produce results within acceptable margins of error. Fortunately, reasonably accurate findings can be obtained with surprisingly small samples.

Again, it is essential to distinguish between theory and practice. Probability tables are based upon mathematical theory. In actual survey work, these tables provide an important guide, but they can't be applied too literally.

With this qualification in mind, the size of samples to be used in national surveys can now be described. Suppose, for example, that a sample comprises only 600 individuals. What is the theoretical margin of error? If the sample is a perfectly drawn random sample, then the chances are 95 in 100 that the results of a poll of 600 in which those interviewed divide 60% in favor, 40% opposed (or the reverse) will be within 4 percentage points of the true figure; that is, the division in the population is somewhere between 56% and 64% in favor. The odds are even that the error will be less than 2 percentage points—between 58% and 62% in favor, 42% to 38% opposed.

What this means, in the example cited above, is that the odds are 19 to 1 that in repeated samplings the figure for the issue would vary in the case of those favoring the issue from 56% to 64%; the percentage of those opposed would vary between 44% and 36% in repeated samples. So, on the basis of a national sample of only 600 cases, one could say that the odds are great that the addition of many cases—

even millions of cases—would not likely change the majority side to the minority side.

Now, if this sample is doubled in size—from 600 to 1,200—the error factor using the 95 in 100 criterion or confidence level is decreased from 4 percentage points to 2.8 percentage points; if it is doubled again—from 1,200 to 2,400—there is a further decrease—from 2.8 to 2.0, always assuming a mathematically random sample.

Even if a poll were to embrace a total of 2,000,000 individuals, there would still be a chance of error, although tiny. Most survey organizations try to operate within an error range of 4 percentage points at the 95 in 100 confidence level. Accuracy greater than this is not demanded on most issues, nor in most elections, except, of course, those that are extremely close.

Obviously, in many fields an error factor as large as 4 percentage points would be completely unacceptable. In fact, in measuring the rate of unemployment, the government and the press place significance on a change as small as 0.1%. At present, unemployment figures are based upon nationwide samples carried out by the U.S. Bureau of Labor Statistics in the same general manner as polls are conducted. The government bases its findings on samples of some 50,000 persons. But samples even of this size are not sufficient to warrant placing confidence in a change as small as 0.1%. And yet such a change is often headlined on the front pages as indicating a real and significant change in the employment status of the nation.

Even if one were totally unfamiliar with the laws of probability, empirical evidence would suffice to demonstrate that the amassing of thousands of cases does not change results except to a minor extent.

An experiment conducted early in the Gallup Poll's history will illustrate this point. At the time—in the middle 1930s—the National Recovery Act (N.R.A.) was a hotly debated issue. Survey results were tabulated as the ballots from all areas of the United States were returned. The figures below are those actually obtained as each lot of new ballots was tabulated.

NUMBER OF RETURNED BALLOTS	PERCENT VOTING IN FAVOR OF THE N.R.A.
First 500	54.9%
First 1,000	53.9
First 5,000	55.4
First 10,000	55.4
First 30,000	55.5

From these results it can be seen that if only 500 ballots had been received, the figure would have differed little from the final result. In fact the greatest difference found in the whole series is only 1.6 percentage points from the final result.

This example represents a typical experience of researchers in this field. But one precaution needs to be observed. The returns must come from a representative sample of the population being surveyed; otherwise they could be as misleading as trying to project the results of a national election from the vote registered late in the afternoon of election day in a New Hampshire village.

The theoretical error, as noted earlier, can be used only as a guide. The expected errors in most surveys are usually somewhat larger. In actual survey practice, some sample design elements tend to reduce the range of error, as stratification does; some tend to increase the range of error as, for example, clustering. But these are technical matters to be dealt with in textbooks on statistics.

Survey organizations should, on the basis of their intimate knowledge of their sampling procedures and the analysis of their data, draw up their own tables of suggested tolerances to enable laymen to interpret their survey findings intelligently.

The normal sampling unit of the Gallup Poll consists of 1,500 individuals of voting age, that is, eighteen years and over. A sample of this size gives reasonable assurance that the margin of error for results representing the entire country will be less than 3 percentage points based on the factor of size alone.

The margin for sampling error is obviously greater for subgroups. For example, the views of individuals who have attended college are frequently reported. Since about one-fourth of all persons over eighteen years have attended college, the margin of error must be computed on the basis of one-fourth the total sample of 1,500, or 375. Instead of a margin of error of 3 percentage points, the error factor increases to 6 or 7 percentage points in the typical cluster sample.

In dealing with some issues, interest focuses on the views of subgroups such as Blacks, labor union members, Catholics, or young voters—all representing rather small segments of the total population. Significant findings for these subgroups are possible only by building up the size of the total sample.

This can be done in the case of the Gallup Poll by including the same question or questions in successive surveys. Since different, but comparable, persons are interviewed in each study, subgroup samples can be enlarged accordingly. Thus, in a single survey approximately 165 Blacks and other nonwhites would be interviewed in a sample of 1,500, since they constitute 11% of the total voting-age population. On three successive surveys a total of 495 would be reached—enough to provide a reasonably stable base to indicate their views on important political and social issues.

Since much interest before and after elections is directed toward the way different groups in the population vote, it has been the practice of the Gallup Poll to increase the size of its samples during the final month before election day to be in a position to report the political preferences of the many groups that make up the total population—information that cannot be obtained by analyzing the actual election returns. Election results, for example, do not reveal how women voted as opposed to men, how the different age groups voted, how different religious groups voted, how different income levels voted. Many other facts about the public's voting habits can be obtained only through the survey method.

During the heat of election campaigns, critics have asserted on occasion that the Gallup Poll increases its sample size solely to make more certain of being "right." Examination of trend figures effectively answers this criticism. The results reported on the basis of the standard sampling unit have not varied, on the average, more than 1 or 2 percentage points from the first enlarged sample in all of the national elections of the last two decades, and this, of course, is within the margin of error expected.

Persons unfamiliar with the laws of probability invariably assume that the size of the sample must bear a fixed relationship to the size of the "universe" sampled. For example, such individuals are likely to assume that if a polling organization is sampling opinions of the whole United States, a far larger sample is necessary than if the same kind of survey is to be conducted in a single state, or in a single city. Or, to put this in another way, the assumption is that since the population of the United States is roughly ten times that of New York State, then the sample of the United States should be ten times as large.

The laws of probability, however, do not work in this fashion. Whenever the population to be surveyed is many times the size of the sample (which it typically is), the size of samples must be almost the same. If one were conducting a poll in Baton Rouge, Louisiana, on a mayoralty race, the size of the sample should be virtually the same as for the whole United States. The same principle applies to a state.

Two examples, drawn from everyday life, may help to explain this rather mystifying fact. Suppose that a hotel cook has two kinds of soup on the stove—one in a very large pot, another in a small pot. After thoroughly stirring the soup in both pots, the cook need not take a greater number of spoonsful from the large pot or fewer spoonsful from the small pot to taste the quality of the soup, since the quality should be the same.

The second example, taken from the statistician's world, may shed further light on this phenomenon. Assume that 100,000 black and white balls are placed in a large cask. The white balls number 70,000; the black balls, 30,000. Into another cask, a much smaller one, are placed 1,000 balls, divided in exactly the same proportion: 700 white balls, 300 black balls.

Now the balls in each cask are thoroughly mixed and a person, blindfolded, is asked to draw out of each cask exactly 100 balls. The likelihood of drawing 70 white balls and 30 black balls is virtually the same, despite the fact that one cask contains 100 times as many balls as the other.

If this principle were understood then hours of Senate floor time could have been saved in recent years. Senator Albert Gore, of Tennessee, a few years ago, had this to say about the Gallup Poll's sampling unit of 1,500—as reported in the *Congressional Record*:

As a layman I would question that a straw poll of less than 1 per cent of the people could under any reasonable circumstance be regarded as a fair and meaningful cross-section. This would be something more than 500 times as large a sample as Dr. Gallup takes.

In the same discussion on the Senate floor, Senator Russell Long of Lousiana added these remarks:

I believe one reason why the poll information could not be an accurate reflection of what the people are thinking is depicted in this example. Suppose we should try to find how many persons should be polled in a city the size of New Orleans in order to determine how an election should go. In a city that size, about 600,000 people, a number of 1,000 would be an appropriate number to sample to see how the election was likely to go. . . . In my home town of Baton Rouge, Lousiana, I might very well sample perhaps 300 or 400 people and come up with a fairly accurate guess as to how the city or the parish would go, especially if a scientific principle were used. But if I were to sample only a single person or two or three in that entire city, the chances are slim that I would come up with an accurate guess.

If the reader has followed the explanation of the workings of the laws of probability, and of earlier statements about the size of samples, he will be aware of two errors in the senator's reasoning. Since both cities, New Orleans and Baton Rouge, have populations many times the size of the sample he suggested, both require samples of the same size. The second is his assumption that any good researcher would possibly attempt to draw conclusions about either city on the basis of "a single person or two."

The size of the "universe" to be sampled is typically very great in the case of most surveys; in fact, it is usually many times the size of the samples to be obtained. A different principle applies when the "universe" is small. The size of a sample needed to assess opinions of the residents of a community of 1,000 voters is obviously different from that required for a city that is much larger. A sample of 1,000 in such a town would not be a sample; it would be a complete canvass.

DEVELOPING POLL QUESTIONS

Nothing is so difficult, nor so important, as the selection and wording of poll questions. In fact, most of my time and effort in the field of polling has been devoted to this problem.

The questions included in a national survey of public opinion should meet many tests: they must deal with the vital issues of the day, they must be worded in a way to get at the heart of these issues, they must be stated in language understandable to the least well educated, and finally, they must be strictly impartial in presenting the issue.

If any reader thinks this is easy, let him try to word questions on any present-day issue. It is a tough and trying mental task. And even years of experience do not make the problem less onerous.

One rule must always be followed. No question, no matter how simple, must reach the interviewing stage without first having gone through a thorough pretesting procedure. Many tests must be applied to see that each question meets required standards.

Every survey organization has its own methods of testing the wording of questions. Here it will suffice to describe in some detail how the Gallup Poll goes about this task.

Pretesting of questions dealing with complicated issues is carried on in the Interviewing Center maintained in Hopewell, New Jersey, by the Gallup organizations. Formerly, this center was a motion-picture theater. In the early 1950s it was converted into an interviewing center. The town of Hopewell is located in the middle of an area with a total population of 500,000—an area that includes the cities of Trenton and Princeton, suburban communities, small towns, and rural districts. Consequently, people from many walks of life are available for interviewing.

Pretesting procedures normally start with "in-depth" interviews with a dozen or more individuals invited to come to the center. The purpose of these interviews is to find out how much thought each participant has given to the issue under consideration, the level of his or her knowledge about the issue, and the important facets that must be probed. Most of the questions asked in these sessions are "open" questions—that is, questions which ask: "What do you know about the XX problem? What do you think about it? What should the government do about it?" and so forth.

In conversations evoked by questions of this type, it is possible, in an unhurried manner, to discover how much knowledge average persons have of a given issue, the range of views regarding it, and the special aspects of the issue that need to be probed if a series of questions is to be developed.

The next step is to try out the questions, devised at this first stage, on a new group of respondents, to see if the questions are understandable and convey the meaning intended. A simple test for this can be employed. After reading the question, the respondent is asked to "play back" what it says to him. The answer quickly reveals whether the person being interviewed understands the language used and whether he grasps the main point of the question. This approach can also reveal, to the trained interviewer, any unsuspected biases in the wording of the question. When the language in which a question is stated is not clear to the interviewee, his typical reaction is: "Will you read that question again?" If questions have to be repeated, this is unmistakable evidence that they should be worded in a simpler and more understandable manner.

Another procedure that has proved valuable in testing questions is the self-administered interview. The respondent, without the benefit of an interviewer, writes out the answers to the questions. The advantages of this procedure are many. Answers show whether the individual has given real thought to the issue and reveal, also, the degree of his interest. If he has no opinion, he will typically leave the question blank. If he has a keen interest in the issue, he will spell out his views in some detail. And if he is misinformed, this becomes apparent in what he writes.

Self-administered questionnaires can be filled out in one's own home, or privately in an interviewing center. Since the interviewer is not at hand, many issues, such as those dealing with sex, drug addiction, alcoholism, and other personal matters, can be covered in this manner. The interviewer's function is merely to drop off the questionnaire, and pick it up in a sealed envelope the next day—or the respondent can mail it directly to the Princeton office.

Even with all of these precautions, faulty question wordings do sometimes find their way onto the survey interviewing form. Checks for internal consistency, made when the ballots are returned and are tabulated, usually bring to light these shortcomings.

Most important, the reader himself must be the final judge. The Gallup Poll, from its establishment in 1935, has followed the practice of including the exact wording of questions, when this is important, in the report of the poll findings. The reader is thus in a position to decide whether the question is worded impartially and whether the interpretation of the results, based upon the question asked, is fair and objective.

A United States senator has brought up another point about questions:

How do pollsters like yourself determine what questions to ask from time to time? It seems to me that pollsters can affect public opinion simply by asking the question. The results could be pro or anti the president depending upon the questions asked and the president's relation to it.

To be sure, a series of questions could be asked that would prove awkward to the administration, even though worded impartially, and interpreted objectively. But this would be self-defeating because it would soon become apparent to readers and commentators that the survey organization was not engaged solely in fact-finding but was trying to promote a cause.

One way to prevent unintentional biases from creeping into survey operations is to have a staff that is composed of persons representing the different shades of political belief—from right to left. If not only the questions but also the written reports dealing with the results have to run this gamut—as is the practice in the Gallup office—the dangers of unintentional bias are decreased accordingly.

Still one more safeguard in dealing with biases of any type comes about through the financial support of a poll. If sponsors represent all shades of political belief, then economic pressures alone help to keep a poll on the straight and narrow path.

So much for bias in the wording and selection of questions. This still does not answer the question posed by some who wish to know what standards or practices are followed in deciding what issues to present to the public.

Since the chief aim of a modern public opinion poll is to assess public opinion on the important issues of the day and to chart the trend of sentiment, it follows that most subjects chosen for investigation must deal with current national and international issues, and particularly those that have an immediate concern for the typical citizen. Newspapers, magazine, and the broadcast media are all useful sources of ideas for polls. Suggestions for poll subjects come from individuals and institutions—from members of Congress, editors, public officials, and foundations. Every few weeks the public itself is questioned about the most important problems facing the nation, as they see them. Their answers to this question establish priorities, and provide an up-to-date list of areas to explore through polling.

A widely held assumption is that questions can be twisted to get any answer you want. In the words of one publisher: "If you word a question one way you get a result which may differ substantially from the result you get if you word the question in a different way."

It's not that easy. Questions can be worded in a manner to bring confusing and misleading results. But the loaded question is usually self-defeating because it is obvious that it is biased.

Hundreds of experiments with a research procedure known as the split-ballot technique (one-half the cross-section gets Question A, the other half Question B) have proved that even a wide variation in question wordings did not bring substantially different results if the basic meaning or substance of the question remained the same.

Change the basic meaning of the question, add or leave out an essential part, and the results will change accordingly, as they should. Were people insensitive to words—if they were unable to distinguish between one concept and another—then the whole *raison d'être* of polling would vanish.

Often the interpreters of poll findings draw inferences that are not warranted or make assumptions that a close reading of the question does not support. Consider, for example, these two questions:

"Do you feel the United States should have gotten involved in Vietnam in the first place?"

"Do you feel the United States should have helped South Vietnam to defend itself?"

While at first glance these questions seem to deal with the same point—America's involvement—actually they are probing widely different aspects of involvement. In the first case, the respondent can read in that we helped Vietnam "with our own troops"; in the second question, that our help would have been limited to materials. Many polls have shown that the American people are willing to give military supplies to almost any nation in the world that is endangered by the communists, but they are unwilling to send troops.

If the two questions cited above did not bring substantially different results, then all the other poll results dealing with this issue would be misleading.

Questions must be stated in words that everyone understands, and results are likely to be misleading to the extent that the words are not fully understood. Ask people whether they are disturbed about the amount of pornography in their magazines and newspapers and you will get one answer; if you talk about the amount of smut you will get another.

Word specialists may insist that every word in the language conveys a slightly different connotation to every individual. While this may be true, the world (and polls) must operate on the principle that commonly used words convey approximately the same meaning to the vast majority. And this fact can easily be established in the pretesting of questions. When a question is read to a respondent and he is then asked to "play it back" in his own words, it becomes quickly evident whether he has understood the words, and in fact, what they mean to him.

Some questions that pass this test can still be faulty. The sophisticated poll watcher should be on the alert for the "desirable goal" question. This type of question ties together a desirable goal with a proposal for reaching this end. The respondent typically reacts to the goal as well as to the means. Here are some examples of desirable goal questions:

> "To win the war quickly in Vietnam, would you favor all-out bombing of North Vietnam?"
> "To reduce crime in the cities, would you favor increasing jail and prison sentences?"
> "In order to improve the quality of education in the United States, should teachers be paid higher salaries?"

These questions, which present widely accepted goals accompanied by the tacit assumption that the means suggested will bring about the desired end, produce results biased on the favorable side.

The more specific questions are, the better. One of the classic arguments between newspapers and television has centered around a question that asks the public: "Where do you get most of your news about what's going on in the world today—from the newspaper, or radio, or television, or magazines, or talking to people, or where?" The answers show TV ahead of daily newspapers. But when this question is asked in a way to differentiate between international news, and local and state news, TV wins on international news, but the daily newspaper has a big lead on local news. A simple explanation is that the phrase, "What is going on in the *world?*" is interpreted by the average citizen to mean in the faraway places—not his home city.

People are extremely literal minded. A farmer in Ontario, interviewed by the Canadian Gallup Poll, was asked at the close of the interview how long he had lived in the same house; specifically, the length of his residence there. The answer that came back was "Twenty-six feet and six inches."

Whenever it is possible, the questions asked should state both sides of the issue. Realistic alternatives should be offered, or implied.

Looking back through more than four decades of polling, this aspect of question wording warrants the greatest criticism. There is probably little need to state the other side, or offer an alternative, in a question such as this: "Should the voting age be lowered to include those eighteen years of age?" The alternative implied is to leave the situation as it is.

An excellent observation has been made by a political scientist on the faculty of a New England college:

> Somehow more realism must be introduced into polls. . . . People often affirm abstract principles but will not be willing to pay the price of their concrete application. For example, would you be willing to pay more for each box of soap you buy in order to reduce ground pollution—or $200 more for your next car in order to reduce air pollution, etc.?

This type of question is similar to the desirable goal question. The public wants to clear the slums, wants better medical care, improved racial relations, better schools, better housing. The real issue is one of priorities and costs. The role of the public opinion poll in this situation is to shed light on the public's concern about each major problem, establish priorities, and then discover whether the people are willing to foot the bill.

The well-informed person is likely to think of the costs involved by legislation that proposes to deal with these social problems. But to the typical citizen there is no immediate or direct relationship between legislation and the amount he has to pay in taxes. Congress usually tries to disguise costs by failing to tie taxes or costs to large appropriations, leaving John Doe with the impression that someone else will pay the bill.

Still another type of question that is suspect has to do with good intentions. Questions of this type have meaning only when controls are used and when the results are interpreted with a full understanding of their shortcomings.

Examples of questions that fall into this category are those asking people if they "plan to go to church," "read a book," "listen to good music," "vote in the coming election," and so forth.

To the typical American the word "intend" or "plan" connotes many things, such as "Do I think this is a good idea?" "Would I like to do it?" "Would it be good for me?" "Would it be good for other people?" These and similar questions of a prestige nature reveal attitudes, but they are a poor guide to action.

Behavior is always the best guide. The person who attended church last Sunday is likely to go next Sunday, if he says he plans to. The citizen who voted in the last election and whose name is now on the registration books is far more likely to vote than the person who hasn't bothered to vote or to register, even though he insists that he "plans" to do both.

Probably the most difficult of all questions to word is the type that offers the respondent several alternatives. Not only is it hard to find alternatives that are mutually exclusive; it is equally difficult to find a series that covers the entire range of opinions. Added to this is the problem of wording each alternative in a way that doesn't give it a special advantage. And finally, in any series of alternatives that ranges from one extreme of opinion to the other, the typical citizen has a strong inclination to choose one in the middle.

As a working principle it can be stated that the more words included in a question, either by way of explanation or in stating alternatives, the greater the possibilities that the question wording itself will influence answers.

A member of the editorial staff of a newsmagazine voiced a common reaction when he observed:

> On more than a few occasions I have found that I could not, were I asked, answer a poll with a "yes" or "no." More likely my answer would be "yes, but" or "yes, if." I wonder whether pollsters can't or just don't want to measure nuances of feeling.

Obviously it is the desire of a polling organization to produce a full and accurate account of the public's views on any given issue, nuances and all.

First, however, it should be pointed out that there are two main categories of questions serving two different purposes—one to *measure* public opinion, the other to *describe* public opinion. The first category has to do with the "referendum" type of question. Since the early years of polling, heavy emphasis has been placed upon this type of question, which serves in effect as an unofficial national referendum on a given issue, actually providing the same results, within a small margin of error, that an official nationwide referendum would if it were held at the same time and on the same issue.

At some point in the decision process, whether it be concerned with an important issue before Congress, a new law before the state legislature, or a school bond issue in Central City, the time comes for a simple "yes" or "no" vote. Fortunately, or unfortunately, there is no lever on a voting machine that permits the voter to register a "yes, if" or a "yes, but" vote. While discussion can and should proceed at length, the only way to determine majority opinion is by a simple count of noses.

If polling organizations limited themselves to the referendum type of question they would severely restrict their usefulness. They can and should use their machinery to reveal the many facets of public opinion of any issue, and to shed light on the reasons why the people hold the views they do; in short, to explore the "why" behind public opinion.

More and more attention is being paid to this diagnostic approach and the greatest improvements in the field of public opinion research in the future are likely to deal with this aspect of polling.

One of the important developments in question technique was the development in the late 1940s of a new kind of question design that permits the investigation of views on any issue of a complex nature.

This design, developed by the Gallup Poll, has been described as the "quintamensional approach" since it probes five aspects of opinion:

1. the respondent's awareness and general knowledge about it,
2. his overall opinions,
3. the reasons why he holds his views,
4. his specific views on specific aspects of the problem,
5. the intensity with which he hold his opinions.

This question design quickly sorts out those who have no knowledge of a given issue—an important function in successful public opinion polling. And it can even reveal the extent or level of knowledge of the interviewee about the issue.

This is how the system works. The first question put to the person being interviewed (on any problem or issue no matter how complex) is this: "Have you heard or read about the XXX problem (proposal or issue)?"

The person being interviewed can answer either "yes" or "no" to this question, or he can add, "I'm not sure." If he answers in the negative, experience covering many years indicates that he is being entirely truthful. If he answers "yes" or "I'm not sure" he is then asked: "Please tell me in your own words what the debate (or the proposal or issue) is about." At this point the person interviewed must produce evidence that reveals whether he has some knowledge of the problem or issue.

The reader might imagine himself in this interviewing situation. You are called upon by an interviewer and in the course of the interview are asked if you have "heard or read about the Bronson proposal to reorganize the Security Council of the United Nations." The answer is likely to be "no." Possibly you might say: "I seem to have heard about it somewhere." Or suppose that, just to impress the interviewer (something that rarely happens) you fall into the trap of saying "yes."

The next question puts you neatly and delicately on the spot. It asks you to describe in your own words what the Bronson proposal is. You have to admit at this point that you do not know, or come up with an answer that immediately indicates you do not know what it is.

At this stage the questioning can be expanded to discover just how well informed you are. If it is an issue or proposal, then you can be asked to give the main arguments for and the main arguments against the plan or issue. In short, by adding questions at this stage, the *level* of knowledge of the respondent can be determined.

The next question in the design is an "open" question that asks simply: "What do you think should be done about this proposal?" or "How do you think this issue should be resolved?" This type of question permits the person being interviewed to give his views without any specifics being mentioned. Answers, of course, are recorded by the interviewer as nearly as possible in the exact words of the respondent.

The third category of questions seeks to find out the "why" behind the respondent's views. This can be done with a simple question asking: "Why do you feel that way?" or variations of this, along with "nondirective" probes such as "What else?" or "Can you explain that in greater detail?"

The fourth category in the design poses specific issues that can be answered in "yes" or "no" fashion. At this fourth stage it is possible to go back to those who were excluded by the first two questions: those who said they had not heard or read about the issue in question or proved, after the second question, that they were uninformed.

By explaining in neutral language to this group what the problem or issue is and the specific proposals that have been made for dealing with it, the uninformed can voice their opinions, which later can be compared with those of the already informed group.

The fifth category attempts to get at the intensity with which opinions are held. How strongly does each side hold to its views? What action is each individual willing to take to see that his opinion prevails? What chance is there that he may change his mind?

This, then, is the quintamensional approach. And its special merit is that it can quickly sort out the informed from the uninformed. The views of the well informed can be compared not only with the less well informed but with those who are learning about the issue for the first time. Moreover, through cross-tabulations, it is possible to show how special kinds of knowledge are related to certain opinions.

The filtering process may screen out nearly all individuals in the sample because they are uninformed, but it is often of interest and importance to know how the few informed individuals divide on a complex issue. When the best informed individuals favor a proposal or issue, experience indicates that their view tends to be accepted by lower echelons as information and knowledge become more widespread.

But this is not the invariable pattern. In the case of Vietnam, it was the best educated and the best informed who reversed their views as the war went on. The least well educated were always more against the war in Vietnam.

It is now proper to ask why, with all of its obvious merits, this question design is not used more often. The answer is that polling organizations generally avoid technical and complex issues, preferring to deal with those on which the vast majority of Americans have knowledge and opinions. Often the design is shortened to embrace only the filter question that seeks to find out if the individual has read or heard about a given issue, and omits the other questions.

In the field of public opinion research, one finds two schools of thought: one is made up largely of those in academic circles who believe that research on public attitudes should be almost entirely descriptive or diagnostic; the other, made up largely of persons in political life or in journalism or allied fields, who want to know the "score." It is the task of the polling organization to satisfy both groups. And to do this, both categories of questions must be included in the surveys conducted at regular intervals.

The long experience of the Gallup Poll points to the importance of reporting trends of opinion on all the continuing problems, the beliefs, the wishes of the people.

In fact, about four out of every ten questions included in a typical survey are for the purpose of measuring trends. Simple "yes" and "no" questions are far better suited to this purpose than "open-ended" questions, and this accounts chiefly for the high percentage of this type of question in the field of polling.

INTERVIEWERS AND INTERVIEWING PROBLEMS

Since the reliability of poll results depends so much on the integrity of interviewers, polling organizations must go to great lengths to see that interviewers follow instructions conscientiously.

A professor at an Ivy League college sums up the problems that have to do with interviewers in this question: "How do you insure quality control over your interviewers, preventing them from either influencing the answers, mis-recording them, or filling in the forms themselves?"

Before these specific points are dealt with, the reader may wish to know who the interviewers are and how they are selected and trained.

Women make the best interviewers, not only in the United States but in virtually every nation where public opinion survey organizations are established. Generally, they are more conscientious and more likely to follow instructions than men. Perhaps the nature of the work makes interviewing more appealing to them. The fact that the work is part-time is another reason why women prefer it.

Most interviewers are women of middle age, with high-school or college education. Most are married and have children.

Very few interviewers devote full time to this work. In fact, this is not recommended. Interviewing is mentally exhausting and the interviewer who works day after day at this task is likely to lose her zeal, with a consequent drop in the quality of her work.

When an area is drawn for the national cross-section, the interviewing department of the polling organization finds a suitable person to serve as the interviewer in this particular district. All the usual methods of seeking individuals who can meet the requirements are utilized, including such sources as school superintendents, newspaper editors, members of the clergy, and the classified columns of the local press.

Training for this kind of work can be accomplished by means of an instruction manual, by a supervisor, or by training sessions. The best training consists of a kind of trial-by-fire process. The interviewer is given test interviews to do after she has completed her study of the instruction manual. The trial interviews prove whether she can do the work in a satisfactory manner; more important, making these interviews enables the interviewer to discover if she really likes this kind of work. Her interviews are carefully inspected and investigated. Telephone conversations often straighten out procedures and clear up any misunderstandings about them.

Special questions added to the interviewing form and internal checks on consistency can be used to detect dishonesty. Also, a regular program of contacting persons who have been interviewed—to see if they in fact have been interviewed—is commonly employed by the best survey organizations.

It would be foolhardy to insist that every case of dishonesty can be detected in this manner, but awareness of the existence of these many ways of checking honesty removes most if not all of the temptation for the interviewers to fill in the answers themselves.

Experience of many years indicates that the temptation to "fudge" answers is related to the size of the work load given to the interviewer. If too many interviews are required in too short a time, the interviewer may hurry through the assignment, being less careful than she otherwise would be and, on occasion, not above the temptation to fill in a last few details.

To lessen this pressure, the assignment of interviews given to Gallup Poll interviewers has been constantly reduced through the years. At the present time, an assignment consists of only five or six interviews, and assignments come at least a week apart. This policy increases the cost per interview but it also keeps the interviewer from being subjected to too great pressure.

In the case of open questions that require the interviewer to record the exact words of the respondent, the difficulties mount. The interviewer must attempt to record the main thought of the respondent as the respondent is talking, and usually without benefit of shorthand. The addition of "probe" questions to the original open-end questions helps to organize the response in a more meaningful way. In certain circumstances, the use of small tape recorders, carried by the interviewer, is highly recommended.

So much for the interviewer's side of this situation. What about the person being interviewed? How honest is he?

While there is no certain way of telling whether a given individual is answering truthfully, the evidence from thousands of surveys is that people are remarkably honest and frank when asked their views in a situation that is properly structured—that is, when the respondent knows the purpose of the interview and is told that his name will not be attached to any of the things he says, and when the questions are properly worded.

It is important to point out that persons reached in a public opinion survey normally do not know the interviewer personally. For this reason, there is little or no reason to try to impress her. And, contrary to a widely held view, people are not inclined to "sound off" on subjects they know little about. In fact, many persons entitled, on the basis of their knowledge, to hold an opinion about a given problem or issue often hesitate to do so. In the development of the quintamensional procedure, described earlier, it was discovered that the opening question could not be stated: "Have you *followed* the discussion about the XX issue?" Far too many said they hadn't. And for this reason the approach had to be changed to ask: "Have you *heard or read* about the XX issue?"

The interviewer is instructed to read the question exactly as it is worded, and not try to explain it or amplify it. If the interviewee says, "Would you repeat that?" (incidentally, this is always the mark of a bad question), the interviewer repeats the question, and if on the second reading the person does not understand or get the point of the question, the interviewer checks the "no opinion" box and goes on to the next question.

But don't people often change their minds? This is a question often asked of poll-takers. The answer is, "Of course." Interviewed on Saturday, some persons may have a different opinion on Sunday. But this is another instance when the law of averages comes to the rescue. Those who shift their views in one direction will almost certainly be counterbalanced by those who change in the opposite direction. The net result is to show no change in the overall results.

Polls can only reflect people as they are—sometimes inconsistent, often uninformed. Democracy, however, does not require that every individual, every voter, be a philosopher. Democracy requires only that the sum total of individual views—the collective judgment—add up to something that makes sense. Fortunately, there now exists some forty years of polling evidence to prove the soundness of the collective judgment of the people.

How many persons refuse to be interviewed? The percentage is very small, seldom more than 10% of all those contacted. Interestingly, this same figure is found in all the nations where public opinion polls are conducted. Refusals are chiefly a function of lack of interviewing skill. Top interviewers are rarely turned down. This does not mean that a man who must get back to work immediately or a woman who has a cake in the oven will take thirty to forty-five minutes to discuss issues of the day. These situations are to be avoided. And that is why the Time-Place interviewing plan was developed by the Gallup Poll.

Readers may wonder how polls allow for the possible embarrassment or guilty conscience factor that might figure in an interviewee's answers to some questions. For example, while a voter might be prepared to vote for a third-party candidate like George Wallace, he might be uneasy about saying so to a stranger sitting in his living room.

When interviews and the interviewing situation are properly structured, however, this does not happen. In the 1968 election campaign, to follow the same example, the Gallup Poll found Wallace receiving at one point as much as 19% of the total vote. Later his popularity declined. The final poll result showed him with 15% of the vote; he actually received 14%. If there had been any embarrassment about admitting being for Wallace, his vote would obviously have been under-estimated by a sizable amount.

Properly approached, people are not reluctant to discuss even personal matters—their private problems, their religion, sex. By using an interesting technique developed in Sweden, even the most revealing facts about the sex life of an individual can be obtained. And the same type of approach is found to be highly successful in finding out the extent of drug use by college students. Many studies about the religious beliefs of individuals have been conducted by the Gallup Poll without meeting interviewing difficulties.

The desire to have one's voice heard on issues of the day is almost universal. An interviewer called upon an elderly man and found him working in his garden. After he had offered his views on many subjects included in the poll, he called to the interviewer who had started for her car, and said: "You know, two of the most important things in my life have happened this week. First, I was asked to serve on a jury, and now I have been asked to give my views in a public opinion poll."

MEASURING INTENSITY

To the legislator or administrator the intensity with which certain voters or groups of voters hold their opinions has special significance. If people feel strongly enough about a given issue they will likely do something about it—write letters, work for a candidate who holds a contrary view, contribute money to a campaign, try to win other voters to their candidate. To cite an example: Citizens who oppose any kind of gun control laws, though constituting a minority of the public, feel so strongly about this issue that they will do anything they can to defeat such legislation. As a result, they have succeeded in keeping strict gun laws from being adopted in most states and by the federal government.

Since most legislation calls for more money, a practical measure of the intensity of feeling about a given piece of legislation is the willingness to have taxes increased to meet the costs.

One politician made this criticism of polling efforts: "Issue polling often fails to differentiate between hard and soft opinion. If the issue is national health insurance, then the real test is not whether the individual favors it but how much more per year he is willing to pay in taxes for such a program."

This is a merited criticism of polls and, as stated earlier, one that points to the need for greater attention on the part of polling organizations. The action that an individual is willing to take—the sacrifice he is willing to undergo—to see that his side of an issue prevails is one of the best ways of sorting out hard from soft opinion.

Questions put to respondents about "how strongly" they feel, "how important it is to them," and "how much they care" all yield added insights into the intensity of opinions held by the public. The fact, however, that they are used as seldom as they are in the regular polls, here and abroad, indicates that the added information gained does not compensate for the time and the difficulties encountered by the survey interviewer. Most attitude scales are, in fact, better suited to the classroom with students as captive subjects than to the face-to-face interviews undertaken by most survey organizations.

The best hope, in my opinion, lies in the development of new questions that are behavior- or action-oriented. Here, then, is an important area where both academicians and practitioners can work together in the improvement of present research procedures.

The specific complaint mentioned above—that of providing a more realistic presentation of an issue—can probably be dealt with best in the question wording, as noted earlier.

While verbal scales to measure intensity can be usefully employed in many situations, two nonverbal scales have gained wide acceptance and use throughout the world. Since they do not depend upon words, language is no barrier to their use in any nation. Moreover, they can be employed in normal interviewing situations, and on a host of problems.

The scales were devised by Jan Stapel of the Netherlands Institute of Public Opinion and by Hadley Cantril and a colleague, F. P. Kilpatrick. While the scales seem to be similar, each has its own special merits.

The Stapel scale consists of a column of ten boxes. The five at the top are white, the five at the bottom black.

The boxes are numbered from +5 to −5. The interviewer carries a reproduction of this scale and at the appropriate time in the interview hands it to the respondent. The interviewer explains the scale in these or similar words: "You will notice that the boxes on this card go from the highest position of plus 5—something you like very much—all the way down to the lowest position of minus 5—or something you dislike very much. Now, how far up the scale, or how far down the scale, would you rate the following?"

After this explanation, the interviewer asks the respondent how far up or down the scale he would rate an individual, political party, product, company, proposal, or almost anything at issue. The person is told "put your finger on the box" that best represents his point of view; or, in other situations, to call off the number opposite the box. The interviewer duly records this number on his interviewing form.

One of the merits of the Stapel Scalometer is that it permits the person being interviewed to answer two questions with one response: whether he has a positive or a negative feeling toward the person or party or institution being rated, and at the same time the degree of his liking or disliking. By simply calling off a number he indicates that he has a favorable or unfavorable opinion of the F.B.I., of Jimmy Carter, or of the Equal Rights Amendment, and how much he likes or dislikes each. In actual use, researchers have found the extreme positions on the scale are most indicative and most sensitive to change. These are the +4 and +5 positions on the favorable side and the −4 and −5 positions on the negative side. Normally these two positions are combined to provide a "highly favorable" or a "highly unfavorable" rating.

Scale ratings thus obtained are remarkably consistent and remarkably reliable in ranking candidates and parties. In fact, the ratings given to the two major-party candidates have paralleled the relative standings of the candidates in elections, especially when the party ratings are averaged with the candidate ratings.

Cantril and Kilpatrick devised the "Self-Anchoring Scale."* Cantril and his associate, Lloyd Free, used this scale to measure the aspirations and fears of people in different nations of the world—both those living in highly developed countries and those in the least developed. They sought "to get an overall picture of the reality worlds in which people lived, a picture expressed by individuals in their own terms and to do this in such a way . . . as to enable meaningful comparisons to be made between different individuals, groups of individuals, and societies."

The Self-Anchoring scale is so simple that it can be used with illiterates and with people without any kind of formal education. A multination survey in which this measuring instrument was employed included nations as diverse in their educational and living standards as Nigeria, India, the United States, West Germany, Cuba, Israel, Japan, Poland, Panama, Yugoslavia, Philippines, Brazil, and the Dominican Republic.

---

*F. P. Kilpatrick and Hadley Cantril, "Self-Anchoring Scale." *Journal of Individual Psychology,* November 1960.

The scale makes use of a ladder device.

```
———— 10 ————
————  9  ————
————  8  ————
————  7  ————
————  6  ————
————  5  ————
————  4  ————
————  3  ————
————  2  ————
————  1  ————
————  0  ————
```

The person being interviewed describes his own wishes and hopes, the realization of which would constitute the best possible life. This is the top anchoring point of the scale. At the other extreme, the same individual describes his worries and fears embodied in the worst possible life he can imagine. With the use of this device, he is asked where he thinks he stands on the ladder today. Then he is asked where he thinks he stood in the past, and where he thinks he will stand in the future.

This same procedure was used by Albert Cantril and Charles Roll in a survey called *Hopes and Fears of the American People*—a revealing study of the mood of the American people in the spring of 1971.

Use of this scale would be extremely helpful in pursuing the goal set forth by Alvin Toffler in his book *Future Shock*. He writes:

The time has come for a dramatic reassessment of the directions of change, a reassessment made not by the politicians or the sociologists or the clergy or the elitist revolutionaries, not by technicians or college presidents, but by the people themselves. We need, quite literally, to "go to the people" with a question that is almost never asked of them: "*What kind of a world do you want 10, 20, or 30 years from now?*" We need to initiate, in short, a continuing plebiscite on the future. Toffler points out that "the voter may be polled about specific issues, but not about the general shape of the preferable future."

This is true to a great extent. With the exception of the Cantril-Free studies, this area has been largely overlooked by polling organizations. Toffler advocates a continuing plebiscite in which millions of persons would participate. From a practical point of view, however, sampling offers the best opportunity to discover just what the public's ideas of the future are—and more particularly, the kind of world they want ten years, twenty years, or thirty years from now.

REPORTING AND INTERPRETING POLL FINDINGS

Public opinion polls throughout the world have been sponsored by the media of communication—newspapers, magazines, television, and radio. It is quite proper, therefore, to answer this question: "How well do the various media report and evaluate the results of a given poll?"

Since October 1935, Gallup Poll reports have appeared weekly in American newspapers in virtually all of the major cities. During this period, I am happy to report, no newspaper has changed the wording of poll releases sent to them to make the findings fit the newspaper's editorial or political views. Editors, however, are permitted to write their own headlines because of their own special type and format policies; they can shorten articles or, in fact, omit them if news columns are filled by other and more pressing material.

Since the funds for the Gallup Poll come from this source and since the sponsoring newspapers represent all shades of political belief, the need for strict objectivity in the writing and interpretation of poll results becomes an economic as well as a scientific necessity.

At various stages in the history of the Gallup Poll, charges have been made that the poll has a Republican bias, and at other times, a Democratic bias, largely dependent upon whether the political tide is swinging toward one side or the other. Even a cursory examination of the findings dealing with issues of the day, and of election survey results, will disprove this.

The Gallup Poll is a fact-finding organization, or looked at in another way, a kind of scorekeeper in the political world.

When poll findings are not to the liking of critics there is always a great temptation to try to discredit the poll by claiming that it is "biased," that it makes "secret adjustments" and that it manipulates the figures to suit its fancy, and that it is interfering with "democratic dialogue." Such charges were heard often in earlier years, but time has largely stilled this kind of attack on the poll's integrity.

Limitations of space, in the case of newspapers, and of time in the case of television and radio, impose restrictions on the amount of detail and analysis that can be included in any one report. The news media have a strong preference for "hard" news, the kind that reports the most recent score on candidate or party strength, or the division of opinion on highly controversial subjects. This type of news, it should be added, makes up the bulk of their news budgets.

These space and time requirements do require a different kind of poll report form from one that would be written to satisfy those who prefer a full and detailed description of public opinion.

A political writer for a large metropolitan newspaper has raised this point: "Is it not more accurate to report a point spread instead of a simple single figure? . . . If so, would it not be more responsible to state it that way, even though it would take away some of the sharpness in published reports?"

A degree of error is inherent in all sampling and it is important that this fact be understood by those who follow poll findings. The question is how best to achieve this end. One way, of course, is to educate the public to look at all survey results not as fixed realities or absolutes but as reliable estimates only.

The best examples, as noted earlier, are the monthly figures on unemployment and the cost of living. Should these be published showing a point spread or the margin of error? If they were, then the monthly index of unemployment, based as it is on a sample of 50,000, would read, at a given point in time, not 8.8%, but 8.5% to 9.1%. Reporting the cost of living index in such fashion would almost certainly cause trouble, since many labor contracts are based upon changes as small as 0.1%.

In reporting the trend of opinion, especially on issues, the inclusion of a point spread would make poll reports rather meaningless, particularly if the trend were not a sharp one. The character of the trend curve itself normally offers evidence of the variations due to sample size.

In the case of elections, the reporting of the margin of error can, on occasion, be misleading to the reader. The reason is that polling errors come from many sources, and often the least of these in importance is the size of the sample. Yet, the statistical margin of error relates solely to this one factor.

An example may help to shed light on this point. A telephone poll taken in a mayoralty race in a large eastern city, reported the standings of the candidates and added that they were accurate within "a possible error margin of 3.8%." In short, the newspaper in which the results were published and the polling organization assured readers that the results perforce had to be right within this margin, based upon the laws or probability. Actually, the poll figure was 14 percentage points short on the winning candidate. Factors other than the size of the sample were responsible for this wide deviation.

The best guide to a poll's accuracy is its record. If allowance is to be made for variation in the poll's reported figures, then perhaps the best suggestion, to be reasonably certain that the error will not exceed a stated amount in a national election, is to multiply by 2.5 the average deviation of the poll in its last three or four elections.

Still another way to remind readers and viewers of the presence of some degree of error in all survey findings is to find a word or words that convey this fact. A growing practice among statisticians in dealing with sampling data is to refer to results as "estimates." Unfortunately, this word conveys to some the impression that subjective judgments have entered into the process. A better word needs to be found that removes some of the certainty that is too often attached to poll percentages without, at the same time, erring in the opposite direction. The word "assessment" has been adopted by some survey researchers and it is hoped that it will come into general use in the future.

George H. Gallup

DESIGN OF THE SAMPLE

The design of the sample used in the Gallup Poll is that of a replicated probability sample down to the block level in the case of urban areas and to segments of townships in the case of rural areas.

After stratifying the nation geographically and by size of community in order to insure conformity of the sample with the latest available estimates by the Census Bureau of the distribution of the adult population, about 350 different sampling locations or areas are selected on a strictly random basis. The interviewers have no choice whatsoever concerning the part of the city or county in which they conduct their interviews.

Interviewers are given maps of the area to which they are assigned, with a starting point indicated, and are required to follow a specified direction. At each occupied dwelling unit, interviewers are instructed to select respondents by following a prescribed systematic method. This procedure is followed until the assigned number of interviews is completed. The standard sample size for most Gallup Polls is 1500 interviews. This is augmented in specific instances where greater survey accuracy is considered desirable.

Since this sampling procedure is designed to produce a sample that approximates the adult civilian population (18 and older) living in private households in the United States (that is, excluding those in prisons and hospitals, hotels, religious institutions, and on military reservations), the survey results can be applied to this population for the purpose of projecting percentages into numbers of people. The manner in which the sample is drawn also produces a sample that approximates the population of private households in the United States. Therefore, survey results also can be projected in terms of numbers of households when appropriate.

SAMPLING TOLERANCES

It should be remembered that all sample surveys are subject to sampling error; that is, the extent to which the results may differ from what would be obtained if the whole population surveyed had been interviewed. The size of such a sampling error depends largely on the number of interviews. Increasing the sample size lessens the magnitude of possible error and vice versa.

The following tables may be used in estimating sampling error. The computed allowances (the standard deviation) have taken into account the effect of the sample design upon sampling error. They may be interpreted as indicating the range (plus or minus the figure shown) within which the results of repeated samplings in the same time period could be expected to vary, 95 percent of the time (or at a confidence level of .5), assuming the same sampling procedure, the same interviewers, and the same questionnaire.

Table A shows how much allowance should be made for the sampling error of a percentage. The table would be used in the following manner: Say a reported percentage is 33 for a group that includes 1500 respondents. Go to the row "percentage near 30" in the table and then to the column headed "1500." The number at this point is three, which means that the 33 percent obtained in the sample is subject to a sampling error of plus or minus 3 points. Another way of saying it is that very probably (95 chances out of 100) the average of repeated samplings would be somewhere between 30 and 36, with the most likely figure being the 33 obtained.

In comparing survey results in two subsamples, such as men and woman, the question arises as to how large must a difference between them be before one can be reasonably sure that it reflects a statistically significant difference. In Table B and C, the number of points that must be allowed for, in such comparisons, is indicated.

For percentages near 20 or 80, use Table B; for those near 50, Table C. For percentages in between, the error to be allowed for is between that shown in the two tables.

Here is an example of how the tables should be used: Say 50 percent of men and 40 percent of women respond the same way to a question—a difference of 10 percentage points. Can it be said with any assurance that the ten-point difference reflects a significant difference between men and women on the question? (Samples, unless otherwise noted, contain approximately 750 men and 750 women.)

Because the percentages are near 50, consult Table C. Since the two samples are about 750 persons each, look for the place in the table where the column and row labeled "750" converge. The number six appears there. This means the allowance for error should be 6 points, and the conclusion that the percentage among men is somewhere between 4 and 16 points higher than the percentage among women would be wrong only about 5 percent of the time. In other words, there is a considerable likelihood that a difference exists in the direction observed and that it amounts to at least 4 percentage points.

If, in another case, male responses amount to 22 percent, and female to 24 percent, consult Table B because these percentages are near 20. The column and row labeled "750" converge on the number five. Obviously, then, the two-point difference is inconclusive.

TABLE A

Recommended Allowance for Sampling Error of a Percentage

In Percentage Points
(at 95 in 100 confidence level)*
Size of the Sample

	3000	1500	1000	750	600	400	200	100
Percentages near 10	2	2	2	3	4	4	5	7
Percentages near 20	2	3	3	4	4	5	7	9
Percentages near 30	2	3	4	4	4	6	8	10
Percentages near 40	3	3	4	4	5	6	9	11
Percentages near 50	3	3	4	4	5	6	9	11
Percentages near 60	3	3	4	4	5	6	9	11
Percentages near 70	2	3	4	4	4	6	8	10
Percentages near 80	2	3	3	4	4	5	7	9
Percentages near 90	2	2	2	3	4	4	5	7

*The chances are 95 in 100 that the sampling error is not larger than the figures shown.

TABLE B

Recommended Allowance for Sampling Error of the Difference Between Two Subsamples

In Percentage Points
(at 95 in 100 confidence level)*

Percentages near 20 or percentages near 80

Size of the Sample	1500	750	600	400	200
1500	3				
750	4	5			
600	5	6	6		
400	6	7	7	7	
200	8	8	8	9	10

TABLE C

Percentages near 50

Size of the Sample	1500	750	600	400	200
1500	4				
750	5	6			
600	6	8	8		
400	7	8	8	9	
200	10	10	11	11	13

*The chances are 95 in 100 that the sampling error is not larger than the figures shown.

RECORD OF
GALLUP POLL ACCURACY

Year	Gallup Final Survey*		Election Result*	
1978	55.0%	Democratic	54.0%	Democratic
1976	48.0	Carter	50.0	Carter
1974	60.0	Democratic	58.9	Democratic
1972	62.0	Nixon	61.8	Nixon
1970	53.0	Democratic	54.3	Democratic
1968	43.0	Nixon	43.5	Nixon
1966	52.5	Democratic	51.9	Democratic
1964	64.0	Johnson	61.3	Johnson
1962	55.5	Democratic	52.7	Democratic
1960	51.0	Kennedy	50.1	Kennedy
1958	57.0	Democratic	56.5	Democratic
1956	59.5	Eisenhower	57.8	Eisenhower
1954	51.5	Democratic	52.7	Democratic
1952	51.0	Eisenhower	55.4	Eisenhower
1950	51.0	Democratic	50.3	Democratic
1948	44.5	Truman	49.9	Truman
1946	58.0	Republican	54.3	Republican
1944	51.5	Roosevelt	53.3[2]	Roosevelt
1942	52.0	Democratic	48.0[1]	Democratic
1940	52.0	Roosevelt	55.0	Roosevelt
1938	54.0	Democratic	50.8	Democratic
1936	55.7	Roosevelt	62.5	Roosevelt

*The figure shown is the winner's percentage of the Democratic-Republican vote except in the elections of 1948, 1968, and 1976. Because the Thurmond and Wallace voters in 1948 were largely split-offs from the normally Democratic vote, they were made a part of the final Gallup Poll preelection

[1]Final report said Democrats would win control of the House, which they did even though the Republicans won a majority of the popular vote.
[2]Civilian vote 53.3, Roosevelt soldier vote 0.5 = 53.8% Roosevelt. Gallup final survey based on civilian vote.

estimate of the division of the vote. In 1968 Wallace's candidacy was supported by such a large minority that he was clearly a major candidate, and the 1968 percents are based on the total Nixon-Humphrey-Wallace vote. In 1976, because of interest in McCarthy's candidacy and its potential effect on the Carter vote, the final Gallup Poll estimate included Carter, Ford, McCarthy, and all other candidates as a group.

Average Deviation for 22
    National Elections . . . . 2.2 percentage points

Average Deviation for 15
    National Elections
    Since 1950, inclusive . . . . 1.4 percentage points

Trend in Deviation Reduction

Elections	Average Error
1936–48	4.0
1950–58	1.7
1960–68	1.5
1970–78	1.1

CHRONOLOGY

This chronology is provided to enable the reader to relate poll results to specific events or series of events that may have influenced public opinion.

1977

December 2	Unemployment rate in November was 6.9% nationwide, while a record 63% of all working-age Americans were employed.
December 14	Thousands of farmers begin a strike to show their anger over rising costs.
December 15	Congress votes major increases in the social security tax. President Carter signs the bill on December 20.
December 22	President Carter approves $126-billion budget for the Department of Defense for fiscal year 1979.
December 25–26	Egyptian President Anwar Sadat and Israeli Prime Minister Menahem Begin meet in Ismalia, Egypt, to discuss Mideast peace proposals.
December 28	President Carter appoints G. William Miller as chairman of the Federal Reserve Board, replacing Arthur F. Burns.
December 29	President Carter begins nine-day overseas trip.

1978

January 4	The Treasury Department and the Federal Reserve Board announce a plan to end the decline of the dollar. The dollar rises 6% in trading.

1978

January 6	President Carter returns to Washington after a 16,000-mile trip. The president visited Poland, Iran, Saudi Arabia, Egypt, France, and Belgium.
January 7	The Labor Department reported that the national unemployment rate at the end of 1977 was 6.4%.
January 13	Senator Hubert Humphrey of Minnesota dies at age 66.
January 15	The Dallas Cowboys score a 27–10 win over the Denver Broncos in Super Bowl XII.
January 19	President Carter delivers his first State of the Union address, calling for a $25-billion tax cut, ratification of the Panama Canal treaties, a new federal department of education, and a strong energy bill.
	Judge William Webster is named to head the FBI.
January 24	A Soviet spy satellite powered by a nuclear reactor breaks up over northwestern Canada. A United States-Canadian team begins a $1-million search for the remains.
January 30	The Senate Foreign Relations Committee approves the Panama Canal treaties.
February 3	Unemployment for January was 6.3%. Unemployment among Black workers remained unchanged at 12.7%.
	Egyptian President Anwar Sadat visits Washington to confer with President Carter.
	Civil war begins in Nicaragua.
February 7–13	The United States reiterates its opposition to Israeli settlements in occupied Arab territories.
February 14	The United States announces that it will sell $4.8-billion worth of jet warplanes to Egypt, Israel, and Saudi Arabia. On May 15 the Senate votes 54–44 to support the sales after intense lobbying by the president.

1978

February 27   Consumer prices rose 0.8% is January, led by food, housing, and medical-care costs. The January rise was about twice the average monthly increase since July.

February 28   President Carter asks Congress to approve a 24% increase in federal spending on education.

March 2   President Carter asks Congress to approve his plan to revise the federal civil service system to allow more flexibility in rewarding merit and penalizing incompetence.

March 3   Rhodesian Prime Minister Ian Smith and three Black leaders sign an agreement to transfer power to the nation's Black majority by the end of 1978. Transfer is later delayed until April 20, 1979. The State Department denounced the internal settlement as illegal.

March 10   Unemployment for February fell to 6.1%, the lowest since October 1974. Black unemployment fell from 12.7% to 11.8%. The unemployment rate for women declined from 6.1% to 5.7%.

March 13   United States and Germany announce a series of joint actions to stabilize the dollar.

March 14   Israeli troops invade southern Lebanon to "root out terrorist bases" used by Palestinian guerrilas.

March 17   The worst oil spill in history occurs off the coast of France as the supertanker *Amoco Cadiz* runs aground in heavy seas.

March 25   Nation's soft-coal miners ratify a new contract to end 110-day strike, the longest in the industry's history.

March 27   President Carter proposes a broad program to aid the nation's cities.

March 28   Consumer prices rose 0.6% for February, led by a 1.2% increase in food costs.

1978

March 31	The United States trade deficit for February was the largest in history. Imports exceeded exports by $4.52 billion, putting American trade in the red for the twenty-first consecutive month.
April 3	President Carter returns to Washington from a seven-day, 14,000-mile trip to South America and Africa. Carter visited Venezuela, Brazil, Nigeria, and Liberia.
	United States Steel Company reverses its March 30 decision to increase steel prices. President Carter had denounced the increase as "excessive" and "inflationary."
April 6	President Carter signs legislation raising the mandatory retirement age from sixty-five to seventy for most workers.
April 7	Unemployment rose in March to 6.2%.
	President Carter announces decision to defer production of neutron bomb.
April 10	The United Nations and the State Department disclose the defection to the West of Arkady Shevchenko, a high Soviet official in the United Nations Secretariat.
April 11	Israeli troops begin to withdraw from Lebanon.
April 13–26	On the New York Stock Exchange, an unprecedented 431.88 million shares are traded and the Dow Jones industrial average rises 62 points. On April 17 a volume of 63.5 million shares is traded, the heaviest in the exchange's history.
April 18	The Supreme Court rules, by a 7–2 vote, that broadcasters and recording companies would not have automatic access to former President Nixon's White House tapes.
	The Senate ratifies the second of the Panama Canal treaties by a vote of 68–32, one vote more than the two-thirds majority needed. The first of the two treaties had been ratified by the same vote on March 16.
April 19	Economic growth declined 0.6% for the first quarter of 1978. The severe winter weather and the coal miners' strike were blamed.

1978

April 22   According to a special report in *Business Week,* the United States "is caught in the grip of the worst, most prolonged, and most pernicious inflation in its history."

May 5   Unemployment in April fell to 6%, the lowest in three and a half years. Consumer prices rose 0.6%, led by a record 6.6% increase in the price of beef.

May 8–11   Antigovernment riots sweep Iran, with dozens reported killed.

May 9   Urban guerrillas kill former Italian Prime Minister Aldo Moro.

May 15   Patricia Hearst returns to prison to resume a seven-year sentence for bank robbery. She had been on bail since November 19, 1976.

May 23   A special five-week United Nations General Assembly session on disarmament opens.

May 26   Legalized casino gambling begins in Atlantic City, New Jersey, home of the nation's first legal casino outside of Nevada.

May 30   President Carter attacks Cuba and the Soviet Union for intervention in Africa.

May 31   The Supreme Court rules, by a 5–3 vote, that police can obtain warrants to search newspaper property without prior warning.

June 2   The Bureau of Labor Statistics reports that May wholesale prices and unemployment increased only slightly, indicating that inflation might be slowing down.

June 6   Californians set off a nationwide tax revolt by approving Proposition 13, a ballot initiative to cut property taxes in the state by 57%.

June 7   In an address at the United States Naval Academy, President Carter warns the Soviet Union to end confrontation with the United States. The president attacks the Soviet definition of detente, which, he said, "seems to mean a continuing aggressive struggle for political advantage and increased influence."

1978

June 9	The Mormon church revokes its 148-year-old policy barring Black men from the priesthood.
June 15	The Supreme Court halts construction on the Tennessee Valley Authority's nearly completed Tellico dam to protect the habitat of the tiny snail darter, an endangered species.
June 16	President Carter and General Omar Torrijos of Panama exchange the ratification documents of the new Panama Canal treaties at a ceremony in Panama City.
June 22	American Nazis call off a planned march through Skokie, Illinois. The Supreme Court had earlier denied the town's request to prohibit the march.
June 28	The Supreme Court orders Allan Bakke, a thirty-eight-year-old white engineer who claimed he had been a victim of "reverse discrimination," to be admitted to the University of California at Davis Medical School. At the same time, the Court upholds the concept of affirmative action provided that firm quotas are not imposed.
June 30	The Carter administration, in a gesture to the Chinese government in Peking, announced that sixty F-4 fighter-bombers would not be sold to Nationalist China. The Consumer Price Index rose 0.9% for May. The trade deficit for May was $2.24 billion, the smallest since September 1977, but nevertheless the twenty-fourth consecutive monthly deficit.
July 7	Unemployment in June was 5.7%, a four-year low.
July 12	United Nations Ambassador Andrew Young states in a Paris newspaper that there are "hundreds, perhaps thousands, of political prisoners in the United States." President Carter later rebukes him for his remarks.
July 16	President Carter begins a two-day economic summit in Bonn with leaders of West Germany, Great Britain, Japan, France, Italy, and Canada.

1

1978

July 17   On the steps of the United States Capitol, more than 1,000 American Indians end their 2,700-mile "longest walk" to focus public attention on the problems of the Indian.

July 20   Dr. Peter Bourne resigns as President Carter's adviser on drug abuse after disclosure that he had written a prescription for a powerful sedative for an aide under a fictitious name.

July 25   An Englishwoman gives birth to the world's first "test-tube baby."

July 28   The price of gold rises above $200 an ounce, reflecting the weakness of the United States dollar and the apparent difficulty in controlling inflation.

     Consumer prices rose 0.9% during June. The annual rate of inflation for the second quarter of 1978 was 11.4%. Food prices rose 1.4% in June, led by a 5.6% increase in beef prices.

July 29   President Carter outlines the principles of his national health plan, which he proposes to phase in slowly depending on the state of the economy. Senator Edward Kennedy, author of a more comprehensive national health insurance plan, criticizes the president.

August 2   Congressman Philip Crane, a conservative Republican from Illinois, becomes the first candidate to enter the 1980 presidential race.

August 3   The New York Stock Market records a volume of 65.4 million shares traded, beating the former record of 63.49 million shares set on April 17.

August 4   Unemployment rose to 6.2% for July.

     New York Times reporter Myron Farber is jailed for refusing to turn over his files on investigations of suspicious hospital deaths that led to the murder trial of a New Jersey doctor. Farber is released on October 24 following the doctor's acquittal.

August 6   Pope Paul VI dies at age eighty.

1978

August 17	President Carter vetoes a $36-billion weapons bill because it includes a $2-billion nuclear-powered aircraft carrier that he opposes.
	Three Americans complete the first transatlantic balloon crossing.
August 22	Jomo Kenyatta, president of Kenya, dies.
August 26	The college of cardinals elects as pope Albino Luciani, formerly patriarch of Venice, who takes the name of John Paul I.
August 29	The dollar falls sharply in value after a $3-billion trade deficit was reported for July.
August 30	Wages rose a record 2.1% for the second quarter of 1978, while the consumer price index rose even faster—2.9%—during the same period.
	Major banks raise the prime interest rate to 9.25%.
September 1	Unemployment fell 0.3% in August to 5.9%.
September 8	Martial law is declared in Iran.
September 9	Guerrillas launch an offensive designed to force the resignation of Nicaraguan strongman Anastasio Somoza. Government troops put down the rebellion within two weeks.
September 15	Muhammad Ali becomes the first boxer to win the heavyweight title three times by defeating Leon Spinks in a unanimous fifteen-round decision.
September 17	The Mideast summit at Camp David ends with the signing of a framework for peace by Egyptian President Anwar Sadat, Israeli Prime Minister Menachem Begin, and President Carter.
September 25	One hundred and forty-four persons are killed when a jetliner and a private plane collide over San Diego in the worst air disaster in United States history.

1978

September 29   Pope John Paul I dies.

October 6   Congress extends for three years the deadline for ratification of the Equal Rights Amendment.

October 13   President Carter signs into law a bill to reform the federal civil service system.

October 15   Congress adopts a $18.7-billion tax-cut bill that includes an increase of $250 in personal exemptions and a $2.1-billion reduction in capital gains taxes.

                After a year and a half debate, Congress approves a modified version of President Carter's energy bill. Legislation includes price increases for natural gas leading to deregulation in 1985 of newly discovered supplies, a ban on gas-guzzling cars, and measures to promote energy conservation.

October 16   Polish Karol Cardinal Wojtyla is elected pope. He is the first non-Italian pope in 456 years. Wojtyla takes the name John Paul II.

October 17   New York Yankees win their second straight baseball championship by defeating the Los Angeles Dodgers in the sixth game of the World Series.

October 20   The stock market closes the worst week in its history with a 59.08 loss in the Dow Jones industrial average, down to 838.01.

October 24   President Carter announces new antiinflation program of voluntary wage and price guidelines.

October 25–30   The United States dollar plunges to record lows against the Japanese yen and the West German mark.

October 31   The Federal Reserve Board raises the discount rate to a record high of 9.5%.

                Oil workers go on strike in Iran.

1978

November 1   President Carter announces a series of emergency measures to bolster the dollar. Measures include a hike in the discount rate, quintupling of gold sales, and intensive intervention in the world currency markets.

November 6   Massive antigovernment demonstrations continue in Iran.

November 7   Republicans score modest gains in midterm elections, picking up three Senate seats, twelve House seats, and six governorships.

November 13   The House formally reprimands three members for misconduct in the South Korean influence-buying scandal, ending an eighteen-month investigation of bribery on Capitol Hill.

November 19   Congressman Leo Ryan of California and four members of his party are killed in Guyana by members of the People's Temple commune. More than 900 members of the cult subsequently commit suicide.

November 27   San Francisco Mayor George Moscone and Supervisor Harvey Milk are killed in their offices.

December 6   Former Cincinnati Red Pete Rose signs a new contract with the Philadelphia Phillies for $3.2 million to become the highest-paid player in baseball history.

December 10   Former Israeli Prime Minister Golda Meir dies.

              Israeli Prime Minister Menachem Begin accepts the Nobel Peace Prize in Oslo; cowinner Egyptian President Anwar Sadat is represented at the presentation ceremony by an aide.

December 15   The United States recognizes the People's Republic of China and the two nations agree to exchange ambassadors. The United States also announces that it will withdraw its recognition of Taiwan.

              The city of Cleveland becomes the first major American city since the Depression to default.

1978

December 18   The Organization of Petroleum Exporting Countries announ-
                 ces a 14.5% increase in oil prices for 1979.

December 23   In Iran, the first American is killed in continuing violence which
                 threatens to overthrow the shah.

JANUARY 5
PREDICTIONS FOR 1978

Interviewing Date: 11/18–21/77
Survey #989-K

As far as you're concerned, do you expect next year—1978—will be better or worse than 1977?

Better 45%
Worse 30
Same 18
No opinion 7

By Sex
Male

Better 47%
Worse 27
Same 21
No opinion 5

Female

Better 42%
Worse 34
Same 16
No opinion 8

By Race
Whites

Better 45%
Worse 30
Same 19
No opinion 6

Nonwhites

Better 41%
Worse 34
Same 12
No opinion 13

By Education
College

Better 51%
Worse 26
Same 18
No opinion 5

JANUARY 1
MOST ADMIRED MAN

Interviewing Date: 12/9–12/77
Survey #990-K

What man that you have heard or read about, living today in any part of the world, do you admire the most? And who would be your second choice?

Following are the top eleven in the voting with first and second choices combined:

Jimmy Carter
Anwar Sadat
Hubert Humphrey
Billy Graham
Gerald Ford
Henry Kissinger
Menahem Begin
Ronald Reagan
Pope Paul VI ⎫
Richard Nixon ⎬ TIED
Bob Hope

Note: Among those receiving a high number of mentions are the following (in alphabetical order): Muhammad Ali, Walter Cronkite, Jesse Jackson, Edward (Ted) Kennedy, Jerry Lewis, Walter Mondale, Ralph Nader, Oral Roberts, Nelson Rockefeller, Eric Sevareid, John Wayne, and Andrew Young.

Survey respondents in these regular audits are asked to give their choices without the aid of a list of names. This procedure, while opening the field to all possible choices, tends to favor those who are in the news.

High School

Better 43%
Worse. 33
Same. 19
No opinion 5

Grade School

Better 38%
Worse. 31
Same. 18
No opinion. 13

By Region
East

Better 43%
Worse. 31
Same. 20
No opinion 6

Midwest

Better 50%
Worse. 25
Same. 20
No opinion. 5

South

Better 40%
Worse. 34
Same. 16
No opinion. 10

West

Better 47%
Worse. 30
Same. 18
No opinion. 5

By Age
18–24 Years

Better 48%
Worse. 31
Same. 13
No opinion. 8

25–29 Years

Better 52%
Worse. 30
Same. 17
No opinion 1

30–49 Years

Better 43%
Worse. 33
Same. 19
No opinion 5

50 Years and Over

Better 42%
Worse. 28
Same. 20
No opinion. 10

By Income
$20,000 and Over

Better 48%
Worse. 28
Same. 21
No opinion. 3

$15,000–$19,999

Better 48%
Worse. 31
Same. 16
No opinion. 5

$10,000–$14,999

Better 47%
Worse. 31
Same. 16
No opinion. 6

$7,000–$9,999

Better 43%
Worse. 28
Same. 22
No opinion. 7

$5,000–$6,999

Better 37%
Worse...................................34
Same....................................20
No opinion.............................. 9

$3,000–$4,999

Better 37%
Worse...................................36
Same....................................19
No opinion.............................. 8

Under $3,000

Better 45%
Worse...................................26
Same....................................14
No opinion..............................15

By Politics
Republicans

Better 37%
Worse...................................38
Same....................................20
No opinion.............................. 5

Democrats

Better 48%
Worse...................................28
Same....................................17
No opinion.............................. 7

Southern Democrats

Better 44%
Worse...................................29
Same....................................19
No opinion.............................. 8

Other Democrats

Better 50%
Worse...................................26
Same....................................17
No opinion.............................. 7

Independents

Better 47%
Worse...................................28
Same....................................19
No opinion.............................. 6

By Religion
Protestants

Better 44%
Worse...................................31
Same....................................18
No opinion.............................. 7

Catholics

Better 46%
Worse...................................29
Same....................................21
No opinion.............................. 4

By Occupation
Professional and Business

Better 51%
Worse...................................27
Same....................................18
No opinion.............................. 4

Clerical and Sales

Better 56%
Worse...................................25
Same....................................13
No opinion.............................. 6

Manual Workers

Better 41%
Worse...................................33
Same....................................20
No opinion.............................. 6

Non-Labor Force

Better 42%
Worse...................................29
Same....................................18
No opinion..............................11

By Community Size
One Million and Over

Better 44%
Worse 31
Same 19
No opinion 6

500,000–999,999

Better 46%
Worse 35
Same 17
No opinion 2

50,000–499,999

Better 48%
Worse 29
Same 17
No opinion 6

2,500–49,999

Better 46%
Worse 26
Same 20
No opinion 8

Under 2,500; Rural

Better 41%
Worse 31
Same 20
No opinion 8

Note: Analysis of the results shows greater optimism among men, whites, persons with a college background, and those under thirty years of age. Midwesterners and persons in the Far West also appear to be more upbeat in their assessment of prospects for the new year than are easterners and southerners. Republicans are slightly less bullish than are Democrats and independents. Persons in upper income groups and those in business or the professions are more optimistic than are those in lower income groups and in manual labor occupations.

JANUARY 8
ECONOMIC OUTLOOK

Interviewing Date: 11/18–21/77
Survey #989-K

Which of these do you think is likely to be true of 1978: a year of economic prosperity or a year of economic difficulty?

Prosperity 24%
Difficulty 52
Same 17
Don't know 7

By Race
Whites

Prosperity 24%
Difficulty 51
Same 18
Don't know 7

Nonwhites

Prosperity 20%
Difficulty 54
Same 15
Don't know 11

By Education
College

Prosperity 30%
Difficulty 49
Same 18
Don't know 3

High School

Prosperity 21%
Difficulty 55
Same 16
Don't know 8

Grade School

Prosperity 20%
Difficulty 44
Same 20
Don't know 16

By Income

$20,000 and Over

Prosperity 27%
Difficulty 50
Same. 17
Don't know 6

$15,000–$19,999

Prosperity 25%
Difficulty 52
Same. 19
Don't know 4

$10,000–$14,999

Prosperity 23%
Difficulty 54
Same. 19
Don't know 4

$7,000–$9,999

Prosperity 25%
Difficulty 53
Same. 16
Don't know 6

$5,000–$6,999

Prosperity 20%
Difficulty 53
Same. 15
Don't know 12

$3,000–$4,999

Prosperity 19%
Difficulty 50
Same. 19
Don't know 12

Under $3,000

Prosperity 21%
Difficulty 50
Same. 9
Don't know 20

Those Who Think 1978 Will Be Better than 1977

Prosperity 41%
Difficulty 34
Same. 19
Don't know 6

Those Who Think 1978 Will Be Worse than 1977

Prosperity 7%
Difficulty 79
Same. 9
Don't know 5

Those Who Think 1978 Will Be the Same as 1977

Prosperity 12%
Difficulty 52
Same. 28
Don't know 8

Those Who Think 1978 Will Be a Year of Rising Prices

Prosperity 23%
Difficulty 55
Same. 15
Don't know 7

Those Who Think 1978 Will Be a Year of Falling Prices

Prosperity 48%
Difficulty 33
Same. 14
Don't know 5

Those Who Think That Prices Will Remain the Same in 1978

Prosperity 20%
Difficulty 30
Same. 44
Don't know 6

Which of these do you think is likely to be true of 1978: a year of rising prices or a year of falling prices?

Rising 85%
Falling 5
Same. 7
Don't know 3

By Race
Whites

Rising 87%
Falling 4
Same. 7
Don't know 2

Nonwhites

Rising 73%
Falling 11
Same. 11
Don't know 5

By Education
College

Rising 87%
Falling 6
Same. 6
Don't know 1

High School

Rising 85%
Falling 5
Same. 8
Don't know 2

Grade School

Rising 80%
Falling 5
Same. 8
Don't know 7

By Income
$20,000 and Over

Rising 89%
Falling 5
Same. 5
Don't know 1

$15,000–$19,999

Rising 87%
Falling 4
Same. 8
Don't know 1

$10,000–$14,999

Rising 88%
Falling 4
Same. 6
Don't know 2

$7,000–$9,999

Rising 86%
Falling 7
Same. 4
Don't know 3

$5,000–$6,999

Rising 79%
Falling 5
Same. 11
Don't know 5

$3,000–$4,999

Rising 71%
Falling 11
Same. 13
Don't know 5

Under $3,000

Rising 81%
Falling 6
Same. 7
Don't know 6

Those Who Think 1978 Will Be Better than 1977

Rising 82%
Falling 7
Same. 9
Don't know 2

Those Who Think 1978 Will Be Worse than 1977

Rising................................92%
Falling 3
Same.................................. 3
Don't know 2

Those Who Think 1978 Will Be the Same as 1977

Rising................................82%
Falling 5
Same.................................. 11
Don't know 2

Those Who Think 1978 Will Be a Year of Economic Prosperity

Rising................................82%
Falling 11
Same.................................. 6
Don't know 1

Those Who Think 1978 Will Be a Year of Economic Difficulty

Rising................................91%
Falling 4
Same.................................. 4
Don't know 1

Those Who Think That the Economic Situation in 1978 Will Remain the Same as in 1977

Rising................................75%
Falling 4
Same.................................. 18
Don't know 3

Which of these do you think is likely to be true of 1978: a year when taxes will rise or a year when taxes will fall?

Rise 74%
Fall...................................10
Same.................................. 11
Don't know 5

By Race
Whites

Rise 76%
Fall................................... 9
Same.................................. 11
Don't know 4

Nonwhites

Rise 62%
Fall................................... 12
Same.................................. 14
Don't know 12

By Education
College

Rise 72%
Fall................................... 12
Same.................................. 13
Don't know 3

High School

Rise 77%
Fall................................... 9
Same.................................. 11
Don't know 3

Grade School

Rise 66%
Fall................................... 11
Same.................................. 9
Don't know 14

By Income
$20,000 and Over

Rise 73%
Fall................................... 12
Same.................................. 13
Don't know 2

$15,000–$19,999

Rise 74%
Fall................................... 12
Same.................................. 10
Don't know 4

$10,000–$14,999

Rise 82%
Fall 6
Same 10
Don't know 2

$7,000–$9,999

Rise 76%
Fall 8
Same 14
Don't know 2

$5,000–$6,999

Rise 68%
Fall 10
Same 15
Don't know 7

$3,000–$4,999

Rise 63%
Fall 12
Same 12
Don't know 13

Under $3,000

Rise 70%
Fall 8
Same 7
Don't know 15

Those Who Think 1978 Will Be Better than 1977

Rise 71%
Fall 14
Same 11
Don't know 4

Those Who Think 1978 Will Be Worse than 1977

Rise 82%
Fall 5
Same 9
Don't know 4

Those Who Think 1978 Will Be the Same as 1977

Rise 72%
Fall 7
Same 17
Don't know 4

Those Who Think 1978 Will Be a Year of Economic Prosperity

Rise 70%
Fall 15
Same 11
Don't know 4

Those Who Think 1978 Will Be a Year of Economic Difficulty

Rise 81%
Fall 8
Same 8
Don't know 3

Those Who Think That the Economic Situation in 1978 Will Remain the Same as in 1977

Rise 65%
Fall 7
Same 23
Don't know 5

Which of these do you think is likely to be true of 1978: a year of strikes and industrial disputes or a year of industrial peace?

Strikes and disputes 54%
Industrial peace 23
Same 12
Don't know 11

By Race

Whites

Strikes and disputes 55%
Industrial peace 23
Same 12
Don't know 10

Nonwhites

Strikes and disputes 52%
Industrial peace. 20
Same. 10
Don't know 18

By Education
College

Strikes and disputes 51%
Industrial peace. 29
Same. 12
Don't know 8

High School

Strikes and disputes 57%
Industrial peace. 22
Same. 12
Don't know 9

Grade School

Strikes and disputes 51%
Industrial peace. 15
Same. 14
Don't know 20

By Income
$20,000 and Over

Strikes and disputes 49%
Industrial peace. 30
Same. 13
Don't know 8

$15,000–$19,999

Strikes and disputes 55%
Industrial peace. 25
Same. 9
Don't know 11

$10,000–$14,999

Strikes and disputes 55%
Industrial peace. 22
Same. 17
Don't know 6

$7,000–$9,999

Strikes and disputes 61%
Industrial peace. 23
Same. 8
Don't know 8

$5,000–$6,999

Strikes and disputes 59%
Industrial peace. 16
Same. 10
Don't know 15

$3,000–$4,999

Strikes and disputes 52%
Industrial peace. 16
Same. 13
Don't know 19

Under $3,000

Strikes and disputes 55%
Industrial peace. 18
Same. 8
Don't know 19

By Occupation
Professional and Business

Strikes and disputes 52%
Industrial peace. 27
Same. 13
Don't know 8

Clerical and Sales

Strikes and disputes 54%
Industrial peace. 25
Same. 12
Don't know 9

Manual Workers

Strikes and disputes 57%
Industrial peace. 22
Same. 12
Don't know 9

Non-Labor Force

Strikes and disputes 52%
Industrial peace. 21
Same. 11
Don't know 16

Labor Union Families Only

Strikes and disputes 56%
Industrial peace. 24
Same. 11
Don't know 9

Non-Labor Union Families Only

Strikes and disputes 54%
Industrial peace. 22
Same. 13
Don't know 11

Which of these do you think is likely to be true of 1978: a year of full employment or a year of rising unemployment?

Unemployment. 49%
Full employment. 17
Same. 27
Don't know 7

By Race
Whites

Unemployment. 49%
Full employment. 17
Same. 27
Don't know 7

Nonwhites

Unemployment. 49%
Full employment. 16
Same. 24
Don't know 11

By Education
College

Unemployment. 46%
Full employment. 16
Same. 33
Don't know 5

High School

Unemployment. 51%
Full employment. 19
Same. 24
Don't know 6

Grade School

Unemployment. 47%
Full employment. 13
Same. 27
Don't know 13

By Income
$20,000 and Over

Unemployment. 48%
Full employment. 18
Same. 29
Don't know 5

$15,000–$19,999

Unemployment. 45%
Full employment. 20
Same. 28
Don't know 7

$10,000–$14,999

Unemployment. 49%
Full employment. 17
Same. 28
Don't know 6

$7,000–$9,999

Unemployment. 56%
Full employment. 17
Same. 21
Don't know 6

$5,000–$6,999

Unemployment. 50%
Full employment. 13
Same. 28
Don't know 9

$3,000–$4,999

Unemployment......................54%
Full employment....................13
Same.............................23
Don't know 10

Under $3,000

Unemployment......................52%
Full employment....................15
Same.............................20
Don't know 13

By Occupation
Professional and Business

Unemployment......................47%
Full employment....................16
Same.............................31
Don't know 6

Clerical and Sales

Unemployment......................49%
Full employment....................26
Same.............................20
Don't know 5

Manual Workers

Unemployment......................54%
Full employment....................16
Same.............................24
Don't know 6

Non-Labor Force

Unemployment......................45%
Full employment....................14
Same.............................30
Don't know 11

Labor Union Families Only

Unemployment......................52%
Full employment....................15
Same.............................27
Don't know 6

Non-Labor Union Families Only

Unemployment......................49%
Full employment....................17
Same.............................27
Don't know 7

Note: In their feeling that prices and taxes will be higher in 1978 than in the preceding year, Americans are among the most bearish of the publics polled in a multinational survey. Only the Finns, Japanese, and Mexicans express a comparable degree of pessimism regarding prices. With regard to taxes, Americans are exceeded in their expectancy of a bigger tax bill only by the French and Brazilians, and they express about the same degree of pessimism as the Swiss and Uruguayans.

In their view on strikes and industrial problems, Americans are among the most pessimistic in the sixteen-nation group. Leading the list in this respect are the British, among whom 65% expect a year of strikes. Following the British, but significantly less pessimistic, are Australians (57% predict a year of strikes) Americans (54%), Swedes (53%), and Canadians (51%).

On the question of joblessness during 1978, Americans are closer to the middle point of the nations surveyed. Six publics (those in France, Sweden, Finland, Japan, Canada, and India) take a more pessimistic view of the employment picture. About the same percentage of Germans as Americans predict more joblessness in 1978; the remaining eight publics surveyed are significantly less pessimistic.

JANUARY 12
PEACE PREDICTIONS

Interviewing Date: 11/18–21/77
Survey #989-K

Which of these do you think is likely to be true of 1978: a peaceful year, more or less free of international disputes, or a troubled year with much international discord?

Peaceful year. 35%
Troubled year 45
Same. 12
Don't know 8

By Sex
Male

Peaceful year. 38%
Troubled year 43
Same. 12
Don't know 7

Female

Peaceful year. 33%
Troubled year 47
Same. 12
Don't know 8

By Education
College

Peaceful year. 45%
Troubled year 38
Same. 14
Don't know 3

High School

Peaceful year. 32%
Troubled year 49
Same. 12
Don't know 7

Grade School

Peaceful year. 25%
Troubled year 46
Same. 10
Don't know 19

By Region
East

Peaceful year. 34%
Troubled year 44
Same. 15
Don't know 7

Midwest

Peaceful year. 40%
Troubled year 41
Same. 12
Don't know 7

South

Peaceful year. 30%
Troubled year 48
Same. 11
Don't know 11

West

Peaceful year. 36%
Troubled year 49
Same. 10
Don't know 5

By Age
18–24 Years

Peaceful year. 38%
Troubled year 45
Same. 10
Don't know 7

25–29 Years

Peaceful year. 44%
Troubled year 41
Same. 11
Don't know 4

30–49 Years

Peaceful year. 37%
Troubled year 41
Same. 17
Don't know 5

50 Years and Over

Peaceful year. 29%
Troubled year 50
Same. 9
Don't know 12

By Income

$20,000 and Over

Peaceful year........................40%
Troubled year 41
Same..................................14
Don't know 5

$15,000–$19,999

Peaceful year........................40%
Troubled year 42
Same..................................13
Don't know 5

$10,000–$14,999

Peaceful year........................37%
Troubled year 45
Same..................................12
Don't know 6

$7,000–$9,999

Peaceful year........................36%
Troubled year 45
Same..................................11
Don't know 8

$5,000–$6,999

Peaceful year........................21%
Troubled year 55
Same..................................12
Don't know 12

$3,000–$4,999

Peaceful year........................27%
Troubled year 49
Same.................................. 9
Don't know 15

Under $3,000

Peaceful year........................24%
Troubled year 52
Same.................................. 7
Don't know 17

By Politics

Republicans

Peaceful year........................34%
Troubled year 50
Same..................................11
Don't know 5

Democrats

Peaceful year........................34%
Troubled year 45
Same..................................13
Don't know 8

Southern Democrats

Peaceful year........................30%
Troubled year 48
Same..................................13
Don't know 9

Other Democrats

Peaceful year........................36%
Troubled year 44
Same..................................12
Don't know 8

Independents

Peaceful year........................38%
Troubled year 41
Same..................................14
Don't know 7

Note: Despite recent peace initiatives in the Middle East, Americans tend to view overall prospects for peace in the world in a somewhat gloomy light.

A recent eighteen-nation survey shows Americans to be among the more pessimistic publics, with 45% in the United States predicting a "troubled year with much international discord," compared to 35% who think 1978 will be a "peaceful year, more or less free of international disputes."

While the United States joins eight of the eighteen nations surveyed where pessimists are dominant, Americans are considerably more encouraged about peace prospects today than they were three years ago. At the beginning of 1975, a large majority of Americans, 61%, predicted international discord, while 29% believed that year would be more or less peaceful.

Analysis of the United States findings show persons with a college background and younger adults to be somewhat less pessimistic than persons with less formal education and older adults. Differences by political party affiliation and by sex are slight.

JANUARY 15
POWER EXPECTATIONS

Interviewing Date: 11/18–21/77
Survey #989-K

Which of these do you think is likely to be true of 1978: a year when America will increase her power in the world, or a year when American power will decline?

Increase 42%
Decline............................. 26
Same................................ 24
Don't know 8

By Education
College

Increase 31%
Decline............................. 31
Same................................ 33
Don't know 5

High School

Increase 46%
Decline............................. 26
Same................................ 21
Don't know 7

Grade School

Increase 47%
Decline............................. 15
Same................................ 20
Don't know 18

By Region
East

Increase 36%
Decline............................. 28
Same................................ 30
Don't know 6

Midwest

Increase 42%
Decline............................. 21
Same................................ 28
Don't know 9

South

Increase 48%
Decline............................. 25
Same................................ 16
Don't know 11

West

Increase 41%
Decline............................. 30
Same................................ 24
Don't know 5

By Politics
Republicans

Increase 40%
Decline............................. 30
Same................................ 25
Don't know 5

Democrats

Increase 47%
Decline............................. 22
Same................................ 23
Don't know 8

Southern Democrats

Increase 52%
Decline............................. 22
Same................................ 15
Don't know 11

Other Democrats

Increase 44%
Decline 23
Same 26
Don't know 7

Independents

Increase 38%
Decline 27
Same 28
Don't know 7

Which of these do you think is likely to be true of 1978: a year when Russia will increase her power in the world, or a year when Russian power will decline?

Increase 53%
Decline 16
Same 20
Don't know 11

By Education
College

Increase 45%
Decline 22
Same 27
Don't know 6

High School

Increase 59%
Decline 14
Same 18
Don't know 9

Grade School

Increase 47%
Decline 13
Same 13
Don't know 27

By Region
East

Increase 49%
Decline 16
Same 25
Don't know 10

Midwest

Increase 50%
Decline 16
Same 23
Don't know 11

South

Increase 57%
Decline 13
Same 15
Don't know 15

West

Increase 58%
Decline 20
Same 17
Don't know 5

By Politics
Republicans

Increase 60%
Decline 14
Same 19
Don't know 7

Democrats

Increase 50%
Decline 19
Same 20
Don't know 11

Southern Democrats

Increase 57%
Decline 14
Same 15
Don't know 14

Other Democrats

Increase 47%
Decline 21
Same 22
Don't know 10

Independents

Increase 54%
Decline 13
Same 22
Don't know 11

Which of these do you think is likely to be true of 1978: a year when China will increase her power in the world, or a year when Chinese power will decline?

Increase 56%
Decline 11
Same 18
Don't know 15

By Education
College

Increase 55%
Decline 12
Same 24
Don't know 9

High School

Increase 61%
Decline 10
Same 15
Don't know 14

Grade School

Increase 40%
Decline 13
Same 14
Don't know 33

By Region
East

Increase 55%
Decline 10
Same 22
Don't know 13

Midwest

Increase 56%
Decline 11
Same 19
Don't know 14

South

Increase 53%
Decline 12
Same 12
Don't know 23

West

Increase 62%
Decline 12
Same 17
Don't know 9

By Politics
Republicans

Increase 58%
Decline 11
Same 20
Don't know 11

Democrats

Increase 58%
Decline 11
Same 14
Don't know 17

Southern Democrats

Increase 56%
Decline 8
Same 13
Don't know 23

Other Democrats

Increase 59%
Decline 12
Same 15
Don't know 14

Increase 53%
Decline 12
Same 22
Don't know 13

Which statement on this card best describes how you would rate Russia's power in the world?

Most powerful 8%
One of the most powerful 68
Powerful as other large countries 16
One of the least powerful 1
Not at all powerful 1
Don't know 6

Which statement on this card best describes how you would rate China's power in the world?

Most powerful 3%
One of the most powerful 34
Powerful as other large countries 43
One of the least powerful 9
Not at all powerful 2
Don't know 9

Which statement on this card best describes how you would rate America's power in the world?

Most powerful 34%
One of the most powerful 50
Powerful as other large countries 13
One of the least powerful 1
Not at all powerful . . . . *
Don't know 2

*Less than 1%.

Note: Although fewer Americans today than one year ago predict that United States power and influence in the world will grow, we still continue to believe our nation to be the dominant one among the three superpowers—Russia, China, and the United States.

At the present time, 42% of Americans believe America will increase her power in 1978, while 26% believe that American power will decline. Another 32% see little change or express uncertainty. Last year at this time, 57% of Americans said United States power would increase, 25% said it would decline, and far fewer than today, 18%, saw United States power remaining about the same or expressed uncertainty.

Rather remarkably, the United States public's perceptions of the relative strength of the three superpowers differ little on the basis of educational level, age, or political party affiliation.

An eighteen-nation Gallup survey shows almost unanimous agreement that the three superpowers will increase their power this year. Only Brazil (where more see a decline in Russian power than see an increase), Japan (where American power is seen to be static), and Mexico (where a decline in Chinese and Russian power is seen) are the exceptions to this general feeling of increasing power.

There is also almost full agreement on the superpowers' "pecking order." People were asked to rate each of the three countries on a "power scale," running from the most powerful country down to the least powerful.

Of the fifteen countries in which these particular questions were asked, thirteen rate the United States as the most powerful, followed by Russia and then China.

The two exceptions are Britain and Uruguay. In Britain, Russia is rated the most powerful (24%), followed by America (17%) and China (5%). In Uruguay, America is thought to be the most powerful (43%), but China is ranked second (36%), and Russia is a poor third (9%).

Of particular importance are the views of the publics in those nations that share mutual defense treaties with the United States.

Probably the most important defense pact in which the United States is now a partner is NATO, the North Atlantic Treaty Organization. Of the nations surveyed, four—Canada, France, West Germany, and Great Britain—are members of NATO.

Their views concerning American power vis-à-vis Russia and China indicate that, generally, residents of these allied nations take a pessimistic view of the developing power balance in the world. This is particularly true in West Germany and Great Britain. In Germany only 26% feel America will increase her power during the current year, while 33% and 40%, respectively, take the same view of Russian and Chinese power. At the same time, 12% of Germans feel United States prestige will slide this year, while the comparable percentages for Russia and China are 8% and 4%, respectively. The same pattern obtains for Great Britain.

In Canada and France, opinion is not so pessimistic as in the other two nations when the United States is compared to Russia. But when compared to the outlook for China, attitudes toward America's prestige suffer significantly.

The following illustrates these comparisons:

Views of NATO Nations

Canada

AMERICAN POWER

Increase 35%
Decrease 20
Same, don't know 45

RUSSIAN POWER

Increase 37%
Decrease 12
Same, don't know 51

CHINESE POWER

Increase 44%
Decrease 7
Same, don't know 49

France

AMERICAN POWER

Increase 27%
Decrease 19
Same, don't know 54

RUSSIAN POWER

Increase 23%
Decrease 20
Same, don't know 57

CHINESE POWER

Increase 45%
Decrease 6
Same, don't know 49

West Germany

AMERICAN POWER

Increase 26%
Decrease 12
Same, don't know 62

RUSSIAN POWER

Increase 33%
Decrease 8
Same, don't know 59

CHINESE POWER

Increase 40%
Decrease 4
Same, don't know 56

Great Britain

AMERICAN POWER

Increase 30%
Decrease 16
Same, don't know 54

RUSSIAN POWER

Increase 39%
Decrease 9
Same, don't know 52

CHINESE POWER

Increase 42%
Decrease 5
Same, don't know 53

How these perceptions—those of Americans as well as NATO nations and other allies—will manifest themselves politically, if at all, remains the concern of the Carter administration.

JANUARY 19
PRESIDENT CARTER

Interviewing Date: 12/9–12/77
Survey #990-K

Do you approve or disapprove of the way

*Jimmy Carter is handling his job as president?**

Approve.............................57%
Disapprove 27
No opinion..........................16

By Race
Whites

Approve.............................56%
Disapprove 28
No opinion..........................16

Northern Whites

Approve.............................55%
Disapprove 29
No opinion..........................16

Southern Whites

Approve.............................57%
Disapprove 26
No opinion..........................17

Nonwhites

Approve.............................64%
Disapprove 20
No opinion..........................16

Northern Blacks

Approve.............................59%
Disapprove 20
No opinion..........................21

Southern Blacks

Approve.............................74%
Disapprove 19
No opinion......................... 7

By Region
East

Approve.............................54%
Disapprove 32
No opinion..........................14

*Gallup questionnaires do not include the first name of the president in surveys on presidential popularity.

Midwest

Approve.............................55%
Disapprove 27
No opinion..........................18

South

Approve.............................60%
Disapprove 25
No opinion..........................15

Deep South

Approve.............................58%
Disapprove 22
No opinion..........................20

Rest of South

Approve.............................61%
Disapprove 26
No opinion..........................13

West

Approve.............................58%
Disapprove 26
No opinion..........................16

By Age
18–24 Years

Approve.............................64%
Disapprove 17
No opinion..........................19

25–29 Years

Approve.............................56%
Disapprove 28
No opinion..........................16

30–49 Years

Approve.............................60%
Disapprove 25
No opinion..........................15

50 Years and Over

Approve.............................51%
Disapprove 34
No opinion..........................15

By Politics

Republicans

Approve.............................43%
Disapprove 44
No opinion.........................13

Democrats

Approve.............................67%
Disapprove 19
No opinion.........................14

Southern Democrats

Approve.............................71%
Disapprove 18
No opinion.........................11

Other Democrats

Approve.............................66%
Disapprove 20
No opinion.........................14

Independents

Approve.............................53%
Disapprove 28
No opinion.........................19

By Religion

Protestants

Approve.............................56%
Disapprove 14
No opinion.........................14

Catholics

Approve.............................61%
Disapprove 20
No opinion.........................19

How much trust and confidence do you have in President Carter, the man—a great deal, some, hardly any, or none?

A great deal.........................30%
Some................................52
Hardly any..........................9
None................................4
No opinion..........................5

By Race

Whites

A great deal.........................29%
Some................................53
Hardly any..........................9
None................................4
No opinion..........................5

Northern Whites

A great deal.........................26%
Some................................56
Hardly any..........................10
None................................3
No opinion..........................5

Southern Whites

A great deal.........................35%
Some................................44
Hardly any..........................8
None................................6
No opinion..........................7

Nonwhites

A great deal.........................38%
Some................................41
Hardly any..........................10
None................................7
No opinion..........................4

Northern Blacks

A great deal.........................29%
Some................................39
Hardly any..........................15
None................................10
No opinion..........................7

Southern Blacks

A great deal.........................47%
Some................................45

Hardly any........................ 3
None............................. 5
No opinion........................ *

By Region
East

A great deal....................... 23%
Some............................. 54
Hardly any........................ 12
None............................. 4
No opinion........................ 7

Midwest

A great deal....................... 26%
Some............................. 57
Hardly any........................ 9
None............................. 5
No opinion........................ 3

South

A great deal....................... 36%
Some............................. 44
Hardly any........................ 8
None............................. 6
No opinion........................ 6

Deep South

A great deal....................... 36%
Some............................. 38
Hardly any........................ 7
None............................. 10
No opinion........................ 9

Rest of South

A great deal....................... 36%
Some............................. 47
Hardly any........................ 8
None............................. 4
No opinion........................ 5

West

A great deal....................... 32%
Some............................. 51
Hardly any........................ 9
None............................. 3
No opinion........................ 5

By Age
18–24 Years

A great deal....................... 22%
Some............................. 60
Hardly any........................ 5
None............................. 5
No opinion........................ 8

25–29 Years

A great deal....................... 21%
Some............................. 60
Hardly any........................ 13
None............................. 2
No opinion........................ 4

30–49 Years

A great deal....................... 29%
Some............................. 55
Hardly any........................ 9
None............................. 3
No opinion........................ 4

50 Years and Over

A great deal....................... 36%
Some............................. 43
Hardly any........................ 11
None............................. 5
No opinion........................ 5

By Politics
Republicans

A great deal....................... 22%
Some............................. 56
Hardly any........................ 15
None............................. 6
No opinion........................ 1

Democrats

A great deal....................... 38%
Some............................. 47
Hardly any........................ 7
None............................. 3
No opinion........................ 5

Southern Democrats

A great deal 42%
Some 43
Hardly any 7
None 3
No opinion 5

Other Democrats

A great deal 37%
Some 49
Hardly any 7
None 2
No opinion 5

Independents

A great deal 22%
Some 55
Hardly any 10
None 6
No opinion 7

By Religion
Protestants

A great deal 32%
Some 50
Hardly any 10
None 4
No opinion 4

Catholics

A great deal 28%
Some 55
Hardly any 7
None 3
No opinion 7

Those Who Approve of the Way President Carter Is Handling His Job

A great deal 44%
Some 52
Hardly any 2
None 1
No opinion 1

Those Who Disapprove of the Way President Carter Is Handling His Job

A great deal 10%
Some 52
Hardly any 25
None 12
No opinion 1

Those Who Think President Carter's Record Is Excellent

A great deal 93%
Some 6
Hardly any . . . . *
None 1
No opinion . . . . *

Those Who Think President Carter's Record Is Good

A great deal 48%
Some 46
Hardly any 2
None 1
No opinion 3

Those Who Think President Carter's Record Is Fair

A great deal 18%
Some 69
Hardly any 9
None 2
No opinion 2

Those Who Think President Carter's Record Is Poor

A great deal 7%
Some 33
Hardly any 34
None 25
No opinion 1

*Less than 1%.

How would you rate President Carter's record to date—do you think he's done an excellent job in dealing with the problems facing the nation, a good job, a fair job, or a poor job?

Excellent	5%
Good	32
Fair	46
Poor	12
No opinion	5

By Race
Whites

Excellent	5%
Good	31
Fair	47
Poor	13
No opinion	4

Northern Whites

Excellent	3%
Good	32
Fair	48
Poor	13
No opinion	4

Southern Whites

Excellent	8%
Good	31
Fair	43
Poor	12
No opinion	6

Nonwhites

Excellent	11%
Good	36
Fair	37
Poor	10
No opinion	6

Northern Blacks

Excellent	8%
Good	35
Fair	33
Poor	13
No opinion	11

Southern Blacks

Excellent	15%
Good	36
Fair	42
Poor	7
No opinion	*

By Region
East

Excellent	3%
Good	32
Fair	44
Poor	15
No opinion	6

Midwest

Excellent	4%
Good	29
Fair	50
Poor	13
No opinion	4

South

Excellent	9%
Good	32
Fair	43
Poor	11
No opinion	5

Deep South

Excellent	10%
Good	34
Fair	36
Poor	12
No opinion	8

Rest of South

Excellent	8%
Good	31
Fair	46
Poor	11
No opinion	4

West

Excellent	4%
Good	35
Fair	46
Poor	12
No opinion	3

By Age
18–24 Years

Excellent	3%
Good	39
Fair	44
Poor	6
No opinion	8

25–29 Years

Excellent	3%
Good	35
Fair	49
Poor	7
No opinion	6

39–49 Years

Excellent	6%
Good	34
Fair	45
Poor	13
No opinion	2

50 Years and Over

Excellent	6%
Good	27
Fair	46
Poor	17
No opinion	4

By Politics
Republicans

Excellent	6%
Good	20
Fair	52
Poor	21
No opinion	1

Democrats

Excellent	6%
Good	37
Fair	44
Poor	8
No opinion	5

Southern Democrats

Excellent	11%
Good	35
Fair	42
Poor	9
No opinion	3

Other Democrats

Excellent	4%
Good	38
Fair	45
Poor	7
No opinion	6

Independents

Excellent	3%
Good	34
Fair	44
Poor	14
No opinion	5

By Religion
Protestants

Excellent	6%
Good	30
Fair	46
Poor	14
No opinion	4

Catholics

Excellent	3%
Good	38
Fair	45
Poor	9
No opinion	5

Those Who Approve of the Way President Carter Is Handling His Job

Excellent 9%
Good 49
Fair................................ 40
Poor 1
No opinion......................... 1

Those Who Disapprove of the Way President Carter Is Handling His Job

Excellent .... *%
Good 4
Fair................................ 57
Poor 38
No opinion......................... 1

Those Who Have a Great Deal of Trust in President Carter

Excellent 16%
Good 52
Fair................................ 28
Poor 3
No opinion......................... 1

Those Who Have Some Trust in President Carter

Excellent 1%
Good 29
Fair................................ 61
Poor 8
No opinion......................... 1

Those Who Have Hardly Any Trust in President Carter

Excellent .... *%
Good 7
Fair................................ 45
Poor 46
No opinion......................... 2

Those Who Have No Trust in President Carter

Excellent 2%
Good 5
Fair................................ 17
Poor 72
No opinion......................... 4

*Less than 1%.

Note: If there is one word that best describes the American public's feeling about President Carter after one year in office, that word might well be "ambivalence."

While Carter once had the approval of 75% of Americans for the way he was handling his job as president, his rating fluctuated as much as 24 percentage points and by the end of his first year in office had declined to 52%—virtually matching his low point during the year of 51%. While Americans evince a great deal of confidence in Jimmy Carter, the man, they seem unwilling to accord him more than a restrained amount of praise for his first year's efforts. Finally, while virtually no one questions the president's moral standards and personal attributes, there are growing doubts about his ability to govern competently.

Two weeks after he was inaugurated, Carter's approval rating showed two in every three people, 66%, endorsing the president's stewardship. This rating eventually reached a high of 75% in a survey conducted after his speech before the United Nations affirming this country's commitment to human rights.

Throughout the first part of the year, approval of Carter's handling of the presidency never dipped below the 60% mark. However, between mid-August and early September, as the controversy over then-Budget Director Bert Lance's financial affairs grew, approval of the president dropped from 66% to 54% and never topped the 60% mark during the rest of his first year in office.

Carter's final approval rating during his first year, 52%, virtually matched his low point and was recorded immediately after the president dismissed United States Attorney David Marston—a step viewed by many as a purely political move.

Not only the Marston removal itself but the way in which the Carter administration handled the affair left the president with a black mark from the public.

In a special telephone survey conducted shortly after the event, sentiment among the 52% of respondents who had heard or read about the firing was four-to-one against the Philadelphia attorney's removal and five-to-one in disapproval of the way the Carter administration handled the situation.

Here are the questions asked in a telephone survey of those who said they had either heard or read about the Marston firing, and the results:

From what you have heard or read, do you think that Marston should or should not have been removed from office?

Should have been fired................. 6%
Should not have been fired.............. 26
No opinion............................ 20
Not heard/read about firing............ 48

Do you approve or disapprove of the way the Carter administration handled the Marston firing?

Approve............................. 6%
Disapprove 32
No opinion........................... 14
Not heard/read about firing............ 48

Intensity of Approval

Periodically during Carter's first year, the Gallup Poll also sought to determine the intensity of the public's support for the president's actions and policies.

Results from the final such survey during that first year, conducted in mid-November, showed one-fifth of Americans, 20%, approving very strongly of the way in which Carter was handling his duties and 36% expressing a milder degree of approval. At the other end of the spectrum, 15% disapproved very strongly of the president's actions, and the same percentage expressed mild disapproval.

Viewing these figures in another way, of the people expressing approval of the president's actions, one-third (35%) registered strong approval and the other two-thirds (65%) were not so generous with their praise. Among those disapproving, the majority, 53%, described their disapproval as mild while 47% fell into the group strongly disapproving.

Following is the trend in the intensity of Carter's approval during his first year in office, using those who approved and those who disapproved as separate bases for analysis:

Intensity of Carter Popularity

Among Those Approving

	Strong approval	Mild approval
Nov. 18–21, 1977........	35%	65%
Nov. 4–7	36	64
Oct. 21–24..............	35	65
Oct. 14–17	39	61
Sept. 30–Oct. 3..........	41	59
May 6–9.................	49	51
March 18–21............	56	44

Among Those Disapproving

	Strong disapproval	Mild disapproval
Nov. 18–21, 1977 ..	53%	47%
Nov. 4–7	51	49
Oct. 21–24	60	40
Oct. 14–17	52	48
Sept. 30–Oct. 3.....	52	48
May 6–9	52	48
March 18–21	53	47

Comparative Standing

Compared to that of his six immediate predecessors, Carter's popularity during his first year in office is not particularly impressive.

His average rating, 62% approval, is exceeded by four; Gerald Ford's is lower, and Richard Nixon's average rating, 61%, is not significantly different from Carter's.

His highest rating, 65%, betters those achieved by both Ford and Nixon during their first years, matches Eisenhower's, but falls below those of the three other men. For lowest first-year rating figures, only Ford's is worse than Carter's, 37% to 51% respectively.

From his high point to his low point in popularity, Carter dropped 24 percentage points. Only Ford, who dropped 34 points, and Truman, who also slipped 24 points, come anywhere close to the inconsistency measured for Carter. Among Presidents Eisenhower, Kennedy, Johnson, and Nixon, only Eisenhower's 17-percentage-point spread comes close to the range measured for Carter.

Further Indicators

In addition to his popularity rating, there is additional survey evidence of the tempered enthusiasm the public now has for Carter.

After he had been in office nearly eleven months, just 5% of Americans said they would characterize Carter's record at that point (the survey was conducted between December 9 and 12, 1977) as excellent, while 32% rated his record as good. About half the public, 46%, gave the president a fair rating on his record, and 12% said it was poor.

In addition to rating his record this way, Americans were hard pressed to think of a significant Carter achievement. When asked what they considered Carter's most important achievement during his first year in office, half of Americans said either that he hadn't accomplished anything of note (26%) or they couldn't cite anything (22%).

Among those who were able to think of something they considered to be an important accomplishment, most cited his efforts in the area of foreign affairs and specifically his attempts to bring about peace in the Middle East.

Rating Domestic Policy

Although at the end of the year Americans generally could not recall an achievement in the domestic field that they were willing to call Carter's most important one, earlier in the year they endorsed his domestic policies.

In early July 1977 nearly six people in ten, 58%, said they approved of the way Carter was handling the nation's domestic problems. Only half as many, 29%, found fault with the president's efforts in this field.

One of Carter's most conspicuous failures during the year, however, was in the field of domestic policy. Not only did he fail to convince an increasing number of Americans that the energy situation called for a commitment that was "the moral equivalent of war," but as the year wore on he progressively lost support for his efforts in the energy field.

In February 1977 61% said they approved of the way Carter was dealing with the energy situation. But by August, nearly as many disapproved (39%) as approved (44%) of his efforts.

Rating Foreign Policy

In the foreign policy arena, the president won the midsummer endorsement of Americans (49% approved of his handling of our foreign policy problems and 32% disapproved), but on two specific decisions relating directly to foreign policy, Carter did not fare as well.

Early in his administration, the president was faced with a decision concerning production of the B-1 bomber. Carter decided to halt production, and this choice was backed by a plurality of those who, at the time of the survey, had heard or read about the subject. Nearly half, 47%, of those familiar with Carter's decision supported the president, while 33% disapproved. Carter's judgment found particular support among people critical of the size of the defense budget.

In another major decision concerning foreign policy, however, Carter split the informed public opinion. After the president announced a phased withdrawal of United States ground troops from South Korea, the Gallup Poll asked those who had heard or read about the decision their views on the subject. Among the eight people in ten, 78%, who had heard or read about the president's plan, 40% backed him while nearly as many, 38%, disapproved.

Disappointed Expectations

Another part of the president's problem with the American public is the fact that he has not lived up to the expectations of many people.

Although 23% said he had been a better president than they expected, 38% said he had not been as good as they thought he would be. Another 29% said Carter had been about what they expected.

An examination of the reasoning used here indicates that the group who approved of Carter felt he had brought new ideas and values to the job and needed more time to work things out. Among those critical of the president, the majority said simply that he was not keeping his campaign promises. Others cited such faults as indecisiveness, insufficient command of the economy, and a weak foreign policy.

In his first year in office, Carter managed to cause disappointment among the public in general, but particularly significant was his loss of popularity with many of the minority groups that played an important role in his election. For example, among nonwhites (of whom 85% voted for Carter), 30% said he had not lived up to their expectations; his popularity rating with this group dropped from 62% to 54%.

Carter had another problem with Black opinion during his first summer as president. National Urban League Executive Director Vernon Jordan accused the Carter administration of forgetting the Black voters who helped put the Democrat in office. Jordan took Carter to task for neglecting issues that mattered to Blacks—unemployment, rebuilding of cities, welfare reform, affirmative action programs, and economic development. As many as one-fourth of Blacks who were polled, 26%, expressed the opinion that they were being unfairly treated by the Carter administration—a viewpoint with which only 4% of whites concurred.

In fact, Americans nationwide were more likely to single out several other groups more often than Blacks as being unfairly treated by the administration. Cited most often as suffering from discrimination were senior citizens (named by 18%) and small-business people (16%).

On the positive side, however, was the finding that 42% in the survey said none of the twelve groups listed on the survey—Blacks, senior citizens, small-business people, women, people on welfare, unemployed people, farmers, labor union members, corporate executives, Catholics, Jews, and "people like yourself"—were being unfairly treated by the Carter administration.

Other groups disappointed in the president included those in his home region. Among southerners (54% support during the election), 33% said he is not the president they expected him to be, and his rating declined from 74% to 54%. With members of labor union families (among who 63% voted for Carter), 40% said he had disappointed them, and his approval rating dipped from its original 71% to 55%.

Possibly most troublesome, though, is the fact that as many as four Democrats in ten, 38%, are disillusioned with Carter as president. And, among his own party members, his popularity dropped from 77% in February 1977 to 60% one year later.

Carter, the Man

Despite their reservations about the president's record during his first year in office, Americans continue to have a high degree of confidence in Carter as an individual.

For example, eleven months after he had been in office, fully 82% of the public said they had either a great deal (30%) or some (52%) confidence in Carter, the man, as distinct from his performance in office. This confidence was recorded among all groups of Americans, including those most likely to be antagonistic toward the president—for example, Republicans.

In addition, huge proportions of the public rate the president as an intelligent (80%), moral (80%) man. Although he is sometimes portrayed as cool and aloof, 78% of Americans view him as a likable person.

Probably the perception that is potentially most damaging to the Carter image, however, is his failure to convince large numbers of Americans that he has a coherent, well-defined program for guiding the nation.

During the campaign and early in his administration, the percentage of Americans who viewed Carter as a man with good ideas and programs for moving the country ahead outnumbered those with the opposite viewpoint by about a two-to-one margin.

After eight months in office, however, these percentages had evened out, with just as many holding the view that the president didn't have well-defined programs for improving America (44%) as those who thought he indeed had conceived a clear agenda for change (43%). This trend is further substantiated by the finding that 49% of the American public viewed Carter as a man of average abilities, a significantly larger number than the 41% who believed he had exceptional abilities.

Finally, the president is once again subject to the view that he is unclear, if not inconsistent, on the issues. Nearly half the public, 47%, said it was hard to know where he stood on the issues, while 42% had no such problem. These numbers represent a setback in the president's ability to communicate his stand on the problems facing America.

The Lance Affair

Without doubt, the number one presidential headache during the first year stemmed from the financial dealings of presidential friend, adviser, and budget director Bert Lance.

Carter barely had time to unpack before allegations began to appear in the media concerning Lance's personal and business financial dealings. The affair dragged through the summer, and although the president stood by his friend, Lance was forced to resign after appearing before a Senate committee to "clear his name."

Although the president steadfastly refused to condemn Lance's dealings, the public clearly did. In a survey completed approximately one week before Lance resigned, three out of four people, 74%, who said they had been following the discussions concerning the Lance affair expressed the view that the budget director had handled his financial dealings improperly, and 69% expressed the view he should resign.

Perhaps more important for Carter, however, is the finding that one-fourth of those who saw, heard, or read about the Lance testimony before the Senate Governmental Affairs Committee came away with a more critical view of the president's ethical standards. At the same time, 8% said their view of Carter's standards had improved, and 58% said the Lance matter hadn't made any difference in their feelings in this regard.

Although the public seems to have quickly forgotten about the Lance problem (it received virtually no mention in end-of-year surveys regarding Carter), it may well have been the most serious rupture of the bond of trust Carter had worked so hard to create between his administration and the public it serves.

JANUARY 22
ABORTION

Interviewing Date: 12/9–12/77
Survey #990-K

Do you think abortions should be legal under any circumstances, legal only under certain circumstances, or illegal in all circumstances?

Legal, any circumstances 22%
Legal, certain circumstances 55
Illegal, all circumstances 19
No opinion 4

By Sex
Male

Legal, any circumstances 22%
Legal, certain circumstances 55
Illegal, all circumstances 17
No opinion 6

Female

Legal, any circumstances 22%
Legal, certain circumstances 55
Illegal, all circumstances 20
No opinion 3

By Marital Status

Married

Legal, any circumstances	21%
Legal, certain circumstances	58
Illegal, all circumstances	17
No opinion	4

Single

Legal, any circumstances	23%
Legal, certain circumstances	53
Illegal, all circumstances	20
No opinion	4

Widowed

Legal, any circumstances	19%
Legal, certain circumstances	45
Illegal, all circumstances	29
No opinion	7

Separated

Legal, any circumstances	35%
Legal, certain circumstances	33
Illegal, all circumstances	17
No opinion	15

Divorced

Legal, any circumstances	34%
Legal, certain circumstances	44
Illegal, all circumstances	18
No opinion	4

By Race

Whites

Legal, any circumstances	23%
Legal, certain circumstances	56
Illegal, all circumstances	17
No opinion	4

Northern Whites

Legal, any circumstances	24%
Legal, certain circumstances	55
Illegal, all circumstances	17
No opinion	4

Southern Whites

Legal, any circumstances	19%
Legal, certain circumstances	60
Illegal, all circumstances	19
No opinion	2

Nonwhites

Legal, any circumstances	14%
Legal, certain circumstances	41
Illegal, all circumstances	32
No opinion	13

Northern Blacks

Legal, any circumstances	22%
Legal, certain circumstances	28
Illegal, all circumstances	39
No opinion	11

Southern Blacks

Legal, any circumstances	2%
Legal, certain circumstances	59
Illegal, all circumstances	24
No opinion	15

By Region

East

Legal, any circumstances	26%
Legal, certain circumstances	48
Illegal, all circumstances	20
No opinion	6

Midwest

Legal, any circumstances	17%
Legal, certain circumstances	54
Illegal, all circumstances	24
No opinion	5

South

Legal, any circumstances	17%
Legal, certain circumstances	60
Illegal, all circumstances	19
No opinion	4

Deep South

Legal, any circumstances 7%
Legal, certain circumstances........... 68
Illegal, all circumstances 20
No opinion......................... 5

Rest of South

Legal, any circumstances 21%
Legal, certain circumstances........... 56
Illegal, all circumstances 19
No opinion......................... 4

West

Legal, any circumstances 31%
Legal, certain circumstances........... 58
Illegal, all circumstances 9
No opinion......................... 2

By Age
18–24 Years

Legal, any circumstances 19%
Legal, certain circumstances........... 60
Illegal, all circumstances 19
No opinion......................... 2

25–29 Years

Legal, any circumstances 32%
Legal, certain circumstances........... 49
Illegal, all circumstances 16
No opinion......................... 3

30–49 Years

Legal, any circumstances 23%
Legal, certain circumstances........... 58
Illegal, all circumstances 15
No opinion......................... 4

50 Years and Over

Legal, any circumstances 19%
Legal, certain circumstances........... 52
Illegal, all circumstances 23
No opinion......................... 6

By Income
$20,000 and Over

Legal, any circumstances 31%
Legal, certain circumstances........... 59
Illegal, all circumstances 9
No opinion......................... 1

$15,000–$19,999

Legal, any circumstances 20%
Legal, certain circumstances........... 60
Illegal, all circumstances 14
No opinion......................... 6

$10,000–$14,999

Legal, any circumstances 21%
Legal, certain circumstances........... 53
Illegal, all circumstances 22
No opinion......................... 4

$7,000–$9,999

Legal, any circumstances 16%
Legal, certain circumstances........... 56
Illegal, all circumstances 22
No opinion......................... 6

$5,000–$6,999

Legal, any circumstances 11%
Legal, certain circumstances........... 59
Illegal, all circumstances 27
No opinion......................... 3

$3,000–$4,999

Legal, any circumstances 17%
Legal, certain circumstances........... 41
Illegal, all circumstances 29
No opinion......................... 13

Under $3,000

Legal, any circumstances 21%
Legal, certain circumstances........... 38
Illegal, all circumstances 35
No opinion......................... 6

By Religion
Protestants

Legal, any circumstances 18%
Legal, certain circumstances 58
Illegal, all circumstances 19
No opinion 5

Catholics

Legal, any circumstances 20%
Legal, certain circumstances 53
Illegal, all circumstances 23
No opinion 4

By Occupation
Professional and Business

Legal, any circumstances 31%
Legal, certain circumstances 57
Illegal, all circumstances 11
No opinion 1

Clerical and Sales

Legal, any circumstances 27%
Legal, certain circumstances 58
Illegal, all circumstances 15
No opinion . . . . *

Manual Workers

Legal, any circumstances 17%
Legal, certain circumstances 57
Illegal, all circumstances 20
No opinion 6

Skilled Workers

Legal, any circumstances 17%
Legal, certain circumstances 65
Illegal, all circumstances 14
No opinion 4

Unskilled Workers

Legal, any circumstances 17%
Legal, certain circumstances 51
Illegal, all circumstances 25
No opinion 7

Non-Labor Force

Legal, any circumstances 17%
Legal, certain circumstances 49
Illegal, all circumstances 26
No opinion 8

By Community Size
One Million and Over

Legal, any circumstances 28%
Legal, certain circumstances 46
Illegal, all circumstances 19
No opinion 7

500,000–999,999

Legal, any circumstances 28%
Legal, certain circumstances 52
Illegal, all circumstances 16
No opinion 4

50,000–499,999

Legal, any circumstances 26%
Legal, certain circumstances 56
Illegal, all circumstances 15
No opinion 3

2,500–49,999

Legal, any circumstances 15%
Legal, certain circumstances 61
Illegal, all circumstances 20
No opinion 4

Under 2,500; Rural

Legal, any circumstances 15%
Legal, certain circumstances 58
Illegal, all circumstances 23
No opinion 4

*Less than 1%.

Asked of those who said abortions should be legal only under certain circumstances:

Now, thinking about the first three months of pregnancy, under which of these circumstances [respondents were handed a card with six circumstances listed] do you think abortions should be legal?

When the woman's life is endangered 77%
When the pregnancy is a result of rape
    or incest 65
When the woman may suffer severe
    physical health damage 54
When there is a chance the baby will be
    born deformed 45
When the woman's mental health is
    endangered....................... 42
If the family cannot afford to have the
    child 16
Don't know 2

Also asked of those who said abortions should be legal under certain circumstances: Thinking about the second three months of pregnancy, under which of these circumstances [respondents retained card] do you think abortions should be legal?

When the woman's life is endangered 64%
When the pregnancy is a result of rape
    or incest 38
When the woman may suffer severe
    physical health damage 46
When there is a chance the baby will
    be born deformed................. 39
When the woman's mental health is
    endangered....................... 31
If the family cannot afford to have the
    child 9
Don't know 9

Also asked of those who said abortions should be legal under certain circumstances: Thinking about the last three months of pregnancy, under which of these circumstances [respondents retained card] do you think abortions should be legal?

When the woman's life is endangered 60%
When the pregnancy is a result of rape
    or incest 24
When the woman may suffer severe
    physical health damage 34
When there is a chance the baby will
    be born deformed.................. 28
When the woman's mental health is
    endangered....................... 24
If the family cannot afford to have the
    child 6
Don't know 20

Suppose you had a fifteen-year-old unmarried daughter who told you she had recently become pregnant. Would you advise her to have an abortion or not?

Would 24%
Would not 62
No opinion.......................... 14

By Sex
Male

Would 26%
Would not 57
No opinion.......................... 17

Female

Would 22%
Would not 66
No opinion.......................... 12

By Marital Status
Married

Would 23%
Would not 63
No opinion.......................... 14

Single

Would 28%
Would not 51
No opinion.......................... 21

Widowed

Would 17%
Would not 72
No opinion.........................11

Separated

Would 21%
Would not 69
No opinion.........................10

Divorced

Would 33%
Would not 60
No opinion......................... 7

By Race
Whites

Would 25%
Would not 61
No opinion.........................14

Northern Whites

Would 27%
Would not 59
No opinion.........................14

Southern Whites

Would 21%
Would not 66
No opinion.........................13

Nonwhites

Would 12%
Would not 69
No opinion.........................19

Northern Blacks

Would 16%
Would not 58
No opinion.........................26

Southern Blacks

Would 2%
Would not 90
No opinion......................... 8

By Region
East

Would 29%
Would not 53
No opinion.........................18

Midwest

Would 21%
Would not 66
No opinion.........................13

South

Would 19%
Would not 69
No opinion.........................12

Deep South

Would 10%
Would not 77
No opinion.........................13

Rest of South

Would 23%
Would not 66
No opinion.........................11

West

Would 29%
Would not 57
No opinion.........................14

By Age
18–24 Years

Would 25%
Would not 58
No opinion.........................17

25–29 Years

Would 32%
Would not 57
No opinion.........................11

30–49 Years

Would 26%
Would not 62
No opinion.........................12

50 Years and Over

Would 19%
Would not 66
No opinion.........................15

By Income
$20,000 and Over

Would 34%
Would not 52
No opinion.........................14

$15,000–$19,999

Would 24%
Would not 62
No opinion.........................14

$10,000–$14,999

Would 25%
Would not 60
No opinion.........................15

$7,000–$9,999

Would 19%
Would not 66
No opinion.........................15

$5,000–$6,999

Would 12%
Would not 74
No opinion.........................14

$3,000–$4,999

Would 15%
Would not 72
No opinion.........................13

Under $3,000

Would 14%
Would not 75
No opinion.........................11

By Religion
Protestants

Would 23%
Would not 63
No opinion.........................14

Catholics

Would 18%
Would not 70
No opinion.........................12

By Occupation
Professional and Business

Would 32%
Would not 55
No opinion.........................13

Clerical and Sales

Would 26%
Would not 65
No opinion.......................... 9

Manual Workers

Would 22%
Would not 63
No opinion.........................15

Skilled Workers

Would 25%
Would not 60
No opinion.........................15

Unskilled Workers

Would 20%
Would not 65
No opinion.........................15

Non-Labor Force

Would 17%
Would not 71
No opinion........................... 12

By Community Size
One Million and Over

Would 30%
Would not 52
No opinion........................... 18

500,000–999,999

Would 30%
Would not 53
No opinion........................... 17

50,000–499,999

Would 27%
Would not 62
No opinion........................... 11

2,500–49,999

Would 17%
Would not 69
No opinion........................... 14

Under 2,500; Rural

Would 19%
Would not 69
No opinion........................... 12

Just your own opinion, at what point do you think a fetus becomes a human being?

At conception 36%
During first three months of pregnancy ... 23
During last six months of pregnancy 12
When the baby is actually born 10
Other answers 2
Can't say 17

By Religion
Protestants

At conception 33%
During first three months of pregnancy ... 24
During last six months of pregnancy 12
When baby is actually born............ 8
Other answers 5
Can't say 18

Catholics

At conception 47%
During first three months of pregnancy ... 21
During last six months of pregnancy 12
When the baby is actually born.......... 5
Other answers 1
Can't say 14

Note: Despite the strenuous lobbying efforts of "right to life" groups who are opposed to legal abortions, a large majority of Americans (77%) believe abortions should be legal. However, within this group, most (55%) would restrict the circumstances under which the operation can be performed.

Not surprisingly, the stage of pregnancy during which an abortion is performed has an important bearing on determining people's attitudes. More significant, however, are the specific circumstances beyond pregnancy stage under which the public would permit legal abortions.

Analysis by groups reveals a remarkable agreement in the views of both men and women toward abortion in every circumstance tested. Perhaps even more interesting, though, is the unaniminity in the attitudes of Protestants and Catholics, with only a slightly smaller percentage of Catholics believing that abortion should be legal under certain circumstances (53%) than Protestants (58%).

The socioeconomic groups most likely to favor legal abortions under any circumstances include the college-educated, young people between the ages of 25 and 29, those making $20,000 per year or more, and people in the professions and business. Conversely, greatest opposition to abortion is found among non-whites, persons with little formal education, those in the lower income brackets, and residents of smaller cities and rural areas.

JANUARY 23
SEX EDUCATION

Interviewing Date: 12/9–12/77
Survey #990-K

Do you approve or disapprove of schools giving courses in sex education?

Approve...........................77%
Disapprove 16
No opinion......................... 7

By Education
College

Approve...........................88%
Disapprove 9
No opinion......................... 3

High School

Approve...........................80%
Disapprove 14
No opinion......................... 6

Grade School

Approve...........................50%
Disapprove 35
No opinion........................15

By Age
18–24 Years

Approve...........................90%
Disapprove 6
No opinion......................... 4

25–29 Years

Approve...........................86%
Disapprove 9
No opinion......................... 5

30–49 Years

Approve...........................84%
Disapprove 11
No opinion......................... 5

50 Years and Over

Approve...........................64%
Disapprove 26
No opinion........................10

By Income
$20,000 and Over

Approve...........................88%
Disapprove 9
No opinion......................... 3

$15,000–$19,999

Approve...........................84%
Disapprove 12
No opinion......................... 4

$10,000–$14,999

Approve...........................77%
Disapprove 14
No opinion......................... 9

$7,000–$9,999

Approve...........................73%
Disapprove 19
No opinion......................... 8

$5,000–$6,999

Approve...........................74%
Disapprove 21
No opinion......................... 5

$3,000–$4,999

Approve...........................59%
Disapprove 30
No opinion........................11

Under $3,000

Approve...........................49%
Disapprove 34
No opinion........................17

By Religion
Protestants

Approve.............................75%
Disapprove 18
No opinion............................ 7

Catholics

Approve.............................80%
Disapprove 15
No opinion............................ 5

Those Who Favor Making Birth-Control Devices Available to Teenagers

Approve.............................90%
Disapprove 8
No opinion............................ 2

Those Who Oppose Making Birth-Control Devices Available to Teenagers

Approve.............................62%
Disapprove 31
No opinion............................ 7

Asked of those who approve of schools giving courses in sex education: Would you approve or disapprove if these courses discussed birth control?

Approve 89%*
Disapprove 8
No opinion............................ 3

Asked of the total sample: Do you favor or oppose making birth-control devices available to teenage boys and girls?

---

*When shown as a percentage of the total sample, the results are:

Approve.............................69%
Disapprove 6
No opinion............................ 2
                                  ———
                                  77%

The 69% figure is a marked increase over the 36% figure recorded in 1970.

Approve.............................56%
Disapprove 35
No opinion............................ 9

By Education
College

Approve.............................67%
Disapprove 27
No opinion............................ 6

High School

Approve.............................56%
Disapprove 34
No opinion............................10

Grade School

Approve.............................35%
Disapprove 51
No opinion............................14

By Age
18–24 Years

Approve.............................72%
Disapprove 21
No opinion............................ 7

25–29 Years

Approve.............................66%
Disapprove 28
No opinion............................ 6

30–49 Years

Approve.............................61%
Disapprove 31
No opinion............................ 8

50 Years and Over

Approve.............................42%
Disapprove 46
No opinion............................12

By Income

$20,000 and Over

Approve...........................65%
Disapprove 26
No opinion........................ 9

$15,000–$19,999

Approve...........................57%
Disapprove 35
No opinion........................ 8

$10,000–$14,999

Approve...........................56%
Disapprove 33
No opinion........................11

$7,000–$9,999

Approve...........................55%
Disapprove 37
No opinion........................ 8

$5,000–$6,999

Approve...........................49%
Disapprove 45
No opinion........................ 6

$3,000–$4,999

Approve...........................47%
Disapprove 40
No opinion........................13

Under $3,000

Approve...........................36%
Disapprove 51
No opinion........................13

By Religion

Protestants

Approve...........................54%
Disapprove 37
No opinion........................ 9

Catholics

Approve...........................52%
Disapprove 38
No opinion........................10

Those Who Approve of Schools Giving Courses in Sex Education

Approve...........................65%
Disapprove 28
No opinion........................ 7

Those Who Oppose Schools Giving Courses in Sex Education

Approve...........................27%
Disapprove 68
No opinion........................ 5

Note: Social scientists and others are calling the ever-increasing number of unwanted teenage pregnancies an epidemic. It is estimated that last year there were 700,000 unplanned pregnancies among the nation's teens. According to the Planned Parenthood Federation of America, 3,000 thirteen-year-old girls became mothers last year.

Widespread concern over teenage pregnancies is reflected in the sharply increasing number of Americans who favor sex education in the schools, including discussion of birth control. In addition, a majority supports making birth-control devices available to teenagers.

Interestingly, there are no significant differences on these questions in the attitudes of Protestants and Catholics, even though the Roman Catholic Church officially opposes the use of artificial means of birth control.

If anything, Catholics are slightly more in favor of sex education in the schools (80% approve) than Protestants (75%). Members of both groups are equally supportive of birth-control discussion and the availability of contraceptive devices for teenagers.

Demographic analysis also reveals that those most likely to react favorably to (1) supporting the teaching of sex education; (2) including discussion of birth control in these classes; and

(3) making birth-control devices available to teens are those in the upscale socioeconomic groups—that is, those in the upper income and education brackets and people in the professions, business, and other white-collar positions.

The survey also indicates consistent differences of opinion on these questions by geographic region. People living in the South and Midwest are less supportive in all three instances than are those living in the East and Far West.

Not unexpectedly, attitudes toward the teaching of sex education and the inclusion of birth-control discussions in the classes correlate closely with views on making birth-control devices available to teens.

Large majorities of those who approve of sex education classes (65%) and birth-control discussions (71%) also support birth-control devices for teenagers. Conversely, those who disapprove in both cases overwhelmingly disapprove of making contraceptives available to teens.

However, support for the teaching of sex education in schools is found in the majority of both people who favor and people who oppose making contraceptives available to teenagers.

JANUARY 29
LEISURE ACTIVITIES

Interviewing Date: 12/9–12/77
Survey #990-K

> *Thinking about how you spend your non-working time each day, do you think that you spend too much time or too little time watching television?*

Too much.	31%
Too little.	17
About right.	48
Don't know	4

By Sex
Male

Too much.	35%
Too little.	15

About right.	47
Don't know	3

Female

Too much.	28%
Too little.	18
About right.	49
Don't know	5

By Race
Whites

Too much.	32%
Too little.	15
About right.	49
Don't know	4

Nonwhites

Too much.	19%
Too little.	36
About right.	40
Don't know	5

By Education
College

Too much.	32%
Too little.	14
About right.	49
Don't know	5

High School

Too much.	33%
Too little.	17
About right.	46
Don't know	4

Grade School

Too much.	21%
Too little.	20
About right.	56
Don't know	3

By Age
18–24 Years

Too much. 42%
Too little. 19
About right. 32
Don't know 7

25–29 Years

Too much. 39%
Too little. 13
About right. 47
Don't know 1

30–49 Years

Too much. 35%
Too little. 17
About right. 44
Don't know 4

50 Years and Over

Too much. 21%
Too little. 16
About right. 59
Don't know 4

Thinking about how you spend your non-working time each day, do you think that you spend too much time or too little time reading newspapers?

Too much. 5%
Too little. 47
About right. 45
Don't know 3

By Sex
Male

Too much. 6%
Too little. 43
About right. 49
Don't know 2

Female

Too much. 3%
Too little. 52
About right. 42
Don't know 3

By Race
Whites

Too much. 5%
Too little. 47
About right. 46
Don't know 2

Nonwhites

Too much. 3%
Too little. 52
About right. 38
Don't know 7

By Education
College

Too much. 5%
Too little. 46
About right. 47
Don't know 2

High School

Too much. 4%
Too little. 50
About right. 44
Don't know 2

Grade School

Too much. 3%
Too little. 40
About right. 49
Don't know 8

By Age
18–24 Years

Too much. 6%
Too little. 62
About right. 28
Don't know 4

25–29 Years

Too much..................... 2%
Too little..................... 69
About right..................... 29
Don't know .... *

30–49 Years

Too much..................... 4%
Too little..................... 51
About right..................... 42
Don't know 3

50 Years and Over

Too much..................... 5%
Too little..................... 31
About right..................... 61
Don't know 3

*Less than 1%.

Thinking about how you spend your non-working time each day, do you think that you spend too much time or too little time reading magazines?

Too much..................... 6%
Too little..................... 49
About right..................... 39
Don't know 6

By Sex
Male

Too much..................... 5%
Too little..................... 51
About right..................... 39
Don't know 5

Female

Too much..................... 7%
Too little..................... 48
About right..................... 38
Don't know 7

By Race
Whites

Too much..................... 6%
Too little..................... 49
About right..................... 40
Don't know 5

Nonwhites

Too much..................... 8%
Too little..................... 48
About right..................... 30
Don't know 14

By Education
College

Too much..................... 10%
Too little..................... 44
About right..................... 45
Don't know 1

High School

Too much..................... 5%
Too little..................... 53
About right..................... 36
Don't know 6

Grade School

Too much..................... 2%
Too little..................... 44
About right..................... 38
Don't know 16

By Age
18–24 Years

Too much..................... 8%
Too little..................... 49
About right..................... 38
Don't know 5

25–29 Years

Too much..................... 5%
Too little..................... 61
About right..................... 30
Don't know 4

30–49 Years

Too much.............................. 6%
Too little............................53
About right...........................35
Don't know 6

50 Years and Over

Too much.............................. 5%
Too little............................42
About right...........................45
Don't know 8

Note: These findings, suggesting that the hold of television may not be as great as believed, offer some good news for the print media in their competition for a greater share of the average person's leisure time.

In recent years newspapers have been particularly concerned about shrinking readership among young people. This concern is vindicated by past Gallup surveys indicating that only about half of young people say they read a newspaper daily.

Perhaps not too surprising is the fact that those people with the most leisure time—that is, those not in the labor force (largely retirees) are most satisfied with their reading/viewing habits. In all three cases (watching television, reading newspapers, and reading magazines), this group expresses significantly higher satisfaction with their reading and viewing than do Americans nationwide. The same finding is true of those in the oldest age bracket—50 years of age and older. There is, of course, a good deal of overlap between these two groups.

JANUARY 30
PRESIDENT CARTER

Interviewing Date: 1/6–9/78
Survey #991-K

Do you approve or disapprove of the way Jimmy Carter is handling his job as president?

Approve..............................55%
Disapprove 27
No opinion............................18

By Race
Whites

Approve..............................54%
Disapprove 29
No opinion............................17

Nonwhites

Approve..............................63%
Disapprove 15
No opinion............................22

Southern Whites

Approve..............................54%
Disapprove 28
No opinion............................18

Northern Blacks

Approve..............................64%
Disapprove 14
No opinion............................22

Southern Blacks

Approve..............................64%
Disapprove 15
No opinion............................21

By Education
College

Approve..............................53%
Disapprove 36
No opinion............................11

High School

Approve..............................56%
Disapprove 24
No opinion............................20

Grade School

Approve..............................53%
Disapprove 20
No opinion............................27

By Region
East
Approve.............................57%
Disapprove 24
No opinion...........................19

Midwest
Approve.............................58%
Disapprove 26
No opinion...........................16

South
Approve.............................56%
Disapprove 26
No opinion...........................18

West
Approve.............................46%
Disapprove 34
No opinion...........................20

By Politics
Republicans
Approve.............................34%
Disapprove 52
No opinion...........................14

Democrats
Approve.............................65%
Disapprove 17
No opinion...........................18

Southern Democrats
Approve.............................64%
Disapprove 18
No opinion...........................18

Other Democrats
Approve.............................66%
Disapprove 16
No opinion...........................18

Independents
Approve.............................53%
Disapprove 28
No opinion...........................19

By Religion
Protestants
Approve.............................59%
Disapprove 27
No opinion...........................14

Catholics
Approve.............................51%
Disapprove 26
No opinion...........................23

President Carter is completing his first year in office. What do you regard as his most important achievement to date?

Nothing 26%
Middle East talks 11
Foreign relations......................11
Stand on energy...................... 5
Stand on human rights 4
Peace efforts 4
His open style 3
Getting people back to work 3
Restoring faith in government 3
Other 17
Don't know 22
                                    ___
                                    109%

*Total adds to more than 100% due to multiple responses.

FEBRUARY 2
PANAMA CANAL

Interviewing Date: 1/6–9/78
Survey #991-K

Have you heard or read about the debate over the Panama Canal treaties?

                                     Yes
National..............................81%

By Sex

Male	86%
Female	77

By Race

Whites	85%
Nonwhites	54

By Education

College	93%
High school	80
Grade school	65

By Politics

Republicans	86%
Democrats	80
Southern Democrats	78
Other Democrats	81
Independents	85

Asked of those who had heard or read about the debate: As far as you know, in what year is the Panama Canal to be turned over completely to the Republic of Panama by terms of the treaties?

2000 (correct)	25%
1999 (accepted as correct)	1
Incorrect	29
Don't know	45

By Sex

Male

2000 (correct)	34%
1999 (accepted as correct)	1
Incorrect	27
Don't know	38

Female

2000 (correct)	16%
1999 (accepted as correct)	*
Incorrect	30
Don't know	54

By Race

Whites

2000 (correct)	26%
1999 (accepted as correct)	1
Incorrect	30
Don't know	43

Nonwhites

2000 (correct)	13%
1999 (accepted as correct)	*
Incorrect	19
Don't know	68

By Education

College

2000 (correct)	36%
1999 (accepted as correct)	1
Incorrect	31
Don't know	32

High School

2000 (correct)	22%
1999 (accepted as correct)	1
Incorrect	29
Don't know	48

Grade School

2000 (correct)	10%
1999 (accepted as correct)	*
Incorrect	22
Don't know	68

By Politics

Republicans

2000 (correct)	38%
1999 (accepted as correct)	1
Incorrect	27
Don't know	34

Democrats

2000 (correct)	18%
1999 (accepted as correct)	1
Incorrect	29
Don't know	52

Southern Democrats

2000 (correct)........................21%
1999 (accepted as correct) 1
Incorrect.............................23
Don't know 55

Other Democrats

2000 (correct)........................16%
1999 (accepted as correct) 1
Incorrect.............................32
Don't know 51

Independents

2000 (correct)........................25%
1999 (accepted as correct) 1
Incorrect.............................32
Don't know 42

*Less than 1%.

Asked of those who had heard or read about the debate: To the best of your knowledge, how much do the biggest United States aircraft carriers and supertankers now use the Panama Canal—a great deal, quite a lot, not very much, or not at all?

Great deal 16%
Quite a lot 17
Not very much........................21
Not at all (correct) 20
Don't know 26

By Sex
Male

Great deal 17%
Quite a lot 16
Not very much........................19
Not at all (correct) 29
Don't know 19

Female

Great deal 15%
Quite a lot 19
Not very much........................22
Not at all (correct) 11
Don't know 33

By Race
Whites

Great deal 17%
Quite a lot 17
Not very much........................21
Not at all (correct) 20
Don't know 25

Nonwhites

Great deal 12%
Quite a lot 19
Not very much........................16
Not at all (correct) 12
Don't know 41

By Education
College

Great deal 16%
Quite a lot 19
Not very much........................22
Not at all (correct) 28
Don't know 15

High School

Great deal 17%
Quite a lot 17
Not very much........................21
Not at all (correct) 17
Don't know 28

Grade School

Great deal 12%
Quite a lot 14
Not very much........................18
Not at all (correct) 8
Don't know 48

By Politics
Republicans

Great deal 17%
Quite a lot 19
Not very much........................15
Not at all (correct) 27
Don't know 22

Democrats

Great deal 17%
Quite a lot 17
Not very much...................... 22
Not at all (correct) 16
Don't know 28

Southern Democrats

Great deal 14%
Quite a lot 16
Not very much...................... 25
Not at all (correct) 16
Don't know 29

Other Democrats

Great deal 19%
Quite a lot 18
Not very much...................... 20
Not at all (correct) 16
Don't know 27

Independents

Great deal 13%
Quite a lot 17
Not very much...................... 25
Not at all (correct) 21
Don't know 24

Asked of those who had heard or read about the debate: As far as you know, will the United States have the right to defend the Panama Canal against third-nation attacks after Panama takes full control?

Will (correct) 54%
Will not 21
Don't know 25

By Sex
Male

Will (correct) 61%
Will not 21
Don't know 18

Female

Will (correct) 48%
Will not 20
Don't know 32

By Race
Whites

Will (correct) 55%
Will not 21
Don't know 24

Nonwhites

Will (correct) 42%
Will not 19
Don't know 39

By Education
College

Will (correct) 62%
Will not 23
Don't know 15

High School

Will (correct) 53%
Will not 20
Don't know 27

Grade School

Will (correct) 41%
Will not 18
Don't know 41

By Politics
Republicans

Will (correct) 56%
Will not 21
Don't know 23

Democrats

Will (correct) 57%
Will not 18
Don't know 25

Southern Democrats

Will (correct) 53%
Will not 17
Don't know 30

Other Democrats

Will (correct) 59%
Will not 19
Don't know 22

Independents

Will (correct) 51%
Will not 25
Don't know 24

Asked of those who had heard or read about the debate: Actually, the treaties would give Panama full control over the Panama Canal and the Canal Zone by the year 2000, but the United States would retain the right to defend the canal against a third nation. Do you favor or oppose these treaties between the United States and Panama?

Favor 45%
Oppose 42
No opinion 13

By Sex
Male

Favor 47%
Oppose 44
No opinion 9

Female

Favor 45%
Oppose 39
No opinion 16

By Race
Whites

Favor 45%
Oppose 43
No opinion 12

Nonwhites

Favor 49%
Oppose 29
No opinion 22

By Education
College

Favor 55%
Oppose 37
No opinion 8

High School

Favor 42%
Oppose 45
No opinion 13

Grade School

Favor 36%
Oppose 42
No opinion 22

By Politics
Republicans

Favor 37%
Oppose 52
No opinion 11

Democrats

Favor 50%
Oppose 38
No opinion 12

Independents

Favor 44%
Oppose 42
No opinion 14

Asked of those who had not heard or read about the debate over the treaties: The treaties would give Panama full control over the Panama Canal and the Canal Zone by the year 2000, but the United States would retain the right to defend the canal against a third nation. Do you favor or oppose these treaties between the United States and Panama?

Favor 33%
Oppose 17
No opinion 50

By Sex
Male

Favor 29%
Oppose 17
No opinion 54

Female

Favor 36%
Oppose 17
No opinion 47

By Race
Whites

Favor 42%
Oppose 42
No opinion 16

Nonwhites

Favor 15%
Oppose 19
No opinion 66

By Education
College

Favor 52%
Oppose 31
No opinion 17

High School

Favor 39%
Oppose 14
No opinion 47

Grade School

Favor 15%
Oppose 17
No opinion 68

By Politics
Republicans

Favor 35%
Oppose 26
No opinion 39

Democrats

Favor 33%
Oppose 16
No opinion 51

Independents

Favor 39%
Oppose 15
No opinion 46

Asked of those correctly answering the questions regarding (1) the year the Republic of Panama will completely take over the canal and Canal Zone; (2) whether the United States retains the right to defend the canal against third-nation attacks; and (3) how much the largest United States ships use the canal: Do you favor or oppose these treaties between the United States and Panama?

Favor 57%
Oppose 39
No opinion 4

By Sex
Male

Favor 57%
Oppose 39
No opinion 4

Female

Favor 57%
Oppose 36
No opinion 7

By Race

Whites

Favor 55%
Oppose............................. 40
No opinion......................... 5

Nonwhites

Favor 100%
Oppose............................. *
No opinion......................... *

By Education

College

Favor 59%
Oppose............................. 39
No opinion......................... 2

High School

Favor 53%
Oppose............................. 38
No opinion......................... 9

Grade School

Favor 63%
Oppose............................. 37
No opinion......................... *

By Politics

Republicans

Favor 49%
Oppose............................. 48
No opinion......................... 3

Democrats

Favor 71%
Oppose............................. 22
No opinion......................... 7

Independents

Favor 55%
Oppose............................. 41
No opinion......................... 4

Note: The Carter administration's efforts to educate the public concerning the Panama Canal treaties, in order to promote Senate ratification, have resulted in some degree of success, both in increased awareness of the issue itself and in slightly higher approval nationwide. In the current survey, 81% of respondents say they have heard or read about the debate over the proposed treaties, an increase of 7% from an identical survey in late September—early October 1977.

Along with the public's heightened awareness of the issue, approval for the treaties has also increased, to almost the same degree, since the original survey on the subject. Among those who have followed the treaty debates, opinion is about evenly split, with 45% favoring the pact between the United States and Panama, 42% opposed, and 13% undecided. In the previous survey, the margin was slightly greater, with 40% approving and 48% opposed to the canal treaties.

Analysis of the attitudes of the "informed" segment of the population (those who have followed the debate concerning the treaties) indicates that support for the treaties is highest among the college-educated, young people under the age of 30, those in the upper income brackets ($20,000 per year or more), those in the professions and business, and people living in the East and primarily nonrural areas. Democrats, not surprisingly, are more inclined to support the treaties than are Republicans or independents.

Perhaps of more interest to proponents of the treaties is the fact that approval has increased to an even greater extent among the "uninformed" segment of the survey. In a question that explains the terms of the treaties and asks whether the respondent approves or disapproves of the treaties, 33% in the current survey favor the proposed treaties, as opposed to 23% in the earlier survey. Opposition has also decreased significantly, with 17% now opposed to the treaties, versus 39% in September and October. In addition, many more people are now undecided (50%) than a few months earlier (38%).

The greatest increases in approval for the

treaties among the "uninformed" are found among the college-educated, people in the upper and middle income brackets, those employed in clerical and sales positions, and residents of medium-sized cities.

Although the American public could benefit from further knowledge concerning the particulars of the proposed Panama Canal treaties, it is apparent that the administration's educational efforts in this regard have met with some degree of success. It appears likely that the more informed the public becomes regarding the issue, the more they will tend to favor returning the canal to Panama.

FEBRUARY 5
LABOR UNIONS

Interviewing Date: 1/6–9/78
Survey #991-K

In general, do you approve or disapprove of labor unions?

Approve.............................59%
Disapprove 31
No opinion..........................10

By Sex
Male

Approve.............................60%
Disapprove 32
No opinion.......................... 8

Female

Approve.............................58%
Disapprove 30
No opinion..........................12

By Race
Whites

Approve.............................58%
Disapprove 33
No opinion.......................... 9

Nonwhites

Approve.............................65%
Disapprove 16
No opinion..........................19

By Education
College

Approve.............................58%
Disapprove 36
No opinion.......................... 6

High School

Approve.............................59%
Disapprove 31
No opinion..........................10

Grade School

Approve.............................58%
Disapprove 25
No opinion..........................17

By Region
East

Approve.............................63%
Disapprove 25
No opinion..........................12

Midwest

Approve.............................59%
Disapprove 33
No opinion.......................... 8

South

Approve.............................55%
Disapprove 32
No opinion..........................13

West

Approve.............................58%
Disapprove 36
No opinion.......................... 6

By Age
18–24 Years

Approve............................58%
Disapprove 33
No opinion.........................9

25–29 Years

Approve............................65%
Disapprove 26
No opinion.........................9

30–49 Years

Approve............................58%
Disapprove 32
No opinion.........................10

50 Years and Over

Approve............................57%
Disapprove 31
No opinion.........................12

By Income
$20,000 and Over

Approve:...........................61%
Disapprove 34
No opinion.........................5

$15,000–$19,999

Approve............................56%
Disapprove 36
No opinion.........................8

$10,000–$14,999

Approve............................60%
Disapprove 27
No opinion.........................13

$7,000–$9,999

Approve............................58%
Disapprove 29
No opinion.........................13

$5,000–$6,999

Approve............................55%
Disapprove 31
No opinion.........................14

$3,000–$4,999

Approve............................58%
Disapprove 29
No opinion.........................13

Under $3,000

Approve............................58%
Disapprove 27
No opinion.........................15

By Politics
Republicans

Approve............................43%
Disapprove 51
No opinion.........................6

Democrats

Approve............................66%
Disapprove 24
No opinion.........................10

Southern Democrats

Approve............................60%
Disapprove 28
No opinion.........................12

Other Democrats

Approve............................70%
Disapprove 21
No opinion.........................9

Independents

Approve............................56%
Disapprove 31
No opinion.........................13

By Religion
Protestants

Approve............................53%
Disapprove 37
No opinion.........................10

Catholics

Approve............................68%
Disapprove 22
No opinion.........................10

By Occupation
Professional and Business

Approve............................53%
Disapprove 42
No opinion......................... 5

Clerical and Sales

Approve............................62%
Disapprove 26
No opinion.........................12

Manual Workers

Approve............................66%
Disapprove 24
No opinion.........................10

Skilled Workers

Approve............................61%
Disapprove 32
No opinion......................... 7

Unskilled Workers

Approve............................67%
Disapprove 22
No opinion.........................11

Non-Labor Force

Approve............................56%

Disapprove 31
No opinion.........................13

Labor Union Families Only

Approve............................84%
Disapprove 9
No opinion......................... 7

Non-Labor Union Families Only

Approve............................51%
Disapprove 38
No opinion.........................11

Note: At first glance, a 59% majority approval of labor unions might be considered a positive finding. Analysis of the figures, however, will not hearten union sympathizers.

First, the current approval rating represents a continued low point in public support for unions. Although there has been no change since the previous survey in 1972, this figure is well below the 76% figure recorded in 1957. Prior to the current and previous surveys, the low point in union approval was 63%, recorded in May 1961. While there has been no change in the percentage approving of unions, there has been a significant increase in those disapproving. Previously, the 26% disapproval recorded in 1972 represented the nadir of public sentiment toward unions. The current figure has climbed to 31%.

Unions find their strongest opposition in the upscale groups—those people in the higher education and income brackets as well as those in the professions and business. (The fact that upscale groups are as likely as downscale groups to approve of unions indicates a greater certainty of opinion in the former groups—in other words, fewer people registering "no opinion.")

These findings come at a time when confidence in labor unions remains at a low ebb in the United States.

Only 16% of the American public, for example, expresses "a great deal" of confidence in organized labor, a view shared by only 25% of labor union families. In addition, only 13% of Americans give labor union leaders a "very high" rating for their honesty and ethical standards, while 47% give them a rating of "low" or "very low."

Nonetheless, a majority of Americans nationwide and among almost all population groups do endorse the concept of unionism. Only Republicans, among whom 51% disapprove, reject unionism in principle.

As in the United States, recent Gallup Polls in Great Britain have shown the public standing of unions there to be at one of the lowest levels observed in the past two decades.

For example, two-thirds of Britons believe that the views of the trade union (labor union) leaders do not represent the views of the rank and file. There has also been an increase in the percentage who believe that unions are becoming too powerful.

The right of British firemen and police to strike is opposed by 50% and 49%, respectively, while 43% support the right to strike of both groups.

However, in Great Britain too, the principle of unionism is generally supported. A majority of 53% of Britons, according to Gallup surveys, believe trade unions are, on the whole, a "good thing" for Britain, while 33% view them as a "bad thing."

FEBRUARY 5
PUBLIC EMPLOYEE STRIKES

Interviewing Date: 1/6–9/78
Survey #991-K

Here are some questions about strikes in various occupations. Should policemen be permitted to strike, or not?

Should 33%
Should not 61
No opinion........................... 6

By Race
Whites

Should 33%
Should not 62
No opinion........................... 5

Nonwhites

Should 35%
Should not 56
No opinion........................... 9

By Education
College

Should 30%
Should not 68
No opinion........................... 2

High School

Should 35%
Should not 60
No opinion........................... 5

Grade School

Should 31%
Should not 55
No opinion........................... 14

By Region
East

Should 29%
Should not 65
No opinion........................... 6

Midwest

Should 37%
Should not 56
No opinion........................... 7

South

Should 33%
Should not 61
No opinion........................... 6

West

Should 34%
Should not 62
No opinion. 4

By Age
18–24 Years

Should 40%
Should not 56
No opinion. 4

25–29 Years

Should 40%
Should not 52
No opinion. 8

30–49 Years

Should 34%
Should not 61
No opinion. 5

50 Years and Over

Should 27%
Should not 66
No opinion. 7

Labor Union Families Only

Should 46%
Should not 51
No opinion. 3

Non-Labor Union Families Only

Should 30%
Should not 64
No opinion. 6

Should firemen be permitted to strike, or not?

Should 32%
Should not 62
No opinion. 6

By Race
Whites

Should 32%
Should not 63
No opinion. 5

Nonwhites

Should 35%
Should not 58
No opinion. 7

By Education
College

Should 30%
Should not 68
No opinion. 2

High School

Should 33%
Should not 62
No opinion. 5

Grade School

No opinion. 31%
Should not 54
No opinion. 13

By Region
East

Should 27%
Should not 67
No opinion. 6

Midwest

Should 36%
Should not 59
No opinion. 5

South

Should 32%
Should not 61
No opinion. 7

West

Should 33%
Should not 62
No opinion............................ 5

By Age
18–24 Years

Should 37%
Should not 58
No opinion............................ 5

25–29 Years

Should 38%
Should not 55
No opinion............................ 7

30–49 Years

Should 34%
Should not 61
No opinion............................ 5

50 Years and Over

Should 27%
Should not 67
No opinion............................ 6

Labor Union Families Only

Should 47%
Should not 50
No opinion............................ 3

Non-Labor Union Families Only

Should 28%
Should not 65
No opinion............................ 7

Should teachers be permitted to strike, or not?

Should 43%
Should not 51
No opinion............................ 6

By Race
Whites

Should 43%
Should not 52
No opinion............................ 5

Nonwhites

Should 49%
Should not 41
No opinion............................ 10

By Education
College

Should 49%
Should not 49
No opinion............................ 2

High School

Should 42%
Should not 52
No opinion............................ 6

Grade School

Should 38%
Should not 51
No opinion............................ 11

By Region
East

Should 38%
Should not 57
No opinion............................ 5

Midwest

Should 45%
Should not 49
No opinion............................ 6

South

Should 46%
Should not 47
No opinion............................ 7

West

Should	45%
Should not	50
No opinion	5

By Age
18–24 Years

Should	57%
Should not	38
No opinion	5

25–29 Years

Should	56%
Should not	37
No opinion	7

30–49 Years

Should	46%
Should not	48
No opinion	6

50 Years and Over

Should	30%
Should not	64
No opinion	6

Labor Union Families Only

Should	58%
Should not	40
No opinion	2

Non-Labor Union Families Only

Should	39%
Should not	54
No opinion	7

Note: Americans may support the concept of unionism, but they are dead set against the right of public employees to strike—particularly those employed in the safety-related services of police work and fire fighting. By roughly two-to-one margins, the public opposes allowing people in these two professions to strike.

The general public also stands against allowing teachers the right to strike; however, opinion on this issue is more closely divided (five to four opposed).

Older people, those who are not members of labor union households, and the college-educated are the groups registering the strongest opposition to strikes by police and fire personnel. But while the former two groups are also the most strongly opposed to teachers' strikes, college-educated Americans show more support for such actions than do those with less education.

FEBRUARY 9
THE MIDDLE EAST

Interviewing Date: 1/20–23/78
Survey #992-K

Have you followed the recent developments in the Middle East?

	Yes
National	63%

By Sex

Male	72%
Female	55

By Race

Whites	67%
Nonwhites	37

By Education

College	79%
High school	58
Grade school	49

By Region

East	64%
Midwest	62
South	59
West	69

By Age

18–24 years	50%
25–29 years	64
30–49 years	64
50 years and over	68

By Income

$20,000 and over	73%
$15,000–$19,999	70
$10,000–$14,999	65
$7,000–$9,999	60
$5,000–$6,999	49
$3,000–$4,999	49
Under $3,000	44

By Politics

Republicans	73%
Democrats	60
Southern Democrats	54
Other Democrats	64
Independents	63

By Religion

Protestants	60%
Catholics	69

By Occupation

Professional and business	76%
Clerical and sales	61
Manual workers	58
Non-labor force	63

Asked of those who have followed the recent developments in the Middle East: Do you approve or disapprove of the way President Carter is dealing with the Middle East situation?

Approve	56%
Disapprove	26
No opinion	18

By Sex
Male

Approve	56%
Disapprove	31
No opinion	13

Female

Approve	56%
Disapprove	20
No opinion	24

By Race
Whites

Approve	56%
Disapprove	27
No opinion	17

Nonwhites

Approve	57%
Disapprove	19
No opinion	24

By Education
College

Approve	62%
Disapprove	23
No opinion	15

High School

Approve	51%
Disapprove	29
No opinion	20

Grade School

Approve	57%
Disapprove	25
No opinion	18

By Region
East

Approve	59%
Disapprove	26
No opinion	15

Midwest

Approve	54%
Disapprove	29
No opinion	17

South

Approve.............................56%
Disapprove 23
No opinion.........................21

West

Approve.............................55%
Disapprove 26
No opinion.........................19

By Age
18–24 Years

Approve.............................54%
Disapprove 24
No opinion.........................22

25–29 Years

Approve.............................58%
Disapprove 24
No opinion.........................18

30–49 Years

Approve.............................61%
Disapprove 25
No opinion.........................14

50 Years and Over

Approve.............................52%
Disapprove 28
No opinion.........................20

By Income
$20,000 and Over

Approve.............................63%
Disapprove 25
No opinion.........................12

$15,000–$19,999

Approve.............................60%
Disapprove 23
No opinion.........................17

$10,000–$14,999

Approve.............................46%
Disapprove 33
No opinion.........................21

$7,000–$9,999

Approve.............................63%
Disapprove 19
No opinion.........................18

$5,000–$6,999

Approve.............................54%
Disapprove 23
No opinion.........................23

$3,000–$4,999

Approve.............................58%
Disapprove 22
No opinion.........................20

Under $3,000

Approve.............................33%
Disapprove 40
No opinion.........................27

By Politics
Republicans

Approve.............................42%
Disapprove 37
No opinion.........................21

Democrats

Approve.............................63%
Disapprove 19
No opinion.........................18

Southern Democrats

Approve.............................58%
Disapprove 17
No opinion.........................25

Other Democrats

Approve.............................65%
Disapprove 19
No opinion.........................16

Independents

Approve...........................58%
Disapprove 29
No opinion........................13

By Religion
Protestants

Approve...........................52%
Disapprove 28
No opinion........................20

Catholics

Approve...........................62%
Disapprove 23
No opinion........................15

By Occupation
Professional and Business

Approve...........................57%
Disapprove 29
No opinion........................14

Clerical and Sales

Approve...........................50%
Disapprove 25
No opinion........................25

Manual Workers

Approve...........................60%
Disapprove 23
No opinion........................17

Non-Labor Force

Approve...........................47%
Disapprove 32
No opinion........................21

Also asked of those who have followed the recent developments in the Middle East:

Do you think President Carter is leaning too much in favor of Israel, too much in favor of Egypt, or do you feel that he is treating both sides equally fairly?

Favor Israel......................16%
Favor Egypt 6
Both equally 62
No opinion........................16

By Sex
Male

Favor Israel......................20%
Favor Egypt 6
Both equally 63
No opinion........................11

Female

Favor Israel......................11%
Favor Egypt 6
Both equally 60
No opinion........................23

By Race
Whites

Favor Israel......................16%
Favor Egypt 6
Both equally 63
No opinion........................15

Nonwhites

Favor Israel......................16%
Favor Egypt 6
Both equally 49
No opinion........................29

By Education
College

Favor Israel......................16%
Favor Egypt 8
Both equally 64
No opinion........................12

High School

Favor Israel	17%
Favor Egypt	5
Both equally	60
No opinion	18

Grade School

Favor Israel	9%
Favor Egypt	5
Both equally	61
No opinion	25

By Region
East

Favor Israel	22%
Favor Egypt	6
Both equally	59
No opinion	13

Midwest

Favor Israel	18%
Favor Egypt	5
Both equally	59
No opinion	18

South

Favor Israel	11%
Favor Egypt	7
Both equally	63
No opinion	19

West

Favor Israel	11%
Favor Egypt	6
Both equally	67
No opinion	16

By Age
18–24 Years

Favor Israel	12%
Favor Egypt	7
Both equally	65
No opinion	16

25–29 Years

Favor Israel	11%
Favor Egypt	11
Both equally	55
No opinion	23

30–49 Years

Favor Israel	20%
Favor Egypt	7
Both equally	59
No opinion	14

50 Years and Over

Favor Israel	15%
Favor Egypt	4
Both equally	64
No opinion	17

By Income
$20,000 and Over

Favor Israel	16%
Favor Egypt	6
Both equally	66
No opinion	12

$15,000–$19,999

Favor Israel	18%
Favor Egypt	4
Both equally	63
No opinion	15

$10,000–$14,999

Favor Israel	16%
Favor Egypt	10
Both equally	58
No opinion	16

$7,000–$9,999

Favor Israel	12%
Favor Egypt	4
Both equally	69
No opinion	15

$5,000–$6,999

Favor Israel	16%
Favor Egypt	5
Both equally	54
No opinion	25

$3,000–$4,999

Favor Israel	15%
Favor Egypt	*
Both equally	63
No opinion	22

Under $3,000

Favor Israel	10%
Favor Egypt	12
Both equally	36
No opinion	42

By Politics
Republicans

Favor Israel	20%
Favor Egypt	8
Both equally	51
No opinion	21

Democrats

Favor Israel	10%
Favor Egypt	5
Both equally	70
No opinion	15

Southern Democrats

Favor Israel	8%
Favor Egypt	4
Both equally	71
No opinion	17

Other Democrats

Favor Israel	11%
Favor Egypt	5
Both equally	69
No opinion	15

Independents

Favor Israel	22%
Favor Egypt	6
Both equally	60
No opinion	12

By Religion
Protestants

Favor Israel	15%
Favor Egypt	6
Both equally	61
No opinion	18

Catholics

Favor Israel	17%
Favor Egypt	4
Both equally	66
No opinion	13

By Occupation
Professional and Business

Favor Israel	19%
Favor Egypt	8
Both equally	59
No opinion	14

Clerical and Sales

Favor Israel	20%
Favor Egypt	6
Both equally	60
No opinion	14

Manual Workers

Favor Israel	15%
Favor Egypt	5
Both equally	64
No opinion	16

Non-Labor Force

Favor Israel	14%
Favor Egypt	5

Both equally 60
No opinion........................... 21

*Less than 1%.

Also asked of those who have followed the recent developments in the Middle East: Do you think Israel is or is not doing all it should do to bring about peace in the Middle East?

Is................................... 25%
Is not................................ 57
No opinion............................ 18

By Sex
Male

Is................................... 25%
Is not................................ 61
No opinion............................ 14

Female

Is................................... 24%
Is not................................ 53
No opinion............................ 23

By Race
Whites

Is................................... 25%
Is not................................ 58
No opinion............................ 17

Nonwhites

Is................................... 21%
Is not................................ 46
No opinion............................ 33

By Education
College

Is................................... 27%
Is not................................ 60
No opinion............................ 13

High School

Is................................... 23%
Is not................................ 60
No opinion............................ 17

Grade School

Is................................... 25%
Is not................................ 37
No opinion............................ 38

By Region
East

Is................................... 22%
Is not................................ 63
No opinion............................ 15

Midwest

Is................................... 23%
Is not................................ 60
No opinion............................ 17

South

Is................................... 26%
Is not................................ 52
No opinion............................ 22

West

Is................................... 29%
Is not................................ 51
No opinion............................ 20

By Age
18–24 Years

Is................................... 21%
Is not................................ 63
No opinion............................ 16

25–29 Years

Is................................... 29%
Is not................................ 54
No opinion............................ 17

30–49 Years

Is	25%
Is not	61
No opinion	14

50 Years and Over

Is	24%
Is not	53
No opinion	23

By Income
$20,000 and Over

Is	27%
Is not	61
Is not	12

$15,000–$19,999

Is	27%
Is not	61
No opinion	12

$10,000–$14,999

Is	17%
Is not	64
No opinion	19

$7,000–$9,999

Is	21%
Is not	49
No opinion	30

$5,000–$6,999

Is	23%
Is not	55
No opinion	22

$3,000–$4,999

Is	33%
Is not	38
No opinion	29

Under $3,000

Is	26%
Is not	43
No opinion	31

By Politics
Republicans

Is	25%
Is not	53
No opinion	22

Democrats

Is	24%
Is not	58
No opinion	18

Southern Democrats

Is	23%
Is not	53
No opinion	24

Other Democrats

Is	24%
Is not	60
No opinion	16

Independents

Is	26%
Is not	60
No opinion	14

By Religion
Protestants

Is	23%
Is not	57
No opinion	20

Catholics

Is	19%
Is not	64
No opinion	17

By Occupation
Professional and Business

Is...26%
Is not.......................................60
No opinion..................................14

Clerical and Sales

Is...32%
Is not.......................................55
No opinion..................................13

Manual Workers

Is...22%
Is not.......................................59
No opinion..................................19

Non-Labor Force

Is...22%
Is not.......................................54
No opinion..................................24

Also asked of those who have followed the recent developments in the Middle East: Do you think Egypt is or is not doing all it should to bring about peace in the Middle East?

Is...32%
Is not.......................................50
No opinion..................................18

By Sex
Male

Is...36%
Is not.......................................51
No opinion..................................13

Female

Is...27%
Is not.......................................48
No opinion..................................25

By Race
Whites

Is...32%
Is not.......................................51
No opinion..................................17

Nonwhites

Is...26%
Is not.......................................37
No opinion..................................37

By Education
College

Is...38%
Is not.......................................50
No opinion..................................12

High School

Is...27%
Is not.......................................55
No opinion..................................18

Grade School

Is...30%
Is not.......................................31
No opinion..................................39

By Region
East

Is...36%
Is not.......................................49
No opinion..................................15

Midwest

Is...33%
Is not.......................................49
No opinion..................................18

South

Is...27%
Is not.......................................51
No opinion..................................22

West

Is	30%
Is not	51
No opinion	19

By Age
18–24 Years

Is	23%
Is not	61
No opinion	16

25–29 Years

Is	31%
Is not	51
No opinion	18

30–49 Years

Is	31%
Is not	54
No opinion	15

50 Years and Over

Is	36%
Is not	42
No opinion	22

By Income
$20,000 and Over

Is	36%
Is not	54
No opinion	10

$15,000–$19,999

Is	39%
Is not	50
No opinion	11

$10,000–$14,999

Is	24%
Is not	58
No opinion	18

$7,000–$9,999

Is	25%
Is not	45
No opinion	30

$5,000–$6,999

Is	29%
Is not	43
No opinion	28

$3,000–$4,999

Is	30%
Is not	34
No opinion	36

Under $3,000

Is	25%
Is not	42
No opinion	33

By Politics
Republicans

Is	29%
Is not	51
No opinion	20

Democrats

Is	32%
Is not	49
No opinion	19

Southern Democrats

Is	26%
Is not	49
No opinion	25

Other Democrats

Is	35%
Is not	49
No opinion	16

Independents

Is..................................36%
Is not..............................50
No opinion..........................14

By Religion
Protestants

Is..................................30%
Is not..............................51
No opinion..........................19

Catholics

Is..................................32%
Is not..............................51
No opinion..........................17

By Occupation
Professional and Business

Is..................................36%
Is not..............................52
No opinion..........................12

Clerical and Sales

Is..................................26%
Is not..............................61
No opinion..........................13

Manual Workers

Is..................................30%
Is not..............................50
No opinion..........................20

Non-Labor Force

Is..................................31%
Is not..............................44
No opinion..........................25

Also asked of those who have followed the recent developments in the Middle East:

Do you think Israel should or should not withdraw its military forces and civilian settlements from the Sinai Peninsula?

Should..............................40%
Should not..........................30
No opinion..........................30

By Education
College

Should..............................43%
Should not..........................31
No opinion..........................26

High School

Should..............................40%
Should not..........................32
No opinion..........................28

Grade School

Should..............................29%
Should not..........................18
No opinion..........................53

By Region
East

Should..............................44%
Should not..........................29
No opinion..........................27

Midwest

Should..............................41%
Should not..........................26
No opinion..........................33

South

Should..............................35%
Should not..........................33
No opinion..........................32

West

Should 37%
Should not 32
No opinion............................ 31

By Politics
Republicans

Should 35%
Should not 36
No opinion............................ 29

Democrats

Should 42%
Should not 25
No opinion............................ 33

Independents

Should 43%
Should not 33
No opinion............................ 24

By Religion
Protestants

Should 38%
Should not 32
No opinion............................ 30

Catholics

Should 44%
Should not 23
No opinion............................ 33

Also asked of those who have followed the recent developments in the Middle East: How likely do you think it is that there will be peaceful settlement of differences between Israel and Egypt—very likely, fairly likely, or not at all likely?

Very likely........................... 8%
Fairly likely 48
Not at all likely 37
No opinion........................... 7

By Education
College

Very likely........................... 8%
Fairly likely 52
Not at all likely 35
No opinion........................... 5

High School

Very likely........................... 7%
Fairly likely 46
Not at all likely 41
No opinion........................... 6

Grade School

Very likely........................... 13%
Fairly likely 38
Not at all likely 30
No opinion........................... 19

By Region
East

Very likely........................... 9%
Fairly likely 52
Not at all likely 33
No opinion........................... 6

Midwest

Very likely........................... 8%
Fairly likely 47
Not at all likely 38
No opinion........................... 7

South

Very likely........................... 6%
Fairly likely 44
Not at all likely 42
No opinion........................... 8

West

Very likely........................... 9%
Fairly likely 46
Not at all likely 37
No opinion........................... 8

By Politics
Republicans

Very likely.......................... 6%
Fairly likely........................42
Not at all likely 46
No opinion.......................... 6

Democrats

Very likely.......................... 9%
Fairly likely........................48
Not at all likely 34
No opinion.......................... 9

Independents

Very likely.......................... 8%
Fairly likely........................50
Not at all likely 39
No opinion.......................... 3

By Religion
Protestants

Very likely.......................... 8%
Fairly likely........................45
Not at all likely 40
No opinion.......................... 7

Catholics

Very likely.......................... 6%
Fairly likely........................54
Not at all likely 32
No opinion.......................... 8

Also asked of those who have followed the recent developments in the Middle East: How likely do you think it is that there will be a peaceful settlement of differences between Israel and all the Arab nations— very likely, fairly likely, or not at all likely?

Very likely.......................... 6%
Fairly likely........................32
Not at all likely 53
No opinion.......................... 9

By Education
College

Very likely.......................... 5%
Fairly likely........................35
Not at all likely 54
No opinion.......................... 6

High School

Very likely.......................... 5%
Fairly likely........................31
Not at all likely 56
No opinion.......................... 8

Grade School

Very likely..........................14%
Fairly likely........................30
Not at all likely 34
No opinion..........................22

By Region
East

Very likely.......................... 7%
Fairly likely........................33
Not at all likely 52
No opinion.......................... 8

Midwest

Very likely.......................... 8%
Fairly likely........................34
Not at all likely 48
No opinion..........................10

South

Very likely.......................... 4%
Fairly likely........................31
Not at all likely 56
No opinion.......................... 9

West

Very likely.......................... 6%
Fairly likely........................31
Not at all likely 55
No opinion.......................... 8

By Politics

Republicans

Very likely	6%
Fairly likely	27
Not at all likely	58
No opinion	9

Democrats

Very likely	7%
Fairly likely	35
Not at all likely	48
No opinion	10

Independents

Very likely	6%
Fairly likely	30
Not at all likely	59
No opinion	5

By Religion

Protestants

Very likely	7%
Fairly likely	31
Not at all likely	53
No opinion	9

Catholics

Very likely	6%
Fairly likely	36
Not at all likely	49
No opinion	9

Asked of the entire sample: Have you heard or read about the PLO, that is, the Palestine Liberation Organization?

	Yes
National	77%

By Education

College	88%
High school	75
Grade school	52

By Region

East	78%
Midwest	75
South	72
West	86

By Politics

Republicans	80%
Democrats	72
Independents	84

By Religion

Protestants	76%
Catholics	77

Asked of those who have followed the recent developments in the Middle East and have heard or read about the Palestine Liberation Organization: Do you think the PLO does or does not represent the point of view of a majority of Palestinians?

Does	14%
Does not	63
No opinion	23

By Education

College

Does	13%
Does not	65
No opinion	22

High School

Does	16%
Does not	62
No opinion	22

Grade School

Does	11%
Does not	55
No opinion	34

By Region

East

Does	9%
Does not	71
No opinion	20

Midwest

Does..............................19%
Does not...........................59
No opinion.........................22

South

Does..............................15%
Does not...........................58
No opinion.........................27

West

Does..............................15%
Does not...........................63
No opinion.........................22

By Politics
Republicans

Does..............................11%
Does not...........................66
No opinion.........................23

Democrats

Does..............................17%
Does not...........................59
No opinion.........................24

Independents

Does..............................14%
Does not...........................66
No opinion.........................20

By Religion
Protestants

Does..............................12%
Does not...........................63
No opinion.........................25

Catholics

Does..............................18%
Does not...........................64
No opinion.........................18

Asked of those who have followed the recent developments in the Middle East

and have heard or read about the Palestine Liberation Organization: Which of the plans listed on this card would you prefer with regard to the Palestinians? [Respondents were handed a card listing three plans—Plan A: They should have a separate, independent nation on the West Bank of the Jordan River in the area that was formerly Jordan but is now occupied by Israel; Plan B: They should have a state on the West Bank of the Jordan River that is not totally independent and is linked with Jordan; and Plan C: They should go on living as they are now in Israel and in the existing Arab nations.]

Plan A 24%
Plan B.............................22
Plan C.............................30
Don't know 24

By Education
College

Plan A 26%
Plan B.............................28
Plan C.............................29
Don't know 17

High School

Plan A 24%
Plan B.............................18
Plan C.............................31
Don't know 27

Grade School

Plan A 15%
Plan B.............................11
Plan C.............................35
Don't know 39

By Region
East

Plan A 29%
Plan B.............................19
Plan C.............................29
Don't know 23

Midwest

Plan A 25%
Plan B. 28
Plan C. 26
Don't know 21

South

Plan A 18%
Plan B. 15
Plan C. 32
Don't know 35

West

Plan A 23%
Plan B. 25
Plan C. 36
Don't know 16

By Politics
Republicans

Plan A 27%
Plan B. 17
Plan C. 32
Don't know 24

Democrats

Plan A 23%
Plan B. 23
Plan C. 31
Don't know 23

Independents

Plan A 25%
Plan B. 23
Plan C. 29
Don't know 23

By Religion
Protestants

Plan A 21%
Plan B. 21
Plan C. 32
Don't know 26

Catholics

Plan A 34%
Plan B. 24
Plan C. 23
Don't know 19

Note: Although President Jimmy Carter may not yet have been able to exert enough pressure on the parties involved to bring about a true peace in the Middle East, he can at least rest assured that those Americans who have been following developments in that area of the world approve of the way in which he is approaching the problem.

Fully 56% of those following developments in the Middle East say they approve of Carter's dealings, while less than half as many in this group, 26%, disapprove. Carter's efforts win the approval of a majority in almost every population group, with the greatest disparity evident by political affiliation. While 63% and 58% of Democrats and independents, respectively, back Carter's efforts, only 42% of Republicans express the same view. Much of this approval is a product, no doubt, of Carter's perceived fairness in the matter. While 16% of those following Middle East developments think Carter is leaning too much in favor of Israel and another 6% see him as too much favoring Egypt, the vast majority (62%) feels he is treating both sides with equal fairness. This is the majority point of view among all population groups nationwide (except those in the very lowest income category, among whom 42% have no opinion).

While Carter receives backing for his even-handed approach to Middle East problems, informed American opinion holds the view that neither Israel not Egypt is doing all it should do to achieve peace.

However, although most Americans say their sympathies are with neither side (25%) or have no opinion (30%), among those who do take sides, 37% sympathize with Israel and 8% with the Arab nations. These results, based on a survey completed in December 1977 of those who said they had heard or read about the situation in the Middle East, represent a continuation of a trend evident since April 1975.

After the first such survey, in December 1973, support for the Israelis declined from 50% to the current 37% figure, first recorded in April 1975. At the same time, though, it should be noted that sympathy for the Arab position has neither increased nor decreased since the December 1973 survey.

At the heart of the peace issue is the disposition of Arabs lands captured by Israel in the 1967 war.

In the December 1977 survey, opinion among those who had heard or read about the situation in the Middle East favored the return of at least some portion of these lands. A plurality, 34%, favored returning part of the land controlled by Israel since 1967, and another 16% believed all the land should be returned. One person in five, 20%, favored Israel retention of all the land, and an unusually high number, 30%, were undecided.

In a subsequent survey, completed after Egyptian diplomats were called home from the peace talks with Israel by President Anwar Sadat, 40% of those who had been following developments in the Middle East expressed the view that Israel should withdraw its military forces and civilian settlements from the Sinai Peninsula—a step Egypt has been insisting on as a prerequisite for peace between the two nations. Three persons in ten, 30%, felt Israel should retain those settlements and its military presence in the Sinai, and 30% were undecided.

Not surprisingly, among those who thought Israel was not doing all it could do to achieve peace, 54% believed the settlements and military forces should be removed. And even among those who believed Israel was doing all it could in the cause of peace, 23% wanted the settlements and military forces out of the Sinai.

Two other major disagreements between Israel and the Arab nations are the role of the Palestine Liberation Organization (PLO) and the fate of the Palestinian people.

While leaders of the PLO claim the organization is the only legitimate representative of the Palestinians, they have yet to make their case convincing to informed Americans. Among those people who followed developments in the Middle East and who had heard or read about the PLO, only 14% believed the organization represented the point of view of a majority of Palestinians. A large majority, 63%, rejected this belief, and the remaining 23% were undecided.

As for the political destiny of the Palestinians, survey respondents were presented with three options and asked which they preferred. Opinion split very evenly, with the largest number, 30%, holding the view that the Palestinians should go on living as they are now in Israel and the Arab nations. Another 24% felt the Palestinians should be given a separate, independent nation on the West Bank of the Jordan River in the area now controlled by Israel and formerly known as Trans-Jordan. Nearly as many, 22%, opted for the same location for such a state but wanted it controlled by and linked to Jordan.

In view of the direct negotiations taking place between Israel and Egypt, it is not surprising that those who had been following the developments in the Middle East would rate the chances of peace between these two nations as better than the chances of peace between Israel and the other Arab nations.

FEBRUARY 12
SATISFACTION INDEX

Interviewing Date: 11/18–21/77
Survey #989-K

How satisfied or dissatisfied are you with life in the nation today?

---

*To measure the level or degree of satisfaction or dissatisfaction, a ten-point scale was used. Each respondent was asked to point to the step on the scale that best represented his or her feelings of satisfaction or dissatisfaction.

The top step represented the highest level of satisfaction and the bottom step, the lowest level of dissatisfaction.

In the results reported here, the percentage represents the total score for the top three steps of the scale and describes the "highly satisfied."

	Highly Satisfied
National	57%

By Sex

Male	57%
Female	57

By Race

Whites	59%
Blacks	41

By Age

18–29 years	48%
30–49 years	56
50 years and over	65

By Education

College	56%
High school	55
Grade school	65

Note: President Jimmy Carter's positive assessment of the state of the union would likely meet with little challenge from a majority of Americans. A recent Gallup survey gives further evidence that the somber post-Watergate mood of the public has given way to an increase in national pride.

In a survey in the fall of 1974, only one-third of Americans (34%) expressed a high level of satisfaction with life in the nation at that time. Today a clear majority of 57% do so. An increasingly upbeat mood is recorded for all major population groups, although sharp differences remain. Blacks, for example, are far less satisfied with life in the nation today than are whites, with 41% of Blacks compared to 59% of whites expressing a high level of satisfaction. Young adults of all races are generally less content than are their elders about the state of the nation.

FEBRUARY 16
TAXES

Interviewing Date: 1/3–15, 20–26/78
Special Telephone Survey

Please tell me the extent to which you agree or disagree with the following statements. Even with a tax cut, the amount taken out of my paycheck in taxes and Social Security deductions will go up this year. Would you say you agree strongly, agree, disagree, or disagree strongly?

	Before Carter's State of the Union Message	After Carter's State of the Union Message
Strongly agree	17%	19%
Agree	55	44
Disagree	18	24
Strongly disagree	5	4
No opinion	5	9

Controlling inflation is more important than cutting taxes. Would you say you agree strongly, agree, disagree, or disagree strongly?

Strongly agree	19%
Agree	66
Disagree	7
Strongly disagree	2
No opinion	6

It has been said that tax cuts would lead to a bigger deficit in the federal budget and would make it very difficult for the president to fulfill his promise to balance the budget by 1981. Do you think it is more important to work toward balancing the budget or to cut taxes at this time?

Work toward balancing budget	53%
Cut taxes	39
Don't know	8

Note: The American people are not convinced that President Jimmy Carter's proposed tax cut will have a major effect on the amount of money in their pay envelopes each week.

In Gallup surveys conducted both before and after Carter revealed his tax cut plans for individuals and businesses, the overwhelming majority of Americans agreed that their taxes and payroll deductions would continue to increase.

However, Carter's speech appears to have had some effect. Among those questioned before Carter spoke, 72% agreed that their taxes and deductions would continue to rise. After his speech, 63% held this opinion. Although this represents a significant decline in the percentage with this viewpoint, the president obviously has a long way to go before a majority believes his proposed tax cut will help them gain ground in their personal economic situations.

The survey also reveals two other important findings regarding tax cuts and the economy: first, the public agrees nine to one that controlling inflation is more important than achieving a tax cut; and second, by a five-to-four count, Americans view balancing the budget as more important than cutting taxes.

FEBRUARY 18
PRESIDENT CARTER

Interviewing Date: 1/20–23/78
Survey #992-K

Do you approve or disapprove of the way Jimmy Carter is handling his job as president?

Approve...............................52%
Disapprove 28
No opinion............................20

By Region
East

Approve...............................50%
Disapprove 32
No opinion............................18

Midwest

Approve...............................53%
Disapprove 28
No opinion............................19

South

Approve...............................54%
Disapprove 24
No opinion............................22

Deep South

Approve...............................59%
Disapprove 20
No opinion............................21

West

Approve...............................49%
Disapprove 31
No opinion............................20

FEBRUARY 19
RELIGIOUS DISCIPLINES AND MOVEMENTS

Interviewing Date: 1/20–23/78
Survey #992-K

Which, if any, of these are you involved in or do you practice:

Yoga?

	Yes
National..............................	3%

By Sex

Male.................................	3%
Female...............................	3

By Education

College..............................	6%
High school	2
Grade school	*

By Region

East	4%
Midwest..............................	2
South	2
West.................................	4

By Age

18–24 years	4%
25–29 years	4
30–49 years	4
50 years and over	*

By Religion

Protestants	2%
Catholics	5

*Less than 1%.

Transcendental Meditation?

	Yes
National	25%

By Sex

Male	2%
Female	2

By Education

College	4%
High school	1
Grade school	*

By Region

East	2%
Midwest	*
South	1
West	3

By Age

18–24 years	*%
25–29 years	5
30–49 years	2
50 years and over	*

By Religion

Protestants	2%
Catholics	2

*Less than 1%.

Eastern religions?

	Yes
National	1%

By Sex

Male	1%
Female	1

By Education

College	3%
High school	*
Grade school	*

By Region

East	2%
Midwest	*
South	*
West	2

By Age

18–24 years	2%
25–29 years	1
30–49 years	1
50 years and over	*

By Religion

Protestants	1%
Catholics	1

*Less than 1%.

The Charismatic Movement?

	Yes
National	2%

By Sex

Male	2%
Female	3

By Education

College	2%
High school	2
Grade school	*

By Region

East 2%
Midwest........................... 2
South 1
West............................... 4

By Age

18–24 years....................... 3%
25–29 years....................... 8
39–49 years....................... 1
50 years and over 1

By Religion

Protestants......................... 3%
Catholics 2

*Less than 1%.

Bible study groups?

| | Yes |
National.............................19%

By Sex

Male...............................15%
Female.............................22

By Education

College.............................21%
High school 18
Grade school.......................17

By Region

East 8%
Midwest...........................21
South 26
West...............................21

By Age

18–24 years.......................15%
25–29 years.......................22
30–49 years.......................19
50 years and over 20

By Religion

Protestants.........................27%
Catholics 4

Speaking in tongues?

| | Yes |
National........................... 3%

By Sex

Male............................... 3%
Female............................. 4

By Education

College............................. 3%
High school 4
Grade school....................... 4

By Region

East 2%
Midwest........................... 3
South 3
West............................... 6

By Age

18–24 years....................... 4%
25–29 years....................... 8
30–49 years....................... 3
50 years and over 2

By Religion

Protestants......................... 4%
Catholics 2

Inner or spiritual healing?

| | Yes |
National........................... 6%

By Sex

Male............................... 5%
Female............................. 7

By Education

College	7%
High school	6
Grade school	5

By Region

East	3%
Midwest	4
South	9
West	10

By Age

18–24 years	4%
25–29 years	10
30–49 years	7
50 years and over	5

By Religion

Protestants	8%
Catholics	2

Note: One of the most remarkable trends in the 1970s is the continuing interest in the inner or spiritual life.

A recent nationwide Gallup survey designed to test interest and involvement in three religious disciplines and four religious movements shows that in terms of disciplines, a projected five million Americans are involved in yoga, three million in TM, and two million in Eastern religions. In terms of religious movements, a projected twenty-nine million are involved in Bible study groups, nine million in inner or spiritual healing, five million in speaking in tongues, and three million in the Charismatic Movement.

Broadly speaking, practitioners of TM and yoga and those involved in Eastern religions tend to be younger adults with a college background who live on either of the two coasts. Little difference is found between men and women in terms of level of interest or involvement. In addition, about equal proportions of Protestants and Catholics practice these disciplines.

Although those involved in these three religious disciplines are not as likely to be churchgoers as are others, they are just as likely to say their religious beliefs are "very important" in their lives.

Turning to the four religious movements tested, it is interesting to note that young persons are just as likely to be involved in Bible study groups as are old persons, although earlier surveys have shown young people to be far less likely than their elders to read the Bible on a regular basis.

Differences in terms of educational background are slight in the case of each of the four movements. However, those who say they are "very religious" are far more likely to be involved in these movements than are those who indicate they are "not too" or "not at all" religious.

Protestants are more likely than Catholics to be involved in Bible study groups, inner or spiritual healing, and speaking in tongues, but both groups are about equally likely to be involved in the Charismatic Movement.

FEBRUARY 23
TAXES

Interviewing Date: 1/20–26/78
Special Telephone Survey

Of these groups, low-income people, high-income people, middle-income people, businesses, and people like yourself, which do you feel would benefit the most from any tax cuts?

Low-income people	28%
Middle-income people	17
High-income people	32
Businesses	17
People like yourself	3
Don't know	3

By Income
$20,000 and Over

Low-income people	39%
Middle-income people	14

High-income people 25
Businesses 16
People like yourself 3
Don't know 3

$15,000–$19,999

Low-income people 25%
Middle-income people 22
High-income people 32
Businesses 16
People like yourself 5
Don't know . . . . *

$10,000–$14,999

Low-income people 23%
Middle-income people 17
High-income people 32
Businesses 24
People like yourself 2
Don't know 2

$5,000–$9,999

Low-income people 23%
Middle-income people 17
High-income people 40
Businesses 14
People like yourself 2
Don't know 4

Under $5,000

Low-income people 24%
Middle-income people 17
High-income people 44
Businesses 11
People like yourself 3
Don't know 1

*Less than 1%.

For each group I will mention please tell me whether you think this group would benefit a lot, some, or not very much from any tax cuts:

Businesses?

A lot 35%
Some 32
Not very much 21
Don't know 12

High-income people?

A lot 35%
Some 24
Not very much 36
Don't know 5

Middle-income people?

A lot 16%
Some 51
Not very much 29
Don't know 4

Low-income people?

A lot 21%
Some 31
Not very much 46
Don't know 2

People like yourself?

A lot 8%
Some 42
Not very much 44
Don't know 6

Have you heard or read about the recent increase in Social Security taxes?

	Yes
National	82%

Asked of those who replied in the affirmative: Do you think a tax cut, if approved, would be more than your increase in Social Security taxes, less than the increase, or about the same as the increase in Social Secirty taxes?

More than Social Security increase 14%
Less than Social Security increase 26
About the same 44
Don't know 16

Note: President Jimmy Carter faces a difficult task in convincing the public that it has much to gain from his proposed tax cuts.

In the latest Gallup Poll, people who are aware that Social Security taxes were recently increased take the position that Carter's proposals, even if they are passed, would do no more than offset what has already been removed from their take-home pay by the Social Security tax increase.

When asked what group—businesses, high-income people, middle-income people, low-income people, or "people like yourself"—has the most to gain from the tax cuts, fewer than one person in ten singles out someone like himself or herself. When asked if each of the same groups would benefit "a lot," "some," or "not very much" from the cuts, only about one in ten claims people like himself or herself will benefit a lot.

Nationwide, only 3% say people like themselves would benefit most from the tax cuts. About three persons in ten, 32%, single out those in the upper income brackets as the major beneficiaries of the tax cut; another 28% think those in the lower income categories would benefit most, and 17% name either those in the middle income brackets or businesses.

A plurality of people in the highest income bracket sees those with the lowest incomes as benefiting the most from Carter's proposed cuts. In every other income bracket, a plurality thinks those in the highest income bracket will benefit the most.

Americans not only see people like themselves as least likely to receive the most benefit from the tax cuts but also are convinced they are least likely to benefit "a lot" if the proposals become law.

FEBRUARY 26
CIGARETTE SMOKING

Interviewing Date: 1/20–23/78
Survey #992-K

Have you yourself smoked any cigarettes in the past week?

	Yes
National	36%

By Sex

Male	39%
Female	34

By Race

Whites	37%
Nonwhites	35

By Education

College	30%
High school	43
Grade school	28

By Age

18–24 years	42%
25–29 years	41
30–49 years	42
50 years and over	27

By Occupation

Professional and business	34%
Clerical and sales	49
Manual workers	41
Skilled workers	37
Unskilled workers	44
Non-labor force	29

Asked of those who replied in the affirmative: About how many cigarettes do you smoke each day?

Less than one pack	34%
One–two packs	61
More than two packs	4
Unsure	1

By Sex

Male

Less than one pack	28%
One–two packs	67
More than two packs	4
Unsure	1

Female

Less than one pack 41%
One–two packs 55
More than two packs 3
Unsure 1

By Race
Whites

Less than one pack 30%
One–two packs 65
More than two packs 4
Unsure 1

Nonwhites

Less than one pack 62%
One-two Packs 37
More than two packs 1
Unsure . . . . *

By Education
College

Less than one pack 39%
One–two packs 58
More than two packs 3
Unsure . . . . *

High School

Less than one pack 32%
One–two packs 63
More than two packs 4
Unsure 1

Grade School

Less than one pack 38%
One–two packs 60
More than two packs 2
Unsure . . . . *

By Age
18–24 Years

Less than one pack 41%
One–two packs 50
More than two packs 7
Unsure 1

25–29 Years

Less than one pack 41%
One–two packs 59
More than two packs. . . . . *
Unsure . . . . *

30–49 Years

Less than one pack 26%
One–two packs 70
More than two packs 4
Unsure . . . . *

50 Years and Over

Less than one pack 37%
One–two packs 59
More than two packs 3
Unsure 1

By Occupation
Professional and Business

Less than one pack 28%
One–two packs 67
More than two packs 4
Unsure 1

Clerical and Sales

Less than one pack 28%
One–two packs 63
More than two packs 5
Unsure 4

Manual Workers

Less than one pack 36%
One–two packs 60
More than two packs 4
Unsure . . . . *

Skilled Workers

Less than one pack 33%
One–two packs 63
More than two packs 3
Unsure 1

Unskilled Workers

Less than one pack 39%
One–two packs 57
More than two packs 4
Unsure . . . . *

Non-Labor Force

Less than one pack 36%
One–two packs 58
More than two packs 5
Unsure 1

*Less than 1%.

Do you think the broadcasting industry should or should not be encouraged to increase the number of antismoking messages on television and radio?

Should 51%
Should not 40
No opinion. 9

Smokers Only

Should 38%
Should not 55
No opinion. 7

Nonsmokers Only

Should 59%
Should not 31
No opinion. 10

Do you think the present eight-cents-per-pack federal tax on cigarettes should or should not be increased?

Should 45%
Should not 41
No opinion. 14

Smokers Only

Should 24%
Should not 71
No opinion. 5

Nonsmokers Only

Should 57%
Should not 24
No opinion. 19

Do you think that cigarette smoking on commercial airplanes should or should not be banned completely?

Should 43%
Should not 47
No opinion. 10

Smokers Only

Should 23%
Should not 70
No opinion. 7

Nonsmokers Only

Should 56%
Should not 33
No opinion. 11

Do you think the amount of money the Department of Health, Education, and Welfare spends on antismoking educational efforts should or should not be increased?

Should 40%
Should not 50
No opinion. 10

Smokers Only

Should 28%
Should not 65
No opinion. 7

Nonsmokers Only

Should 48%
Should not 40
No opinion. 12

Note: Four of the antismoking proposals recently set forth by Health, Education, and Welfare Secretary Joseph Califano meet with mixed public reaction.

In January, Califano, formerly a heavy smoker himself, announced a major campaign against cigarette smoking, calling the practice "public health enemy number one."

The new HEW program has several facets, including labels for birth-control pills warning those who use them that a combination of the pills and smoking may be hazardous to health, a study to determine whether the federal excise tax on cigarettes should be increased (it is now eight cents), an attempt to ban smoking on all commercial airline flights, and a proposal that would expand smoking prohibitions in government buildings and public places.

The new program would also create an office of smoking and health assigned to counteract the estimated $500 million per year spent by the tobacco industry on cigarette advertising. Tentative plans call for a budget for the new office of $6 million per year to discourage smoking.

To test public reaction to the Califano program, the Gallup Poll recently asked a representative sample of Americans about their views on the following aspects of the program: (1) encouraging the broadcasting industry to increase antismoking messages; (2) increasing the current eight-cent-per-pack federal tax; (3) banning smoking on all commercial airline flights; and (4) increasing the amount of money spent by HEW on antismoking messages.

The most dramatic contrasts in the survey are found in a comparison of the views of smokers with those of nonsmokers.

In the case of all four questions, nonsmokers support the Califano proposals, while smokers are opposed to all four. However, as many as four in ten smokers do support encouraging the broadcast media to increase antismoking messages. The three other aspects tested all have the backing of about one smoker in four.

The Califano program has been criticized by the tobacco industry for going too far and by antismoking groups for not going far enough.

Antismoking groups have pointed out that the federal government spends more than $60 million a year subsidizing tobacco crops.

MARCH 2
URBAN AMERICA—A SPECIAL GALLUP REPORT, PART I

Many observers of the urban scene maintain that the survival of America's cities depends to a major extent on the rejuvenation of neighborhoods. If the decline of the neighborhoods can be arrested, or if neighborhood quality can be improved, the cities will inevitably benefit.

Findings from a just-released Gallup survey—sponsored by the Charles F. Kettering and Charles Stewart Mott Foundations—indicate that although the picture is mixed, the prospects for improving the quality of the neighborhoods, and therefore the cities, appear promising.

On the debit side, the neighborhoods seem to be in a more vulnerable position than the cities. Although as many as a third of the nation's urban residents say they would like to move away from the cities, an even larger proportion would like to move out of their neighborhoods.

This somewhat gloomy evidence is offset, however, by the survey findings that fully three-quarters of those residents who express a desire to move out of their neighborhoods say that they would be willing to remain if changes or improvements were carried out.

Furthermore, the vast majority of urban residents—including a majority of those wanting to leave their neighborhood—say they would be willing to volunteer their time and effort to help solve urban problems at the neighborhood level.

Desire to Leave

The percentage of residents who would like to move out of their neighborhoods is as high in the smaller and medium-sized cities as it is in the nation's largest cities. In the large and medium-sized cities, it is as high in the suburbs as in the center city areas.

The following table illustrates these findings:

Percent Who Would Like to Move

	Center City	Suburbs
Large cities:		
1 million and over	38%	36%
Medium-sized cities:		
250,000–999,999	39	36
Small cities:		
50,000–249,999	38	28

Neighborhoods Pessimistic

While urban residents generally rate their neighborhoods better than the city as a whole, they are more pessimistic about the future of their neighborhood than they are about the prospects for their city.

For example, when the nation's urban population is asked to rate their city as it is today, as it was five years ago, and as it will be five years hence on a scale from zero to ten, with zero representing the "worst possible city" and ten the "ideal city," the differences between the perceived standing of the city at the three points in time is marginal—6.4, 6.3, 6.1

In contrast, the neighborhood is felt to have declined markedly since five years ago, with the average ratings decreasing from 7.2 to 6.9. Moreover anticipations are that it will deteriorate even more in the next five years, as seen in the further drop in the ratings from 6.9 to 6.4. Offsetting this negative evidence are the following findings:

1. Only a third of those residents expressing the desire to move out of their neighborhoods say that "nothing" could be done to change or improve their neighborhoods to induce them to remain. Six in ten cite areas in which improvements could be made, such as upgrading housing quality, appearances, and maintenance (19%); lowering crime (10%); improving the traffic situation (9%); and cleaning up the neighborhood (7%).

2. The vast majority of city-dwellers (80%) say they would be willing to volunteer their time and efforts to help in solving their cities' problems at the ground level—i.e., in their own neighborhoods—by participating in such activities as signing petitions, attending meetings, writing letters, picketing, and making financial contributions.

The table below indicates the percentage of the nation's urban residents who state they would be willing to volunteer their time in various activities and the percentage who have already done so within the last five years.

	Would be willing to	Have done so within 5 years
Sign petition	63%	36%
Attend meetings concerning the threat	53	21
Participation in face-to-face discussions with public officials	43	9
Write letters to public officials	42	12
Volunteer time to or serve on neighborhood committee	36	9
Testify at public hearing	33	4
Make small financial donation	29	15
Picket city office or public officials' offices	11	2
Picket in the neighborhood	10	1
Any of these activities	89	52
None of these activities	11	4

Further evidence of this desire to improve or strengthen the neighborhoods is seen in the finding that although only one urban resident in eight (12%) belongs to a neighborhood organization, another 29% state they would like to belong to one if such were available. An additional 17% say they might, depending on the circumstances.

The reservoir of talent available to the neighborhoods is representative of virtually the entire urban population, including the young and the lower socioeconomic groups as well as the better-educated and more affluent citizens.

Even those who are most pessimistic about the future of the neighborhood—and those who would move out given the opportunity—are as willing to become involved as those who are most optimistic about its future.

Finally, since these human energies could be tapped without a significant outlay of public money, they would represent a primary resource for strengthening America's neighborhoods—and ultimately the nation's cities.

The findings reported here are based on personal interviews conducted during the last three months of 1977 with 3,242 residents of cities with populations over 50,000.

MARCH 5
URBAN AMERICA—A SPECIAL GALLUP REPORT, PART II

If America's urban residents had their wish, more than one-third would move away from their cities. This proportion holds true for the smaller and medium-size cities as well as for the nation's largest cities, and for the suburbs as well as for the center city areas.

Those residents expressing a desire to leave their cities represent essentially the same socio-economic groups who have been moving away for the last three decades—and whom the cities can least afford to lose. These are the younger, better educated, more affluent, primarily working people who provide the largest share of tax revenues as well as the talent needed to fill public and private leadership roles.

Conversely, those least likely to want to move away are the older, less educated, less affluent population segments, including so-called public-service dependent groups, such as the retired and the unemployed. An important exception among the lower socioeconomic population, however, are Blacks, who are as likely to say they want to leave their cities as are whites.

Underscoring the statistic that as many as one-third of the nation's city dwellers would like to move away is the finding that in smaller communities (under 50,000 inhabitants) only 15% express the desire to move; and in rural areas the percentage wanting to leave declines to 12%.

Desired Location

This desire to move away from one's city does not represent a wish to live in the suburbs but a desire for a complete change of scenery. Only 16% of those center city residents indicating they would like to leave say they would like to move to the suburbs.

Evidence from other Gallup surveys reveals that the nation's city-dwellers, given a choice, would prefer to live in America's smaller, less urbanized communities and in rural areas. For example, although only one-third of America's population lives in communities of under 10,000 inhabitants or in open country, a recent survey reveals that as many as six in ten, given the opportunity, would like to live in such places.

These findings are reflected in census data showing that, on a percentage basis, the largest population increases recorded during the last decade have been in the small towns and rural districts, outside the nation's major metropolitan areas.

Other data from the current survey tend to confirm this apparent preference for less populated areas. When asked to describe the "ideal city," the nation's city-dwellers choose words and phrases that more appropriately describe smaller communities, such as towns and villages—with emphasis on residential attractiveness. Examples include: a lack of crime, over-crowding, traffic congestion, and pollution; clean, attractive, well-maintained housing; friendly people.

Mentioned relatively infrequently are the attributes and advantages associated with large urban environments, such as employment and business opportunities, recreational and cultural facilities, and good municipal services.

The comparison is shown in the following table:

	Desire to Move Away
Cities over 50,000	36%
1,000,000 and over	39
Center city	39
Suburbs	39

250,000 to 999,999	36
Center city	36
Suburbs.....................	38
50,000 to 249,999	34
Center city	36
Suburbs.....................	29
Communities under 50,000, rural areas (open country)	15

The next table indicates the percentage among key population groups in all cities containing more than 50,000 inhabitants who would like to move away.

Desire to Move Away

All urban residents	36%
REGION	
East	36%
Midwest...........................	40
South	32
West..............................	37
AGE	
18–34 years.........................	49%
35–49 years.........................	35
50 years and over	22
EDUCATION	
College............................	40%
High school	37
Grade school.......................	23
RACE	
Whites	26%
Nonwhites.........................	35

People Are Pessimistic

Undoubtedly contributing to this desire to leave the cities is the feeling that the cities have declined as desirable places to live and that they will likely deteriorate still more in the future. Again, it is in the nation's largest cities, those experiencing the biggest problems, in which residents see the most precipitous decline.

For example, when residents of cities with populations over 1,000,000 are asked how they would rate their own city today as a place to live on a scale from zero to ten, with zero representing the worst possible city and ten the ideal city, the average rating is 5.8.

When asked how they felt their city rated five years ago, the average rating is 6.4, or somewhat higher than today's rating. But when large-city residents are asked how they anticipate their city will rate as a place to live five years from today, the average score is lower than today—5.4.

Reasons for Leaving

To determine why urban residents want to leave their cities, an analysis was made of responses to two indirect questions concerning perceptions of th "ideal" and the "worst possible" cities, as well as to several direct questions concerning the reasons for leaving, views as to the cities' most important problems, etc.

Key factors in the desire to move away from the cities are crime; overcrowding or population congestion; the poor condition, appearance, and maintenance of residential housing; unemployment or low pay; air pollution; dirt, traffic congestion; racial problems; and poor climate.

The degree to which crime currently dominates the thinking of the nation's urban residents is apparent from the following findings:

1. Twenty years ago less than 5% of urban dwellers mentioned crime as their city's most important problem. Today that number has risen to 40% among residents of center city areas in the nation's largest cities.

2. A low crime rate is named by 34% as the most important attribute of the "ideal city," with a high crime rate cited most frequently (by 49%) as a description of the "worst possible" city.

3. Crime runs a close second to population congestion or overcrowding as the most frequently mentioned reason for wanting to move away from one's city.

The findings reported today are based on 3,242 interviews with adults, 18 years and older, in more than 300 scientifically selected localities across the nation. The survey, conducted during the last three months of 1977, was sponsored by the Charles F. Kettering and Charles Stuart Mott Foundations.

MARCH 8
PRESIDENT CARTER

Interviewing Date: 2/10–13/78
Survey #993-K

Do you approve or disapprove of the way Jimmy Carter is handling his job as president?

Approve.............................47%
Disapprove 34
No opinion..........................19

By Race
Whites

Approve.............................45%
Disapprove 36
No opinion..........................19

Nonwhites

Approve.............................55%
Disapprove 21
No opinion..........................24

Northern Blacks

Approve.............................54%
Disapprove 18
No opinion..........................28

Southern Blacks

Approve.............................57%
Disapprove 26
No opinion..........................17

By Education
College

Approve.............................50%
Disapprove 35
No opinion..........................15

High School

Approve.............................44%
Disapprove 36
No opinion..........................20

Grade School

Approve.............................49%
Disapprove 26
No opinion..........................25

By Region
East

Approve.............................50%
Disapprove 29
No opinion..........................21

Midwest

Approve.............................38%
Disapprove 44
No opinion..........................18

South

Approve.............................52%
Disapprove 32
No opinion..........................16

Deep South

Approve.............................57%
Disapprove 27
No opinion..........................16

West

Approve.............................46%
Disapprove 32
No opinion..........................22

MARCH 9
WAGE-PRICE CONTROLS

Interviewing Date: 2/10–13/78
Survey #993-K

Would you favor or oppose having the government bring back wage and price controls?

Favor 44%
Oppose..............................40
No opinion..........................16

By Education
College
Favor 37%
Oppose 52
No opinion 11

High School
Favor 46%
Oppose 37
No opinion 17

Grade School
Favor 49%
Oppose 27
No opinion 24

By Region
East
Favor 44%
Oppose 37
No opinion 19

Midwest
Favor 48%
Oppose 42
No opinion 10

South
Favor 40%
Oppose 38
No opinion 22

West
Favor 43%
Oppose 43
No opinion 14

By Income
$20,000 and Over
Favor 34%
Oppose 55
No opinion 11

$15,000–$19,999
Favor 46%
Oppose 43
No opinion 11

$10,000–$14,999
Favor 45%
Oppose 35
No opinion 20

$7,000–$9,999
Favor 47%
Oppose 33
No opinion 20

$5,000–$6,999
Favor 56%
Oppose 26
No opinion 18

$3,000–$4,999
Favor 45%
Oppose 30
No opinion 25

Under $3,000
Favor 50%
Oppose 24
No opinion 26

By Occupation
Professional and Business
Favor 39%
Oppose 50
No opinion 11

Clerical and Sales
Favor 46%
Oppose 40
No opinion 14

Manual Workers

Favor 46%
Oppose 36
No opinion 18

Non-Labor Force

Favor 45%
Oppose 36
No opinion 19

Labor Union Families Only

Favor 42%
Oppose 44
No opinion 14

Non-Labor Union Families Only

Favor 44%
Oppose 39
No opinion 17

Note: Fear of growing inflation has again focused attention on a return to wage-price controls, last imposed in 1974. While anathema to most labor and business groups, controls have consistently met with support from the general public, particularly during wars and periods of severe inflation.

The current results closely parallel those recorded in the previous survey on the subject in December 1976, when 46% expressed support for a "freeze" and 40% were opposed. Support for controls, however, is slightly lower than that recorded in an August 1974 survey, at a time when the nation was suffering double-digit inflation. That survey showed 50% in favor of a return to controls, 39% opposed, and 11% undecided.

The Carter administration has expressed opposition to wage-price controls and has recently established a policy that seeks by voluntary restraint to reduce both wage and price increases to below the average levels of the last two years.

While labor and business leaders, in general, have been opposed to controls, support for a freeze was recently expressed by the Federal Reserve Bank of New York, which maintained in its annual report that controls may be necessary to break the inflationary psychology created when pressure for wage and price increases continue to build in anticipation of future inflation.

Nearly four decades of public opinion measurements have found the public in favor of wage-price controls during periods of war and severe inflation. Twelve years ago, in 1966, opinion was fairly evenly divided between those who favored and those who opposed wage-price curbs, but as inflationary pressures increased during the late sixties, opinion began to shift toward support for a wage-price freeze.

MARCH 12
MOST IMPORTANT NATIONAL PROBLEM

Interviewing Date: 2/10–13/78
Survey #993-K

What do you think is the most important problem facing the country today?

High cost of living, inflation 33%
Energy problems 29
Unemployment 17
International problems, foreign policy 7
Crime and lawlessness 4
Moral decline, lack of religious
   commitment 3
Excessive government spending 2
Dissatisfaction with government 2
Drug abuse 2
Poverty 2
Race relations 1
All others 17
Can't say 4
                                 123%*

*Total adds to more than 100% due to multiple responses.

Asked of those who named one of the top three problems above as the most important problem: Which political party do you think could do a better job of handling the problem you have just mentioned—the Republican party or the Democratic party?

Those Who Named the High Cost of Living

Democratic 29%
Republican. 22
No difference. 40
No opinion. 9

Those Who Named Unemployment

Democratic 46%
Republican. 15
No difference. 30
No opinion. 9

Those Who Named Energy Problems

Democratic 35%
Republican. 19
No difference. 33
No opinion. 13

Note: The problem facing the Republican party is illustrated by the fact that the Republicans have failed to convince voters they can handle the top problems better than the Democrats can.

Each person in the survey who named a problem was then asked which party was better able to deal with the particular problem they named. While the Democrats hold a wide (36% to 19%) margin on this measurement—a leading indicator of political trends—the GOP can take some hope from the fact that the gap between parties today is less than at this time in the beginning of the 1974 congressional election year. At that time the Democratic party held a 40% to 16% advantage. In that survey (reported in late January), the top problems named by the public were the energy situation (46%), the high cost of living (25%), dissatisfaction with government/lack of trust in government (15%), and corruption in government/Watergate (7%).

The division of the national popular vote in the 1974 congressional elections was 58.9% Democratic and 41.1% Republican.

MARCH 16
PRESIDENT CARTER

Interviewing Date: 2/24–27/78
Survey #994-K

Do you approve or disapprove of the way Jimmy Carter is handling his job as president?

Approve. 51%
Disapprove 33
No opinion. 16

By Race
Whites

Approve. 50%
Disapprove 35
No opinion. 15

Northern Whites

Approve. 48%
Disapprove 36
No opinion. 16

Southern Whites

Approve. 54%
Disapprove 31
No opinion. 15

Nonwhites

Approve. 56%
Disapprove 21
No opinion. 23

Northern Blacks

Approve. 55%
Disapprove 22
No opinion. 23

Southern Blacks

Approve. 59%
Disapprove 18
No opinion. 23

By Education
College
Approve.............................45%
Disapprove 42
No opinion.........................13

High School
Approve.............................53%
Disapprove 32
No opinion.........................15

Grade School
Approve.............................49%
Disapprove 22
No opinion.........................29

By Region
East
Approve.............................51%
Disapprove 35
No opinion.........................14

Midwest
Approve.............................47%
Disapprove 33
No opinion.........................20

South
Approve.............................55%
Disapprove 28
No opinion.........................17

Deep South
Approve.............................47%
Disapprove 32
No opinion.........................21

West
Approve.............................47%
Disapprove 38
No opinion.........................15

By Politics
Republicans
Approve.............................32%
Disapprove 54
No opinion.........................14

Democrats
Approve.............................63%
Disapprove 22
No opinion.........................15

Southern Democrats
Approve.............................68%
Disapprove 18
No opinion.........................14

Independents
Approve.............................48%
Disapprove 35
No opinion.........................17

Asked of those who approve: How strongly would you say you approve—very strongly or not so strongly?

Very strongly........................18%
Not so strongly 31
No opinion......................... 2
                                    ─────
                                    51%

Asked of those who disapprove: How strongly would you say you disapprove— very strongly or not so strongly?

Very strongly........................15%
Not so strongly 17
No opinion......................... 1
                                    ─────
                                    33%

Note: These results represent the first increase in the president's ratings since early December 1977, when 57% expressed approval. Carter's popularity had declined since the December survey, reaching a low point of 47% approval in early February.

Carter's job rating after thirteen months in office is slightly higher than the one recorded after a similar time for the man he defeated for the presidency, Gerald Ford. In a survey completed in September 1975, thirteen months after Ford assumed the presidency, 47% approved of his conduct in office and 36% disapproved.

Aside from Ford and President Harry Truman (who had 50% approval at a comparable time), Carter's rating after thirteen months in office falls significantly below those of his six immediate predecessors. For example, at a comparable time in his administration, President Richard Nixon had the support of 56% of the public. Presidents Lyndon Johnson and Dwight Eisenhower received 69% and 68% ratings respectively, and President John Kennedy had the backing of 78%.

Survey Differences

Observers of polls have asked why various national surveys of the president's standing differ. While such factors as the time the survey was conducted often account for differences, poll results should always be interpreted in the light of the exact question asked.

Polls that focus on the achievements of the president presently give Carter a low rating. On the other hand, one national poll that focuses on confidence in the president himself shows a much higher rating for Carter.

The Gallup Poll, which has asked the same question for four decades, takes both of these aspects into account. The question asked the respondent is this: "Do you approve or disapprove of the way (name of incumbent) is handling his job as president?" Those who are evenly balanced in their opinion or who are in doubt typically fall into the "don't know" category.

Gallup Poll surveys of the president's standing are based on face-to-face interviews with a scientifically selected cross-section of adults in all parts of the nation.

PRESIDENT CARTER'S POPULARITY— A GALLUP ANALYSIS

Few presidents in the Gallup Poll's history have had to deal with so many critical issues as has Jimmy Carter. His failure to impress the public with his achievement accounts, at least in part, for the sharp decline in his popularity since March 1977, when his approval rating stood at 75%.

From that high point, Carter's popularity declined to a low of 47%, registered in a Gallup Poll survey early this February. The latest soundings by the Gallup Poll indicate this long decline has halted, at least for the time being. His latest approval figure, 51% (recorded February 24–27), represents a gain of 4 percentage points over the 47% recorded in early February.

While every president in the forty-three-year period covered by the Gallup Poll has suffered a decline in popularity from the honeymoon days following his inauguration, this decline can vary widely among different segments of the public.

Comparison of Carter's popularity (based on an average of three surveys conducted since the end of January) with the vote given him in the 1976 presidential election brings to light this unusual finding: the Democratic president is given a surprisingly high approval vote by upper income groups, predominantly Republican in their viewpoints. In contrast, he has suffered his greatest loss in popularity among voters in the lower income groups, which are predominantly Democratic.

Perhaps the most interesting difference that emerges is Carter's relative strength with the college-educated. This group includes a high proportion of people in the business and professional groups, a majority of whom are Republicans or independents. However, this is the only educational group in which Carter's popularity is higher than his share of the election vote in 1976.

The following table shows how the president's popularity (averaged from the last three surveys) compares with his share of the popular vote in the 1976 presidential election:

By Education

	Carter popularity	Carter share of 1976 vote
College	49%	42%
High school	46	54
Grade school	56	58

Business and professional groups also give Carter a surprisingly high approval vote despite their Republican leanings. The approval rate of manual workers is appreciably lower than their vote for Carter in the 1976 election.

By Occupation

	Carter popularity	Carter share of 1976 vote
Business and professional	46%	42%
Clerical and sales	53	50
Manual workers	52	58

The Midwest is the area of the nation where Carter's popularity is lowest. This is the section of the country where Republican candidates have the best chance of winning seats in the coming congressional elections.

There is a close relationship between a president's popularity and the success of his party in winning congressional seats in an off-year election. On the basis of off-year elections since 1936, it appears that when a president slips below a 55% approval rating, the opposing party stands to win more than the normal number of seats.

The following shows how Carter's popularity in the four major geographical regions compares with his share of the 1976 vote:

By Region

	Carter popularity	Carter share of 1976 vote
East	50%	51%
Midwest	46	48
South	54	54
West	47	46

One of the sharpest declines in Carter's popularity is found among nonwhite voters. In 1976, 85% of their vote went to Carter. Nonwhites now give Carter an approval rating of 55%—a loss of 30 percentage points.

Here are the comparisons, based on race, of Carter's popularity and his share of the 1976 popular vote:

By Race

	Carter popularity	Carter share of 1976 vote
Whites	49%	46%
Nonwhites	55	85

The results reported here for the demographic groups shown are based on face-to-face interviews with 4,603 adults, 18 years and older, in more than 300 scientifically selected localities across the nation. Interviewing for the first two surveys took place during the periods of January 20–23 and February 10–13. Interviewing for the most recent survey took place February 24–27 and included 1,553 adults.

MARCH 23
COST OF LIVING

Interviewing Date: 2/10–13/78
Survey #993-K

What is the smallest amount of money a family of four (husband, wife, and two children) needs each week to get along in this community?

	Median Average
National	$201*

By Region

East	$201
Midwest	$201
South	$200
West	$200

By Community Size

One million and over	$248
500,000–999,999	$201
50,000–499,999	$201
2,500–49,999	$200
Under 2,500; rural	$199

By Income

$15,000 and over	$202
$10,000–$14,999	$200
$5,000–$9,999	$199
Under $5,000	$199

By Occupation

Professional and business	$226
Clerical and sales	$201
Manual workers	$200
Non-labor force	$198

*Farm families were excluded from the survey since many farmers raise their own food.

What is the smallest amount of money your family needs each week to get along in this community?

	Median Average
National	$198*

By Region

East	$198
Midwest	$173
South	$176
West	$199

By Community Size

One million and over	$200
500,000–999,999	$199
50,000–499,999	$175
2,500–49,999	$173
Under 2,500; rural	$152

By Income

$15,000 and over	$236
$10,000–$14,999	$173
$5,000–$9,999	$128
Under $5,000	$ 99

By Occupation

Professional and business	$227
Clerical and sales	$177
Manual workers	$198
Non-labor force	$102

By Size of Household

Single person	$ 99
Two-person family	$151
Three-person family	$199
Four-person family	$201
Five-or-more-person family	$202

*Farm families were excluded from the survey since many farmers raise their own food.

Note: By their own estimate, Americans believe that it requires $201 per week, as a minimum, for a family of four to make ends meet today.

The public's median estimate of living costs for a four-person family in this latest Gallup Poll is the highest amount recorded since these surveys began in 1937.

The extent to which inflation, now cited by the American people as the number one problem facing the nation, has affected living costs comes to light in a comparison of poll results obtained by the Gallup Poll during the last forty years. In 1937, when the Gallup Poll first asked this question, the median answer given was $30. A decade later the figure was $43, and by 1957 the amount had risen to $72. In 1967 the figure hit three digits, $101, for the first time. During the last decade, inflation and a rising standard of living have doubled this amount to $201 per week. In short, while it took four decades for the sum to reach $100, it took only one decade, 1967–77, to double that amount.

In earlier years, marked differences in living costs were found in the different geographic regions of the nation. In this latest survey, consumer estimates of living costs are virtually the same from region to region. Previously, people living in the thirteen southern states had always gauged costs for a family of four lower than had residents of the three other geographic regions. Currently the median average estimate in the South, $200, almost exactly equals estimates from other parts of the nation. Similarly, residents of the Midwest, who until 1976 estimated needs in that region as being significantly lower than those recorded on both coasts, peg their cost of living at the same level ($200) as do those living in the East ($201). Predictably, inhabitants of the nation's largest cities (one million or more residents) cite a significantly higher figure ($248 per week) than do those living in smaller cities, towns, or rural areas.

The dollar estimates arrived at in these surveys are based on national samples of the adult, civilian, nonfarm population. While estimates may seem unreasonably low to some readers, it should be remembered that the question asked respondents for "the smallest amount of money."

MARCH 26
CONGRESSIONAL ELECTIONS

Interviewing Date: 2/10–13, 24–27/78
Survey #993-K, 994-K

Asked of registered voters in the Midwest: If the elections for Congress were being held today, which party would you like to see win in this congressional district, the Democratic party of the Republican party?

Midwest Only

Democratic	42%
Republican	40
Other	4
Undecided	14

Asked of those who were undecided: As of today, do you lean more to the Democratic party or to the Republican party?

Here are the results when those who are undecided are allocated between the two major parties:

Democratic	51%
Republican	49

Note: Republican hopes for gaining a substantial number of seats in the House of Representatives in the coming congressional elections rest chiefly with the Midwest.

The twelve states that form the Midwest hold a total of 121 of the 435 seats in the lower house. Of these 121 seats, 68 are now held by Democrats, 53 by Republicans.

The Midwest will be the chief battleground for a simple reason: more seats in this region are held by a small margin than is the case in any other section of the nation. In other words, any loss in Democratic voting strength there will result in more seat changes than in other areas.

The latest Gallup survey measuring congressional preference today in the Midwest shows an uptrend for the Republicans. In the last off-year congressional elections, in 1974, Democrats won sixty-nine seats compared to fifty-two for the GOP. In that election, Democratic candidates won 55% of all votes cast for House races; GOP candidates, 45%. The current survey assumes a turnout comparable to that of 1970 and 1974.

Off-Year Losses

The party occupying the White House traditionally loses seats in off-year congressional elections. In fact, in only one election during this century has the party in power gained seats. In the 1934 elections the Democratic party not only did not lose any seats but added nine to an already substantial majority of 310.

The average seat loss for the president's party in recent decades has been slightly more than thirty. Various reasons have been advanced to explain this voting behavior. Certainly three factors, judging from polling experience, are important: the popularity of the president at the time of the election, the issues that voters regard as most important and their perceptions as to which party can deal better with these problems, and the turnout on election day.

Carter's Popularity in the Midwest

When poll results showing a president's popularity at the time of off-year elections are related to the number of seats gained or lost, a low nationwide approval rating is reflected in the election outcome. When a president's approval rating falls below 55% nationally, seat gains for the opposition tend to be substantially larger than normal.

In the most recently reported survey, Carter's approval rating nationwide is 51%. This rating represents an upturn in Carter's popularity after his low of 47% in early February. In the Midwest, however, Carter's approval rating stands at 47%.

Most Important Issues to Midwestern Voters

In the opinion of midwestern voters the most important problem facing the nation is inflation (the high cost of living). Energy is a close second, and unemployment ranks third among the many problems mentioned. When asked which party they believe can deal better with the problem they think most important, midwestern voters give a smaller edge to the Democrats than does the rest of the nation.

When those who think there is no difference in the ability of the parties to deal with these problems or who have no opinion on the question are divided equally between the parties, the results show the Democrats with a slight advantage—53% to 47%. This contrasts with the nationwide figure of 58% for the Democrats and 42% for the Republicans.

The Effect of Turnout

As a general rule, low turnout tends to favor Republican candidates, especially in areas outside the South. Persons most likely to vote generally come from the upper income levels and from older age groups. Since a high proportion of Republicans are found in these groups, a low turnout usually favors GOP candidates.

Fewer than half of all Americans take the trouble to vote in off-year elections. The average turnout in the last two off-year elections has been 40% of those of voting age. This turnout level has been assumed in developing the figures reported here.

Interviewing Date: 2/10–13/78
Survey #993-K

Asked of the entire sample: Do you happen to know the name of the present representative in Congress from your district?

Yes	40%
No	43
Not sure	17

By Sex
Male

Yes	44%
No	41
Not sure	15

Female

Yes	37%
No	45
Not sure	18

By Race
Whites

Yes	42%
No	41
Not sure	17

Nonwhites

Yes	23%
No	61
Not sure	16

Northern Blacks

Yes	19%
No	72
Not sure	9

Southern Blacks

Yes 22%
No 53
Not sure 25

By Education
College

Yes 50%
No 36
Not sure 14

High School

Yes 37%
No 47
Not sure 16

Grade School

Yes 32%
No 42
Not sure 26

By Region
East

Yes 45%
No 44
Not sure 11

Midwest

Yes 41%
No 38
Not sure 21

South

Yes 39%
No 39
Not sure 22

West

Yes 33%
No 56
Not sure 11

MARCH 30
COST OF LIVING

Interviewing Date: 2/10–13/78
Surey #993-K

On the average, about how much does your family spend on food, including milk, each week?

	Median Average
National	$50*

By Region

East	$50
Midwest	$48
South	$49
West	$49

By Community Size

One million and over	$59
500,000–999,999	$51
50,000–499,999	$49
2,500–49,999	$47
Under 2,500; rural	$45

By Size of Household

Single person	$26
Two-person family	$44
Three-person family	$50
Four-person family	$60
Five-or-more-person family	$74

*Farm families were excluded from the survey since many farmers raise their own food.

Note: After two years at the same level, average family food expenditures are on the rise again.

In this year's Gallup Poll survey of the public's weekly expenditures for food, the median average amount cited is $50 per week—an increase of two dollars from last year, or more than $100 per year.

The latest figure, based on nonfarm families, is the highest amount ever recorded since the Gallup Poll began charting family expenditures in 1937. At that time, the median figure mentioned by survey respondents was $11 per week.

The amount rose at a relatively moderate pace throughout the 1940s and the ensuing twenty years. However, during the current decade the increase has been dramatic—from $34 in 1970 to the $50 figure reported today—a 47% increase.

Some of the sharpest contrasts in reported spending for food each week are by geographic region and city size of the respondent. As has been the case in the past, residents of eastern states report spending a significantly higher amount per week ($58) than do those in the other three major regions ($48 or $49). Following the trend in years past, inhabitants of the nation's largest cities (one million or more residents) say they spend much more per week ($59) than do those living in smaller cities or rural areas. People in the highest income bracket spend more per week ($58) than others (ranging from $49 to $38).

The survey also reveals that, at least on a per capita basis, those in multiple-person households eat more cheaply than single people, and the gap may be widening a bit.

The following illustrates the changes in per capita spending for food reported in surveys during the last four years:

Per Capita Food Expenditures, 1975–1978

Single-Person Household

1975	$25.00
1976	$25.00
1977	$23.00
1978	$26.00

Two-Person Household

1975	$18.00
1976	$18.00
1977	$20.00
1978	$22.00

Three-Person Household

1975	$15.33
1976	$16.00
1977	$14.33
1978	$16.67

Four-Person Household

1975	$12.00
1976	$16.50
1977	$15.50
1978	$15.00

These figures were recorded before the last surge in food prices reported by the federal government—increases that may propel the median average expenditure over the $50-per-week mark.

APRIL 2
CONGRESSIONAL ELECTIONS

Interviewing Date: 2/10–13, 24–27/78
Survey #993-K, 994-K

Asked of registered voters: If the elections for Congress were being held today, which party would you like to see win in this congressional district?

Democratic	49%
Republican	36
Other	3
Undecided	12

By Region
East

Democratic	48%
Republican	39
Other	3
Undecided	10

Midwest

Democratic	42%
Republican	40
Other	4
Undecided	14

South

Democratic	58%
Republican	23
Other	3
Undecided	16

West

Democratic	51%
Republican	37
Other	4
Undecided	8

Note: As the 1978 congressional election campaign gets underway, Republican hopes for substantial gains in the race for the House of Representatives have yet to materialize.

Since World War II, the party that holds the White House has lost some thirty to thirty-five seats in off-year elections. Although nationally the GOP is slightly stronger today than at election time in 1974—the last off-year election—Gallup Poll findings at this time point to only modest Republican gains.

Republican chances to win seats, as reported earlier, are greatest in the Midwest, chiefly because more Democratic seats are held by narrow margins there.

In the South and the West, Democrats are holding their strength. Actually, in the South the poll findings show the party slightly stronger than it was in 1974. While the South has cast its vote for certain Republican presidential candidates in elections since World War II, voters there continue to elect a preponderance of Democratic congressional candidates. Of the 121 seats in this area, Democratic candidates won eighty-nine to the Republicans' thirty-two in 1976. In 1974, the Democrats won ninety-two of the 121 seats. Losses for the Democrats in voting strength in the East parallel those found in the Midwest—5% in both cases.

APRIL 6
THE MIDDLE EAST

Interviewing Date: 3/3–6/78
Survey #995-K

Have you heard or read about the situation in the Middle East?

Yes	83%
No	17

Among the college-educated, people in the upper income brackets, and those in the professions and business, the figure reaches 93% or better.

Asked of those who replied in the affirmative: In the Middle East situation, are your sympathies more with Israel or more with the Arab nations?

Israel	38%
Arabs	11
Neither	33
No opinion	18

By Sex
Male

Israel	38%
Arabs	12
Neither	35
No opinion	15

Female

Israel	39%
Arabs	10
Neither	30
No opinion	21

By Race
Whites

Israel	39%
Arabs	11
Neither	33
No opinion	17

Nonwhites

Israel	30%
Arabs	10
Neither	29
No opinion	31

By Education
College
Israel 49%
Arabs 13
Neither.............................. 28
No opinion........................... 10

High School
Israel 35%
Arabs 10
Neither.............................. 35
No opinion........................... 20

Grade School
Israel 26%
Arabs 10
Neither.............................. 35
No opinion........................... 29

By Region
East
Israel 33%
Arabs 14
Neither.............................. 36
No opinion........................... 17

Midwest
Israel 37%
Arabs 11
Neither.............................. 34
No opinion........................... 18

South
Israel 40%
Arabs 10
Neither.............................. 29
No opinion........................... 21

West
Israel 46%
Arabs 7
Neither.............................. 32
No opinion........................... 15

By Age
18–29 Years
Israel 46%
Arabs 8
Neither.............................. 32
No opinion........................... 14

30–49 Years
Israel 41%
Arabs 8
Neither.............................. 32
No opinion........................... 19

50 Years and Over
Israel 31%
Arabs 15
Neither.............................. 34
No opinion........................... 20

By Politics
Republicans
Israel 39%
Arabs 13
Neither.............................. 32
No opinion........................... 16

Democrats
Israel 38%
Arabs 9
Neither.............................. 32
No opinion........................... 21

Independents
Israel 38%
Arabs 12
Neither.............................. 35
No opinion........................... 15

By Religion
Protestants
Israel 38%
Arabs 10
Neither.............................. 32
No opinion........................... 20

Catholics

Israel 32%
Arabs 13
Neither...............................39
No opinion...........................16

Also asked of those who have heard or read about the situation in the Middle East: Do you think the United States should supply arms and materiel to Israel?

Yes 31%
No....................................56
No opinion...........................13

By Sex
Male

Yes 38%
No....................................52
No opinion...........................10

Female

Yes 24%
No....................................60
No opinion...........................16

By Race
Whites

Yes 32%
No....................................56
No opinion...........................12

Nonwhites

Yes 19%
No....................................58
No opinion...........................23

By Education
College

Yes 45%
No....................................48
No opinion........................ 7

High School

Yes 27%
No....................................60
No opinion...........................13

Grade School

Yes 16%
No....................................59
No opinion...........................25

By Region
East

Yes 30%
No....................................59
No opinion...........................11

Midwest

Yes 28%
No....................................59
No opinion...........................13

South

Yes 34%
No....................................51
No opinion...........................15

West

Yes 35%
No....................................55
No opinion...........................10

By Age
18–29 Years

Yes 31%
No....................................60
No opinion........................ 9

30–49 Years

Yes 32%
No....................................55
No opinion...........................13

50 Years and Over

Yes 31%
No. 53
No opinion. 16

By Politics
Republicans

Yes 37%
No. 50
No opinion. 13

Democrats

Yes 28%
No. 55
No opinion. 17

Independents

Yes 32%
No. 62
No opinion. 6

By Religion
Protestants

Yes 30%
No. 56
No opinion. 14

Catholics

Yes 28%
No. 59
No opinion. 13

Also asked of those who have heard or read about the situation in the Middle East: Do you think the United States should supply arms and materiel to the Arabs?

Yes 16%
No. 72
No opinion. 12

By Sex
Male

Yes 22%
No. 67
No opinion. 11

Female

Yes 10%
No. 76
No opinion. 14

By Race
Whites

Yes 17%
No. 72
No opinion. 11

Nonwhites

Yes 8%
No. 65
No opinion. 27

By Education
College

Yes 25%
No. 68
No opinion. 7

High School

Yes 13%
No. 74
No opinion. 13

Grade School

Yes 8%
No. 68
No opinion. 24

By Region
East

Yes 15%
No. 74
No opinion. 11

Midwest

Yes 14%
No 75
No opinion 11

South

Yes 17%
No 67
No opinion 16

West

Yes 21%
No 69
No opinion 10

By Age
18–29 Years

Yes 11%
No 81
No opinion 8

30–49 Years

Yes 17%
No 72
No opinion 11

50 Years and Over

Yes 20%
No 64
No opinion 16

By Politics
Republicans

Yes 24%
No 64
No opinion 12

Democrats

Yes 13%
No 71
No opinion 16

Independents

Yes 16%
No 79
No opinion 5

By Religion
Protestants

Yes 15%
No 71
No opinion 14

Catholics

Yes 17%
No 71
No opinion 12

Note: While the average citizen cannot be expected to be aware of the diplomatic and military complexities of the situation, the current results are nevertheless another clear indication of the post-Vietnam mood of the American public and the desire not to get involved militarily in developments overseas.

These findings are recorded at a time of intense debate in Washington over the Carter administration's plan to sell Israel, Egypt, and Saudi Arabia a total of 200 fighter aircraft over the next five years. The issues under discussion include whether and how the $4.8 billion package will affect Israel's future military security and the course of diplomatic efforts to achieve a Middle East peace settlement, and how the plan to sell arms squares with President Carter's overall policy of restraining arms sales.

APRIL 9
PRESIDENT CARTER

Interviewing Date: 2/24–27; 3/3–6, 10–13/78
Survey #994-K, 995-K, 996-K

Do you approve or disapprove of the way Jimmy Carter is handling his job as president?

Approve............................49%
Disapprove 34
No opinion.........................17

By Race
Whites

Approve............................48%
Disapprove 36
No opinion.........................16

Northern Whites

Approve............................47%
Disapprove 37
No opinion.........................16

Southern Whites

Approve............................51%
Disapprove 32
No opinion.........................17

Nonwhites

Approve............................59%
Disapprove 20
No opinion.........................21

Northern Blacks

Approve............................55%
Disapprove 21
No opinion.........................24

Southern Blacks

Approve............................65%
Disapprove 18
No opinion.........................17

By Education
College

Approve............................48%
Disapprove 39
No opinion.........................13

High School

Approve............................50%
Disapprove 33
No opinion.........................17

Grade School

Approve............................50%
Disapprove 26
No opinion.........................24

By Income
$20,000 and Over

Approve............................48%
Disapprove 41
No opinion.........................11

$15,000–$19,999

Approve............................50%
Disapprove 36
No opinion.........................14

$10,000–$14,999

Approve............................51%
Disapprove 35
No opinion.........................14

$7,000–$9,999

Approve............................50%
Disapprove 29
No opinion.........................21

$5,000–$6,999

Approve............................49%
Disapprove 31
No opinion.........................20

$3,000–$4,999

Approve............................52%
Disapprove 29
No opinion.........................19

Under $3,000

Approve.............................51%
Disapprove 27
No opinion...........................22

By Religion
Protestants

Approve.............................48%
Disapprove 34
No opinion...........................18

Catholics

Approve.............................54%
Disapprove 32
No opinion...........................14

Interviewing Date: 3/3–6, 3/10–13/78
Survey #996-K, 997-K

Now, here's another kind of question about the way Carter is handling his job as president. [Respondent is handed a card.] You notice that the numbers on this card go from zero, meaning the strongest disapproval of the way Carter is handling his job as president, up to ten, meaning the strongest approval of the way Carter is handling his job. To indicate how you feel, would you select a number between zero and ten—the lower the number, the stronger you disapprove—the higher the number, the stronger you approve?

	3/3-6/78	3/10-13/78
Zero	4%	4%
One	3	2
Two	3	4
Three	7	7
Four	8	10
Five	22	19
Six	13	11
Seven	13	14
Eight	11	14
Nine	3	3
Ten	7	7
Don't know	6	5

By Sex
Male

Zero	5%	5%
One	3	3
Two	4	4
Three	8	8
Four	10	10
Five	18	18
Six	12	11
Seven	15	16
Eight	12	13
Nine	3	3
Ten	6	6
Don't know	4	3

Female

Zero	3%	4%
One	3	2
Two	3	3
Three	6	6
Four	7	10
Five	25	21
Six	14	11
Seven	11	12
Eight	11	15
Nine	3	3
Ten	8	7
Don't know	6	6

By Race
Whites

Zero	4%	5%
One	3	2
Two	3	4
Three	8	8
Four	8	11
Five	22	20
Six	14	10
Seven	13	14
Eight	11	14
Nine	3	3
Ten	6	6
Don't know	5	5

Northern Whites

Zero	4%	4%
One	3	2
Two	3	4
Three	8	9
Four	9	11
Five	21	21
Six	14	10
Seven	13	13
Eight	12	13
Nine	3	3
Ten	6	5
Don't know	4	5

Southern Whites

Zero	3%	7%
One	2	3
Two	3	2
Three	7	6
Four	8	8
Five	24	16
Six	14	9
Seven	13	16
Eight	10	17
Nine	3	3
Ten	8	8
Don't know	5	5

Nonwhites

Zero	4%	1%
One	3	1
Two	2	3
Three	*	3
Four	7	3
Five	20	16
Six	10	17
Seven	14	12
Eight	11	14
Nine	6	6
Ten	14	16
Don't know	9	8

Northern Blacks

Zero	5%	0%
One	5	1
Two	3	1
Three	*	6
Four	10	3
Five	21	15
Six	8	15
Seven	12	10
Eight	14	21
Nine	5	2
Ten	8	18
Don't know	9	8

Southern Blacks

Zero	2%	2%
One	*	1
Two	2	5
Three	*	0
Four	2	2
Five	16	12
Six	13	21
Seven	12	13
Eight	9	10
Nine	7	12
Ten	25	17
Don't know	10	5

By Education

College

Zero	2%	4%
One	2	2
Two	4	3
Three	10	10
Four	12	14
Five	19	17
Six	19	14
Seven	17	16
Eight	10	12
Nine	2	1
Ten	2	4
Don't know	1	1

High School

Zero	5%	4%
One	3	2
Two	3	4
Three	7	7
Four	8	9

Five	23	20
Six	12	10
Seven	13	14
Eight	11	15
Nine	4	3
Ten	6	5
Don't know	5	6

Grade School

Zero	4%	5%
One	5	2
Two	3	4
Three	4	3
Four	4	5
Five	22	20
Six	7	4
Seven	8	10
Eight	13	13
Nine	4	5
Ten	18	18
Don't know	8	11

By Region

East

Zero	3%	2%
One	3	2
Two	3	4
Three	7	8
Four	6	12
Five	20	22
Six	12	10
Seven	12	15
Eight	18	11
Nine	5	2
Ten	6	6
Don't know	5	6

Midwest

Zero	5%	4%
One	3	2
Two	4	5
Three	8	8
Four	10	8
Five	21	20
Six	14	11
Seven	13	13

Eight	9	15
Nine	2	3
Ten	7	7
Don't know	5	3

South

Zero	3%	6%
One	2	3
Two	3	3
Three	6	5
Four	7	7
Five	23	15
Six	13	11
Seven	12	15
Eight	10	15
Nine	4	4
Ten	11	10
Don't know	6	6

West

Zero	3%	6%
One	4	1
Two	2	3
Three	9	9
Four	11	13
Five	23	20
Six	14	10
Seven	15	11
Eight	9	15
Nine	1	3
Ten	5	3
Don't know	4	6

By Age

18–24 Years

Zero	*%	3%
One	*	2
Two	2	2
Three	10	6
Four	10	11
Five	22	17
Six	19	15
Seven	16	17
Eight	8	16
Nine	3	3
Ten	3	4
Don't know	6	4

25–29 Years

Zero	5%	3%
One	2	3
Two	3	3
Three	6	14
Four	7	10
Five	20	16
Six	17	17
Seven	18	11
Eight	10	14
Nine	3	1
Ten	2	4
Don't know	7	5

30–49 Years

Zero	2%	2%
One	3	1
Two	4	4
Three	6	8
Four	10	13
Five	26	18
Six	12	10
Seven	14	17
Eight	11	14
Nine	2	2
Ten	6	5
Don't know	4	5

50 Years and Over

Zero	6%	7%
One	5	2
Two	2	5
Three	7	6
Four	7	7
Five	18	22
Six	10	7
Seven	9	10
Eight	14	13
Nine	4	4
Ten	12	10
Don't know	6	7

By Income

$20,000 and Over

Zero	5%	3%
One	3	3
Two	3	4
Three	10	10
Four	11	16
Five	19	18
Six	15	12
Seven	14	17
Eight	14	11
Nine	1	1
Ten	3	3
Don't know	2	2

$15,000–$19,999

Zero	5%	4%
One	*	2
Two	2	3
Three	6	8
Four	8	12
Five	23	17
Six	17	12
Seven	15	15
Eight	10	15
Nine	3	3
Ten	6	6
Don't know	4	3

$10,000–$14,999

Zero	3%	5%
One	3	2
Two	2	5
Three	7	7
Four	11	6
Five	29	18
Six	11	14
Seven	13	13
Eight	8	17
Nine	3	2
Ten	4	4
Don't know	6	8

$7,000–$9,999

Zero	2%	2%
One	5	*
Two	3	5
Three	4	6
Four	7	6
Five	21	24

Six	11	6
Seven	16	10
Eight	8	16
Nine	6	6
Ten	7	10
Don't know	10	9

$5,000–$6,999

Zero	5%	4%
One	4	2
Two	5	3
Three	7	6
Four	3	9
Five	15	16
Six	10	9
Seven	13	13
Eight	19	14
Nine	4	3
Ten	10	13
Don't know	5	8

$3,000–$4,999

Zero	2%	4%
One	4	4
Two	2	3
Three	5	4
Four	4	7
Five	22	24
Six	11	7
Seven	7	11
Eight	13	15
Nine	6	5
Ten	18	10
Don't know	6	5

Under $3,000

Zero	2%	10%
One	4	3
Two	3	3
Three	3	0
Four	6	1
Five	17	24
Six	12	3
Seven	12	18
Eight	10	12
Nine	4	8

Ten	21	12
Don't know	6	7

By Occupation

Professional and Business

Zero	4%	4%
One	2	2
Two	4	4
Three	10	11
Four	13	13
Five	19	17
Six	19	12
Seven	13	15
Eight	11	14
Nine	1	2
Ten	2	3
Don't know	1	3

Clerical and Sales

Zero	4%	1%
One	6	2
Two	5	1
Three	5	9
Four	10	11
Five	24	24
Six	10	12
Seven	17	12
Eight	8	15
Nine	4	1
Ten	4	6
Don't know	3	6

Manual Workers

Zero	4%	3%
One	2	2
Two	2	4
Three	6	6
Four	6	8
Five	24	16
Six	13	13
Seven	15	15
Eight	12	15
Nine	3	4
Ten	7	7
Don't know	6	7

Non-Labor Force

Zero	4%	8%
One.................	4	2
Two	3	5
Three	7	6
Four................	7	9
Five	19	23
Six	8	6
Seven	9	11
Eight................	14	11
Nine................	4	4
Ten.................	15	10
Don't know	6	5

*Less than 1%.

Note: President Jimmy Carter is making polling history in one important respect. Rarely in the forty-three years of the Gallup Poll has so little difference been found between rich and poor in their approval rating of a president.

In the 1930s, economic concerns became the chief basis for determining party preference. Poorer people turned to the Democratic party and gave their support to Democratic candidates; upper-income voters remained loyal to the Republican party. These differing viewpoints have consistently manifested themselves in the approval ratings given incumbent presidents.

At least for the present, Carter has obliterated these traditional differences. His current approval rating (based on three successive surveys) is virtually the same with persons in upper income levels as with those in lower income levels.

Just as little difference is found in Carter's ratings across income level, his popularity across educational levels is also remarkably similar. College-educated Americans accord the president about the same degree of support as do people whose formal education ended at the high-school level or earlier.

Carter Losses

If any one group of Americans can claim to have "elected" Jimmy Carter it is the nation's nonwhite population. Nonwhites gave Carter 85% of their vote in 1976—the largest share of any single group's vote received by the president. Today, however, Carter's job rating among nonwhites has declined to 59%, from a high of 85% in March 1977.

A more detailed look at Carter's rating among the Black population reveals a split by geographical region. Among northern Blacks, 55% say they approve of Carter's handling of the presidency. Among southern Blacks 65% back the president.

More Catholics approve of Carter than Protestants do (54% to 48%).

Carter's popularity among labor union families does not compare favorably with the vote they gave him in the election. In 1976 63% of labor union families voted for Carter, but today his popularity is only 52%—not radically different from the 49% approval rating he receives from non-union family members.

The first findings by groups reported today are based on the results from three surveys combined and reflect personal interviews with more than 4,500 Americans across the nation.

APRIL 13
CAPITAL PUNISHMENT

Interviewing Date: 3/3–6/78
Survey #996-K

Are you in favor of the death penalty for persons convicted of murder?

Yes	62%
No.................................	22
No opinion..........................	11

By Sex
Male

Yes	70%
No.................................	22
No opinion..........................	8

Female

Yes 55%
No. 32
No opinion. 13

By Race
Whites

Yes 64%
No. 26
No opinion. 10

Nonwhites

Yes 42%
No. 44
No opinion. 14

By Education
College

Yes 61%
No. 31
No opinion. 8

High School

Yes 65%
No. 26
No opinion. 9

Grade School

Yes 53%
No. 29
No opinion. 18

By Age
18–29 Years

Yes 57%
No. 35
No opinion. 8

30–49 Years

Yes 64%
No. 26
No opinion. 10

50 Years and Over

Yes 65%
No. 22
No opinion. 13

By Politics
Republicans

Yes 72%
No. 20
No opinion. 8

Democrats

Yes 59%
No. 29
No opinion. 12

Independents

Yes 61%
No. 30
No opinion. 9

Are you in favor of the death penalty for persons convicted of treason?

Yes 36%
No. 50
No opinion. 14

By Sex
Male

Yes 45%
No. 45
No opinion. 10

Female

Yes 28%
No. 55
No opinion. 17

By Race
Whites

Yes 37%
No. 49
No opinion. 14

Nonwhites

Yes 28%
No. 54
No opinion. 18

By Education
College

Yes 33%
No. 58
No opinion. 9

High School

Yes 39%
No. 47
No opinion. 14

Grade School

Yes 32%
No. 46
No opinion. 22

By Age
18–29 Years

Yes 22%
No. 68
No opinion. 10

30–49 Years

Yes 39%
No. 46
No opinion. 15

50 Years and Over

Yes 43%
No. 40
No opinion. 17

By Politics
Republicans

Yes 43%
No. 43
No opinion. 14

Democrats

Yes 34%
No. 51
No opinion. 15

Independents

Yes 34%
No. 53
No opinion. 13

Are you in favor of the death penalty for persons convicted of rape?

Yes 32%
No. 56
No opinion. 12

By Sex
Male

Yes 34%
No. 54
No opinion. 12

Female

Yes 31%
No. 57
No opinion. 12

By Race
Whites

Yes 32%
No. 56
No opinion. 12

Nonwhites

Yes 33%
No. 55
No opinion. 12

By Education
College

Yes 26%
No. 64
No opinion. 10

High School

Yes 35%
No. 54
No opinion. 11

Grade School

Yes 32%
No. 45
No opinion. 23

By Age
18–29 Years

Yes 29%
No. 60
No opinion. 11

30–49 Years

Yes 31%
No. 57
No opinion. 12

50 Years and Over

Yes 35%
No. 51
No opinion. 14

By Politics
Republicans

Yes 27%
No. 60
No opinion. 13

Democrats

Yes 35%
No. 53
No opinion. 12

Independents

Yes 30%
No. 58
No opinion. 12

Are you in favor of the death penalty for persons convicted of hijacking an airplane?

Yes 37%
No. 52
No opinion. 11

By Sex
Male

Yes 44%
No. 45
No opinion. 11

Female

Yes 30%
No. 58
No opinion. 12

By Race
Whites

Yes 38%
No. 51
No opinion. 11

Nonwhites

Yes 28%
No. 57
No opinion. 15

By Education
College

Yes 35%
No. 57
No opinion. 8

High School

Yes 37%
No. 53
No opinion. 10

Grade School

Yes 38%
No. 40
No opinion. 22

18–29 Years

Yes 23%
No 67
No opinion 10

30–49 Years

Yes 38%
No 52
No opinion 10

50 Years and Over

Yes 46%
No 40
No opinion 14

By Politics

Republicans

Yes 41%
No 48
No opinion 11

Democrats

Yes 36%
No 52
No opinion 12

Independents

Yes 35%
No 55
No opinion 10

Note: With the debate in the New York state legislature having focused national attention on the death penalty, the Gallup Poll sought to determine current attitudes on capital punishment for four major crimes—murder, treason, rape, and airplane hijacking.

This survey indicates that the American public believes in letting the punishment fit the crime. Six in ten Americans (62%) nationwide favor the death penalty for murder, but the public votes 56% to 32% against it for rape, 52%

to 37% against it for hijacking, and 50% to 36% against it for treason.

Current views on the death penalty for murder are similar to those recorded two years ago, when public support was at a twenty-three-year high point. Support is down slightly from two years ago, but opposition is also down approximately to the same extent.

Women are far more likely to oppose the death penalty than men are except in the case of rape, where their views are similar. Nonwhites are more likely to oppose it than whites, but these groups also agree when the crime considered is rape. The educational background and age of respondents are also important factors; younger persons and those with a college background are more likely to oppose the death penalty for all four crimes tested.

Background

In 1972 the United States Supreme Court found the death penalty, as then administered, unconstitutional. Since that time, however, thirty-five states have enacted new death penalty statutes. Both the senate and the assembly in New York recently voted in favor of a death penalty bill. The margin in both houses, however, appears insufficient to override a promised veto by Governor Hugh Carey.

Fear of Crime Has Grown in Last Decade

The nationwide increase in support of the death penalty over the last decade coincides with a sharply rising fear of crime on the part of the American people. The Gallup Poll's most recent study on crime showed nearly half of the public fearful of venturing out after dark in their own neighborhoods. One person in five nationally says he or she has been physically assaulted, had his or her home broken into, or had property vandalized during a twelve-month period tested.

Reasons Pro and Con

Survey respondents give a number of disparate reasons for their position on the death penalty.

Those in favor of capital punishment frequently cite these arguments: (1) the death penalty acts as a crime deterrent; (2) jail sentences are an economic burden on society; (3) criminals today "get off too easily"; (4) vengence—"eye for an eye"; (5) jail is not rehabilitative.

Those opposed to capital punishment give these reasons: (1) religion forbids it, the Bible stating, "Thou shalt not kill"; (2) the death penalty is not a deterrent; (3) there should be life imprisonment with no parole; (4) people can be rehabilitated; (5) the legal system is not equitable; (6) taking a second life will not solve anything.

The following table shows the trend since 1953, when the current question dealing with persons convicted of murder was first used:

Death Penalty for Murderers

Latest Survey

Favor 62%
Oppose 27
No opinion 11

April 1976

Favor 65%
Oppose 28
No opinion 7

November 1972

Favor 57%
Oppose 32
No opinion 11

March 1972

Favor 50%
Oppose 41
No opinion 9

1971

Favor 49%
Oppose 40
No opinion 11

1969

Favor 51%
Oppose 40
No opinion 9

1966

Favor 42%
Oppose 47
No opinion 11

1965

Favor 45%
Oppose 43
No opinion 12

1960

Favor 51%
Oppose 36
No opinion 13

1953

Favor 68%
Oppose 25
No opinion 7

APRIL 16
URBAN AMERICA—A SPECIAL GALLUP REPORT, PART III

To halt or at least reduce the exodus of residents from the nation's cities, it will be necessary to significantly improve the quality of urban life—or, more specifically, the quality of the many services, facilities, and institutions provided by the cities.

To determine which features of city life are considered most satisfactory as well as those most in need of improvement, residents of the nation's cities were asked to rate fifty urban services, facilities, and institutions.

Among the key findings of the study, which was co-sponsored by the Charles F. Kettering and Charles Stewart Mott Foundations, are the following:

As a group, the uniformed services rate higher than any other aspect of urban life studied, with the fire department receiving the highest favorable rating.

Public transportation, local government, and the courts and correctional facilities are rated lowest.

The younger, better educated, and more affluent citizens—those residents that the cities can least afford to lose—register the greatest dissatisfaction with urban services, facilities, and institutions.

It is residents of the cities that are now experiencing the most difficulties—the largest cities and those in the East and Midwest—who express the highest degree of dissatisfaction with urban services and facilities.

Uniformed Services

When the nation's urban residents rate city services and facilities on a zero-to-ten scale, the uniformed services—police, fire, and sanitation—score highest collectively. The fire department receives a highly favorable rating—one of the top three grades—from 64% of city dwellers, which represents the highest score for any feature of city life tested.

The sanitation department ranks close behind, receiving a highly favorable rating from 59%. Although the police department trails the other two uniformed services, it is assigned highly favorable ratings by a relatively high percentage (47%) of city dwellers.

Also rating relatively high are the city hospitals and health care facilities (54%), the public schools (42%), and the parks and playgrounds (42%).

Ranking relatively far down the list of services are public transportation, rated highly favorably by only 28%, downtown shopping (28%), traffic and parking facilities (15%), and local government (21%).

At the bottom of the list are the courts and the corectional facilities, which receive only 19% and 14% highly favorable ratings respectively.

The tables below show how some of the more important features of urban life, of the fifty items tested, compare in terms of *highly favorable* ratings. Results are shown for all cities and by city size, small (50,000–249,999), medium (250,000–999,999), and large (1 million and over):

To find out how you feel about various aspects of life in this city, would you use this card [respondents were handed a card]. You will notice that this card goes from zero—or something you have a highly unfavorable opinion about—up to ten—for something you have a highly favorable opinion about. The higher the number, the more favorable you feel about something. What rating from zero to ten would you give this city for the following:

All cities

UNIFORMED SERVICES
Fire.................................64%
Sanitation............................59
Police...............................47
EDUCATION/HEALTH
Hospitals, health care 54%
Public schools.......................42
RECREATION
Parks and playgrounds.................42%
Recreational opportunities 40
Cultural opportunities 39
ENVIRONMENT
Climate 43%
Noise level..........................40
Air quality..........................31
TRANSPORTATION
Highway system.......................38%
Public transportation 28
Traffic (downtown)....................15
Parking (downtown)...................15
MUNICIPAL GOVERNMENT
Mayor 22%
Local government.....................21
City council..........................19
Councilman..........................19

JUSTICE

Courts 19%
Correctional facilities................. 14

Small cities

UNIFORMED SERVICES

Fire................................ 67%
Sanitation........................... 60
Police.............................. 48

EDUCATION/HEALTH

Hospitals, health care 63%
Public schools 48

RECREATION

Parks and playgrounds................. 39%
Recreational opportunities 31
Culturai opportunities 30

ENVIRONMENT

Climate 51%
Noise level.......................... 43
Air quality 44

TRANSPORTATION

Highway system...................... 43%
Public transportation 33
Traffic (downtown)................... 19
Parking (downtown)................... 20

MUNICIPAL GOVERNMENT

Mayor 22%
Local government..................... 22
City council 19
Councilman.......................... 18

JUSTICE

Courts 23%
Correctional facilities................. 20

Medium cities

UNIFORMED SERVICES

Fire................................ 68%
Sanitation........................... 66
Police.............................. 51

EDUCATION/HEALTH

Hospitals, health care 57%
Public schools 41

RECREATION

Parks and playgrounds................. 48%
Recreational opportunities 46
Cultural opportunities 45

ENVIRONMENT

Climate 46%
Noise level.......................... 41
Air quality 32

TRANSPORTATION

Highway system...................... 38%
Public transportation 29
Traffic (downtown)................... 14
Parking (downtown)................... 13

MUNICIPAL GOVERNMENT

Mayor 24%
Local government..................... 22
City council 20
Councilman.......................... 22

JUSTICE

Courts 22%
Correctional facilities................. 14

Large cities

UNIFORMED SERVICES

Fire................................ 58%
Sanitation........................... 51
Police.............................. 42

EDUCATION/HEALTH

Hospitals, health care 42%
Public schools 36

RECREATION

Parks and playgrounds................. 36%
Recreational opportunities 42
Cultural opportunities 42

ENVIRONMENT

Climate 31%
Noise level.......................... 37
Air quality 17

TRANSPORTATION

Highway system...................... 33%
Public transportation 20
Traffic (downtown)................... 10
Parking (downtown)................... 13

MUNICIPAL GOVERNMENT

Mayor 19%
Local government..................... 18
City council 17
Councilman.......................... 16

JUSTICE

Courts 12%
Correctional facilities................. 9

Consistent Ratings

Analysis of the findings by different population groups reveals that fifty ratings vary considerably by the size of the city and the region of the country in which respondents live, whether they reside in the center city or the suburbs, and their age, education, and race.

For example, in the largest cities, residents are much less likely to assign a highly favorable rating to any of their municipal services or facilities than those living in small or medium-sized cities. The largest differences by city size are recorded in the case of air quality, the uniformed services, public transportation, highway systems, public schools, hospitals, and medical care facilities. The exceptions are the recreational and cultural opportunities, which receive highest ratings from big-city dwellers.

In the case of the nation's small cities and medium-sized cities, relatively little difference is noted between the service ratings of those residents in the center city and in the suburbs.

In the larger cities, however, the ratings are significantly lower for almost all items tested among those living in the center city areas when compared to the ratings of suburban residents.

Differences in ratings by geographical region are less pronounced than those by city size; generally, however, residents in the East and Midwest are less likely to assign highly favorable ratings to urban environment, services, and facilities than are people living in the South and West. This is particularly so in the case of air quality and climate.

Residents of eastern cities are especially discontented, being consistently less likely to give highly favorable ratings to any aspect of urban life than residents in other major regions. The one exception is the quality of the downtown stores. In contrast, residents of western cities are more likely to give city parks and playgrounds and the urban highway system highly favorable ratings than people living in cities in other regions of the nation.

In terms of socioeconomic background, those least likely to assign highly favorable ratings to any urban services or facilities include the younger, the better educated, and more affluent residents—and Blacks.

Blacks, in fact, represent the most discontented group in the urban population, consistently rating virtually every aspect of city life lower than do whites.

Those most likely to rate urban services highly favorably are the older population and—with the exception of Blacks—the less educated, less affluent city residents.

The findings reported today are based on personal interviews with 3,242 adult residents of cities with populations of 50,000 or more. The survey was conducted during the last three months of 1977.

APRIL 18
COAL STRIKE

Interviewing Date: 3/31–4/3/78
Survey #998-K

With respect to President Carter's handling of the coal situation, do you think he has done a good job, only a fair job, or a poor job?

Good job 22%
Fair job.............................. 44
Poor job 26
Don't know 8

By Region
East

Good job 24%
Fair job.............................. 41
Poor job 28
Don't know 7

Midwest

Good job 21%
Fair job.............................. 43
Poor job 27
Don't know 9

South

Good job 24%
Fair job 45
Poor job 23
Don't know 8

West

Good job 18%
Fair job 50
Poor job 25
Don't know 7

Those Who Approve of Carter

Good job 35%
Fair job 48
Poor job 12
Don't know 5

Those Who Disapprove of Carter

Good job 9%
Fair job 40
Poor job 47
Don't know 4

APRIL 19
THE MIDDLE EAST

Interviewing Date: 3/31–4/3/78
Survey #998-K

Have you heard or read about the situation in the Middle East?

	Yes
National	88%

Asked of those who replied in the affirmative: Which of the plans listed on this card would you prefer with regard to the Palestinians? [Respondents were handed a card listing the following—Plan A: They should have a separate, independent nation on the West Bank of the Jordan River in the area that was formerly Jordan but is now occupied by Israel; Plan B: They should have a state on the West Bank of the Jordan River that is not totally independent and is linked with Jordan; Plan C: They should go on living as they are now in Israel and in the existing Arab nations.]

Plan A 32%
Plan B 25
Plan C 22
Don't know 21

By Education
College

Plan A 34%
Plan B 31
Plan C 21
Don't know 14

High School

Plan A 33%
Plan B 24
Plan C 22
Don't know 21

Grade School

Plan A 27%
Plan B 16
Plan C 20
Don't know 37

By Politics
Republicans

Plan A 29%
Plan B 27
Plan C 25
Don't know 19

Democrats

Plan A 35%
Plan B 22
Plan C 21
Don't know 22

Independents

Plan A	33%
Plan B	28
Plan C	20
Don't know	19

Note: Aside from the question of whether or not to sell arms to the Middle East adversaries, a question central to a solution to the Middle East situation is the disposition of the Palestinian people.

To determine how informed Americans view the situation, this segment of the public was presented three alternatives and asked to indicate a preference. Support is about equally divided among the three alternatives. Even among this informed group, however, an unusually large number, 21%, do not express an opinion.

APRIL 20
TAX CREDITS FOR COLLEGE EXPENSES

Interviewing Date: 3/20–4/3/78
Special Telephone Survey

Congress is now discussing ways to increase financial aid to college students. One plan would increase tuition aid and expand existing student loan programs for students from middle-income families.

The other plan would provide tax credits, which would enable parents of students to deduct the amount of the credit from their tax bill.

Which would you prefer, the plan which would increase tuition aid and student loans or the plan which would provide tax credits for parents of students?

Tax credit	51%
Tuition aid	34
Don't know	15

By Education
College

Tax credit	57%
Tuition aid	35
Don't know	8

High School

Tax credit	48%
Tuition aid	34
Don't know	18

Grade School

Tax credit	45%
Tuition aid	35
Don't know	20

By Income
$20,000 and Over

Tax credit	60%
Tuition aid	34
Don't know	6

$15,000–$19,999

Tax credit	55%
Tuition aid	36
Don't know	9

$10,000–$14,999

Tax credit	53%
Tuition aid	30
Don't know	17

Under $10,000

Tax credit	41%
Tuition aid	40
Don't know	19

Parents Only

Tax credit	54%
Tuition aid	34
Don't know	12

Nonparents Only

Tax credit 48%
Tuition aid 35
Don't know 17

Note: Financial aid for students from middle-income families is an issue that has assumed new urgency in recent years. While inflation has made tuition costs difficult for middle-income parents to afford, what financial aid is now available goes primarily to students from low-income families.

The bill currently before Congress would liberalize financial aid through such programs as educational grants, college work-study jobs, and guaranteed student loans. There are other proposals being formulated in both the House and the Senate that would allow tax credits of up to $250 per student per year. Under the Senate version, credits would be increased to $500 in 1980 and expanded to include elementary and secondary schooling.

A tax credit is money subtracted directly from the amount of money owed to the government (as opposed to a tax deduction, which is subtracted from the total taxable income of a family or individual). President Carter has said he would veto any tax credit legislation because it would be too costly for the government.

APRIL 23
ECONOMIC SITUATION

Interviewing Date: 4/14–17/78
Survey #999-K

Would you favor or oppose having the government bring back wage and price controls?

Favor 52%
Oppose 37
No opinion 11

By Education
College

Favor 43%
Oppose 49
No opinion 8

High School

Favor 51%
Oppose 36
No opinion 13

Grade School

Favor 66%
Oppose 22
No opinion 12

By Region
East

Favor 54%
Oppose 37
No opinion 9

Midwest

Favor 50%
Oppose 39
No opinion 11

South

Favor 51%
Oppose 35
No opinion 14

West

Favor 52%
Oppose 39
No opinion 9

By Income
$20,000 and Over

Favor 44%
Oppose 50
No opinion 6

$15,000–$19,999

Favor 58%
Oppose 34
No opinion 8

$10,000–$14,999

Favor 46%
Oppose 41
No opinion 13

$7,000–$9,999

Favor 55%
Oppose 34
No opinion 11

$5,000–$6,999

Favor 61%
Oppose 23
No opinion 16

$3,000–$4,999

Favor 55%
Oppose 29
No opinion 16

Under $3,000

Favor 55%
Oppose 29
No opinion 16

By Occupation
Professional and Business

Favor 47%
Oppose 45
No opinion 8

Clerical and Sales

Favor 52%
Oppose 40
No opinion 8

Manual Workers

Favor 53%
Oppose 35
No opinion 12

Non-Labor Force

Favor 57%
Oppose 29
No opinion 14

Labor Union Families Only

Favor 55%
Oppose 37
No opinion 8

Non-Labor Union Families Only

Favor 51%
Oppose 38
No opinion 11

Those Who Favor Working Toward Balancing the Budget

Favor 53%
Oppose 39
No opinion 8

Those Who Favor a Cut in Taxes at This Time

Favor 53%
Oppose 37
No opinion 10

It has been said that tax cuts would lead to a bigger deficit in the federal budget and would make it very difficult for the president to fulfill his promise to balance the budget by 1981. Do you think it is more important to work toward balancing the budget or to cut taxes at this time?

Balance budget 45%
Cut taxes 44
No opinion 11

By Education
College

Balance budget 51%
Cut taxes 40
No opinion 9

High School

Balance budget	42%
Cut taxes	46
No opinion	12

Grade School

Balance budget	32%
Cut taxes	48
No opinion	20

By Region
East

Balance budget	40%
Cut taxes	47
No opinion	13

Midwest

Balance budget	45%
Cut taxes	45
No opinion	10

South

Balance budget	46%
Cut taxes	43
No opinion	11

West

Balance budget	42%
Cut taxes	44
No opinion	14

By Income
$20,000 and Over

Balance budget	50%
Cut taxes	41
No opinion	9

$15,000–$19,999

Balance budget	44%
Cut taxes	48
No opinion	8

$10,000–$14,999

Balance budget	44%
Cut taxes	45
No opinion	11

$7,000–$9,999

Balance budget	41%
Cut taxes	47
No opinion	12

$5,000–$6,999

Balance budget	32%
Cut taxes	50
No opinion	18

$3,000–$4,999

Balance budget	40%
Cut taxes	40
No opinion	20

Under $3,000

Balance budget	41%
Cut taxes	45
No opinion	14

Those Who Favor Wage and Price Controls

Balance budget	44%
Cut taxes	47
No opinion	9

Those Who Oppose Wage and Price Controls

Balance budget	45%
Cut taxes	45
No opinion	10

During the next twelve months, do you expect your income to go up more than prices go up, about the same, or less than prices go up?

More than prices	9%
Same as prices	32
Less than prices	54
Don't know	5

By Education

College

More than prices	15%
Same as prices	30
Less than prices	52
Don't know	3

High School

More than prices	8%
Same as prices	34
Less than prices	53
Don't know	5

Grade School

More than prices	4%
Same as prices	30
Less than prices	59
Don't know	7

By Region

East

More than prices	7%
Same as prices	33
Less than prices	53
Don't know	7

Midwest

More than prices	9%
Same as prices	33
Less than prices	53
Don't know	5

South

More than prices	10%
Same as prices	34
Less than prices	54
Don't know	2

West

More than prices	12%
Same as prices	26
Less than prices	55
Don't know	7

By Income

$20,000 and Over

More than prices	13%
Same as prices	32
Less than prices	52
Don't know	3

$15,000–$19,999

More than prices	10%
Same as prices	40
Less than prices	47
Don't know	3

$10,000–$14,999

More than prices	9%
Same as prices	30
Less than prices	55
Don't Know	6

$7,000–$9,999

More than prices	7%
Same as prices	36
Less than prices	52
Don't know	5

$5,000–$6,999

More than prices	8%
Same as prices	23
Less than prices	63
Don't know	6

$3,000–$4,999

More than prices	4%
Same as prices	32
Less than prices	60
Don't know	4

Under $3,000

More than prices	3%
Same as prices	25
Less than prices	65
Don't know	7

Those Who Approve of Carter

More than prices. 10%
Same as prices. 36
Less than prices. 49
Don't know 5

Those Who Disapprove of Carter

More than prices. 8%
Same as prices. 30
Less than prices. 58
Don't know 4

Those Who Favor Wage and Price Controls

More than prices. 8%
Same as prices. 30
Less than prices. 58
Don't know 4

Those Who Oppose Wage and Price Controls

More than prices. 11%
Same as prices. 36
Less than prices. 51
Don't know 2

Those Who Think the Economy Will Improve

More than prices. 10%
Same as prices. 40
Less than prices. 46
Don't know 4

Those Who Think the Economy Will Stay the Same

More than prices. 8%
Same as prices. 39
Less than prices. 50
Don't know 3

Those Who Think the Economy Will Worsen

More than prices. 9%
Same as prices. 25

Less than prices. 61
Don't know 5

Do you think the economic situation in the United States during the next six months will get better or will get worse?

Better 26%
Worse. 52
Same (volunteered) 17
No opinion. 5

By Education
College

Better 31%
Worse. 47
Same (volunteered) 17
No opinion. 5

High School

Better 24%
Worse. 53
Same (volunteered) 18
No opinion. 5

Grade School

Better 22%
Worse. 58
Same (volunteered) 14
No opinion. 6

By Region
East

Better 25%
Worse. 54
Same (volunteered) 17
No opinion. 4

Midwest

Better 28%
Worse. 50
Same (volunteered) 16
No opinion. 6

South

Better	25%
Worse	51
Same (volunteered)	18
No opinion	6

West

Better	24%
Worse	55
Same (volunteered)	16
No opinion	5

By Income
$20,000 and Over

Better	26%
Worse	53
Same (volunteered)	18
No opinion	3

$15,000–$19,999

Better	24%
Worse	53
Same (volunteered)	19
No opinion	4

$10,000–$14,999

Better	27%
Worse	51
Same (volunteered)	17
No opinion	5

$7,000–$9,999

Better	32%
Worse	56
Same (volunteered)	7
No opinion	5

$5,000–$6,999

Better	22%
Worse	51
Same (volunteered)	23
No opinion	4

$3,000–$4,999

Better	24%
Worse	54
Same (volunteered)	15
No opinion	7

Under $3,000

Better	28%
Worse	39
Same (volunteered)	18
No opinion	15

Labor Union Families Only

Better	26%
Worse	55
Same (volunteered)	17
No opinion	2

Non-Labor Union Families Only

Better	25%
Worse	52
Same (volunteered)	17
No opinion	6

Those Who Approve of Carter

Better	34%
Worse	44
Same (volunteered)	17
No opinion	5

Those Who Disapprove of Carter

Better	18%
Worse	61
Same (volunteered)	17
No opinion	4

Those Who Favor Wage and Price Controls

Better	23%
Worse	57
Same (volunteered)	15
No opinion	5

Those Who Oppose Wage and Price Controls

Better 29%
Worse 50
Same (volunteered) 19
No opinion 2

Those Who Think Their Income Will Rise More Than Prices

Better 29%
Worse 52
Same (volunteered) 16
No opinion 3

Those Who Think Their Income Will Rise Same As Prices

Better 32%
Worse 41
Same (volunteered) 21
No opinion 6

Those Who Think Their Income Will Rise Less Than Prices

Better 22%
Worse 59
Same (volunteered) 16
No opinion 3

Note: Increasingly alarmed over inflation, the American people favor far more drastic economic measures than those prescribed by President Jimmy Carter and his administration, by Congress, or by the nation's leading economists.

President Carter's recently announced anti-inflation initiatives include voluntary restraint of wage and price increases by the private sector.

The latest nationwide Gallup survey shows a growing number of Americans in favor of wage and price controls. The public votes 50% to 39% in support of these controls, compared to 44% to 40% just two months ago. A majority of Americans—for the first time since 1974—are ready to accept wage and price controls.

As further proof that the public is willing to take stronger economic medicine, as many favor working toward a balanced budget (45%) as favor the proposed tax cut (44%), even though many taxpayers interviewed in the survey were undoubtedly in the throes of meeting the April 17 tax deadline. It is the view of many that efforts toward balancing the budget will help reduce inflation.

Americans have a decidedly pessimistic outlook in both their short-term evaluations of the overall state of the nation's economy and their appraisals of how well their own family's income will keep pace with inflation.

Twice as many people expect the general economic situation in this country to deteriorate during the next six months as expect it to improve (52% compared to 26%). Another 17% believe the economy will remain relatively unchanged, and 5% express no opinion. These figures mark the lowest degree of confidence in the public's short-term outlook since November 1974, when only 16% thought that things would improve and an overwhelming 71% predicted a downturn.

That the economic situation will worsen in the next six months is the predominant opinion across all groups within the population. Respondents' family income, geographical region, and occupation—all factors that might logically be expected to have a significant effect on opinion— make very little difference on their outlook. Americans with a college background are slightly more optimistic than those with less education, but even in this group the majority is pessimistic.

As would be expected, people who think the effects of inflation will more than offset any income gains they may make during the next year are more dubious about the health of the overall economy during the next six months than those who think their family income will keep pace with or gain on inflation.

The majority of Americans do not expect to be able to keep up with inflation during the next year. As inflation rates threaten to move into the double-digit range for this year, 54% of the public expect to lose ground economically, 32% expect to stay where they are, and 9% expect to gain ground.

Those groups most likely to expect price increases to outstrip income gains are the so-called downscale groups—people in the lowest education and income groups, older people, and those who are not members of the labor force (a group composed mainly of retirees). No group within the population expresses optimism in this respect.

Even among those people who expect the short-term economic outlook to improve, a plurality of 46% expects to lose ground to inflation. Of those who believe the economy will remain relatively unchanged and those who believe it will worsen, 50% and 61% respectively are similarly pessimistic.

Economic and price/income expectations also appear to be directly related to attitudes about the president. Not only are people who approve of the way Carter is handling his job significantly less likely to feel their incomes will not keep pace with inflation but they are also definitely less pessimistic about the overall outlook for the economy during the next six months.

APRIL 24
PRESIDENT CARTER

Interviewing Date: 4/14–17/78
Survey #999-K

Do you approve or disapprove of the way Jimmy Carter is handling his job as president?

Approve.............................40%
Disapprove 44
No opinion..........................16

By Sex
Male

Approve.............................41%
Disapprove 47
No opinion..........................12

Female

Approve.............................40%
Disapprove 41
No opinion..........................19

By Race
Whites

Approve.............................39%
Disapprove 46
No opinion..........................15

Northern Whites

Approve.............................39%
Disapprove 46
No opinion..........................15

Southern Whites

Approve.............................38%
Disapprove 47
No opinion..........................15

Nonwhites

Approve.............................52%
Disapprove 24
No opinion..........................29

Northern Blacks

Approve.............................55%
Disapprove 16
No opinion..........................29

Southern Blacks

Approve.............................52%
Disapprove 34
No opinion..........................14

By Education
College

Approve.............................40%
Disapprove 50
No opinion..........................10

High School

Approve............................39%
Disapprove 43
No opinion..........................18

Grade School

Approve............................44%
Disapprove 38
No opinion..........................18

By Region
East

Approve............................41%
Disapprove 42
No opinion..........................17

Midwest

Approve............................39%
Disapprove 44
No opinion..........................17

South

Approve............................40%
Disapprove 45
No opinion..........................15

Deep South

Approve............................45%
Disapprove 41
No opinion..........................14

West

Approve............................41%
Disapprove 45
No opinion..........................14

By Age
18–24 Years

Approve............................47%
Disapprove 37
No opinion..........................16

25–29 Years

Approve............................39%
Disapprove 52
No opinion..........................9

30–49 Years

Approve............................39%
Disapprove 43
No opinion..........................18

50 Years and Over

Approve............................39%
Disapprove 45
No opinion..........................16

By Politics
Republicans

Approve............................25%
Disapprove 63
No opinion..........................12

Democrats

Approve............................51%
Disapprove 35
No opinion..........................14

Southern Democrats

Approve............................48%
Disapprove 35
No opinion..........................17

Other Democrats

Approve............................52%
Disapprove 36
No opinion..........................12

Independents

Approve............................36%
Disapprove 44
No opinion..........................20

By Religion

Protestants

Approve............................41%
Disapprove 44
No opinion..........................15

Catholics

Approve............................39%
Disapprove 44
No opinion..........................17

By Occupation

Professional and Business

Approve............................34%
Disapprove 53
No opinion..........................13

Clerical and Sales

Approve............................46%
Disapprove 40
No opinion..........................14

Manual Workers

Approve............................44%
Disapprove 40
No opinion..........................16

Non-Labor Force

Approve............................43%
Disapprove 42
No opinion..........................15

By Community Size

One Million and Over

Approve............................41%
Disapprove 43
No opinion..........................16

500,000–999,999

Approve............................49%
Disapprove 41
No opinion..........................10

50,000–499,999

Approve............................42%
Disapprove 41
No opinion..........................17

2,500–49,999

Approve............................41%
Disapprove 44
No opinion..........................15

Under 2,500; Rural

Approve............................34%
Disapprove 48
No opinion..........................18

Labor Union Families Only

Approve............................44%
Disapprove 43
No opinion..........................13

Non-Labor Union Families Only

Approve............................40%
Disapprove 44
No opinion..........................16

Those Who Think the Economic Situation Will Get Better

Approve............................54%
Disapprove 32
No opinion..........................14

Those Who Think the Economic Situation Will Stay the Same

Approve............................40%
Disapprove 43
No opinion..........................17

Those Who Think the Economic Situation Will Get Worse

Approve............................34%
Disapprove 51
No opinion..........................15

Interviewing Date: 3/31–4/3/78
Survey #998-K

Asked of those who had an opinion on the way Carter is handling his job: How strongly would you say you approve/disapprove—very strongly or not so strongly?

Strong approval........................14%
Mild approval 34
Mild disapproval......................22
Strong disapproval 17
No opinion............................13

By Sex
Male

Strong approval........................15%
Mild approval 34
Mild disapproval......................22
Strong disapproval 17
No opinion............................13

Female

Strong approval........................13%
Mild approval 36
Mild disapproval......................22
Strong disapproval 14
No opinion............................15

By Race
Whites

Strong approval........................13%
Mild approval 34
Mild disapproval......................23
Strong disapproval 18
No opinion............................12

Nonwhites

Strong approval........................27%
Mild approval 28
Mild disapproval......................12
Strong disapproval 12
No opinion............................21

By Education
College

Strong approval........................13%
Mild approval 35
Mild disapproval......................26
Strong disapproval 18
No opinion............................ 8

High School

Strong approval........................13%
Mild approval 33
Mild disapproval......................22
Strong disapproval 19
No opinion............................13

Grade School

Strong approval........................21%
Mild approval 31
Mild disapproval......................12
Strong disapproval 11
No opinion............................25

By Region
East

Strong approval........................14%
Mild approval 34
Mild disapproval......................22
Strong disapproval 19
No opinion............................11

Midwest

Strong approval........................14%
Mild approval 34
Mild disapproval......................20
Strong disapproval 18
No opinion............................14

South

Strong approval........................17%
Mild approval 32
Mild disapproval......................18
Strong disapproval 17
No opinion............................16

West

Strong approval	13%
Mild approval	31
Mild disapproval	30
Strong disapproval	15
No opinion	11

By Age

18–24 Years

Strong approval	13%
Mild approval	42
Mild disapproval	23
Strong disapproval	12
No opinion	10

25–29 Years

Strong approval	11%
Mild approval	42
Mild disapproval	20
Strong disapproval	14
No opinion	13

30–49 Years

Strong approval	13%
Mild approval	33
Mild disapproval	22
Strong disapproval	19
No opinion	13

50 Years and Over

Strong approval	17%
Mild approval	27
Mild disapproval	22
Strong disapproval	19
No opinion	15

By Income

$20,000 and Over

Strong approval	9%
Mild approval	35
Mild disapproval	29
Strong disapproval	21
No opinion	6

$15,000–$19,999

Strong approval	12%
Mild approval	30
Mild disapproval	28
Strong disapproval	19
No opinion	11

$10,000–$14,999

Strong approval	13%
Mild approval	39
Mild disapproval	17
Strong disapproval	16
No opinion	15

$7,000–$9,999

Strong approval	23%
Mild approval	30
Mild disapproval	17
Strong disapproval	11
No opinion	19

$5,000–$6,999

Strong approval	20%
Mild approval	30
Mild disapproval	17
Strong disapproval	14
No opinion	19

$3,000–$4,999

Strong approval	19%
Mild approval	33
Mild disapproval	10
Strong disapproval	18
No opinion	20

Under $3,000

Strong approval	17%
Mild approval	28
Mild disapproval	21
Strong disapproval	18
No opinion	16

By Politics
Republicans

Strong approval. 6%
Mild approval 25
Mild disapproval. 29
Strong disapproval 31
No opinion. 9

Democrats

Strong approval. 22%
Mild approval 38
Mild disapproval. 16
Strong disapproval 11
No opinion. 13

Southern Democrats

Strong approval. 25%
Mild approval 37
Mild disapproval. 12
Strong disapproval 10
No opinion. 16

Other Democrats

Strong approval. 21%
Mild approval 38
Mild disapproval. 18
Strong disapproval 11
No opinion. 12

Independents

Strong approval. 10%
Mild approval 34
Mild disapproval. 25
Strong approval 17
No opinion. 14

By Religion
Protestants

Strong approval. 14%
Mild approval 32
Mild disapproval. 23
Strong disapproval 18
No opinion. 13

Catholics

Strong approval. 15%
Mild approval 37
Mild disapproval. 20
Strong disapproval 15
No opinion. 13

By Occupation
Professional and Business

Strong approval. 11%
Mild approval 34
Mild disapproval. 29
Strong disapproval 18
No opinion. 8

Clerical and Sales

Strong approval. 12%
Mild approval 33
Mild disapproval. 26
Strong disapproval 20
No opinion. 9

Manual Workers

Strong approval. 15%
Mild approval 36
Mild disapproval. 19
Strong disapproval 15
No opinion. 15

Non-Labor Force

Strong approval. 18%
Mild approval 29
Mild disapproval. 18
Strong disapproval 18
No opinion. 17

By Community Size
One Million and Over

Strong approval. 10%
Mild approval 36
Mild disapproval. 24
Strong disapproval 16
No opinion. 14

500,000–999,999

Strong approval. 17%
Mild approval 30
Mild disapproval. 21
Strong disapproval 21
No opinion. . . . .⁚. . . 11

50,000–499,999

Strong approval. 14%
Mild approval 37
Mild disapproval. 21
Strong disapproval 16
No opinion. 12

2,500–49,999

Strong approval. 18%
Mild approval 29
Mild disapproval. 21
Strong disapproval 20
No opinion. 12

Under 2,500; Rural

Strong approval. 15%
Mild approval 32
Mild disapproval. 22
Strong disapproval 16
No opinion. 15

Note: For the first time since he took office, more people disapprove of the way President Jimmy Carter is handling his job than approve. In this survey, 40% say they approve of Carter's stewardship and 44% disapprove. This represents the lowest approval rating Carter has received since assuming office in January 1977.

Only two groups among the American people—nonwhites (52%) and Democrats (51%)—accord the president majority approval.

In fact, Carter's current rating from party members is the lowest he has yet received. During his first year in office, the president's average rating among Democrats was 73%. It has averaged 61% for the current year—both figures in stark contrast to the latest reading.

The sharp decline in Carter's nationwide popularity coincides with increasing public concern over the high cost of living and economic well-being. Additional survey findings suggest these attitudes may be having a negative effect on the president's job rating. For example, 54% of the people who believe the economic situation in the United States will improve during the next six months approve of Carter, while 51% of those who believe the economy will worsen disapprove. Similarly, Carter has the support of 45% of the people who feel their income will rise faster than prices over the next year. But the approval figure for people who think their incomes will lag behind the price spiral is only 37%.

Intensity of Approval

There were signs that the president was in trouble even before the last rating. The Gallup Poll periodically records the intensity with which Americans approve or disapprove of the way Carter is handling his job. In a survey completed in early April, the number saying they strongly approved of Carter's performance declined to 14%—the lowest such mark he has received in these surveys.

To look more closely at approval intensity, the survey results were examined using just two groups as bases—those who approve and those who disapprove of Carter. The following table shows the trends in the intensity of Carter's approval and disapproval so far in his presidency. Of particular note here is the fact that of those approving of Carter, a steadily declining number have voiced *strong* approval.

Intensity of Carter Popularity

	Among those approving	
	Strong approval	Mild approval
March 31–April 3.	30%	70%
Feb. 24–27, 1978.	35	65
Nov. 18–21, 1977.	35	65
Nov. 4–7	36	64

Oct. 21–24...............	35	65
Oct. 14–17...............	39	61
Sept. 30–Oct. 3...........	41	59
May 6–9..................	49	51
March 18–21..............	56	44

	Among those disapproving	
	Strong disapproval	Mild disapproval
March 31–April 3.....	56%	44%
Feb. 24–27, 1978.....	54	46
Nov. 18–21, 1977.....	53	47
Nov. 4–7.............	51	49
Oct. 21–24...........	60	40
Oct. 14–17...........	52	48
Sept. 30–Oct. 3.......	52	48
May 6–9.............	52	48
March 18–21.........	53	47

Comparative Standing

Ironically, Carter's popularity in the most recent survey stands almost exactly where that of his predecessor, Gerald Ford, was after Ford had been in office a comparable period of time. In November 1975, fifteen months after he was sworn in as president, Ford had the approval of 41% of Americans, compared to 46% disapproval.

Of the four men who directly preceded Ford, all had significantly higher approval ratings at comparable times. The following table shows how Carter compares with his five immediate predecessors:

Presidential Popularity After 15 Months in Office

	Approve	Disapprove
Jimmy Carter............	40%	44%
Gerald Ford.............	41	46
Richard Nixon...........	56	31
Lyndon Johnson	68	18
John Kennedy	77	13
Dwight Eisenhower.......	68	21

And the following table presents a capsule review of Carter's job rating to this point in his administration:

Carter Popularity

Current approval rating	40%
Average approval in current year	49
Average approval while in office.........	59
High point (recorded in March 1977)	75
Low point (recorded in April 1978)......	40

Carter's low point in popularity to date, the current 40%, is below the low points recorded for Presidents Kennedy (56%), Eisenhower (48%), and Roosevelt (54%), but above the low points recorded for Presidents Ford (37%), Nixon (24%), Johnson (35%), and Truman (23%).

APRIL 30
ENERGY SITUATION

Interviewing Date: 3/31–4/3/78
Survey #998-K

How serious would you say the energy situation is in the United States—very serious, fairly serious, or not at all serious?

Very................................	41%
Fairly..............................	39
Not at all	15
No opinion..........................	5

By Education
College

Very................................	51%
Fairly..............................	40
Not at all	7
No opinion..........................	2

High School

Very................................	38%
Fairly..............................	40
Not at all	17
No opinion..........................	5

Grade School

Very 30%
Fairly 35
Not at all 19
No opinion 16

By Region
East

Very 44%
Fairly 35
Not at all 14
No opinion 7

Midwest

Very 35%
Fairly 45
Not at all 16
No opinion 4

South

Very 43%
Fairly 39
Not at all 12
No opinion 6

West

Very 41%
Fairly 39
Not at all 16
No opinion 4

Those Who Favor Gasoline Rationing

Very 42%
Fairly 41
Not at all 13
No opinion 4

Those Who Favor an Increase
in the Gasoline Tax

Very 47%
Fairly 40
Not at all 10
No opinion 3

Those Who Are Opposed to Gasoline
Rationing and Opposed to an
Increase in the Gasoline Tax

Very 34%
Fairly 37
Not at all 25
No opinion 4

*From what you have heard or read, do you
think we produce enough oil in this country
to meet our present energy needs, or do we
have to import some oil from other countries?*

Produce enough 27%
Must import 60
Don't know 13

By Education
College

Produce enough 17%
Must import 75
Don't know 8

High School

Produce enough 30%
Must import 58
Don't know 12

Grade School

Produce enough 33%
Must import 44
Don't know 23

By Region
East

Produce enough 23%
Must import 65
Don't know 12

Midwest

Produce enough 29%
Must import 60
Don't know 11

South

Produce enough 28%
Must import. 57
Don't know 15

West

Produce enough 27%
Must import. 61
Don't know 12

Those Who Think the Energy Situation Is Very Serious

Produce enough 21%
Must import. 70
Don't know 9

Those Who Think the Energy Situation Is Fairly Serious

Produce enough 25%
Must import. 64
Don't know 11

Those Who Think the Energy Situation Is Not At All Serious

Produce enough 52%
Must import. 38
Don't know 10

Asked of those who responded that the United States must import oil from other countries: About how much—that is, what percent—of the oil used in this country do we presently import from other countries?

Up to 9%. 2%
10%–19%. 3
20%–29%. 11
30%–39% (accepted as correct) 9
40%–49% (correct). 19
50%–59% (accepted as correct) 12
60%–69%. 12
70%–79%. 6
80%–89%. 2
90%–100%. 1
Don't know 23

By Education
College

Up to 9%. 1%
10%–19% 1
20%–29%. 11
30%–39% (accepted as correct) 11
40%–49% (correct). 22
50%–59% (accepted as correct) 15
60%–69%. 16
70%–79%. 5
80%–89%. 3
90%–100%. . . . . *
Don't know 15

High School

Up to 9%. 2%
10%–19%. 3
20%–29%. 11
30%–39% (accepted as correct) 7
40%–49% (correct). 19
50%–59% (accepted as correct) 11
60%–69%. 11
70%–79%. 9
80%–89%. 2
90%–100%. 1
Don't know 24

Grade School

Up to 9% . . . . *%
10%–19% 6
20%–29%. 10
30%–39% (accepted as correct). 9
40%–49% (correct) 12
50%–59% (accepted as correct). 8
60%–69%. 7
70%–79%. 1
80%–89% . . . . *
90%–100% . . . . *
Don't know 47

*Less than 1%.

If the consumption of oil and gas is reduced in the United States, which of these two ways would you prefer as a way to achieve this: start a rationing program that would require drivers to reduce the miles they drive by about one-fourth, or raise the tax on gasoline so that a gallon will cost twenty-five cents more than it currently does?

Ration 55%
Raise tax 20
Neither............................ 18
No opinion......................... 7

By Education
College

Ration 51%
Raise tax 28
Neither............................ 18
No opinion......................... 3

High School

Ration 57%
Raise tax 18
Neither............................ 18
No opinion......................... 7

Grade School

Ration 56%
Raise tax 11
Neither............................ 16
No opinion......................... 17

Note: The Carter administration's year-long effort to convince the public of the seriousness of the energy situation has come to naught.

In April 1977, President Jimmy Carter termed the energy situation the moral equivalent of war. However, twelve months after that pronouncement the percentage of Americans who describe the energy picture as "very serious" is exactly the same as it was before Carter made his declaration. While 41% of the public term the energy situation "very serious," nearly as many, 39%, say it is only "fairly serious," and 15% label it "not at all" serious. These figures nearly duplicate those recorded in April 1977, before Carter made three separate television appearances in one week to plug his

energy bill. For that matter, even after Carter's television appearances the percentage calling the energy situation "very serious" increased only marginally, from 41% to 44%.

Though most Americans believe the energy situation is something less than very serious, members of some groups—specifically, the college-educated, those at the top of the income scale, and those in the professions and business —are more inclined to agree with the president.

Knowledge of Imports

One of the most frustrating facts for the Carter administration must be the finding that one American in four, 27%, still believes the United States produces enough petroleum domestically to meet its energy requirements. Of the balance, 60% are cognizant of America's needs to import oil and 13% are unsure. Still, Carter must work with the realization that four people in ten either are laboring under the mistaken impression the United States does not need to import oil or are not sure.

This is not to suggest that the administration has made no progress in educating Americans to this most basic fact of the American energy situation. One year ago, one person in three, 33%, believed America to be energy self-sufficient, while only 52% were aware of the need to import petroleum.

While most Americans know the United States must import oil, people in the upscale socioeconomic groups—the college-educated, those in the upper income levels, and those in the professions and business—are generally more aware of this need. Differences also exist by sex and race: men and whites are better informed on the subject than are women and nonwhites.

Further analysis seem to indicate that inadequate public education lies at the root of the president's failure to convince the public of the seriousness of the energy situation. People who erroneously believe that enough oil is produced in the United States to meet the nation's energy needs tend to doubt the seriousness of the energy crisis. Those who realize we must import oil are significantly more likely to agree with the president that the energy situation is very serious.

A second factor in the knowledge Americans possess concerning import needs is the matter of how much—that is, what percent—of the oil the United States needs is bought from other nations. On this subject, Americans' knowledge is particularly unimpressive.

Before this survey was completed, Federal Energy Administration figures indicated that the United States imported 49% of the oil it needed in the previous month. Allowing for roughly a 10% error in either direction, only about one-third, 31%, of those who know we import oil offer a guess close to this figure. The remainder either underestimate (25%), overestimate (21%), or cannot even offer a guess (23%). The percentage not able even to guess how much oil the United States imports is considerably lower than was the case last year, when 34% were unable to do so.

Rationing vs. Tax Increase

The major culprit in the American energy picture is the automobile.

The two most frequently discussed methods of reducing consumption of gasoline have been the institution of a rationing program or the increase of gasoline taxes to discourage drivers from driving any more than necessary.

In many other nations, there have been substantial increases in gasoline prices that have boosted the price for a gallon into a range between $1.50 and $2.50, compared to an average of around $.70 in this country.

Just how large an increase in the price of gasoline would be sufficient to significantly reduce consumption is a matter of conjecture. However, survey results suggest that the American public is not willing to pay prices as high as those in other nations.

The public would opt for rationing if the choice came down to either a rationing program that would force drivers to cut the number of miles they drive by about one-fourth or an increase of twenty-five cents per gallon for gasoline. More than half, 55%, say they would prefer rationing to an increased tax, while 20% would rather pay more for the gasoline they need. The rest either dislike both alternatives (18%) or are undecided (7%). Rationing as an alternative to increased taxes had majority support nationwide as well as among most socioeconomic groups. And, in fact, no more than three people in ten in any single group (28% of the college-educated) vote for an increased gasoline tax.

Clearly, if the president is to mobilize public opinion behind him in his attempt to portray the energy situation as a true crisis, a more effective educational program is almost certainly a prime requisite. Specifically, Carter and his administration have failed to convey a full realization of the amount of oil the nation must import and the effect this has in cheapening the dollar, thus driving up inflation.

MAY 4
REPUBLICAN PRESIDENTIAL CANDIDATES

Interviewing Date: 3/31–4/3/78
Survey #998-K

Asked of Republicans and independents: Would you please look over this list [respondents were handed a card with six names] and tell me which of these persons, if any, you have heard something about?

Republicans Only

Gerald Ford	97%
Ronald Reagan	96
John Connally	82
Robert Dole	79
Howard Baker	65
Elliot Richardson	53

Independents Only

Ford	94%
Reagan	94

Connally 71
Dole 66
Baker 48
Richardson. 40

Asked of Republicans and independents: Which one would you like to see nominated as the Republican candidate for president in 1980?

Choice of Republicans

Ford 40%
Reagan 30
Baker 11
Richardson. 4
Dole 4
Connally 4
Undecided 7

Choice of Independents

Reagan. 39%
Ford 28
Baker 6
Richardson. 6
Connally 3
Dole 2
Undecided 16

Asked of Republicans and independents: Suppose the choice for president in the Republican convention in 1980 narrows down to Gerald Ford and Ronald Reagan. Which would you prefer to have the Republican convention select?

Choice of Republicans

Ford 54%
Reagan 42
Undecided 4

Choice of Independents

Reagan. 46%
Ford 44
Undecided 10

Asked of Republicans and independents: Suppose the choice for president in the Republican convention in 1980 narrows down to Ronald Reagan and Howard Baker. Which one would you prefer to have the Republican convention select?

Choice of Republicans

Reagan. 65%
Baker 24
Undecided 11

Choice of Independents

Reagan. 61%
Baker 23
Undecided 16

Asked of Republicans and independents: Suppose the choice for president in the Republican convention in 1980 narrows down to Gerald Ford and Howard Baker. Which one would you prefer to have the Republican convention select?

Choice of Republicans

Ford 71%
Baker 21
Undecided 8

Choice of Independents

Ford 61%
Baker 21
Undecided 18

Note: With speculation mounting that Ford will seek the GOP nomination in 1980, the Gallup Poll included his name in a list of six prominent Republicans in this early look at the 1980 race.

The current findings show a gain for Ford since last September and undoubtedly reflect his increased media exposure and activity on the speaking circuit.

The list of Republicans used in the September survey was considerably longer. At that time, Ford trailed Reagan.

Name Recognition

Jimmy Carter was almost unknown outside Georgia two years before the 1976 Democratic primaries. In fact, if White House aspirants learn anything from Carter's rise to the presidency it should be the value of early and intensive campaigning at the grassroots level to register one's name and one's views.

The latest Gallup Poll shows that only a half-dozen of those Republicans mentioned as possible nominees in 1980 are known to a majority of their party members.

The two contestants for the 1976 GOP nomination, Gerald Ford and Ronald Reagan, are known to virtually all party members. John Connally, with an 82% recognition figure, ranks below Ford and Reagan and about even with 1976 vice-presidential nominee Robert Dole of Kansas, whose name awareness registers 79%. Howard Baker of Tennessee, 65%, and Elliot Richardson, 53%, are the only other two men known by more than half of Republican party members.

While Connally, Dole, and Baker have lower recognition scores than Ford and Reagan, they have registered name-awareness gains since September, when Connally had a 72% recognition score, Dole 65%, and Baker 57%. Richardson's score shows little change.

Ford also leads Reagan among Republicans when the two men are matched head-to-head in a showdown test.

MAY 7

DEMOCRATIC PRESIDENTIAL CANDIDATES

Interviewing Date: 3/31–4/3/78
Survey #998-K

Asked of Democrats and independents: Here is a list of people who have been mentioned as possible presidential candidates for the Democratic party in 1980. [Respondents were handed a card with six names listed.] Which one would you like to see nominated as the Democratic candidate for president in 1980?

Choice of Democrats

Edward Kennedy	36%
Jimmy Carter	29
Edmund Brown, Jr.	12
Walter Mondale	8
Henry Jackson	5
Morris Udall	3
Undecided	7

Choice of Independents

Kennedy	35%
Carter	21
Brown	15
Jackson	9
Mondale	8
Udall	2
Undecided	10

Asked of Democrats and independents: Suppose the choice for president in the Democratic convention in 1980 narrows down to Jimmy Carter and Edward Kennedy. Which one would you prefer to have the Democratic convention select?

Choice of Democrats

Kennedy	53%
Carter	40
Undecided	7

Choice of Independents

Kennedy	53%
Carter	39
Undecided	8

Asked of Democrats and independents: Suppose the choice for president in the Democratic convention in 1980 narrows down to Edward Kennedy and Edmund Brown, Jr. Which one would you prefer to have the Democratic convention select?

Choice of Democrats

Kennedy 64%
Brown................................ 27
Undecided 9

Choice of Independents

Kennedy 60%
Brown................................ 27
Undecided 13

Asked of Democrats and independents: Suppose the choice for president in the Democratic convention in 1980 narrows down to Jimmy Carter and Edmund Brown, Jr. Which one would you prefer to have the Democratic convention select?

Choice of Democrats

Carter............................... 63%
Brown................................ 30
Undecided 7

Choice of Independents

Carter............................... 56%
Brown................................ 32
Undecided 12

Note: The greatest threat to Jimmy Carter's reelection may come not from his eventual Republican opponent but from within the ranks of his own party.

An early assessment of nationwide Democratic sentiment about the 1980 election indicates it is *not* Carter but Senator Edward Kennedy who is the first choice of party members to be the 1980 standard-bearer. Kennedy not only is the first choice of Democrats from a list of six possible Democratic nominees in 1980 but also holds an impressive lead when paired against Carter alone.

Only once before in the forty-three-year history of the Gallup Poll has an incumbent president eligible for reelection been defeated in a showdown test of strength. In September 1967, Senator Robert Kennedy was the choice of 51% of Democrats for the 1968 nomination, while 39% preferred then-President Lyndon Johnson.

Also attesting to Edward Kennedy's strength are the findings by region. In Carter's native South, his stronghold in the 1976 election, Kennedy holds the president to a stand-off, winning 46% of the vote compared to 44% for Carter. Outside the South, however, Kennedy is a clear 56%–38% winner.

That Kennedy should make such a strong showing, even against an incumbent president of his own party, is not a total surprise. He has long been a favorite of the Democratic voters and was their top choice even after he declared that he would not be a candidate. In fact, as late as January 1976, Kennedy was an easy first choice among Democrats for the nomination, winning 32% of the vote. Senator Hubert Humphrey of Minnesota was the Democrats' second choice, taking 20% of their vote.

Because of recurring speculation that Edmund Brown, Jr., will run for the nomination if he succeeds in winning reelection as governor of California, this survey also sought to gauge his current strength against the two Democratic front-runners.

MAY 11
PRESIDENTIAL TRIAL HEAT

Interviewing Date: 3/31–4/3/78
Survey #998-K

Asked of registered voters: Suppose the presidential election were being held today. If President Jimmy Carter were the Democratic candidate and Gerald Ford were the Republican candidate, which would you like to see win? [Those who named another person or who were undecided were asked: As of today, do you lean more to Carter, the Democrat, or to Ford, the Republican?]

Carter............................... 51%
Ford 43
Other 2
Undecided 4

By Sex

Male

Carter.............................49%
Ford 46
Other 2
Undecided......................... 3

Female

Carter.............................53%
Ford 41
Other 1
Undecided......................... 5

By Race

Whites

Carter.............................47%
Ford 47
Other 2
Undecided......................... 4

Northern Whites

Carter.............................48%
Ford 46
Other 2
Undecided......................... 4

Southern Whites

Carter.............................47%
Ford 48
Other 1
Undecided......................... 4

Nonwhites

Carter.............................80%
Ford 10
Other 2
Undecided......................... 8

Northern Blacks

Carter.............................80%
Ford 13
Other 3
Undecided......................... 4

Southern Blacks

Carter.............................81%
Ford 5
Other............................. *
Undecided.........................14

By Education

College

Carter.............................47%
Ford 50
Other 1
Undecided......................... 2

High School

Carter.............................49%
Ford 45
Other 2
Undecided......................... 4

Grade School

Carter.............................64%
Ford 25
Other 3
Undecided......................... 8

By Region

East

Carter.............................49%
Ford 44
Other 2
Undecided......................... 5

Midwest

Carter.............................50%
Ford 45
Other 1
Undecided......................... 4

South

Carter.............................51%
Ford 43
Other 1
Undecided......................... 5

Deep South

Carter...............................57%
Ford 34
Other 1
Undecided.......................... 8

Rest of South

Carter...............................49%
Ford 46
Other 1
Undecided.......................... 4

West

Carter...............................56%
Ford 41
Other 3
Undecided.......................... *

By Age
18–24 Years

Carter...............................56%
Ford 39
Other 2
Undecided.......................... 3

25–29 Years

Carter...............................49%
Ford 49
Other 1
Undecided.......................... 1

30–49 Years

Carter...............................47%
Ford 47
Other 2
Undecided.......................... 4

50 Years and Over

Carter...............................53%
Ford 39
Other 2
Undecided.......................... 6

By Income
$20,000 and Over

Carter...............................43%
Ford 53
Other 1
Undecided.......................... 3

$15,000–$19,999

Carter...............................48%
Ford 49
Other 2
Undecided.......................... 1

$10,000–$14,999

Carter...............................53%
Ford 39
Other 1
Undecided.......................... 7

$7,000–$9,999

Carter...............................57%
Ford 38
Other 1
Undecided.......................... 4

$5,000–$6,999

Carter...............................65%
Ford 28
Other 1
Undecided.......................... 6

$3,000–$4,999

Carter...............................63%
Ford 29
Other 2
Undecided.......................... 6

Under $3,000

Carter...............................46%
Ford 38
Other 6
Undecided..........................10

By Politics
Republicans

Carter.................................15%
Ford 81
Other 1
Undecided.........................3

Democrats

Carter.................................71%
Ford 24
Other 1
Undecided.........................4

Southern Democrats

Carter.................................71%
Ford 23
Other.................................*
Undecided.........................5

Other Democrats

Carter.................................71%
Ford 24
Other 2
Undecided.........................3

Independents

Carter.................................47%
Ford 46
Other 2
Undecided.........................5

By Religion
Protestants

Carter.................................47%
Ford 48
Other 1
Undecided.........................4

Catholics

Carter.................................57%
Ford 37
Other 2
Undecided.........................4

By Occupation
Professional and Business

Carter.................................46%
Ford 50
Other 1
Undecided.........................3

Clerical and Sales

Carter.................................36%
Ford 60
Other 2
Undecided.........................2

Manual Workers

Carter.................................53%
Ford 41
Other 2
Undecided.........................4

Non-Labor Force

Carter.................................59%
Ford 35
Other 1
Undecided.........................5

By Community Size
One Million and Over

Carter.................................53%
Ford 37
Other 3
Undecided.........................7

500,000–999,999

Carter.................................59%
Ford 37
Other 4
Undecided.........................*

50,000–499,999

Carter.................................52%
Ford 43
Other 1
Undecided.........................4

2,500–49,999

Carter............................... 50%
Ford 44
Other 1
Undecided.......................... 5

Under 2,500; Rural

Carter............................... 45%
Ford 51
Other 1
Undecided.......................... 3

Labor Union Families Only

Carter............................... 58%
Ford 36
Other 3
Undecided.......................... 3

Non-Labor Union Families Only

Carter............................... 49%
Ford 45
Other 1
Undecided.......................... 5

*Less than 1%.

Note: On a two-way basis (with the undecided vote allocated equally to the two men) and assuming the 1976 voter-turnout ratio, the results are as follows:

Carter............................... 53%
Ford 47

By way of comparison, the popular vote for the major party candidates in the 1976 presidential election was as follows:

Carter............................... 51.1%
Ford 48.9

Asked of registered voters: Suppose the presidential election were being held today. If President Jimmy Carter were the Democratic candidate and Ronald Reagan were the Republican candidate, which would you like to see win? [Those who named another person or who were undecided were asked: As of today, do you lean more to Carter, the Democrat, or to Reagan, the Republican?]

Carter............................... 51%
Reagan............................. 45
Other 1
Undecided.......................... 3

By Sex
Male

Carter............................... 50%
Reagan............................. 47
Other 1
Undecided.......................... 2

Female

Carter............................... 52%
Reagan............................. 43
Other 1
Undecided.......................... 4

By Race
Whites

Carter............................... 48%
Reagan............................. 48
Other 1
Undecided.......................... 3

Northern Whites

Carter............................... 50%
Reagan............................. 46
Other 1
Undecided.......................... 3

Southern Whites

Carter............................... 42%
Reagan............................. 55
Other................................ *
Undecided.......................... 3

Nonwhites

Carter............................... 81%
Reagan............................. 14
Other 0
Undecided.......................... 5

Northern Blacks

Carter.................................87%
Reagan................................12
Other..................................*
Undecided.............................1

Southern Blacks

Carter.................................71%
Reagan................................17
Other..................................*
Undecided............................12

By Education
College

Carter.................................52%
Reagan................................45
Other 1
Undecided.............................2

High School

Carter.................................47%
Reagan................................49
Other 1
Undecided.............................3

Grade School

Carter.................................63%
Reagan................................30
Other 1
Undecided.............................6

By Region
East

Carter.................................57%
Reagan................................38
Other 1
Undecided.............................4

Midwest

Carter.................................48%
Reagan................................49
Other..................................*
Undecided.............................3

South

Carter.................................47%
Reagan................................49
Other..................................*
Undecided.............................4

Deep South

Carter.................................47%
Reagan................................48
Other..................................*
Undecided.............................5

Rest of South

Carter.................................46%
Reagan................................50
Other..................................*
Undecided.............................4

West

Carter.................................53%
Reagan................................43
Other 3
Undecided.............................1

By Age
18–24 Years

Carter.................................63%
Reagan................................31
Other 2
Undecided.............................4

25–29 Years

Carter.................................49%
Reagan................................48
Other..................................*
Undecided.............................3

30–49 Years

Carter.................................51%
Reagan................................46
Other 1
Undecided.............................2

50 Years and Over

Carter................................49%
Reagan.............................47
Other....................................*
Undecided.........................4

By Income
$20,000 and Over

Carter................................45%
Reagan.............................51
Other 1
Undecided..........................3

$15,000–$19,999

Carter................................52%
Reagan.............................47
Other.....................................*
Undecided..........................1

$10,000–$14,999

Carter................................47%
Reagan.............................48
Other......................................*
Undecided..........................5

$7,000–$9,999

Carter................................58%
Reagan.............................40
Other.....................................*
Undecided..........................2

$5,000–$6,999

Carter................................57%
Reagan.............................38
Other 2
Undecided..........................3

$3,000–$4,999

Carter................................67%
Reagan.............................27
Other 1
Undecided..........................5

Under $3,000

Carter................................53%
Reagan.............................31
Other 10
Undecided..........................6

By Politics
Republicans

Carter................................23%
Reagan.............................73
Other......................................*
Undecided..........................4

Democrats

Carter................................69%
Reagan.............................27
Other 1
Undecided..........................3

Southern Democrats

Carter................................63%
Reagan.............................30
Other......................................*
Undecided..........................7

Other Democrats

Carter................................72%
Reagan.............................26
Other......................................*
Undecided..........................2

Independents

Carter................................43%
Reagan.............................53
Other 1
Undecided..........................3

By Religion
Protestants

Carter................................45%
Reagan.............................52
Other......................................*
Undecided..........................3

Catholics

Carter............................59%
Reagan............................35
Other 1
Undecided..........................5

By Occupation

Professional and Business

Carter............................47%
Reagan............................50
Other 1
Undecided..........................2

Clerical and Sales

Carter............................35%
Reagan............................64
Other................................*
Undecided..........................1

Manual Workers

Carter............................53%
Reagan............................44
Other................................*
Undecided..........................3

Non-Labor Force

Carter............................58%
Reagan............................36
Other 1
Undecided..........................5

By Community Size

One Million and Over

Carter............................56%
Reagan............................38
Other 1
Undecided..........................5

500,000–999,999

Carter............................55%
Reagan............................41
Other 1
Undecided..........................3

50,000–499,999

Carter............................56%
Reagan............................39
Other 1
Undecided..........................4

2,500–49,999

Carter............................46%
Reagan............................51
Other 1
Undecided..........................2

Under 2,500; Rural

Carter............................44%
Reagan............................51
Other 1
Undecided..........................4

Labor Union Families Only

Carter............................55%
Reagan............................41
Other................................*
Undecided..........................4

Non-Labor Union Families Only

Carter............................50%
Reagan............................46
Other 1
Undecided..........................3

*Less than 1%.

Note: On a two-way basis (with the undecided vote allocated equally to the two men) and assuming the 1976 voter-turnout ratio, the results are as follows:

Carter............................52%
Reagan............................48

It is important to bear in mind that these test races are indicative of present strength of potential, not actual, candidates and should be interpreted in this light.

The current test election findings are recorded at a time when President Carter's popularity rating is at his low point to date, with 39% expressing approval of his performance in office.

Asked of registered voters: Suppose the presidential election were being held today. If Edmund Brown, Jr., were the Democratic candidate and Gerald Ford were the Republican candidate, which would you like to see win? [Those who named another person or who were undecided were asked: As of today, do you lean more to Brown, the Democrat, or to Ford, the Republican?]

Ford 52%
Brown 40
Other 1
Undecided 7

By Sex
Male

Ford 52%
Brown 42
Other 1
Undecided 5

Female

Ford 52%
Brown 37
Other 2
Undecided 9

By Race
Whites

Ford 54%
Brown 38
Other 1
Undecided 7

Northern Whites

Ford 53%
Brown 39
Other 1
Undecided 7

Southern Whites

Ford 58%
Brown 33
Other 2
Undecided 7

Nonwhites

Ford 30%
Brown 58
Other 2
Undecided 10

Northern Blacks

Ford 20%
Brown 73
Other 2
Undecided 5

Southern Blacks

Ford 39%
Brown 42
Other 1
Undecided 18

By Education
College

Ford 54%
Brown 42
Other 1
Undecided 3

High School

Ford 55%
Brown 35
Other 2
Undecided 8

Grade School

Ford 35%
Brown 50
Other 2
Undecided 13

By Region

East

Ford	48%
Brown	42
Other	1
Undecided	9

Midwest

Ford	57%
Brown	35
Other	1
Undecided	7

South

Ford	55%
Brown	34
Other	2
Undecided	9

Deep South

Ford	59%
Brown	27
Other	4
Undecided	10

Rest of South

Ford	53%
Brown	37
Other	*
Undecided	9

West

Ford	43%
Brown	55
Other	2
Undecided	3

By Age

18–24 Years

Ford	55%
Brown	39
Other	2
Undecided	4

25–29 Years

Ford	57%
Brown	36
Other	3
Undecided	4

30–49 Years

Ford	52%
Brown	38
Other	1
Undecided	9

50 Years and Over

Ford	49%
Brown	42
Other	1
Undecided	8

By Income

$20,000 and Over

Ford	58%
Brown	37
Other	1
Undecided	4

$15,000–$19,999

Ford	57%
Brown	37
Other	*
Undecided	5

$10,000–$14,999

Ford	49%
Brown	37
Other	3
Undecided	11

$7,000–$9,999

Ford	50%
Brown	43
Other	*
Undecided	7

$5,000–$6,999

Ford 34%
Brown 55
Other .... *
Undecided 11

$3,000–$4,999

Ford 48%
Brown 43
Other 2
Undecided 7

Under $3,000

Ford 43%
Brown 34
Other 9
Undecided 14

By Politics
Republicans

Ford 78%
Brown 15
Other 1
Undecided 6

Democrats

Ford 36%
Brown 54
Other 2
Undecided 8

Southern Democrats

Ford 39%
Brown 48
Other 2
Undecided 10

Other Democrats

Ford 34%
Brown 57
Other 1
Undecided 8

Independents

Ford 56%
Brown 36
Other 1
Undecided 7

By Religion
Protestants

Ford 56%
Brown 36
Other 1
Undecided 7

Catholics

Ford 47%
Brown 44
Other 1
Undecided 7

By Occupation
Professional and Business

Ford 60%
Brown 34
Other 1
Undecided 5

Clerical and Sales

Ford 62%
Brown 36
Other .... *
Undecided 2

Manual Workers

Ford 49%
Brown 41
Other 1
Undecided 9

Non-Labor Force

Ford 44%
Brown 46
Other 1
Undecided 9

*Less than 1%.

By Community Size
One Million and Over

Ford 38%
Brown 50
Other 1
Undecided 11

500,000–999,999

Ford 44%
Brown 48
Other 1
Undecided 6

50,000–499,999

Ford 55%
Brown 37
Other 2
Undecided 6

2,500–49,999

Ford 58%
Brown 35
Other 1
Undecided 6

Under 2,500; Rural

Ford 58%
Brown 34
Other 1
Undecided 7

Labor Union Families Only

Ford 51%
Brown 39
Other 1
Undecided 9

Non-Labor Union Families Only

Ford 52%
Brown 40
Other 1
Undecided 7

Asked of registered voters: Suppose the presidential election were being held today. If Edmund Brown, Jr., were the Democratic candidate and Ronald Reagan were the Republican candidate, which would you like to see win? [Those who named another person or who were undecided were asked: As of today, do you lean more to Brown, the Democrat, or to Reagan, the Republican?]

Reagan 53%
Brown 37
Other 2
Undecided 8

By Sex
Male

Reagan 54%
Brown 38
Other 1
Undecided 7

Female

Reagan 52%
Brown 36
Other 3
Undecided 9

By Race
Whites

Reagan 55%
Brown 35
Other 2
Undecided 8

Northern Whites

Reagan 53%
Brown 37
Other 2
Undecided 7

Southern Whites

Reagan................................61%
Brown................................28
Other 2
Undecided............................ 9

Nonwhites

Reagan................................31%
Brown................................58
Other.................................. *
Undecided............................11

Northern Blacks

Reagan................................21%
Brown................................68
Other.................................. *
Undecided............................11

Southern Blacks

Reagan................................44%
Brown................................42
Other 1
Undecided............................13

By Education
College

Reagan................................48%
Brown................................47
Other 1
Undecided............................ 4

High School

Reagan................................59%
Brown................................31
Other 2
Undecided............................ 8

Grade School

Reagan................................42%
Brown................................39
Other 3
Undecided............................15

By Region
East

Reagan................................47%
Brown................................42
Other 1
Undecided............................ 9

Midwest

Reagan................................58%
Brown................................31
Other 3
Undecided............................ 8

South

Reagan................................58%
Brown................................30
Other 2
Undecided............................ 9

Deep South

Reagan................................64%
Brown................................24
Other 2
Undecided............................10

Rest of South

Reagan................................56%
Brown................................33
Other 2
Undecided............................ 9

West

Reagan................................45%
Brown................................50
Other 2
Undecided............................ 3

By Age
18–24 Years

Reagan................................49%
Brown................................34
Other 3
Undecided............................14

25–29 Years

Reagan........................56%
Brown.........................36
Other 2
Undecided..................... 6

30–49 Years

Reagan........................55%
Brown.........................36
Other 2
Undecided..................... 7

50 Years and Over

Reagan........................51%
Brown.........................39
Other 2
Undecided..................... 8

By Income
$20,000 and Over

Reagan........................56%
Brown.........................37
Other 2
Undecided..................... 5

$15,000–$19,999

Reagan........................55%
Brown.........................38
Other 1
Undecided..................... 6

$10,000–$14,999

Reagan........................57%
Brown.........................30
Other 2
Undecided.....................11

$7,000–$9,999

Reagan........................48%
Brown.........................40
Other 3
Undecided..................... 8

$5,000–$6,999

Reagan........................53%
Brown.........................34
Other 3
Undecided.....................10

$3,000–$4,999

Reagan........................36%
Brown.........................53
Other 1
Undecided.....................10

Under $3,000

Reagan........................51%
Brown.........................21
Other 9
Undecided.....................19

By Politics
Republicans

Reagan........................74%
Brown.........................18
Other 1
Undecided..................... 7

Democrats

Reagan........................40%
Brown.........................49
Other 2
Undecided..................... 9

Southern Democrats

Reagan........................42%
Brown.........................44
Other 2
Undecided.....................11

Other Democrats

Reagan........................39%
Brown.........................52
Other 2
Undecided..................... 7

Independents

Reagan............................59%
Brown.............................31
Other 2
Undecided......................... 8

By Religion
Protestants

Reagan............................57%
Brown.............................34
Other 1
Undecided......................... 8

Catholics

Reagan............................51%
Brown.............................39
Other 2
Undecided......................... 8

By Occupation
Professional and Business

Reagan............................53%
Brown.............................39
Other 2
Undecided......................... 6

Clerical and Sales

Reagan............................60%
Brown.............................35
Other 0
Undecided......................... 5

Manual Workers

Reagan............................57%
Brown.............................33
Other 2
Undecided......................... 7

Non-Labor Force

Reagan............................43%
Brown.............................45
Other 1
Undecided.........................11

By Community Size
One Million and Over

Reagan............................47%
Brown.............................43
Other 1
Undecided......................... 9

500,000–999,999

Reagan............................48%
Brown.............................46
Other 1
Undecided......................... 5

50,000–499,999

Reagan............................53%
Brown.............................34
Other 3
Undecided.........................10

2,500–49,999

Reagan............................52%
Brown.............................40
Other 2
Undecided......................... 6

Under 2,500; Rural

Reagan............................60%
Brown.............................29
Other 2
Undecided......................... 8

Labor Union Families Only

Reagan............................53%
Brown.............................39
Other 2
Undecided......................... 6

Non-Labor Union Families Only

Reagan............................53%
Brown.............................36
Other 2
Undecided......................... 8

*Less than 1%.

MAY 14
VOTER INITIATIVE

Interviewing Date: 1/6–9/78
Survey #991-K

The United States Senate will consider a proposal that would require a national vote—that is, a referendum—on any issue when three percent of all voters who voted in the most recent presidential election sign petitions ask for such a nationwide vote. How do you feel about this plan—do you favor or oppose such a plan?

Favor 57%
Oppose 21
No opinion 22

By Education
College

Favor 59%
Oppose 30
No opinion 11

High School

Favor 59%
Oppose 19
No opinion 22

Grade School

Favor 46%
Oppose 11
No opinion 43

By Region
East

Favor 55%
Oppose 19
No opinion 26

Midwest

Favor 56%
Oppose 23
No opinion 21

South

Favor 59%
Oppose 19
No opinion 22

West

Favor 57%
Oppose 23
No opinion 20

By Age
18–29 Years

Favor 59%
Oppose 19
No opinion 22

30–49 Years

Favor 59%
Oppose 22
No opinion 19

50 Years and Over

Favor 52%
Oppose 22
No opinion 26

By Politics
Republicans

Favor 56%
Oppose 25
No opinion 19

Democrats

Favor 59%
Oppose 20
No opinion 21

Independents

Favor 56%
Oppose 22
No opinion 22

Note: Voters of the nation like the idea of being able to pass judgment on proposed national legislation.

A constitutional amendment, described by its

sponsors as the Voter Initiative Amendment, would require a national vote on any issue if 3% of all voters in the previous presidential election sign petitions asking for such a vote. This percentage, applied to the last presidential election, would mean that a national vote could be held on any issue when approximately 2,500,000 people signed petitions.

The initiative, a time-honored device for direct citizen participation in the legislative process, is currently authorized in twenty-three states. According to the Library of Congress, in the past eighty years approximately 1,200 issues have been decided in this manner.

The constitutional amendment that would make the initiative federal policy is sponsored in the Senate by James Abourezk of South Dakota and Mark Hatfield of Oregon and in the House of Representatives by James Jones of Oklahoma and Harold Sawyer of Michigan.

Support for the federal initiative is found among all major groups of the population. Interestingly, nearly identical proportions of Republicans, Democrats, and independents agree the initiative is a good idea. Similarly, about equal majorities in the various geographic regions support such an amendment to the constitution.

Undoubtedly an important reason for the broad support that this amendment receives at this time is the disillusionment experienced by the voters of the nation in the post-Watergate era—disillusionment with both the legislative and executive branches of government.

Those who disapprove of such an amendment generally argue that the public is not well enough informed on many complex issues to arrive at a sound opinion. They point out that the Founding Fathers, in writing the Constitution, intended the nation to be a representative form of democracy, not a pure or direct democracy.

MAY 18
MOST IMPORTANT PROBLEM

Interviewing Date: 4/14–17/78
Survey #999-K

What do you think is the most important problem facing this country today?

Inflation/high cost of living 54%
Unemployment 18
Energy 8
International problems 8
Dissatisfaction with government 3
Crime 3
Moral decline 3
All others 18
Can't say 3
                                                        ___
                                                        118%*

*Total adds to more than 100% due to multiple responses.

Note: The proportion naming the high cost of living as the most important problem facing the nation not only represents a two-thirds increase in this concern but marks the highest degree of anxiety over rising prices recorded in these surveys since early 1977. While worry over rising prices has increased, the proportion citing unemployment has remained constant, and concern over the energy situation has declined to the lowest point since October 1976.

Though rising prices is the predominant problem cited by virtually every demographic group of Americans, several other trends emerge from this survey. Nonwhites continue as they have in the recent past to voice more concern over joblessness (36% cite it as the top problem) than do whites (16%). People in the East worry more about unemployment than those in the three other major regions of the country. Survey results broken down by respondents' education levels indicate an inverse relationship between concern over high prices and unemployment. The higher the level of formal education, the more likely high prices is to be named most important problem; the lower the level of formal education, the more likely joblessness is to be the primary concern.

Which political party do you think can do a better job of handling the problem you have just mentioned—the Republican party or the Democratic party?

Democratic 32%
Republican 22

No difference....................... 34
No opinion.......................... 12

By Race
Whites

Democratic......................... 30%
Republican......................... 23
No difference....................... 35
No opinion.......................... 12

Nonwhites

Democratic......................... 51%
Republican.......................... 8
No difference....................... 32
No opinion.......................... 9

By Region
East

Democratic......................... 34%
Republican......................... 19
No difference....................... 37
No opinion.......................... 10

Midwest

Democratic......................... 30%
Republican......................... 24
No difference....................... 33
No opinion.......................... 13

South

Democratic......................... 38%
Republican......................... 21
No difference....................... 31
No opinion.......................... 10

West

Democratic......................... 21%
Republican......................... 21
No difference....................... 39
No opinion.......................... 19

Those Naming High Cost of Living

Democratic......................... 32%
Republican......................... 23
No difference....................... 33
No opinion.......................... 12

Those Naming Unemployment

Democratic......................... 39%
Republican......................... 15
No difference....................... 37
No opinion.......................... 9

Those Naming Energy Problems

Democratic......................... 28%
Republican......................... 27
No difference....................... 37
No opinion.......................... 8

Note: Whether or not the continuing decline in public confidence in the Democratic party—and, by extension, President Carter and those Democrats facing reelection this November—will become a significant political liability is not yet clear. The fact is, however, that in three successive surveys the public's confidence in the Democratic party's ability to handle national problems, whatever these are perceived to be, has declined steadily, while the GOP has made compensating gains.

The Republican party has also made gains in confidence ratings of its ability to handle the three problems the public cites as being the most important facing the nation today—the high cost of living, unemployment, and the energy crisis. The number of people who believe that the Democratic party is best able to deal with the high cost of living has declined from 36% as of last October to 32% in the present survey, while the comparable figure for the Republican party has increased from 19% to 23%. On the unemployment issue, support for the Democratic party has slid from 43% to 39%, and Republican support has risen from 10% to 15%. The most dramatic change is regarding the problem of the energy situation: Democratic support has dropped from 45% to 28%, while Republican support has climbed from 9% to 27%.

Public's Top Concerns, 1935–1978

An examination of the public's major concerns of the last forty-three years shows the issues of peace and prosperity have almost totally eclipsed every other problem in the minds of Americans.

1978 (to date): The economy (high cost of living, unemployment)

1977: The economy (high cost of living, unemployment)

1976: The economy (high cost of living, unemployment)

1975: The economy (high cost of living, unemployment)

1974: High cost of living, Watergate, energy crisis

1973: High cost of living, Watergate

1974: High cost of living, Watergate, energy crisis

1973: High cost of living, Watergate

1972: Vietnam

1971: Vietnam, high cost of living

1970: Vietnam

1969: Vietnam

1968: Vietnam

1967: Vietnam, high cost of living

1966: Vietnam

1965: Vietnam, race relations

1964: Vietnam, race relations

1963: Keeping peace, race relations

1962: Keeping peace

1961: Keeping peace

1960: Keeping peace

1959: Keeping peace

1958: Unemployment, keeping peace

1957: Race relations, keeping peace

1956: Keeping peace

1955: Keeping peace

1954: Keeping peace

1953: Keeping peace

1952: Korean War

1951: Korean War

1950: Labor unrest

1949: Labor unrest

1948: Keeping peace

1947: High cost of living, labor unrest

1946: High cost of living

1945: Winning war

1944: Winning war

1943: Winning war

1942: Winning war

1941: Keeping out of war, winning war

1940: Keeping out of war

1939: Keeping out of war

1938: Keeping out of war

1937: Unemployment

1936: Unemployment

1935: Unemployment

MAY 21
CONGRESSIONAL ELECTIONS

Interviewing Date: 4/14–17, 4/28–5/1/78
Survey #999-K, 101-G

Asked of registered voters: If the elections for Congress were being held today, which party would you like to see win in this congressional district, the Democratic party or the Republican party? [Those who were undecided were asked: As of today, do you lean more to the Democratic party or to the Republican party?]

Democratic 52%
Republican. 38
Other 4
Undecided 6

When those who were undecided are allocated between the two major parties, the results are:

Democratic 58%
Republican. 42

Note: If the congressional elections were being held today, the GOP would gain very few, if any, seats. In any case the change would be far below the average gain for the "out party" of thirty to thirty-five seats.

If the vote for the House were being cast at this time, survey evidence indicates that Democratic candidates would win 58% of the vote nationwide and Republicans would win 42%, assuming a turnout comparable to those of 1970 and 1974. The Gallup Poll estimates that the current survey results indicate few, if any, losses for the Democratic party.

Analysis of Gallup Polls over the last four decades indicates that a president who has the popular approval of fewer than 55% of the nation's adults finds that his party suffers greater than normal losses in House seats. (The latest approval rating of President Jimmy Carter as reported by the Gallup Poll was 39%.)

At present, however, this normal coattail effect does not seem to be working. Undoubtedly, one important reason is the fact that the Democratic party currently holds a wide margin over the GOP as the party voters believe to be better able to deal with the high cost of living and unemployment. These are considered by voters to be the two top problems currently facing the nation.

While the Democratic party commands a more favorable public opinion concerning the key issues than the GOP, the current race could conceivably develop into a situation analogous to 1946. Voters that year, disgruntled over economic problems and labor relations, decided it was "time for a change" and overturned the fourteen-year Democratic control of Congress. However, no evidence so far suggests that outcome this year.

Ever since the Democratic party wrested control of the House from the GOP in 1932, the 1946 election marks the only time the Republicans were able to regain control in an off-year election.

As a general rule, low turnout tends to favor Republican candidates, especially in areas outside the South. Persons most likely to vote generally come from the upper income levels and from older age groups. A higher proportion of Republicans are found in these groups, so a low turnout usually favors GOP candidates.

Fewer than half of all Americans take the trouble to vote in off-year elections. The average turnout in the last two off-year elections has been 40% of those of voting age. This level of turnout has been assumed in developing the figures reported today.

MAY 25
UNIDENTIFIED FLYING OBJECTS

Interviewing Date: 3/3–6/78
Survey #995-K
Have you heard or read about unidentified flying objects—UFOs?

Yes 93%
No.................................. 7

Asked of those who replied in the affirmative: Have you, yourself, ever seen anything you thought was a UFO?

	Yes
National..........................	9%

By Sex

Male................................	12%
Female	7

By Education

College............................	9%
High school	11
Grade school.....................	5

By Region

East	9%
Midwest...........................	8
South	9
West...............................	14

By Age

18–24 years.......................	15%
25–29 years.......................	11
30–49 years.......................	8
50 years and over	6

By Community Size

One million and over	10%
500,000–999,999..................	10
50,000–499,999...................	8
2,500–49,999	12
Under 2,500; rural	9

Also asked of those who said they have heard or read about UFOs: In your opinion, are they something real, or just people's imagination?

Real 57%
Imagination 27
No opinion........................ 16

By Sex
Male

Real 55%
Imagination 31
No opinion.........................14

Female

Real 59%
Imagination 24
No opinion.........................17

By Education
College

Real 66%
Imagination 23
No opinion.........................11

High School

Real 57%
Imagination 27
No opinion.........................16

Grade School

Real 36%
Imagination 38
No opinion.........................26

By Region
East

Real 53%
Imagination 29
No opinion.........................18

Midwest

Real 61%
Imagination 26
No opinion.........................13

South

Real 48%
Imagination 32
No opinion.........................20

West

Real 69%
Imagination 19
No opinion.........................12

By Age
18–24 Years

Real 66%
Imagination 24
No opinion.........................10

25–29 Years

Real 77%
Imagination 12
No opinion.........................11

30–49 Years

Real 63%
Imagination 23
No opinion.........................14

50 Years and Over

Real 40%
Imagination 38
No opinion.........................22

By Community Size
One Million and Over

Real 59%
Imagination 25
No opinion.........................16

500,000–999,999

Real 57%
Imagination 30
No opinion.........................13

50,000–499,999

Real 53%
Imagination 27
No opinion.........................20

2,500–49,999

Real 60%
Imagination 27
No opinion............................ 13

Under 2,500; Rural

Real 57%
Imagination 29
No opinion............................ 14

Those Who Have Seen a UFO

Real 90%
Imagination 8
No opinion............................ 2

Those Who Have Not Seen a UFO

Real 53%
Imagination 30
No opinion............................ 17

Asked of the entire sample: Do you think there are people somewhat like ourselves living on other planets in the universe, or not?

Yes 51%
No.................................... 33
No opinion............................ 16

By Sex
Male

Yes 51%
No.................................... 33
No opinion............................ 16

Female

Yes 51%
No.................................... 33
No opinion............................ 16

By Education
College

Yes 62%
No.................................... 28
No opinion............................ 10

High School

Yes 53%
No.................................... 30
No opinion............................ 17

Grade School

Yes 24%
No.................................... 53
No opinion............................ 23

By Region
East

Yes 50%
No.................................... 34
No opinion............................ 16

Midwest

Yes 54%
No.................................... 30
No opinion............................ 16

South

Yes 42%
No.................................... 39
No opinion............................ 19

West

Yes 62%
No.................................... 26
No opinion............................ 12

By Age
18–24 Years

Yes 67%
No.................................... 23
No opinion............................ 10

25–29 Years

Yes 67%
No.................................... 19
No opinion............................ 14

30–49 Years

Yes 54%
No 32
No opinion 14

50 Years and Over

Yes 37%
No 43
No opinion 20

By Religion
Protestants

Yes 47%
No 37
No opinion 16

Catholics

Yes 51%
No 32
No opinion 17

By Income
$20,000 and Over

Yes 59%
No 28
No opinion 13

$15,000–$19,999

Yes 56%
No 30
No opinion 14

$10,000–$14,999

Yes 55%
No 29
No opinion 16

$7,000–$9,999

Yes 48%
No 39
No opinion 13

$5,000–$6,999

Yes 39%
No 44
No opinion 17

$3,000–$4,999

Yes 37%
No 42
No opinion 21

Under $3,000

Yes 34%
No 34
No opinion 32

Those Who Have Seen a UFO

Yes 73%
No 17
No opinion 10

Those Who Have Not Seen a UFO

Yes 51%
No 34
No opinion 15

The following is the trend since 1966:

1966

Yes 34%
No 46
No opinion 20

1973

Yes 46%
No 38
No opinion 16

1978

Yes 51%
No 33
No opinion 16

Note: For many Americans, the movie *Close Encounters of the Third Kind* is not so farfetched. In fact, a solid majority of Americans now express a belief in UFOs, the proportion having grown steadily since 1966 when the first measurement was taken.

The growing belief in UFOs coincides with an increase in the percentage of Americans who believe there are humanoids living somewhere else in the universe.

MAY 28
PRESIDENTIAL TRIAL HEAT

Interviewing Date: 5/19–22/78
Survey #103-G

Asked of registered voters: Suppose the presidential election were being held today. If Senator Edward Kennedy were the Democratic candidate and Gerald Ford were the Republican candidate, which would you like to see win? [Those who named another person or who were undecided were asked: As of today, do you lean more to Kennedy, the Democrat, or to Ford, the Republican?]

Kennedy	53%
Ford	41
Other	3
Undecided	3

By Sex
Male

Kennedy	53%
Ford	43
Other	2
Undecided	2

Female

Kennedy	53%
Ford	40
Other	3
Undecided	4

By Race
Whites

Kennedy	49%
Ford	45
Other	3
Undecided	3

Northern Whites

Kennedy	50%
Ford	46
Other	2
Undecided	2

Southern Whites

Kennedy	42%
Ford	45
Other	6
Undecided	7

Nonwhites

Kennedy	45%
Ford	4
Other	*
Undecided	1

Northern Blacks

Kennedy	91%
Ford	7
Other	*
Undecided	2

Southern Blacks

Kennedy	98%
Ford	1
Other	*
Undecided	1

By Education
College

Kennedy	44%
Ford	50
Other	3
Undecided	3

High School

Kennedy	55%
Ford	40
Other	2
Undecided	3

Grade School

Kennedy 65%
Ford 28
Other 4
Undecided 3

By Region
East

Kennedy 58%
Ford 38
Other 1
Undecided 3

Midwest

Kennedy 52%
Ford 44
Other 2
Undecided 2

South

Kennedy 51%
Ford 38
Other 5
Undecided 6

Deep South

Kennedy 49%
Ford 38
Other 3
Undecided 10

Rest of South

Kennedy 52%
Ford 37
Other 7
Undecided 4

West

Kennedy 48%
Ford 49
Other 2
Undecided 1

By Age
18–24 Years

Kennedy 70%
Ford 30
Other .... *
Undecided .... *

25–29 Years

Kennedy 63%
Ford 35
Other 2
Undecided .... *

30–49 Years

Kennedy 49%
Ford 43
Other 4
Undecided 4

50 Years and Over

Kennedy 50%
Ford 44
Other 3
Undecided 3

By Income
$20,000 and Over

Kennedy 39%
Ford 54
Other 4
Undecided 3

$15,000–$19,999

Kennedy 47%
Ford 47
Other 2
Undecided 4

$10,000–$14,999

Kennedy 62%
Ford 34
Other 2
Undecided 2

$7,000–$9,999

Kennedy 67%
Ford 27
Other 3
Undecided 3

$5,000–$6,999

Kennedy 66%
Ford 29
Other 2
Undecided 3

$3,000–$4,999

Kennedy 58%
Ford 37
Other 3
Undecided 2

Under $3,000

Kennedy 68%
Ford 23
Other 4
Undecided 5

By Politics
Republicans

Kennedy 15%
Ford 82
Other 1
Undecided 2

Democrats

Kennedy 79%
Ford 16
Other 2
Undecided 3

Independents

Kennedy 39%
Ford 52
Other 6
Undecided 3

By Religion
Protestants

Kennedy 45%
Ford 49
Other 3
Undecided 3

Catholics

Kennedy 70%
Ford 26
Other 1
Undecided 3

By Occupation
Professional and Business

Kennedy 40%
Ford 53
Other 3
Undecided 4

Clerical and Sales

Kennedy 56%
Ford 41
Other 1
Undecided 2

Manual Workers

Kennedy 63%
Ford 32
Other 3
Undecided 2

Non-Labor Force

Kennedy 54%
Ford 41
Other 2
Undecided 3

By Community Size
One Million and Over

Kennedy 61%
Ford 36
Other .... *
Undecided 3

500,000–999,999

Kennedy 59%
Ford 38
Other 2
Undecided 1

50,000–499,999

Kennedy 55%
Ford 39
Other 4
Undecided 2

2,500–49,999

Kennedy 52%
Ford 40
Other 4
Undecided 4

Under 2,500; Rural

Kennedy 44%
Ford 49
Other 3
Undecided 4

Labor Union Families Only

Kennedy 61%
Ford 33
Other 2
Undecided 4

Non-Labor Union Families Only

Kennedy 49%
Ford 45
Other 3
Undecided 3

*Less than 1%.

Asked of registered voters: Suppose the presidential election were being held today. If Senator Edward Kennedy were the Democratic candidate and Ronald Reagan were the Republican candidate, which would you like to see win? [Those who named another person or who were undecided were asked: As of today, do you lean more to Kennedy, the Democrat, or to Reagan, the Republican?]

Kennedy 57%
Reagan 37
Other 2
Undecided 4

By Sex
Male

Kennedy 57%
Reagan 37
Other 2
Undecided 4

Female

Kennedy 57%
Reagan 36
Other 2
Undecided 5

By Race
Whites

Kennedy 53%
Reagan 40
Other 3
Undecided 4

Northern Whites

Kennedy 56%
Reagan 38
Other 3
Undecided 3

Southern Whites

Kennedy 44%
Reagan 47
Other 2
Undecided 7

Nonwhites

Kennedy 95%
Reagan 4
Other .... *
Undecided 1

Northern Blacks

Kennedy 98%
Reagan 2
Other .... *
Undecided .... *

Southern Blacks

Kennedy 90%
Reagan 7
Other .... *
Undecided 3

By Education
College

Kennedy 51%
Reagan 41
Other 4
Other 4

High School

Kennedy 58%
Reagan 35
Other 2
Undecided 5

Grade School

Kennedy 65%
Reagan 32
Other 1
Undecided 2

By Region
East

Kennedy 64%
Reagan 29
Other 3
Undecided 4

Midwest

Kennedy 59%
Reagan 36
Other 2
Undecided 3

South

Kennedy 52%
Reagan 40
Other 2
Undecided 6

Deep South

Kennedy 49%
Reagan 39
Other .... *
Undecided 12

Rest of South

Kennedy 52%
Reagan 41
Other 3
Undecided 4

West

Kennedy 51%
Reagan 45
Other 2
Undecided 2

By Age
18–24 Years

Kennedy 81%
Reagan 15
Other .... *
Undecided 4

25–29 Years

Kennedy 75%
Reagan 20
Other 2
Undecided 3

30–49 Years

Kennedy 54%
Reagan 37
Other 3
Undecided 6

50 Years and Over

Kennedy 50%
Reagan 45
Other 2
Undecided 3

By Income
$20,000 and Over

Kennedy 44%
Reagan 48
Other 4
Undecided 4

$15,000–$19,999

Kennedy 54%
Reagan 39
Other 1
Undecided 6

$10,000–$14,999

Kennedy 67%
Reagan 27
Other 2
Undecided 4

$7,000–$9,999

Kennedy 66%
Reagan 27
Other 3
Undecided 4

$5,000–$6,999

Kennedy 69%
Reagan 23
Other 3
Undecided 5

$3,000–$4,999

Kennedy 56%
Reagan 43
Other 1
Undecided .... *

Under $3,000

Kennedy 76%
Reagan 21
Other .... *
Undecided 3

By Politics
Republicans

Kennedy 20%
Reagan 73
Other 3
Undecided 4

Democrats

Kennedy 81%
Reagan 14
Other 2
Undecided 3

Independents

Kennedy 47%
Reagan 45
Other 3
Undecided 5

By Religion
Protestants

Kennedy 51%
Reagan 43
Other 2
Undecided 4

Catholics

Kennedy 69%
Reagan 26
Other 2
Undecided 3

By Occupation
Professional and Business

Kennedy 47%
Reagan 42
Other 4
Undecided 7

Clerical and Sales

Kennedy 54%
Reagan 40
Other 5
Undecided 1

Manual Workers

Kennedy 66%
Reagan 28
Other 2
Undecided 4

Non-Labor Force

Kennedy 56%
Reagan 41
Other 2
Undecided 1

By Community Size
One Million and Over

Kennedy 68%
Reagan 29
Other .... *
Undecided 3

500,000–999,999

Kennedy 60%
Reagan 34
Other .... *
Undecided 6

50,000–499,999

Kennedy 56%
Reagan 36
Other 5
Undecided 3

2,500–49,999

Kennedy 54%
Reagan 39
Other 2
Undecided 5

Under 2,500; Rural

Kennedy 52%
Reagan 41
Other 3
Undecided 4

Labor Union Families Only

Kennedy 66%
Reagan 28
Other 1
Undecided 5

Non-Labor Union Families Only

Kennedy 53%
Reagan 41
Other 2
Undecided 4

*Less than 1%.

Note: It should be remembered that these early trial tests are indicative only of potential candidate strength at the time the survey was conducted and should be interpreted in this light only.

MAY 30
HOLOCAUST TELEVISION SERIES

Interviewing Date: 4/28–5/1/78
Survey #101-G

Did you happen to see any of the recent television series Holocaust?

Yes 56%
No 44

Asked of those who replied in the affirmative: About how many of the four programs in the series did you watch all the way through?

One 16%
Two 17
Three 17

Four 35
Don't know 15

JUNE 1
SATISFACTION INDEX

September–December 1977
Special Survey

Now, here are some questions concerning how satisfied—or dissatisfied—you are with various things about your life, such as your standard of living, your education, etc. To indicate this, would you use this card. [Respondents were handed a crd with numbers running from zero to ten.] If you are extremely satisfied with something you would call off the highest number, ten. If you are extremely dissatisfied you would mention the lowest number, zero. If you are neither extremely satisfied or extremely dissatisfied you would mention some number in between zero and ten—the higher the number the more satisfied, the lower the number the more dissatisfied.

	Highly satisfied*
Your family life?	79%
Your relations with other people?	79
Your life overall?	69
Your health?	67
This neighborhood?	61
Your housing?	60
Ways you spend your free time?	59
This country as a place to live?	57
Your education as preparation for work?	53
Your education as preparation for life?	50
Your standard of living?	45
Your household income?	41
The way democracy in this nation is working?	32

*In the results reported above, the percentage for a given question represents the total score for the top three steps of the satisfaction scale, describing the "highly satisfied."

Note: Further evidence that the United States is emerging from its post-Watergate doldrums is apparent from a recent Gallup survey that shows the American people to be far more satisfied with their lives than they were in 1975.

The percentage of Americans who say they are "highly satisfied" with "this country as a place to live," for example, has shot up 23 percentage points since 1975, from 34% to 57%.

Other sharp gains in satisfaction with basic aspects of life are found in terms of Americans' view of the value of their education as preparation for both life and work. Increases are also noted in the cases of "family life" and "health."

Despite the high respondent satisfaction in the survey, the results in terms of the more material aspects of life are not as encouraging. For example, the proportion of persons who indicate a high degree of satisfaction with their standard of living has shown virtually no change since the 1975 survey.

In eight Western European nations, as well as the United States, the publics are less satisfied with the material aspects of life—such as standard of living and household income—than with such factors as family life, leisure time, and relations with other people.

Dissatisfaction with democracy is evident on both sides of the Atlantic. This is particularly true in Italy, where only about one person in fifteen (6%) says he or she is satisfied with the way democracy is working there.

Comparisons between countries show Americans to be the most satisfied with "life as a whole," followed by the citizens of Denmark and Ireland. The Danes are consistently more likely to be highly satisfied with the specific aspects of their life than Americans. The Irish also indicate a high level of satisfaction, except in the case of their standard of living and household income.

The French and Italians are the least satisfied nationalities, falling at the bottom of the list for each item tests. In Italy, for example, only about one person in six indicates a high degree of satisfaction with life, and only one person in eight is highly satisfied with his or her standard of living or household income.

The results reported today are based on a survey carried out in nine nations by Gallup International Research Institutes. It is one in a series of Eurobarometer surveys conducted for the Commission of European Communities.

JUNE 4
PRESIDENT CARTER

Interviewing Date: 5/19–22/78
Survey #103-G

Do you approve or disapprove of the way Jimmy Carter is handling his job as president?

Approve............................43%
Disapprove 43
No opinion..........................14

By Sex
Male

Approve............................44%
Disapprove 46
No opinion..........................10

Female

Approve............................42%
Disapprove 41
No opinion..........................17

By Race
Whites

Approve............................41%
Disapprove 46
No opinion..........................13

Northern Whites

Approve............................39%
Disapprove 48
No opinion..........................13

Southern Whites

Approve............................46%
Disapprove 40
No opinion..........................14

Nonwhites

Approve............................54%
Disapprove 23
No opinion..........................23

Northern Blacks

Approve............................53%
Disapprove 24
No opinion..........................23

Southern Blacks

Approve............................61%
Disapprove 20
No opinion..........................19

By Education
College

Approve............................40%
Disapprove 51
No opinion.......................... 9

High School

Approve............................41%
Disapprove 43
No opinion..........................16

Grade School

Approve............................51%
Disapprove 31
No opinion..........................18

By Region
East

Approve............................44%
Disapprove 41
No opinion..........................15

Midwest

Approve............................38%
Disapprove 47
No opinion..........................15

South

Approve...............................48%
Disapprove 36
No opinion..........................16

Deep South

Approve...............................51%
Disapprove 37
No opinion..........................12

Rest of South

Approve...............................47%
Disapprove 35
No opinion..........................18

West

Approve...............................37%
Disapprove 53
No opinion..........................10

By Age
18–24 Years

Approve...............................44%
Disapprove 36
No opinion..........................20

25–29 Years

Approve...............................57%
Disapprove 38
No opinion......................... 5

30–49 Years

Approve...............................40%
Disapprove 45
No opinion..........................15

50 Years and Over

Approve...............................40%
Disapprove 47
No opinion..........................13

By Politics
Republicans

Approve...............................25%
Disapprove 65
No opinion..........................10

Democrats

Approve...............................55%
Disapprove 32
No opinion..........................13

Southern Democrats

Approve...............................59%
Disapprove 27
No opinion..........................14

Other Democrats

Approve...............................53%
Disapprove 34
No opinion..........................13

Independents

Approve...............................39%
Disapprove 46
No opinion..........................15

By Religion
Protestants

Approve...............................42%
Disapprove 44
No opinion..........................14

Catholics

Approve...............................47%
Disapprove 39
No opinion..........................14

By Occupation
Professional and Business

Approve...............................40%
Disapprove 47
No opinion..........................13

Clerical and Sales

Approve...............................35%
Disapprove 44
No opinion..........................21

Manual Workers

Approve...............................44%
Disapprove 41
No opinion..........................15

Non-Labor Force

Approve.............................45%
Disapprove 44
No opinion...........................11

Labor Union Families Only

Approve.............................44%
Disapprove 44
No opinion...........................12

Non-Labor Union Families Only

Approve.............................42%
Disapprove 43
No opinion...........................15

Asked of those who had an opinion: How strongly would you say you approve/disapprove—very strongly or not so strongly?

Strong approval......................14%
Mild approval 26
Mild disapproval.....................22
Strong disapproval 20
No opinion...........................18

Interviewing Date: 5/5–8/78
Survey #102-G

How much trust and confidence do you have in President Carter, the man—a great deal, some, hardly any, or none?

A great deal.........................26%
Some.................................51
Hardly any...........................14
None................................. 6
No opinion........................... 3

By Sex
Male

A great deal.........................25%
Some.................................50
Hardly any...........................16
None................................. 7
No opinion........................... 2

Female

A great deal.........................27%
Some.................................52
Hardly any...........................13
None................................. 5
No opinion........................... 3

By Race
Whites

A great deal.........................25%
Some.................................51
Hardly any...........................15
None................................. 6
No opinion........................... 3

Northern Whites

A great deal.........................24%
Some.................................53
Hardly any...........................14
None................................. 6
No opinion........................... 3

Southern Whites

A great deal.........................30%
Some.................................44
Hardly any...........................17
None................................. 6
No opinion........................... 3

Nonwhites

A great deal.........................29%
Some.................................52
Hardly any...........................10
None................................. 5
No opinion........................... 4

Northern Blacks

A great deal.........................25%
Some.................................52
Hardly any...........................11
None................................. 8
No opinion........................... 4

Southern Blacks

A great deal.........................35%
Some.................................50

Hardly any..........................11
None...............................2
No opinion........................2

By Education
College

A great deal........................24%
Some.............................55
Hardly any.........................14
None...............................6
No opinion........................1

High School

A great deal........................25%
Some.............................51
Hardly any.........................14
None...............................7
No opinion........................3

Grade School

A great deal........................32%
Some.............................43
Hardly any.........................16
None...............................5
No opinion........................4

By Region
East

A great deal........................25%
Some.............................54
Hardly any.........................14
None...............................6
No opinion........................1

Midwest

A great deal........................23%
Some.............................52
Hardly any.........................14
None...............................6
No opinion........................5

South

A great deal........................31%
Some.............................45

Hardly any.........................16
None...............................5
No opinion........................3

Deep South

A great deal........................33%
Some.............................53
Hardly any.........................9
None...............................3
No opinion........................2

Rest of South

A great deal........................30%
Some.............................42
Hardly any.........................19
None...............................6
No opinion........................3

West

A great deal........................22%
Some.............................53
Hardly any.........................14
None...............................8
No opinion........................3

By Age
18–24 Years

A great deal........................16%
Some.............................60
Hardly any.........................18
None...............................3
No opinion........................3

25–29 Years

A great deal........................20%
Some.............................54
Hardly any.........................16
None...............................7
No opinion........................3

30–49 Years

A great deal........................26%
Some.............................52
Hardly any.........................13
None...............................6
No opinion........................3

50 Years and Over

A great deal	31%
Some	45
Hardly any	14
None	7
No opinion	3

By Politics
Republicans

A great deal	14%
Some	56
Hardly any	20
None	8
No opinion	2

Democrats

A great deal	33%
Some	49
Hardly any	12
None	3
No opinion	3

Southern Democrats

A great deal	34%
Some	47
Hardly any	13
None	3
No opinion	3

Other Democrats

A great deal	32%
Some	50
Hardly any	12
None	3
No opinion	3

Independents

A great deal	22%
Some	52
Hardly any	14
None	9
No opinion	3

By Religion
Protestants

A great deal	27%
Some	51
Hardly any	14
None	6
No opinion	2

Catholics

A great deal	25%
Some	51
Hardly any	15
None	5
No opinion	3

By Occupation
Professional and Business

A great deal	23%
Some	50
Hardly any	17
None	9
No opinion	1

Clerical and Sales

A great deal	25%
Some	55
Hardly any	10
None	10
No opinion	*

Manual Workers

A great deal	22%
Some	55
Hardly any	14
None	5
No opinion	4

Non-Labor Force

A great deal	34%
Some	42
Hardly any	14
None	6
No opinion	4

Labor Union Families Only

A great deal	26%
Some	53
Hardly any	15
None	3
No opinion	3

Non-Labor Union Families

A great deal	25%
Some	50
Hardly any	14
None	7
No opinion	3

*Less than 1%.

How would you rate President Carter's record to date—do you think he's done an excellent job in dealing with the problems facing the nation, a good job, a fair job, or a poor job?

Excellent	4%
Good	24
Fair	48
Poor	22
No opinion	3

By Sex
Male

Excellent	3%
Good	23
Fair	46
Poor	25
No opinion	2

Female

Excellent	4%
Good	25
Fair	49
Poor	18
No opinion	4

By Race
Whites

Excellent	3%
Good	23
Fair	48
Poor	23
No opinion	3

Northern Whites

Excellent	3%
Good	23
Fair	49
Poor	23
No opinion	2

Southern Whites

Excellent	4%
Good	23
Fair	46
Poor	23
No opinion	4

Nonwhites

Excellent	5%
Good	36
Fair	44
Poor	10
No opinion	5

Northern Blacks

Excellent	4%
Good	37
Fair	41
Poor	10
No opinion	8

Southern Blacks

Excellent	7%
Good	36
Fair	46
Poor	11
No opinion	*

By Education
College

Excellent	3%
Good	24
Fair	49
Poor	23
No opinion	1

High School

Excellent	3%
Good	24
Fair	49
Poor	20
No opinion	4

Grade School

Excellent	7%
Good	24
Fair	43
Poor	23
No opinion	3

By Region

East

Excellent	4%
Good	24
Fair	50
Poor	21
No opinion	1

Midwest

Excellent	3%
Good	24
Fair	49
Poor	22
No opinion	3

South

Excellent	5%
Good	25
Fair	45
Poor	21
No opinion	4

Deep South

Excellent	4%
Good	30
Fair	48
Poor	16
No opinion	2

Rest of South

Excellent	5%
Good	23
Fair	44
Poor	24
No opinion	4

West

Excellent	2%
Good	24
Fair	47
Poor	22
No opinion	5

By Age

18–24 Years

Excellent	2%
Good	29
Fair	50
Poor	16
No opinion	3

25–29 Years

Excellent	1%
Good	32
Fair	47
Poor	17
No opinion	3

30–49 Years

Excellent	4%
Good	23
Fair	47
Poor	24
No opinion	3

50 Years and Over

Excellent	4%
Good	21
Fair	48
Poor	24
No opinion	3

By Politics

Republicans

Excellent 2%
Good 14
Fair................................ 49
Poor 34
No opinion.......................... 1

Democrats

Excellent 6%
Good 30
Fair................................ 47
Poor 16
No opinion.......................... 2

Southern Democrats

Excellent 6%
Good 28
Fair................................ 47
Poor 16
No opinion.......................... 3

Other Democrats

Excellent 6%
Good 30
Fair................................ 46
Poor 16
No opinion.......................... 2

Independents

Excellent 2%
Good 22
Fair................................ 50
Poor 22
No opinion.......................... 4

By Religion

Protestants

Excellent 3%
Good 25
Fair................................ 48
Poor 21
No opinion.......................... 3

Catholics

Excellent 4%
Good 25
Fair................................ 48
Poor 21
No opinion.......................... 2

By Occupation

Professional and Business

Excellent 3%
Good 20
Fair................................ 50
Poor 25
No opinion.......................... 2

Clerical and Sales

Excellent 3%
Good 27
Fair................................ 46
Poor 22
No opinion.......................... 2

Manual Workers

Excellent 4%
Good 27
Fair................................ 48
Poor 18
No opinion.......................... 3

Non-Labor Force

Excellent 4%
Good 23
Fair................................ 47
Poor 23
No opinion.......................... 3

Labor Union Families Only

Excellent 4%
Good 25
Fair................................ 50
Poor 20
No opinion.......................... 1

Non-Labor Union Families Only

Excellent 4%
Good 24
Fair 47
Poor 22
No opinion 3

*Less than 1%.

Note: President Jimmy Carter's fortunes have taken a slight turn for the better, after a four-month slide in his popularity. In the latest nationwide survey, 43% of Americans approve of the way the president is handling his job as chief executive, and an equal proportion, 43%, disapprove. The current figure represents a three-point gain in approval from the president's low point in popularity, recorded in mid-April, when 40% expressed approval.

Between December and the mid-April survey, Carter's popularity had declined 17 percentage points. That four-month period was a bleak one for Carter in terms of public confidence. Not only did his overall popularity rating decline during that interim but the percentage of those who "strongly approve" of Carter's performance fell from 20% to 14%. However, the latest survey indicates that this decline may now by leveling off.

Confidence in Carter, the man, also declined in this time period, with the percentage saying they have "a great deal" of trust and confidence in Carter down from 30% in December to 25% in the latest survey. The percentage of people rating the president's record to date as "excellent" or "good" dropped from 37% to 28%.

The loss of public confidence in Carter over the last few months is due primarily to a combination of increased concern over the economy and the growing belief that the president is indecisive and not accomplishing what he should— "he doesn't have the push the other presidents have had" was a typical response. Many people also feel he has not kept his campaign promises.

Some of his supporters, on the other hand, maintain that he is doing the best he can and that it is too early to criticize him for failure to live up to his campaign promises. Others feel that Congress is not giving him the support he needs to pass his legislative programs.

JUNE 8
NEUTRON BOMB

Interviewing Date: 4/28–5/1/78
Survey #101-G

Have you heard or read about the neutron bomb?

                                                    Yes
National 79%

Asked of those who replied in the affirmative: What is the chief military advantage of this bomb—that is, how does it work?

Only kills people (correct) 41%
Incorrect replies 34
Don't know 25

Also asked of those who replied in the affirmative: Do you think the United States should or should not proceed to equip our armed forces and our allies with the neutron bomb?

Should 43%
Should not 44
No opinion 13

Asked of the informed group, that is, those who have heard or read about the neutron bomb and can correctly indicate its military advantage (52% of the total sample): Do you think the United States should or should not proceed to equip our armed forces and our allies with the neutron bomb?

Should 46%
Should not 45
No opinion 9

Note: The neutron bomb is designed to kill primarily through radiation. The neutron warhead has a smaller heat and shock effect than older nuclear weapons, but it generates intense radiation; this radiation can penetrate heavy armor, even tanks, to kill troops but leaves surrounding structures relatively unharmed.

"Informed Americans" are found to be evenly divided over the issue of equipping our armed forces and allies with the neutron bomb. There is a general ambivalence among the public toward this new weapon: while many people feel that its presence in our arsenal will help deter possible Russian aggression by countering Soviet superiority in manpower and thereby promote peace, there is also deep concern about the actual use of any nuclear weapons and the accompanying potential of nuclear war.

An analysis of the views held by the "informed" group indicates that women strongly oppose equipping American and allied forces with this new weapon. Other sharp differences in opinion are found by age and political affiliation. Young adults (eighteen to twenty-nine) oppose the neutron bomb in greater numbers than do older adults, and Democrats are more opposed than Republicans.

On April 7, President Jimmy Carter postponed plans to proceed with the neutron bomb weapon system. In his announcement, Carter said that the ultimate decision on production of neutron weapons would be made later and "will be influenced by the degree to which the Soviet Union shows restraint in its conventional and nuclear arms programs and force deployments affecting the security of the United States and Western Europe."

JUNE 11
CONFIDENCE INDEX

Interviewing Date: 4/21–24/78
Survey #100-G

How much confidence do you, yourself, have in these American institutions? Would you say a great deal, quite a lot, some, very little, or none?

Big business?

A great deal, quite a lot 27%
Some............................... 38
Very little, none...................... 30
No opinion.......................... 5

The church or organized religion?

A great deal, quite a lot 60%
Some............................... 24
Very little, none...................... 14
No opinion.......................... 2

Congress?

A great deal, quite a lot 18%
Some............................... 40
Very little, none...................... 37
No opinion.......................... 5

Labor unions?

A great deal, quite a lot 20%
Some............................... 31
Very little, none...................... 43
No opinion.......................... 6

The military?

A great deal, quite a lot 48%
Some............................... 30
Very little, none...................... 17
No opinion.......................... 5

The public schools?

A great deal, quite a lot 45%
Some............................... 30
Very little, none...................... 22
No opinion.......................... 3

The Supreme Court?

A great deal, quite a lot 39%
Some. 32
Very little, none. 21
No opinion. 8

Television?

A great deal, quite a lot 21%
Some. 37
Very little, none. 40
No opinion. 2

Banks and banking?

A great deal, quite a lot 55%
Some. 12
Very little, none. 31
No opinion. 2

Note: One of the surprises from recent testing of public confidence in key American institutions is a very high rating given to banks and banking and a fairly low rating given to "big business."

Asked to indicate the degree of confidence they have in nine key institutions, a national sample of adults rate the church or organized religion highest, followed by banks and banking, the military, and the public schools.

Six in ten persons (60%) express a "great deal" or "quite a lot" of confidence in the church or organized religion. Earlier tests of public confidence in key institutions have also shown the church or organized religion ranking at the top, attesting to the traditionally prominent role organized religion has played in American life.

Although many observers feel that the Bert Lance affair may have tarnished the image of bankers in America, banks and banking nevertheless are a close second in the rankings, with a confidence rating of 55%.

Evidence of our historical pride in the military can also be found in the survey. Notwithstanding discouragement over Vietnam, a total of 48% express a "great deal" or "quite a lot" of confidence in the military.

JUNE 15
PARANORMAL PHENOMENA

Interviewing Date: 2/24–27/78
Survey #994-K

Which of the following do you believe in? [Respondent was handed a card.]

Ghosts?

	Yes
National.	11%

By Sex

Male.	11%
Female.	10

By Age

18–24 years.	13%
25–29 years.	19
30–49 years.	13
50 years and over	5

The Loch Ness Monster?

	Yes
National.	13%

By Sex

Male.	13%
Female.	13

By Age

18–24 years.	21%
25–29 years.	21
30–49 years.	13
50 years and over	7

Sasquatch (Bigfoot)?

	Yes
National.	13%

By Sex

Male.	13%
Female.	13

By Age

18–24 years	18%
25–29 years	24
30–49 years	13
50 years and over	7

By Age

18–24 years	50%
25–29 years	50
30–49 years	29
50 years and over	17

ESP?

	Yes
National	51%

By Sex

Male	46%
Female	56

By Age

18–24 years	62%
25–29 years	63
30–49 years	54
50 years and over	40

Witches?

	Yes
National	10%

By Sex

Male	11%
Female	9

By Age

18–24 years	14%
25–29 years	11
30–49 years	12
50 years and over	5

Déjà-vu?

	Yes
National	30%

By Sex

Male	29%
Female	31

Precognition?

	Yes
National	37%

By Sex

Male	34%
Female	40

By Age

18–24 years	48%
25–29 years	54
30–49 years	36
50 years and over	28

Astrology?

	Yes
National	29%

By Sex

Male	27%
Female	31

By Age

18–24 years	39%
25–29 years	29
30–49 years	29
50 years and over	24

Angels?

	Yes
National	54%

By Sex

Male	51%
Female	56

18–24 years...........................50%
25–29 years...........................49
30–49 years...........................55
50 years and over 55

Devils?

| | Yes |
National...........................39%

By Sex

Male...............................38%
Female.............................40

By Age

18–24 years...........................41%
25–29 years...........................41
30–49 years...........................39
50 years and over 37

Life after death?

| | Yes |
National...........................62%

By Sex

Male...............................58%
Female.............................66

By Age

18–24 years...........................59%
25–29 years...........................60
30–49 years...........................62
50 years and over 65

Clairvoyance?

| | Yes |
National...........................24%

By Sex

Male...............................22%
Female.............................25

By Age

18–24 years...........................32%
25–29 years...........................31
30–49 years...........................25
50 years and over 16

Note: A surprisingly large number of Americans—particularly the younger and better educated—believe in paranormal phenomena such as the occult and supernatural beings.

This conclusion is based on a recent survey of the nation's adults who were asked to indicate whether they believed in a wide variety of phenomena, ranging from such everyday topics as astrology to such esoterica as déjà vu, the feeling that you have been someplace or done something you haven't.

Here are the main findings:

A majority of 54% believe in angels. The percentage increases to 68% among persons surveyed who say their religious beliefs are very important in their lives.

About half of those interviewed (51%) believe in ESP (extrasensory perception). Two-thirds of persons with college backgrounds (64%) do so.

About four in ten people (39%) believe in devils. This belief is held by 50% of those who say their religious convictions are very important in their lives.

Precognition (the feeling that something is going to happen that hasn't actually happened) and déjà vu (the feeling you have been someplace you haven't been before, or have done something you haven't done before) are common beliefs.

Twenty-nine percent of Americans say they believe in astrology and think their lives are governed by the position of the stars. Attesting to the popularity of astrology in the United States today is the fact that astrology columns are carried by 1,200 of the nation's 1,750 daily newspapers. Interestingly, those who say their religious beliefs are "very important" in their lives are as likely to believe in astrology as those who say their religious beliefs are "fairly" or "not at all" important.

About one person in eight (13%)—and one person in four in the West—believes in Sasquatch, or Bigfoot, a purported 8-foot, 900-pound humanoid living in the Pacific Northwest.

A like proportion believe in the Loch Ness Monster, a creature that supposedly lives in a twenty-four-mile-long, one-mile-wide stretch of water in Scotland called Loch Ness. Although there have been an estimated 2,000 reported sightings of "Nessie," little agreement is found on what the creature looks like.

One American in nine (11%) believes in ghosts. As many as 20% of the British, however, say they believe in ghosts. And 7% report they have actually seen a ghost!

One American in ten (10%) believes in witches, with younger adults far more likely to do so than older persons.

JUNE 18
QUEBEC INDEPENDENCE

Interviewing Date: 5/19–22/78
Survey #103-G

Have you heard or read about the possibility of Quebec Province separating from the rest of Canada and becoming an independent country?

	Yes
National	52%

By Sex
Male	60%
Female	44

By Education
College	74%
High school	45
Grade school	33

By Region
East	53%
Midwest	56

South	42
West	59

By Age
18–29 years	44%
30–49 years	50
50 years and over	58

Asked of those who responded in the affirmative: Would you favor or oppose having Quebec separate from the rest of Canada and become an independent country?

Favor	12%
Oppose	51
No opinion	37

By Sex
Male
Favor	11%
Oppose	56
No opinion	33

Female
Favor	12%
Oppose	45
No opinion	43

By Education
College
Favor	14%
Oppose	59
No opinion	27

High School
Favor	10%
Oppose	46
No opinion	44

Grade School
Favor	10%
Oppose	43
No opinion	47

By Region

East

Favor 14%
Oppose 51
No opinion 35

Midwest

Favor 12%
Oppose 52
No opinion 36

South

Favor 9%
Oppose 47
No opinion 44

West

Favor 10%
Oppose 53
No opinion 37

By Age

18–29 Years

Favor 23%
Oppose 39
No opinion 38

30–49 Years

Favor 9%
Oppose 55
No opinion 36

50 Years and Over

Favor 7%
Oppose 55
No opinion 38

Note: There is a possibility that Canada may soon become two nations.

The issue facing Canada is whether the predominantly French-speaking province of Quebec should become independent. Canadian Prime Minister Pierre Trudeau opposes independence for Quebec, while provincial Premier Rene Levesque leads the separatist movement. In fact, Levesque has promised to hold a province-wide referendum on the issue some time next year.

Despite the potential upheaval just north of our border, only about half of Americans, 52%, have even heard or read about the possibility that Quebec province might separate from the rest of Canada and become an independent nation.

Of those who have heard or read about the issue and voice an opinion on it, a four-to-one majority are against an independent Quebec.

Canadian Outlook

Canadians are also against the Quebec separatist movement. The latest Canadian Gallup Poll reading on the issue (conducted in April) shows that of the total Candian public, just 15% back an independent Quebec, while 71% are opposed. Even in Quebec itself, opinion is opposed to becoming an independent nation by a 60%–20% margin. Current nationwide and province figures are substantially the same as those recorded at the outset of the year. Furthermore, Canadians are relatively unconcerned about the separatist issue. Only 10% cite it as the most important problem facing Canada (well behind the 46% who name inflation/high prices and the 38% who say unemployment). Only 26% think it's likely Quebec will eventually split from the rest of the country; 64% think this possibility is unlikely.

JUNE 22
SOCIAL VALUES

Interviewing Dates: 4/21–24/78
Survey #100-G

Here are some social changes which might occur in coming years. [Respondents were handed a card with eight items listed.] Would you welcome these or not welcome them?

More emphasis on self-expression?

Welcome 75%
Not welcome 15
Don't know 10

By Education
College

Welcome 81%
Not welcome 14
Don't know 8

High School

Welcome 76%
Not welcome 16
Don't know 8

Grade School

Welcome 59%
Not welcome 14
Don't know 27

By Age
18–29 Years

Welcome 84%
Not welcome 12
Don't know 4

30–49 Years

Welcome 79%
Not welcome 14
Don't know 7

50 Years and Over

Welcome 65%
Not welcome 18
Don't know 17

Less emphasis on money?

Welcome 70%
Not welcome 21
Don't know 9

By Education
College

Welcome 77%
Not welcome 18
Don't know 5

High School

Welcome 71%
Not welcome 21
Don't know 8

Grade School

Welcome 55%
Not welcome 24
Don't know 21

By Age
18–29 Years

Welcome 72%
Not welcome 24
Don't know 4

30–49 Years

Welcome 77%
Not welcome 17
Don't know 6

50 Years and Over

Welcome 62%
Not welcome 23
Don't know 15

More acceptance of sexual freedom?

Welcome 29%
Not welcome 62
Don't know 9

By Education
College

Welcome 40%
Not welcome 54
Don't know 6

High School

Welcome	28%
Not welcome	63
Don't know	9

Grade School

Welcome	14%
Not welcome	71
Don't know	15

By Age
18–29 Years

Welcome	54%
Not welcome	37
Don't know	9

30–49 Years

Welcome	28%
Not welcome	64
Don't know	8

50 Years and Over

Welcome	11%
Not welcome	79
Don't know	10

More emphasis on technological improvements?

Welcome	75%
Not welcome	12
Don't know	13

By Education
College

Welcome	78%
Not welcome	15
Don't know	7

High School

Welcome	78%
Not welcome	11
Don't know	11

Grade School

Welcome	59%
Not welcome	13
Don't know	28

By Age
18–29 Years

Welcome	76%
Not welcome	14
Don't know	10

30–49 Years

Welcome	80%
Not welcome	11
Don't know	9

50 Years and Over

Welcome	70%
Not welcome	13
Don't know	17

More respect for authority?

Welcome	89%
Not welcome	6
Don't know	5

By Education
College

Welcome	84%
Not welcome	10
Don't know	6

High School

Welcome	92%
Not welcome	4
Don't know	4

Grade School

Welcome	90%
Not welcome	5
Don't know	5

18–29 Years

Welcome 83%
Not welcome 11
Don't know 6

30–49 Years

Welcome 92%
Not welcome 4
Don't know 4

50 Years and Over

Welcome 90%
Not welcome 5
Don't know 5

More emphasis on traditional family ties?

Welcome 91%
Not welcome 5
Don't know 4

By Education
College

Welcome 92%
Not welcome 5
Don't know 3

High School

Welcome 90%
Not welcome 6
Don't know 4

Grade School

Welcome 90%
Not welcome 3
50 years and over 7

By Age
18–29 Years

Welcome 82%
Not welcome 12
Don't know 6

30–49 Years

Welcome 93%
Not welcome 3
Don't know 4

50 Years and Over

Welcome 95%
Not welcome 2
Don't know 3

Less emphasis on working hard?

Welcome 25%
Not welcome 69
Don't know 6

By Education
College

Welcome 20%
Not welcome 77
Don't know 3

High School

Welcome 27%
Not welcome 66
Don't know 7

Grade School

Welcome 26%
Not welcome 66
Don't know 8

By Age
18–29 Years

Welcome 35%
Not welcome 59
Don't know 6

30–49 Years

Welcome 20%
Not welcome 74
Don't know 6

50 Years and Over

Welcome 21%
Not welcome 74
Don't know 5

More acceptance of marijuana usage?

Welcome 20%
Not welcome 74
Don't know 6

By Education
College

Welcome 26%
Not welcome 65
Don't know 9

High School

Welcome 19%
Not welcome 75
Don't know 6

Grade School

Welcome 9%
Not welcome 87
Don't know 4

By Age
18–29 Years

Welcome 43%
Not welcome 47
Don't know 10

30–49 Years

Welcome 16%
Not welcome 79
Don't know 5

50 Years and Over

Welcome 6%
Not welcome 90
Don't know 4

How many voluntary organizations in your community, other than a church or religious group, do you belong to—such as social clubs, civic groups, fraternal organizations, or political groups? Would you say none, one, two, three, or four or more?

One 17%
Two 8
Three 4
Four or more 4
None 67

Note: Values that the public holds in high esteem today may well shape the decade of the 1980s.

To determine what social values may dominate the coming decade, the Gallup Poll asked the American people to express their views on eight social changes—to indicate which they would welcome and which they would not.

The results show widespread acceptance of some so-called traditional values. Thus, while the sixties and seventies have been labeled decades of revolt and disillusionment, the eighties may turn out to be a period of "return to normalcy."

The sharpest differences between younger and older Americans are found in regard to acceptance of marijuana usage and sexual freedom. Young people are a great deal more likely than are their elders to say they would welcome more acceptance of both marijuana and sexual freedom.

JUNE 25
CONGRESSIONAL ELECTIONS

Interviewing Date: 5/5–8, 19–22/78
Survey #102-G, 103-G

Asked of registered voters: If the elections for Congress were being held today, which party would you like to see win in this congressional district, the Democratic party or the Republican party? Those who were undecided were asked: As of today, do you lean more to the Democratic party or to the Republican party?

Democratic 53%
Republican........................... 35
Other 5
Undecided........................... 7

South Only

Democratic 60%
Republican........................... 24
Other 5
Undecided........................... 11

Interviewing Date: 6/2–5/78
Survey #104-G

Do you, yourself, plan to vote in the elections this November, or not?

Will vote 79%
Will not 14
Don't know 7

By Age
18–24 Years

Will vote 72%
Will not 16
Don't know 12

25–29 Years

Will vote 71%
Will not 17
Don't know 12

30–49 Years

Will vote 81%
Will not 15
Don't know 4

50 Years and Over

Will vote 82%
Will not 10
Don't know 8

Asked of those who said that they will vote in November: How certain are you that you will vote—absolutely certain, fairly certain, or not certain?

Absolutely certain 52%
Fairly certain........................ 21
Not certain........................... 2
Don't know 25

By Age
18–24 Years

Absolutely certain 44%
Fairly certain........................ 23
Not certain........................... 2
Don't know 31

25–29 Years

Absolutely certain 43%
Fairly certain........................ 23
Not certain........................... 2
Don't know 32

30–49 Years

Absolutely certain 57%
Fairly certain........................ 21
Not certain........................... 1
Don't know 21

50 Years and Over

Absolutely certain 58%
Fairly certain........................ 19
Not certain........................... 2
Don't know 21

Asked of the entire sample: Here is a picture of a ladder. [Repondent was handed a card.] Suppose we say the top of the ladder, marked ten, represents a person who definitely will vote in the election this November, and the bottom of the ladder, marked zero, represents a person who definitely will not vote in the election. How far up or down the ladder would you place yourself?

Ten................................. 48%
Nine 9
Eight............................... 9
Seven 5
Six................................. 3

Five	4
Four	3
Three	1
Two	1
One	2
Zero	8
Don't know	7

Note: According to historical pattern, the Republican party should win a large number of seats in the congressional elections this November.

However, the latest Gallup Poll shows that if elections for the House of Representatives were being held now, the political composition of the House would remain pretty much as it is today. The Democrats would win 59% of the vote while Republican candidates would capture 41%, assuming a turnout similar to those of 1974 and 1976. These figures show, if anything, a slight upturn in Democratic fortunes from the 1976 election when Democrats won 57% of the vote and the Republicans 43%.

The current survey also indicates the GOP will not make much headway in turning the South into a two-party region at the congressional level. If the current figures hold, Democrats in the South will win 69% of the vote to 31% for the Republicans. Outside the South the vote is much closer—57% to 43%—but still is solidly Democratic.

These figures point toward a solid Democratic majority for President Jimmy Carter to work with during the second half of his administration. They are no doubt disheartening to GOP strategists, particularly since they contradict three major historical indicators that suggest Republican candidates should win many seats now held by Democrats.

First, the party controlling the White House almost always loses seats in the off-year elections. Only twice during this century—in 1902 and 1934—has the party in power managed to gain seats. Furthermore, the average loss since 1900 has been nearly thirty-five seats.

Second, the personal popularity of President Carter would normally indicate a significant shift in seats. Analysis of Gallup Poll data over the last forty years shows that when the popularity of the president drops below the 55% level, his party generally suffers more than a normal loss in House seats. Carter's rating, in the 40% to 45% approval range since early April, is well below this level.

Third, the electorate is currently far more concerned with domestic problems—namely inflation and unemployment—than with foreign affairs. This usually leads to disenchantment by the public with the party in power. However, voters currently perceive the Democrats as being better able to cope with these problems than the Republicans.

JUNE 29
CASINO GAMBLING

Interviewing Date: 6/2–5/78
Survey #104-G

As you may know, some states have legalized casino gambling. That is, there are certain places where people can go and play slot machines and such games as blackjack, craps, roulette, and the like. Would you favor or oppose having legalized casino gambling in this state?

Favor	39%
Oppose	52
Is already legal	2
Don't know	7

By Education
College

Favor	42%
Oppose	52
Is already legal	2
Don't know	4

High School

Favor	42%
Oppose	48
Is already legal	2
Don't know	8

Grade School

Favor 25%
Oppose 63
Is already legal 1
Don't know 11

By Age
18–29 Years

Favor 40%
Oppose 48
Is already legal 2
Don't know 10

30–49 Years

Favor 47%
Oppose 45
Is already legal 2
Don't know 6

50 Years and Over

Favor 31%
Oppose 60
Is already legal 2
Don't know 7

By Religion
Protestants

Favor 31%
Oppose 60
Is already legal 2
Don't know 7

Catholics

Favor 49%
Oppose 40
Is already legal 2
Don't know 9

If casino gambling were legal in this state, do you think the standard of living would improve, or not?

Would 22%
Would not 50
Don't know 28

Do you think there would be an increase in the number of tourists in this state, or not?

Yes 78%
No 14
Don't know 8

Do you think there would be an increase in the overall crime rate, or not?

Yes 58%
No 32
Don't know 10

Do you think that there would be more incidences of family break-ups and/or divorce, or not?

Yes 53%
No 36
Don't know 11

Do you think that organized crime would get involved in the operation of the casinos, or not?

Would 77%
Would not 13
Don't know 10

Are you, yourself, interested in going to Las Vegas, Nevada, to gamble in a casino, or not?

Interested 23%
Not interested 76
Unsure 1

What about Atlantic City, New Jersey? Are you interested in going to Atlantic City to gamble in a casino, or not?

Interested 14%
Not interested 84
Unsure 2

Have you ever been to a gambling casino?

Yes 36%
No 64

By Education
College

Yes 49%
No....................................... 51

High School

Yes 35%
No....................................... 65

Grade School

Yes 18%
No....................................... 82

By Age
18–29 Years

Yes 27%
No....................................... 73

30–49 Years

Yes 42%
No....................................... 58

50 Years and Over

Yes 37%
No....................................... 63

Note: Legalized casino gambling, similar to that now in full swing in Atlantic City, New Jersey, would not necessarily be welcome in other states.

Regionally, southerners are most opposed to casinos. In the South, 61% say they would oppose the opening of casinos in their state. The comparable figure drops to 53% in the Midwest, 50% in the West, and 46% in the East.

JULY 2, 3
LIQUOR

Interviewing Date: 4/21–24/78
Survey #100-G

Has liquor ever been a cause of trouble in your family?

	Yes
National	22%

By Sex

Male	21%
Female	24

By Race

Whites	23%
Nonwhites	16

By Education

College	21%
High school	24
Grade school	19

By Region

East	17%
Midwest	23
South	20
West	32

By Age

18–24 years	26%
25–29 years	22
30–49 years	24
50 years and over	19

By Marital Status

Married	21%
Single	26
Separated	34
Divorced	31

If you or someone else in your family had a drinking problem, where or to whom would you turn for help?

Alcoholics Anonymous	42%
God/the Lord/prayer/the Bible	9
Priest, minister, rabbi	8
The church and its trained personnel	8
Doctor	7
Family member	6
Counseling, local treatment center	5

Hospital 3
Friend 3
Other responses 2
No one 4
Don't know, no answer 16
                                                    ―――――
                                                    113%*

*Total adds to more than 100% due to multiple responses.

Do you have occasion to use alcoholic beverages such as liquor or wine, or are you a total abstainer?

	Those Who Drink
National	70%

By Sex

Male 75%
Female 64

By Race

Whites 71%
Nonwhites 62

By Education

College 82%
High school 71
Grade school 44

By Region

East 84%
Midwest 68
South 54
West 75

By Age

18–24 years 77%
25–29 years 83
30–49 years 75
50 years and over 59

By Marital Status

Married 70%
Single 78

Separated 61
Divorced 83

Asked of those who drink alcoholic beverages: What would you say are the main reasons you drink?

Social 54%
Relaxation 18
Enjoy it 16
Special occasion 10
Like taste 8
Adds to a meal 6
Thirst quencher 3
Enjoy feeling 2
Medicinal 2
Stimulant 2
Other 1
Don't know 5
                                                    ―――――
                                                    127%*

*Total adds to more than 100% due to multiple responses.

Asked of those who are abstainers: What would you say are the main reasons you do not drink?

Don't like it 36%
Unhealthful 16
No desire 13
Against religious beliefs 9
Afraid of effect 7
Too costly 5
Causes trouble 4
Wasn't raised to drink 3
Bad experience 7
Health reasons 6
Others 2
Do not approve 10
Don't know 5
                                                    ―――――
                                                    123%*

*Total adds to more than 100% due to multiple responses.

Asked of those who are abstainers: Do you approve or disapprove of other people drinking?

Approve............................17%
Disapprove 47
No opinion..........................36

Asked of those who drink alcoholic beverages: Do you have any specific rules or guidelines regarding your own use of alcoholic beverages?

Moderation 24%
One or two drink limit 7
Only on special occasions 4
Know when to stop.................... 3
Don't get drunk....................... 4
Never during day 2
No drinking when driving.............. 2
Only beer and wine................... 1
Never drink alone.................... 3
No rules 1
Other 47
Don't know 2

Asked of those who drink alcoholic beverages: Do you sometimes drink more than you think you should?

                                    Yes
National............................23%

Asked of those who drink alcoholic beverages: Do you feel that your pattern of alcohol use would be a good model for your children to follow, or not?

Yes................................75%
No.................................10
No opinion..........................15

Asked of parents: Do you have any guidelines regarding the use of alcoholic beverages by your children?

Not allowed to drink, no liquor allowed
  in home..........................21%
Moderation 10
Not allowed to drink until of age......... 9
May drink only in home................ 3
No drinking and driving 2

Other............................... *
None; no rules.......................51
No opinion; no answer................. 4

*Less than 1%.

Note: This recent Gallup survey offers further evidence that alcohol abuse has become one of the nation's most serious problems.

In the Gallup study, the proportion of Americans who say that liquor has been a cause of trouble in their families has doubled in just four years.

Currently, one person in four (24%) says an alcohol-related problem has adversely affected his or her family life. The figure in 1974 was 12%. The uptrend since 1974 is recorded among most major socioeconomic groups and in all regions of the nation. The proportion saying liquor has been a cause of trouble is as high as one-third among persons in the study who are separated or divorced.

While most studies have focused on the alcoholic, the current study represents an effort to probe the behavior and attitudes of the "problem drinker." In the current study each survey respondent was asked a series of twenty questions adapted from a list developed by the National Council on Alcoholism, Los Angeles County, Inc.

1. Do you drink alone?
2. Do you drink to escape from worries or troubles?
3. Have you ever had a complete loss of memory, say of the previous night's events, because of drinking?
4. Do you drink to build up your self-confidence?
5. Do you drink because you are shy with other people?
6. Do you feel guilty or terribly sorry after drinking?
7. Do people say that maybe you drink too much?
8. Have you ever been to a hospital or been arrested due to drinking?
9. Do you feel a sense of power when you drink?

10. Have you started hanging out with a different crowd because of your drinking?
11. Does drinking cause you to have trouble sleeping?
12. Is drinking making your home life unhappy?
13. Do you crave a drink in the morning or at a definite time each day?
14. Do you lose time from work or school due to drinking?
15. Is drinking affecting your reputation or jeopardizing your job?
16. Do you neglect your family when you drink?
17. Do you get into financial troubles because of drinking?
18. Do you think you have a problem with liquor?
19. Have you lost friends because of your drinking?
20. Has your ambition or efficiency decreased since drinking?

The results of the current study show that a total of 25% of the total sample say "yes" to at least one or more of the twenty questions, with 14% saying "yes" to one question and the remaining 11% saying "yes" to two or more questions. Among drinkers, a total of 35% say "yes" to at least one of the twenty questions, 20% say "yes" to one question, and the remaining 15% say "yes" to two or more questions.

The current study was undertaken by the Gallup Poll in close cooperation with the Reverend David C. Hancock of Prevention of Alcohol Problems, Inc., Minneapolis, Minnesota, and the Reverend David A. Works of the North Conway Institute, Boston, Massachusetts.

There also appears to be a growing awareness and response to the problem of teenage drinking. A survey conducted for the Charles F. Kettering Foundation shows an overwhelming 84% favoring a required course on the effects of drugs and alcohol. Actually, such courses are now being given in many schools.

A similar survey showed that more than three of every four United States adults approve of the idea of offering courses at school for parents as a regular part of the public-school educational process. And their top choice would be a course dealing with drugs, smoking, and use of alcohol.

JULY 9
GOVERNMENT SPENDING

Interviewing Date: 6/16–19/78
Survey #105-G

Would you favor or oppose a constitutional amendment that would require Congress to balance the federal budget each year—that is, keep taxes and expenditures in balance?

Favor 81%
Oppose 11
No opinion 8

By Politics
Republicans

Favor 79%
Oppose 13
No opinion 8

Democrats

Favor 83%
Oppose 10
No opinion 7

Independents

Favor 82%
Oppose 12
No opinion 6

Do you think the federal government is spending too much money, too little, or about the right amount?

Too much 76%
Too little 5
About right 10
No opinion 9

By Politics

Republicans

Too much.	81%
Too little.	2
About right.	7
No opinion.	10

Democrats

Too much.	70%
Too little.	8
About right.	12
No opinion.	10

Independents

Too much.	82%
Too little.	4
About right.	7
No opinion.	7

Do you think your state government is spending too much money, too little, or about the right amount?

Too much.	52%
Too little.	13
About right.	22
No opinion.	13

By Politics

Republicans

Too much.	54%
Too little.	8
About right.	23
No opinion.	15

Democrats

Too much.	48%
Too little.	17
About right.	24
No opinion.	11

Independents

Too much.	57%
Too little.	10

About right.	20
No opinion.	13

Do you think your local government is spending too much money, too little, or about the right amount?

Too much.	37%
Too little.	15
About right.	34
No opinion.	14

By Politics

Republicans

Too much.	40%
Too little.	11
About right.	33
No opinion.	16

Democrats

Too much.	33%
Too little.	17
About right.	36
No opinion.	14

Independents

Too much.	42%
Too little.	15
About right.	31
No opinion.	12

Which political party—the Republican party or the Democratic party—can do a better job of reducing federal spending?

Republican	27%
Democratic	28
No difference.	30
No opinion.	15

Note: By a seven-to-one margin—81%–11%—the American public favors amending the Constitution to require balancing the federal budget each year.

These figures, while one-sided, actually represent a marginal increase in the percentage saying they would favor such an amendment. In March 1976, when the then presidential candidate Jimmy Carter was making a balanced budget one of his campaign promises, Americans backed the budget-balancing amendment by a 78%–13% margin.

Of particular interest is the political unanimity found on the issue. Equal proportions of Republicans, Democrats, and independents agree that the Constitution should be amended to require a balanced federal budget.

Central to the question of a balanced budget is the matter of federal spending. The Carter administration's budget for the fiscal year 1978 tops the $450 billion mark, with a projected deficit of almost $60 billion.

JULY 13
PRESIDENTIAL TRIAL HEATS

Interviewing Date: 6/16–19/78
Survey #105-G

Asked of Republicans: Suppose the choice for president in the Republican convention in 1980 narrows down to Gerald Ford and Ronald Reagan. Which one would you prefer to have the Republican convention select?

Ford 48%
Reagan 43
Undecided 9

Asked of Democrats: Suppose the choice for president in the Democratic convention in 1980 narrows down to Jimmy Carter and Edward Kennedy. Which one would you prefer to have the Democratic convention select?

Kennedy 51%
Carter 31
Undecided 14

Southern Democrats Only

Kennedy 46%
Carter 35
Undecided 19

Note: Amid reports that both Gerald Ford and Ronald Reagan are seeking the GOP nomination in 1980, Republicans across the nation are evenly divided in their preferences.

The latest results among Republicans represent a decline in support for former President Ford since an April survey. At that time, he enjoyed a 54%–42% edge over Reagan.

Throughout their contest for the nomination in 1976, Reagan never led Ford in these man-to-man preferential showdowns. In several instances, though, the vote among Republicans was very close, and these latest results are almost identical to those recorded in December 1975, before the GOP primaries began. At that time Ford and Reagan were tied, with each man receiving 45% of the vote.

On the other side of the political fence, Massachusetts Senator Edward Kennedy continues to hold a commanding lead over President Jimmy Carter among Democrats if their convention in 1980 comes down to a choice between the two. In fact, Kennedy's current 54%–32% margin represents a widening of the distance between the two men. In April, Kennedy led the president in voter approval by a 52%–42% margin.

The dimensions of Kennedy's lead over Carter among Democrats is not the result of Kennedy gaining ground but of Carter losing it. This development has occurred not only nationwide but also in Carter's home region, the South.

For example, whereas in April southern Democrats split their vote 46% for Kennedy and 44% for Carter, now Kennedy holds a 46%–35% lead. Outside the South, where Kennedy is even more popular, his 56%–38% margin in April has increased to 58%–31% in the current survey.

That a sitting president eligible for reelection should trail a potential challenger from his own party in these two-men showdowns of strength is not without precedent. Throughout 1967 and before he announced he would not be a candidate in 1968, President Lyndon Johnson lagged behind Senator Robert F. Kennedy in similar surveys.

JULY 16
EQUAL RIGHTS AMENDMENT

Interviewing Date: 6/4–12/78
Special Telephone Survey

Have you heard or read about the Equal Rights Amendment to the United States Constitution, which would give women equal rights and equal responsibilities?

	Yes
National	90%

Asked of those who were aware of the amendment: Do you favor or oppose this amendment?

Favor	58%
Oppose	31
No opinion	11

By Sex
Male

Favor	62%
Oppose	29
No opinion	9

Female

Favor	55%
Oppose	33
No opinion	12

Also asked of those who were aware of the amendment: As you may know, Congress is discussing extending the time limit for states to ratify the ERA for another seven years. Would you favor or oppose such a proposal?

Favor	43%
Oppose	40
No opinion	17

By Sex
Male

Favor	42%
Oppose	45
No opinion	13

Female

Favor	43%
Oppose	35
No opinion	22

Note: The American public supports ratification of the Equal Rights Amendment but is divided over the question of extending the time limit for passage.

A total of thirty-eight states must ratify the amendment—which forbids discrimination on the basis of sex—before it becomes part of the federal Constitution, and so far thirty-five states have done so. But lately, lobbying efforts by anti-ERA groups have helped defeat the amendment in several state legislatures.

Because three more states must ratify the amendment before March 22, 1979, for constitutional adoption, its supporters have turned their efforts not only to passage in those states that have not yet done so but also to extending the seven-year time limit for ratification.

JULY 20
PERSONAL PROBLEMS

Interviewing Date: 6/16–19/78
Survey #105-G

What do you consider to be the biggest problem in your own personal life?

Making ends meet	27%
Health problems	13
Job/career-related problems, unemployment	9

Maintaining family harmony............ 6
Procrastination/lack of motivation....... 6
Lack of confidence 3
Raising children 3
Retirement/old age.................... 2
Love life............................ 2
Other responses 9
None............................... 19
No opinion; no answer................ 4
                                    _____
                                    103%*

*Total adds to more than 100% due to multiple responses.

JULY 23
CONGRESSIONAL ELECTIONS

Interviewing Date: 6/16–19/78
Survey #105-G

> *If the elections for Congress were being held today, which party would you like to see win in this congressional district, the Democratic party or the Republican party? Those who were undecided were asked: As of today, do you lean more to the Democratic party or to the Republican party?*

Democratic.......................... 54%
Republican.......................... 32
Other 5
Undecided.......................... 9

Interviewing Date: 3/3–6/78
Survey #995-K

> *Which political party do you think would be more likely to keep the United States out of World War III—the Republican party or the Democratic party?*

Democratic.......................... 31%
Republican.......................... 25
No difference........................ 27
No opinion.......................... 17

> *Looking ahead for the next few years, which political party—the Republican or the Democratic—do you think will do the better job of keeping the country prosperous?*

Democratic.......................... 41%
Republican.......................... 23
No difference........................ 23
No opinion.......................... 13

Note: One of the principal reasons for the GOP's relatively poor showing to date in the race for Congress is its failure to gain the advantage on key voter issues, including an issue on which Republicans have traditionally held an edge over their Democratic rivals—that of reducing federal spending.

The latest Gallup Poll report on the race for Congress shows that if elections for the House of Representatives were being held now, the political composition of the House would remain pretty much as it is today—more than two-to-one Democratic.

The proportion of voters who currently credit the Republican party as better able to reduce federal spending (26%) is matched by the proportion who say the Democrats would perform better in this respect (28%). The balance either say they see no difference in the ability of the two parties to deal with this problem (31%) or do not express an opinion (15%).

Transcending the immediate concern with federal spending are the timeless issues of peace and prosperity. And on this score there is more bad news for the GOP. A Gallup Poll taken earlier this year showed the Democratic party holding a 31% to 25% lead as the party voters see as better able to keep the nation out of World War III; Democrats have an even wider 41% to 23% lead as the "party of prosperity."

JULY 27
MOST IMPORTANT PROBLEM

Interviewing Date: 5/19–22/78
Survey #103-G

> *What do you think is the most important problem facing this country today?*

High cost of living/inflation. 60%
Unemployment 14
International problems/foreign policy 10
Energy situation 4
Crime and lawlessness 3
Moral decline/lack of religion 3
Dissatisfaction with government. 3
Race relations 2
Drug abuse. 1
Others. 18
Can't say 3
                                                        ───────
                                                        121%*

*Total adds to more than 100% due to multiple responses.

Which political party do you think could do a better job of handling the problem you have just mentioned—the Republican party or the Democratic party?

Democratic 33%
Republican. 19
No difference. 37
No opinion. 11

Note: As many as six in ten Americans now name the high cost of living as the nation's top problem, with the proportion having grown steadily since last October when 35% cited this as the number one problem.

Nationwide, more than four times as many people name the high cost of living (60%) as name unemployment, the problem cited next frequently (by 14%). However, among nonwhites alone unemployment is named almost as often as rising prices. Nonwhites have been particularly hard hit by unemployment, with half of all young nonwhites in certain regions of the nation reported to be jobless.

The high cost of living far overshadows concern over the international scene, despite the growing tension between Russia and the West. In the current survey, only about one person in ten names an international or foreign-policy issue as the nation's top problem.

Relatively few—in fact, only 4%—cite energy problems as most important, continuing a downtrend since February when 23% named the energy situation.

JULY 30
PRESIDENT CARTER

Interviewing Date: 7/7–10/78
Survey #106-G

Do you approve or disapprove of the way Jimmy Carter is handling his job as president?

Approve. 40%
Disapprove 41
No opinion. 19

By Sex
Male

Approve. 42%
Disapprove 43
No opinion. 15

Female

Approve. 39%
Disapprove 40
No opinion. 21

By Race
Whites

Approve. 39%
Disapprove 44
No opinion. 17

Northern Whites

Approve. 40%
Disapprove 44
No opinion. 16

Southern Whites

Approve. 36%
Disapprove 44
No opinion. 20

Nonwhites

Approve.............................47%
Disapprove 26
No opinion..........................27

Northern Blacks

Approve.............................41%
Disapprove 34
No opinion..........................25

Southern Blacks

Approve.............................54%
Disapprove 17
No opinion..........................29

By Education
College

Approve.............................35%
Disapprove 51
No opinion..........................14

High School

Approve.............................40%
Disapprove 40
No opinion..........................20

Grade School

Approve.............................51%
Disapprove 26
No opinion..........................23

By Region
East

Approve.............................40%
Disapprove 42
No opinion..........................18

Midwest

Approve.............................38%
Disapprove 46
No opinion..........................16

South

Approve.............................40%
Disapprove 38
No opinion..........................22

Deep South

Approve.............................44%
Disapprove 32
No opinion..........................24

Rest of South

Approve.............................38%
Disapprove 40
No opinion..........................22

West

Approve.............................44%
Disapprove 39
No opinion..........................17

By Age
18–24 Years

Approve.............................46%
Disapprove 34
No opinion..........................20

25–29 Years

Approve.............................44%
Disapprove 43
No opinion..........................13

30–49 Years

Approve.............................39%
Disapprove 42
No opinion..........................19

50 Years and Over

Approve.............................37%
Disapprove 44
No opinion..........................19

By Politics
Republicans

Approve.............................20%
Disapprove 64
No opinion..........................16

Democrats

Approve.............................52%
Disapprove 28
No opinion..........................20

Southern Democrats

Approve............................52%
Disapprove 25
No opinion.........................23

Independents

Approve............................36%
Disapprove 48
No opinion.........................16

By Religion
Protestants

Approve............................40%
Disapprove 42
No opinion.........................18

Catholics

Approve............................44%
Disapprove 37
No opinion.........................19

Note: Despite the dramatic events of recent weeks on both the domestic and international fronts, President Jimmy Carter's popularity rating has remained remarkably stable in seven successive surveys taken since mid-April.

In the latest survey, as in the previous six, those who approve and those who disapprove of his handling of the presidency have been roughly in balance. The current results show 40% expressing approval and 41% saying they disapprove. The president's approval rating has varied no more than 2 percentage points between surveys during this three-month period.

Between last fall and spring of the current year, however, the president's popularity rating declined steadily. A special analysis and comparison of the latest four surveys with four surveys taken at the end of 1977 and beginning of 1978 shows the decline to come about equally among all major population groups.

The average popularity rating for the latest four surveys, nationwide, is 42%, while the comparable rating for the four earlier surveys was 56%.

The latest surveys show the president scoring best with nonwhites (particularly those in the South), adults under thirty, and—as might be expected—those who classify themselves as Democrats. His rating was lowest among Republicans, only 20% of whom currently approve of the way he is handling the presidency.

AUGUST 3
TREATMENT BY THE CARTER ADMINISTRATION

Interviewing Date: 7/7–10/78
Survey #105-G

Which one of these groups, if any, do you think is being unfairly treated by the Carter administration? [Respondents were handed a card listing twelve groups.]

Farmers.............................29%
Senior citizens.........................25
Small businessmen.....................24
People like yourself 21
Unemployed 20
Blacks...............................11
Women.............................. 9
Welfare recipients..................... 9
Union members....................... 5
Corporation executives 4
Jews 4
Catholics 2
None of these, don't know 21
_____
184%*

*Total adds to more than 100% due to multiple responses.

Note: Farmers, senior citizens, and small businessmen are most frequently named as groups not being fairly treated by the Carter administration. These three groups, as well as some of the nine others on a list handed to survey respondents, are named more often today than one year ago, in August 1977. Last August as many as 42% said none of these groups were unfairly treated. Today, the percentage is only half this, 21%.

Three in ten adults (29%) currently name farmers as a group not fairly treated by the administration; senior citizens are named by 25% (up 7% from last year), small businessmen by 24% (up 8%), and the unemployed by 20% (up 6%).

These findings help explain President Carter's decline in popularity since last August, when 66% expressed approval of his performance in office. The latest rating shows 40% approving, closely matching the approval scores recorded in six previous successive surveys taken since mid-April.

AUGUST 6
EXTRAMARITAL SEX

Interviewing Date: 4/14–17/78
Survey #999-K

What is your opinion about a married person having sexual relations with someone other than the marriage partner?

Always wrong	65%
Almost always wrong	16
Wrong only sometimes	11
Not wrong at all	4
No opinion	4

By Sex
Male

Always wrong	60%
Almost always wrong	16
Wrong only sometimes	13
Not wrong at all	5
No opinion	6

Female

Always wrong	69%
Almost always wrong	16
Wrong only sometimes	9
Not wrong at all	3
No opinion	3

By Education
College

Always wrong	53%
Almost always wrong	23
Wrong only sometimes	16
Not wrong at all	5
No opinion	3

High School

Always wrong	66%
Almost always wrong	15
Wrong only sometimes	10
Not wrong at all	4
No opinion	5

Grade School

Always wrong	80%
Almost always wrong	9
Wrong only sometimes	5
Not wrong at all	2
No opinion	4

By Age
18–29 Years

Always wrong	52%
Almost always wrong	20
Wrong only sometimes	16
Not wrong at all	6
No opinion	6

30–49 Years

Always wrong	61%
Almost always wrong	19
Wrong only sometimes	11
Not wrong at all	5
No opinion	4

50 Years and Over

Always wrong	77%
Almost always wrong	11
Wrong only sometimes	7
Not wrong at all	1
No opinion	4

By Religion
Protestants

Always wrong........................71%
Almost always wrong.................12
Wrong only sometimes 9
Not wrong at all..................... 4
No opinion........................... 4

Catholics

Always wrong........................64%
Almost always wrong.................20
Wrong only sometimes 9
Not wrong at all..................... 3
No opinion........................... 4

Churched

Always wrong........................74%
Almost always wrong.................13
Wrong only sometimes 7
Not wrong at all..................... 2
No opinion........................... 4

Unchurched*

Always wrong........................53%
Almost always wrong.................20
Wrong only sometimes 15
Not wrong at all..................... 6
No opinion........................... 6

Note: These findings offer further indication of a sexual revolution in American society and seem particularly surprising to some observers in view of the importance Americans profess to place on religion.

The results here do, however, show sharp differences in terms of respondents' church commitments. Among those who are "unchurched," 53% feel it is "always wrong" to have extramarital sex. Among the churched, the figure is 74%.

---

*The "unchurched" are defined as persons who have not attended church or synagogue in the last six months apart from weddings, funerals, or special holidays such as Christmas, Easter, or Yom Kippur, or who are not members of a church or synagogue.

Differences are not so marked on the basis of sex, although women are slightly more likely than men to say "always wrong."

These findings, revealing sharp differences on the basis of age and education, are consistent with other findings from similar surveys on social changes. Young adults and persons with a college background are far more likely to say they would welcome "more acceptance of sexual freedom" in the years ahead than are older adults and persons with less than a college education.

AUGUST 10
WAGE AND PRICE CONTROLS

Interviewing Date: 7/7–10/78
Survey #106-G

Would you favor or oppose having the government bring back wage and price controls?

Favor...............................53%
Oppose.............................34
No opinion..........................13

By Sex
Male

Favor...............................59%
Oppose.............................39
No opinion..........................11

Female

Favor...............................55%
Oppose.............................29
No opinion..........................16

By Education
College

Favor...............................46%
Oppose.............................46
No opinion.......................... 8

High School

Favor 54%
Oppose 33
No opinion 13

Grade School

Favor 63%
Oppose 13
No opinion 24

By Region
East

Favor 58%
Oppose 30
No opinion 12

Midwest

Favor 52%
Oppose 35
No opinion 13

South

Favor 50%
Oppose 31
No opinion 19

West

Favor 51%
Oppose 41
No opinion 8

By Income
$20,000 and Over

Favor 44%
Oppose 50
No opinion 6

$15,000–$19,999

Favor 51%
Oppose 38
No opinion 11

$10,000–$14,999

Favor 58%
Oppose 29
No opinion 13

$5,000–$9,999

Favor 60%
Oppose 25
No opinion 15

Under $5,000

Favor 58%
Oppose 17
No opinion 25

By Politics
Republicans

Favor 47%
Oppose 42
No opinion 11

Democrats

Favor 56%
Oppose 30
No opinion 14

Independents

Favor 52%
Oppose 35
No opinion 13

Labor Union Families Only

Favor 54%
Oppose 37
No opinion 9

Non-Labor Union Families Only

Favor 53%
Oppose 33
No opinion 14

Note: Even though consumer prices advanced at a rate of better than 10% during the first six months of 1978, it seems as though no one wants to take the radical step of controlling wages and prices—no one, that is, except the American people.

Freezing wages and prices is an idea that is long overdue as far as most Americans are concerned. Three consecutive Gallup surveys since April have shown a majority of the public favoring a return to controls, with support coming from a broad spectrum of people, including members of labor union families and residents of every geographical region.

Although most of the public may be convinced of the wisdom of returning to controls, this step is strongly opposed by the Carter administration and by business and labor leaders.

Last April, President Carter said that even if inflation were to continue to higher levels, mandatory wage and price controls would be counterproductive, and he could foresee no circumstances under which he would favor them.

Business and labor leaders have traditionally opposed controls. Labor leaders believe wage controls unfairly penalize union workers; business people want the ability to raise prices and fear that controls will cause shortages in some commodities.

History of Attitudes

Over a period of almost forty years, the American public has consistently supported wage and price controls during wars or periods of severe inflation.

Just over ten years ago, in 1966, opinion was evenly divided between those who favored and those who opposed wage-price curbs. But as inflationary pressures built during the latter half of the 60s, opinion began to shift in favor of controls.

In a survey conducted just a few weeks prior to President Richard Nixon's imposition of a wage-price freeze as part of his Phase One economic program, public support for controls had reached its highest point since the Korean War, with 50% in favor and 39% opposed. Just after Nixon froze wages and prices, a Gallup Poll showed Americans supported the move by

a margin of six to one. Furthermore, surveys conducted at regular intervals during the three phases of Nixon's economic program showed the public consistently favored stricter controls as opposed to less strict. And, since 1974, at least a plurality of the public has favored a return to controls.

AUGUST 13
DEMOCRATIC PRESIDENTIAL CANDIDATES

Interviewing Date: 7/7–10/78
Survey #106-G

Here is a list of people who have been mentioned as possible presidential candidates for the Democratic party in 1980. [Respondents were handed a card with nine names listed.] Which one would you like to see nominated as the Democratic candidate for president in 1980?

Choice of Democrats

Kennedy	44%
Carter	20
Brown	11
Mondale	5
McGovern	4
Jackson	4
Moynihan	1
Udall	1
Church	1
Undecided	9

Choice of Independents

Kennedy	25%
Carter	15
Brown	14
McGovern	7
Jackson	7
Mondale	6
Moynihan	5
Church	4
Udall	3
Undecided	14

Note: In an earlier survey (late March—early April), Kennedy and Carter were in closer contention, 36% to 29%, but the earlier survey results are not directly comparable because the list did not include the names of McGovern, Moynihan, and Church. The latest results, however, would certainly seem to indicate a decisive gain for Kennedy over Carter.

AUGUST 13
REPUBLICAN PRESIDENTIAL CANDIDATES

Interviewing Date: 7/7–10/78
Survey #106-G

Would you please look over this list and tell me which of these persons, if any, you have heard something about?

	Have Heard
Howard Baker	47%
George Bush	32
John Connally	61
Robert Dole	53
Gerald Ford	90
Ronald Reagan	83
Elliot Richardson	38
James Thompson	15
None of the above	4

Here is a list of people who have been mentioned as possible presidential candidates for the Republican party in 1980. [Respondents were handed a card with eight names.] Which one would you like to see nominated as the Republican candidate for president?

Choice of Republicans

Ford	37%
Reagan	31
Baker	9
Connally	5
Dole	4
Richardson	3
Thompson	2
Bush	*
Undecided	7

Choice of Independents

Reagan	31%
Ford	19
Baker	11
Richardson	7
Connally	7
Dole	4
Thompson	2
Bush	2
Undecided	17

*Less than 1%.

Note: Interviewing was conducted prior to the announcement by Representative Philip Crane of Illinois of his candidacy for the presidency.

AUGUST 14
PRESIDENTIAL TRIAL HEAT

Interviewing Date: 7/7–10/78
Survey #106-G

Asked of registered voters: Suppose the presidential election were being held today. If Senator Edward Kennedy were the Democratic candidate and Gerald Ford were the Republican candidate, which would you like to see win? Those who named another person or who were undecided were asked: As of today, do you lean more to Kennedy, the Democrat, or to Ford, the Republican?

Kennedy	57%
Ford	40
Other	*
Undecided	3

*Less than 1%.

Asked of registered voters: Suppose the presidential election were being held today. If President Jimmy Carter were the Democratic candidate and Gerald Ford were the Republican candidate, which would you like to see win? Those who named another person or who were undecided were asked: As of today, do you lean more to Carter, the Democrat, or to Ford, the Republican?

Carter............................47%
Ford 46
Other 2
Undecided......................... 5

Asked of registered voters: Suppose the presidential election were being held today. If President Carter were the Democratic candidate and Ronald Reagan were the Republican candidate, which would you like to see win? Those who were undecided were asked: As of today, do you lean more to Carter, the Democrat, or to Reagan, the Republican?

Carter............................52%
Reagan...........................43
Other 1
Undecided......................... 4

Asked of registered voters: Suppose the presidential election were being held today. If Senator Kennedy were the Democratic candidate and Ronald Reagan were the Republican candidate, which would you like to see win? Those who were undecided were asked: As of today, do you lean more to Kennedy, the Democrat, or to Reagan, the Republican?

Kennedy 59%
Reagan...........................36
Other 1
Undecided......................... 4

AUGUST 20
PRESIDENT CARTER

Interviewing Date: 7/21–24/78
Survey #107-G

Here is a list of terms [respondents were handed a card with terms listed]—shown as pairs of opposites—that have been used to describe President Jimmy Carter. For each pair of opposites, would you select the term which you feel best describes Carter?

	Sept.-Oct. 1977	Today
Has strong leadership qualities	62%	36%
Decisive, sure of himself....	61	38
Has well-defined program for moving the country ahead	43	29
You know where he stands on issues	42	28
Offers imaginative, innovative solutions to national problems.......	52	42
A man you can believe in ...	52	43
A person of exceptional abilities	41	32
Bright, intelligent	80	72
Puts country's interests ahead of politics	57	49
Displays good judgment in a crisis	71	63
Sides with the average citizen	56	51
Says what he believes even if unpopular	62	59
A likeable person..........	78	76
A religious person	81	81
A man of high moral principles..............	80	80
Sympathetic to problems of the poor	62	63
Takes moderate, middle-of-road positions	67	73

Note: While most Americans continue to view Carter as a man of high moral standards, his personal popularity has suffered dramatically during the last ten months. Accompanying this drop in popularity has been a major decline of confidence in the president's ability as a leader. For example, in September 1977, six in ten Americans characterized Carter as "decisive" and "sure of himself." In the latest survey only 38% use these terms. Similarly, last year 62% believed Carter a man of "strong leadership qualities." Today the comparable figure is 36%.

The president has also suffered a decline in his image as a man with "a well-defined program for moving the nation ahead." Last September, 43% described him with such words, and today only 29% do so.

Finally, Carter is receiving more of the type of criticism that plagued him during his election campaign—that he is "fuzzy" on the issues and "waffles." Whereas in September 42% felt they knew where he stood on the issues, only 28% feel this way today.

On the positive side, the president is still viewed by most Americans as a man of high moral standards. Fully eight in ten people continue to view him as a religious person (81%) and a man of high moral principles (80%)—two findings that exactly match those recorded last year.

The president also gets credit for his moderation. The percentage who see Carter as a man of moderate, middle-of-the-road positions on the issues facing him and the nation has increased from 67% to 73% during the last ten months.

The growing dissatisfaction with Carter as a leader is seen in recent findings showing he is not the first choice of party members to be their nominee in the 1980 election. Recent Gallup Polls indicate that nationwide, Democrats favor Senator Edward Kennedy by about a two-to-one margin over Carter.

AUGUST 21
PRESIDENT CARTER

Interviewing Date: 7/21–24/78
Survey #107-G

Do you approve or disapprove of the way Jimmy Carter is handling his job as president?

Approve...........................39%
Disapprove 44
No opinion.........................17

Asked of those who expressed approval or disapproval: How strongly would you say you approve/disapprove—very strongly or not so strongly?

Strong approval......................11%
Mild approval 19
Mild disapproval.....................17
Strong disapproval 19
No opinion..........................17
                                    ___
                                    83%

President Carter has two main jobs. One concerns the problems outside this country, the other concerns problems here in the United States. Do you approve or disapprove of the way Carter is handling our foreign policy—that is, our relations with other nations?

Approve...........................37%
Disapprove 46
No opinion.........................17

Do you approve or disapprove of the way Carter is handling our domestic problems —that is, our problems here at home?

Approve...........................32%
Disapprove 56
No opinion.........................12

Do you approve or disapprove of the way Carter is dealing with the economic conditions in this country?

Approve...........................28%
Disapprove 62
No opinion.........................10

Do you approve or disapprove of the way Carter is dealing with inflation?

Approve...........................22%
Disapprove 66
No opinion.........................12

Do you approve or disapprove of the way Carter is dealing with unemployment?

Approve.............................36%
Disapprove 45
No opinion.........................19

Do you approve or disapprove of the way Carter is dealing with environmental problems and pollution?

Approve.............................43%
Disapprove 31
No opinion.........................26

Do you approve or disapprove of the way Carter is dealing with the energy situation?

Approve.............................41%
Disapprove 42
No opinion.........................17

Do you approve or disapprove of the way Carter is dealing with the Middle East situation?

Approve.............................39%
Disapprove 36
No opinion.........................25

Do you approve or disapprove of the way Carter is handling our relations with Russia?

Approve.............................34%
Disapprove 43
No opinion.........................23

Note: The latest reading of President Jimmy Carter's standing with the American people offers further bad news for the president, but the picture is not all bleak.

1. Carter's overall popularity rating has drifted downward steadily over the last twelve months—from 67% in July 1977 to 39% in the latest survey. Although there has been a bottoming out in his ratings since April, the current figure of 39% approval represents his low point to date.

2. Paralleling this overall decline in the percentage who say they approve of Carter's performance in office is a decline in the percentage of Carter enthusiasts—that is, those who express strong approval. This proportion has declined from 42% in March 1977 (when the first measurement of intensity was taken) to 11% today.

3. In terms of the president's handling of "domestic problems in general," 56% disapprove and 32% approve. When the focus is narrowed to specific domestic problems—namely, those relating to the economy—the president scores poorly on handling inflation (66% disapprove, 22% approve) and economic conditions (62% disapprove, 28% approve). On the question of Carter's dealing with unemployment, the president fares somewhat better, with 36% expressing approval and 45% disapproving.

The president's ratings improve when it comes to noneconomic issues and his handling of international problems. For example, those who approve of the way Carter is dealing with "environmental problems and pollution" outweigh those who disapprove by a 43% to 31% vote. On the question of the president's dealing with the energy situation, about as many approve (41%) as disapprove (42%).

The president scores better on foreign-policy concerns (46% disapprove, 37% approve) than he does in terms of domestic problems (56% to 32%). Specifically, on the Middle East situation, approval slightly outweighs disapproval 39% to 36%. Carter fares less well in terms of "handling relations with Russia," but the vote is fairly close with 43% expressing disapproval and 34% approval.

As reported, the president continues to be viewed by the overwhelming majority of Americans (eight in ten) as a man of "high moral standards." Solid majorities also continue to regard him as "bright" and "intelligent," as a "likeable person," as "displaying good judgment in a crisis," as "sympathetic to problems of the poor," and as "a religious person"—a decided plus in a religiously oriented America.

In assessing the president's current popularity ratings, it should also be borne in mind that Carter, like other chief executives before him, is to a considerable extent a victim of the times. Earlier Gallup Polls have clearly shown that a president, no matter how much he is admired for personal traits, suffers a loss in popularity in a period of widespread concern over economic conditions such as at present.

The nation's economists, as well as the public, are currently anything but bullish about the economy. But if certain sectors of the economy do happen to improve in the months ahead, the president's popularity rating is also likely to improve.

AUGUST 27
RACE RELATIONS

Interviewing Date: 7/21–24/78
Survey #107-G

Between now and the time of the conventions in 1980 there will be more discussion about the qualifications of presidential candidates—their education, age, religion, race, and the like. If your party nominated a generally well-qualified man for president and he happened to be a Negro, would you vote for him?

Yes 77%
No 18
No opinion 5

By Education
College

Yes 86%
No 10
No opinion 4

High School

Yes 76%
No 19
No opinion 5

Grade School

Yes 61%
No 31
No opinion 8

By Region
East

Yes 78%
No 15
No opinion 7

Midwest

Yes 77%
No 17
No opinion 6

South

Yes 67%
No 28
No opinion 5

Deep South

Yes 53%
No 43
No opinion 4

West

Yes 87%
No 10
No opinion 3

Interviewing Date: 7/7–10/78
Survey #106-G

Asked of white persons: If Blacks came to live next door, would you move?

Yes, definitely 4%
Yes, might 9
No 84
No opinion 3

By Education
College

Yes, definitely 3%
Yes, might 6

No................................... 89
No opinion........................... 2

High School

Yes, definitely...................... 4%
Yes, might 10
No................................... 82
No................................... 4

Grade School

Yes, definitely...................... 5%
Yes, might 10
No................................... 77
No opinion........................... 8

By Region
East

Yes, definitely...................... 2%
Yes, might 8
No................................... 86
No opinion........................... 4

Midwest

Yes, definitely...................... 5%
Yes, might 8
No................................... 84
No opinion........................... 3

South

Yes, definitely...................... 6%
Yes, might 12
No................................... 78
No opinion........................... 4

Deep South

Yes, definitely...................... 4%
Yes, might 20
No................................... 76
No opinion........................... *

West

Yes, definitely...................... 2%
Yes, might 7

No................................... 88
No opinion........................... 3
*Less than 1%.

Asked of white persons: Would you move if Blacks came to live in great numbers in your neighborhood?

Yes, definitely......................20%
Yes, might 31
No................................... 45
No opinion........................... 4

By Education
College

Yes, definitely......................17%
Yes, might 33
No................................... 47
No opinion........................... 3

High School

Yes, definitely......................23%
Yes, might 30
No................................... 44
No opinion........................... 3

Grade School

Yes, definitely......................15%
Yes, might 28
No................................... 49
No opinion........................... 8

By Region
East

Yes, definitely......................19%
Yes, might 31
No................................... 45
No opinion........................... 5

Midwest

Yes, definitely......................20%
Yes, might 31
No................................... 44
No opinion........................... 5

South

Yes, definitely 24%
Yes, might 33
No 41
No opinion 2

Deep South

Yes, definitely 34%
Yes, might 24
No 42
No opinion . . . . *

West

Yes, definitely 16%
Yes, might 27
No 53
No opinion 4

*Less than 1%.

Note: Prejudice toward a Black presidential candidate has declined to the lowest point yet recorded. Today, twice the proportion of Americans (77%) as in 1958 (38%) say they would be willing to vote for a qualified Black for the nation's highest office. Since 1963—the year of the "March on Washington" for civil rights—the percentage has increased 30 points.

While the national climate of public opinion is far more receptive today than in earlier years to a Black candidate, some of the increased political clout of Blacks is offset by the fact that fewer of them vote in presidential elections compared to whites. In 1976, it is estimated that while about 57% of whites of voting age cast a ballot, only 45% of Blacks did so.

A dramatic decline in prejudice toward Blacks as neighbors has also taken place.

The proportion of whites who say they "definitely" or "might" move if Blacks came to live next door has declined from 45% in 1963 to 35% in 1965 to 16% in the latest survey.

In addition, those who say they "definitely" or "might" move if Blacks came to live in great numbers in their neighborhood has declined from 78% in 1963 to 69% in 1965 to 45% in the latest survey.

AUGUST 28
RACE RELATIONS

Interviewing Date: 7/7–10/78
Survey #106-G

Asked of white persons: Do you have any children now in grade school or high school?

Yes 32%
No 68

Asked of white persons who do have children in school: Would you, yourself, have any objection to sending your children to a school where a few of the children are Black?

Yes 5%
No 92
No opinion 3

By Education
College

Yes 6%
No 92
No opinion 2

High School

Yes 5%
No 94
No opinion 1

Grade School

Yes 8%
No 80
No opinion 12

By Region
East

Yes 7%
No 92
No opinion 1

Midwest

Yes 3%
No................................. 95
No opinion......................... 2

South

Yes 7%
No................................. 88
No opinion......................... 5

Deep South

Yes 4%
No................................. 91
No opinion......................... 5

West

Yes 3%
No................................. 97
No opinion .... *

*Less than 1%.

Asked of those persons who responded in the negative: Would you, yourself, have any objection to sending your children to a school where half of the children are Black?

Yes 25%
No................................. 69
No opinion......................... 7

By Education
College

Yes 25%
No................................. 69
No opinion......................... 6

High School

Yes 24%
No................................. 69
No opinion......................... 7

Grade School

Yes 17%
No................................. 66
No opinion......................... 17

By Region
East

Yes 22%
No................................. 69
No opinion......................... 9

Midwest

Yes 26%
No................................. 67
No opinion......................... 7

South

Yes 28%
No................................. 67
No opinion......................... 5

Deep South

Yes 33%
No................................. 67
No opinion......................... *

West

Yes 19%
No................................. 73
No opinion......................... 8

*Less than 1%.

Asked of those who responded in the negative to the above question: Would you, yourself, have any objection to sending your children to a school where more than half of the children are Black?

Yes 41%
No................................. 53
No opinion......................... 6

By Education
College

Yes 47%
No 45
No opinion 8

High School

Yes 39%
No 56
No opinion 5

Grade School

Yes 33%
No 67
No opinion .... *

By Region
East

Yes 31%
No 62
No opinion 7

Midwest

Yes 48%
No 44
No opinion 8

South

Yes 49%
No 45
No opinion 6

Deep South

Yes 66%
No 34
No opinion .... *

West

Yes 31%
No 68
No opinion 1

*Less than 1%.

Interviewing Date: 7/21–24/78
Survey #107-G

Do you approve or disapprove of marriage between whites and nonwhites?

Approve 36%
Disapprove 54
No opinion 10

By Sex
Male

Approve 37%
Disapprove 50
No opinion 13

Female

Approve 35%
Disapprove 57
No opinion 8

By Race
Whites

Approve 32%
Disapprove 58
No opinion 10

Nonwhites

Approve 66%
Disapprove 21
No opinion 13

By Education
College

Approve 53%
Disapprove 40
No opinion 7

High School

Approve 32%
Disapprove 57
No opinion 11

Grade School

Approve 19%
Disapprove 70
No opinion 11

By Region
East

Approve 35%
Disapprove 58
No opinion 7

Midwest

Approve 37%
Disapprove 54
No opinion 9

South

Approve 27%
Disapprove 59
No opinion 14

Deep South

Approve 26%
Disapprove 68
No opinion 6

West

Approve 48%
Disapprove 41
No opinion 11

Interviewing Date: 7/7–10/78
Survey #106-G

In your opinion, how well do you think Blacks are treated in this community—the same as whites are, not very well, or badly?

Same as whites 65%
Not very well 18
Badly 4
Don't know 13

By Race
Whites

Same as whites 71%
Not very well 13
Badly 3
Don't know 13

Blacks*

Same as whites 44%
Not very well 39
Badly 10
Don't know 7

Blacks—Male*

Same as whites 42%
Not very well 42
Badly 7
Don't know 9

Blacks—Female*

Same as whites 45%
Not very well 36
Badly 11
Don't know 8

Blacks—College*

Same as whites 36%
Not very well 41
Badly 11
Don't know 12

Blacks—High School*

Same as whites 44%
Not very well 38
Badly 11
Don't know 7

Blacks—Grade School*

Same as whites 51%
Not very well 37
Badly 6
Don't know 6

Blacks—East*

Same as whites 42%
Not very well 33
Badly 10
Don't know 15

Blacks—Midwest*

Same as whites 50%
Not very well 34
Badly 11
Don't know 5

Blacks—South*

Same as whites 46%
Not very well 44
Badly 6
Don't know 4

Blacks—Deep South*

Same as whites 39%
Not very well 47
Badly 9
Don't know 5

Blacks—West*

Same as whites 32%
Not very well 38
Badly 15
Don't know 15

By Education
College

Same as whites 60%
Not very well 23
Badly 3
Don't know 14

High School

Same as whites 67%
Not very well 16
Badly 4
Don't know 13

Grade School

Same as whites 67%
Not very well 16
Badly 4
Don't know 13

By Region
East

Same as whites 68%
Not very well 13
Badly 4
Don't know 15

Midwest

Same as whites 64%
Not very well 16
Badly 3
Don't know 17

South

Same as whites 64%
Not very well 24
Badly 3
Don't know 9

Deep South

Same as whites 56%
Not very well 34
Badly 5
Don't know 5

West

Same as whites 62%
Not very well 20
Badly 7
Don't know 11

*Interviewing Date: 7/21–24/78

In general, do you think Blacks have as good a chance as white people in your community to get any kind of job for which they are qualified, or don't you think they have as good a chance?

As good 67%
Not so good 24
Don't know 9

By Race
Whites

As good 73%
Not so good 18
Don't know 9

Blacks*

As good 39%
Not so good 53
Don't know 8

Blacks—Male*

As good 39%
Not so good 53
Don't know 8

Blacks—Female*

As good 39%
Not so good 53
Don't know 8

Blacks—College*

As good 29%
Not so good 59
Don't know 12

Blacks—High School*

As good 42%
Not so good 51
Don't know 7

Blacks—Grade School*

As good 45%
Not so good 49
Don't know 6

Blacks—East*

As good 32%
Not so good 57
Don't know 11

Blacks—Midwest*

As good 33%
Not so good 64
Don't know 3

Blacks—South*

As good 52%
Not so good 43
Don't know 6

Blacks—Deep South*

As good 46%
Not so good 46
Don't know 8

Blacks—West*

As good 26%
Not so good 57
Don't know 17

By Education
College

As good 64%
Not so good 27
Don't know 9

High School

As good 69%
Not so good 23
Don't know 8

Grade School

As good 69%
Not so good 21
Don't know 10

By Region
East

As good 70%
Not so good 21
Don't know 9

Midwest

As good	67%
Not so good	23
Don't know	10

South

As good	67%
Not so good	25
Don't know	8

Deep South

As good	59%
Not so good	40
Don't know	1

West

As good	65%
Not so good	28
Don't know	7

*Interviewing Date: 7/21–24/78

Note: The current survey suggests that American society is much more racially tolerant than it was fifteen, ten, or even five years ago.

In the fifteen years since the historic "March on Washington," which took place August 28, 1963, the attitudes of white parents on school integration have changed dramatically. Perhaps most striking is the fact that southern white parents now accept integration in about the same proportion as white parents in other regions of the country. Only 28% of southern white parents currently say they would object to sending their children to a school where half the students are black, down from 78% in 1963. The proportion of white parents living outside the South who object to integration has declined from 33% to 23%.

The public is also becoming more tolerant of interracial marriages. In 1968, 20% of Americans approved of whites marrying nonwhites; in 1972, 29% approved; and in the current survey, 36% approve. This increased tolerance is found across all levels of society and in all geographical regions. Approval of interracial marriage is greatest among young adults, people with a college education, and Roman Catholics.

However, all the figures on racial attitudes are not so optimistic. On the question of treatment given to Blacks in our society, the percentage who say that Blacks are treated "not very well" or "badly" in their communities has changed very little since 1963. But though most whites say that Blacks are treated the "same as whites," Blacks report the opposite.

One area in which Blacks do not fare as well as whites—in the opinion of one-fifth of whites and a majority of Blacks—is that of ability to get jobs. Opinion is 53% to 39% among Blacks that they do not have as good a chance as whites to get jobs for which they are qualified. White attitude on this issue splits 73% to 18% in favor of Blacks having as good a chance to get such jobs.

Other Gallup surveys have shown that in the last decade and a half Blacks have made tremendous improvements in terms of their satisfaction with the basic circumstances of life, including income, jobs, and their children's education. Yet the gap between satisfaction levels of Blacks and whites remains wide. A smaller proportion of Blacks (four in ten) than whites (six in ten) express a high level of satisfaction with life in the nation, and fewer Blacks describe themselves as "very happy" (three in ten compared to four in ten among whites). Nationwide, three Americans in ten say that "making ends meet" is the biggest problem facing them personally. Blacks, however, name this problem twice as often as whites do.

SEPTEMBER 3
PUBLIC EMPLOYEE STRIKES

Interviewing Date: 8/4–7/78
Survey #108-G

Here are some questions about strikes in various occupations. Should policemen be permitted to strike, or not?

Should 30%
Should not 64
No opinion......................... 6

By Education
College

Should 27%
Should not 70
No opinion......................... 3

High School

Should 32%
Should not 61
No opinion......................... 7

Grade School

Should 27%
Should not 65
No opinion......................... 8

Labor Union Families Only

Should 41%
Should not 51
No opinion......................... 8

Should firemen be permitted to strike, or not?

Should 29%
Should not 66
No opinion......................... 5

By Education
College

Should 27%
Should not 71
No opinion......................... 2

High School

Should 31%
Should not 63
No opinion......................... 6

Grade School

Should 29%
Should not 64
No opinion......................... 7

Labor Union Families Only

Should 41%
Should not 53
No opinion......................... 6

Should sanitation workers be permitted to strike, or not?

Should 40%
Should not 53
No opinion......................... 7

By Education
College

Should 41%
Should not 55
No opinion......................... 4

High School

Should 42%
Should not 50
No opinion......................... 8

Grade School

Should 33%
Should not 60
No opinion......................... 7

Labor Union Families Only

Should 52%
Should not 43
No opinion......................... 5

Should teachers be permitted to strike, or not?

Should 44%
Should not 51
No opinion......................... 5

By Education
College
Should 46%
Should not 52
No opinion........................... 2

High School
Should 45%
Should not 50
No opinion........................... 5

Grade School
Should 35%
Should not 54
No opinion........................... 11

Labor Union Families Only
Should 53%
Should not 42
No opinion........................... 5

Should postal workers be permitted to strike, or not?

Should 37%
Should not 58
No opinion........................... 5

By Education
College
Should 38%
Should not 60
No opinion........................... 2

High School
Should 40%
Should not 55
No opinion........................... 5

Grade School
Should 25%
Should not 66
No opinion........................... 9

Labor Union Families Only
Should 51%
Should not 44
No opinion........................... 5

Note: The nation in recent months has been gripped by strikes by municipal workers across the nation. The threat of a postal strike was narrowly averted last week after an agreement was made by the United States Postal Service to reopen negotiations with unions representing more than half a million postal workers.

The United States public—plagued by inflation and confronting a growing militancy on the part of public employees—is taking an increasingly "hard line" on strikes by workers in this category.

The percentage who say policemen should not be permitted to strike has grown from 52% in 1975 to 61% in February 1978 to 64% in the latest survey. The same three surveys show opposition to strikes by firemen having grown from 55% in 1975 to 62% today.

The number of persons who believe sanitation workers should not be permitted to strike has increased from 46% in 1975 to 53% in the latest survey.

In terms of attitudes toward strikes by teachers, 48% in 1975 said teachers should not be allowed to strike, compared to 51% in both the February 1978 and latest surveys.

As might be expected, persons in labor union households are more sympathetic to strikes by public employees. Yet while leaning in favor of the right of teachers and sanitation workers to strike—and evenly divided in the case of postal workers—they side with nonunion people when it comes to strikes by policemen and firemen.

While Americans have traditionally supported the right of public employees to join unions and organize for collective bargaining, they have just as consistently voted against their right to strike. The feeling has been that public employees should relinquish this right when they perform vital health- and life-related roles in society.

SEPTEMBER 5
MIDDLE EAST SITUATION

Interviewing Date: 8/4–7/78
Survey #108-G

Have you heard or read about the situation in the Middle East?

	Yes
National	82%

By Education

College	92%
High school	80
Grade school	70

By Region

East	84%
Midwest	80
South	81
West	84

By Age

18–29 years	76%
30–49 years	84
50 years and over	84

By Occupation

Professional and business	91%
Clerical and sales	86
Manual workers	75
Non-labor force	82

Asked of those who replied in the affirmative: In the Middle East situation, are your sympathies more with Israel or more with the Arab nations?

More with Israel	42%
More with Arab nations	11
Neither	30
No opinion	17

By Education
College

More with Israel	51%
More with Arab nations	12
Neither	27
No opinion	10

High School

More with Israel	40%
More with Arab nations	11
Neither	29
No opinion	20

Grade School

More with Israel	27%
More with Arab nations	6
Neither	42
No opinion	25

By Region
East

More with Israel	39%
More with Arab nations	13
Neither	34
No opinion	14

Midwest

More with Israel	37%
More with Arab nations	10
Neither	31
No opinion	22

South

More with Israel	44%
More with Arab nations	9
Neither	28
No opinion	19

West

More with Israel	51%
More with Arab nations	9
Neither	27
No opinion	13

By Age
18–29 Years

More with Israel 45%
More with Arab nations 13
Neither 27
No opinion 15

30–49 Years

More with Israel 45%
More with Arab nations 9
Neither 28
No opinion 18

50 Years and Over

More with Israel 38%
More with Arab nations 10
Neither 33
No opinion 19

By Occupation
Professional and Business

More with Israel 51%
More with Arab nations 10
Neither 28
No opinion 11

Clerical and Sales

More with Israel 42%
More with Arab nations 13
Neither 27
No opinion 18

Manual Workers

More with Israel 39%
More with Arab nations 12
Neither 29
No opinion 20

Non-Labor Force

More with Israel 36%
More with Arab nations 7
Neither 37
No opinion 20

Also asked of those who replied in the affirmative: Do you think Israel is or is not doing all it should to bring about peace in the Middle East?

Is 18%
Is not 57
No opinion 25

By Education
College

Is 19%
Is not 68
No opinion 13

High School

Is 17%
Is not 54
No opinion 29

Grade School

Is 16%
Is not 43
No opinion 41

By Region
East

Is 19%
Is not 60
No opinion 21

Midwest

Is 12%
Is not 56
No opinion 32

South

Is 20%
Is not 52
No opinion 28

West

Is 20%
Is not 62
No opinion 18

By Age
18–29 Years
Is.....................................19%
Is not..................................63
No opinion.............................18

30–49 Years
Is.....................................19%
Is not..................................55
No opinion.............................26

50 Years and Over
Is.....................................15%
Is not..................................55
No opinion.............................30

By Occupation
Professional and Business
Is.....................................18%
Is not..................................66
No opinion.............................16

Clerical and Sales
Is.....................................17%
Is not..................................55
No opinion.............................28

Manual Workers
Is.....................................18%
Is not..................................54
No opinion.............................28

Non-Labor Force
Is.....................................12%
Is not..................................47
No opinion.............................41

Also asked of those who replied in the affirmative: Do you think Egypt is or is not doing all it should to bring about peace in the Middle East?

Is.....................................20%
Is not..................................54
No opinion.............................26

By Education
College
Is.....................................25%
Is not..................................61
No opinion.............................14

High School
Is.....................................18%
Is not..................................53
No opinion.............................29

Grade School
Is.....................................17%
Is not..................................43
No opinion.............................40

By Region
East
Is.....................................22%
Is not..................................58
No opinion.............................20

Midwest
Is.....................................20%
Is not..................................46
No opinion.............................34

South
Is.....................................18%
Is not..................................54
No opinion.............................28

West
Is.....................................22%
Is not..................................60
No opinion.............................18

By Age
18–29 Years
Is.....................................17%
Is not..................................62
No opinion.............................21

30–49 Years

Is....................................22%
Is not................................52
No opinion...........................26

50 Years and Over

Is....................................21%
Is not................................51
No opinion...........................28

By Occupation

Professional and Business

Is....................................24%
Is not................................59
No opinion...........................17

Clerical and Sales

Is....................................22%
Is not................................52
No opinion...........................26

Manual Workers

Is....................................16%
Is not................................54
No opinion...........................30

Non-Labor Force

Is....................................24%
Is not................................47
No opinion...........................29

Note: The Camp David summit meeting between President Jimmy Carter, Israeli Prime Minister Menahem Begin, and Egyptian President Anwar Sadat opens at a time when American public opinion shapes up as follows: Among the 82% who have heard or read about the Middle East situation, nearly half (47%) say their sympathies are with neither side or do not express an opinion. A total of 42% say their sympathies are more with Israel, while 11% say their sympathies lean toward the Arabs.

The trend on this question, going back eleven years, shows sympathies for Israel having declined from 56% in June 1967, at the time of the Six-Day War, to 33% in February of the current year, following the breakdown in Egypt-Israel peace talks. Since February, however, sympathy for Israel has increased.

A majority of informed Americans think both Israel and Egypt should be doing more to bring about peace in the Middle East. About equal proportions say Egypt (20%) and Israel (18%) are doing all they should to bring about peace in the Middle East.

In assessing these findings, it is important to bear in mind that the basic sympathies of the United States public over the years have consistently been on the side of Israel rather than the Arab nations.

The Camp David summit is viewed as a serious political gamble by many political observers, who feel that an unsuccessful meeting would further damage the president's popularity.

The latest measurement of the president's popularity rating shows 39% expressing approval of his performance in office. This represents a decline of 28 percentage points since July 1977. Although there has been a bottoming-out in Carter's ratings since April, the current approval figure represents his low point to date.

SEPTEMBER 10
CONGRESSIONAL ELECTIONS

Interviewing Date: 7/21–24, 8/4–7/78
Survey #107-G, 108-G

If the elections for Congress were being held today, which party would you like to see win in this congressional district, the Democratic party or the Republican party? Those who were undecided were asked: As of today, do you lean more to the Democratic party or to the Republican party?

Democratic..........................50%
Republican...........................36
Other 3
Undecided 11

South Only

Democratic 58%
Republican. 27
Other 3
Undecided 12

Outside South Only

Democratic 48%
Republican. 39
Other 3
Undecided 10

With "other party" and undecided responses allocated, the result is:

Democratic 57%
Republican. 43

South Only

Democratic 66%
Republican. 34

Outside South Only

Democratic 55%
Republican. 45

Note: The 1978 congressional campaign gets underway on a bleak note for GOP hopes for November 7. If the elections for the House of Representatives were being held now, the political composition of the House would remain solidly Democratic.

Gallup surveys show the Democratic party leading in nationwide popular support, 57% to 43%, assuming a level of turnout comparable to the last two previous midterm elections in 1970 and 1974. The current reading is the same as the actual division of the popular vote for members of the House in the 1976 elections.

While the current results are a carbon copy of the 1976 congressional election vote, the GOP is in somewhat better shape today than a year ago. An early October 1977 survey showed the Democrats with 61% of the national popular vote for Congress, compared to 39% for the Republicans.

Present indications are that if the congressional elections were being held today, the GOP would gain few, if any, seats—or, in any case, the change would be below the average gain for the "out party" of thirty to thirty-five seats.

President Carter's relatively low popularity rating (39% approval) appears to be having little adverse effect on Democratic congressional strength, contrary to the pattern observed since the beginning of scientific polling in the mid-1930s.

Typically, when a president's popularity falls below the 50% line, the party in power loses more than the normal thirty to thirty-five seats.

Striking examples of the negative effect a president's low popularity can have on his party's congressional strength are seen in the 1974, 1966, and 1946 elections.

In 1974, although President Gerald Ford had taken office in August, the political demise of President Nixon cast a pall over his party in the fall elections. In 1966 President Lyndon Johnson's slumping popularity hurt his party in that midterm election, and in 1946 President Harry Truman's low approval score did serious damage to the Democratic chances in that year.

It is interesting to note that while a low presidential popularity rating has a demonstrable effect on congressional strength, a high popularity rating does not necessarily have the reverse effect.

A key reason for the GOP's failure to gain ground in the congressional race thus far is the fact that they have yet to persuade the electorate they can do a better job on the issues voters consider most important.

A recent Gallup survey showed voters holding the view by a nearly two-to-one margin that the Democratic party is better able than the GOP to handle the nation's most pressing problem. The key problems named by the public are inflation (cited by 60%) and unemployment (cited by 14%).

Not only has the GOP failed to gain the advantage on basic issues but they also trail on

an issue on which Republicans have traditionally held the lead over their Democratic
rivals—that of reducing federal spending. A
recent survey showed 24% saying the GOP is
better able to reduce federal spending, but 28%
favoring the Democratic party on this issue.

SEPTEMBER 14
PUBLIC SERVICES VS.
PRIVATE COMPANIES

Interviewing Date: 8/4–7/78
Survey #108-G

*In some communities, certain public ser-
vices such as garbage collection, street
cleaning, and the like have been taken over
by private companies. Would you like to
see this done in your own community, or
not?*

Yes 27%
No................................. 41
Already done........................ 22
No opinion.......................... 10

By Community Size
One Million and Over

Yes 23%
No................................. 48
Already done........................ 18
No opinion.......................... 11

500,000–999,999

Yes 35%
No................................. 40
Already done........................ 16
No opinion.......................... 9

50,000–499,999

Yes 30%
No................................. 45
Already done........................ 19
No opinion.......................... 6

2,500–49,999

Yes 22%
No................................. 46
Already done........................ 21
No opinion.......................... 11

Under 2,500; Rural

Yes 25%
No................................. 28
Already done........................ 33
No opinion.......................... 14

*Asked of all persons except those who said
that public services have already been
taken over by some private companies: If
private companies did take over, do you
think that public services would be more
efficient or less efficient?*

More.............................. 42%
Less 28
No difference....................... 13
No opinion.......................... 17

By Community Size
One Million and Over

More.............................. 37%
Less 28
No difference....................... 16
No opinion.......................... 19

500,000–999,999

More.............................. 50%
Less 26
No difference....................... 11
No opinion.......................... 13

50,000–499,999

More.............................. 42%
Less 34
No difference....................... 12
No opinion.......................... 12

2,500–49,999

More.............................. 36%
Less 28

No difference.........................15
No opinion...........................21

Under 2,500; Rural

More................................46%
Less 21
No difference.........................11
No opinion...........................22

Note: One person in every five across the nation says public services such as garbage collection have been taken over by private companies in his or her community, a trend that may gain momentum in post-Proposition 13 America. In addition, nearly three citizens in every ten would like to see such a change brought about in their own communities. A key factor is the belief that public services would be more efficient if private companies were to take over.

These findings are recorded at a time when the American people—plagued by inflation and confronting growing militancy on the part of public employees—are taking an increasingly "hard line" on strikes by public employees. For example, those who believe sanitation workers should not be permitted to strike have increased from 46% in 1975 to 53% in a recent Gallup survey.

SEPTEMBER 17
POLITICAL VIEWS

Interviewing Date: 8/11–14/78
Survey #109-G

People who are conservative in their political views are referred to as being right of center and people who are liberal in their political views are referred to as being left of center. [Respondents were handed a card with eight positions on the left-right continuum.] Which one of these categories best describes your own political position?

Far left..............................3%
Substantially left of center............. 5
Moderately left of center 12
Just slightly left of center 10
Middle of the road (volunteered) 10
Just slightly right of center..............16
Moderately right of center 17
Substantially right of center............. 6
Far right............................. 4
Don't know 17

Registered Voters Only*

Far left..............................2%
Substantially left of center............. 5
Moderately left of center 12
Just slightly left of center 10
Middle of the road (volunteered) 10
Just slightly right of center..............18
Moderately right of center 19
Substantially right of center............. 8
Far right............................. 4
Don't know 12

*Approximately 70% of the total adult population.

Note: In the six weeks between now and the congressional elections, contenders for the 435 House seats will be seeking votes from an electorate that leans heavily to a conservative point of view.

The results reported today graphically illustrate one of the oddities of American politics. While more voters perceive themselves as conservative than liberal, they nevertheless consistently vote Democrats into office. In fact, the Democrats have controlled both Houses of Congress in all twelve congressional elections since 1954. The latest Gallup Poll results show little likelihood that this pattern will be disrupted.

SEPTEMBER 20
CAMP DAVID SUMMIT AGREEMENTS

Interviewing Date: 9/19/78
Special Telephone Survey
Do you approve or disapprove of the way Jimmy Carter is handling his job as president?

Approve..............................56%
Disapprove 30
No opinion.........................14

Asked of those who had heard or read about the Camp David summit: In your opinion, how important a role did President Carter play in getting Sadat and Begin to come to an agreement at the Camp David summit?

Very important 67%
Fairly important 25
Not too important.................... 7
Don't know 1

Also asked of those who had heard or read about the summit: How would you rate President Carter's efforts to try to bring peace to the Mideast—excellent, good, only fair, or poor?

Excellent...........................42%
Good 38
Only fair...........................14
Poor 3
Don't know......................... 3

Also asked of those who had heard or read about the summit: What about President Anwar Sadat of Egypt?

Excellent...........................30%
Good 39
Only fair...........................20
Poor 3
Don't know......................... 8

Also asked of those who had heard or read about the summit: What about Prime Minister Menahem Begin of Israel?

Excellent...........................21%
Good 39
Only fair...........................26

Poor 5
Don't know 9

Also asked of those who had heard or read about the summit: In your opinion, which country, Israel or Egypt, made the most concessions in order to come to an agreement at the meeting:

Israel 35%
Egypt 28
Neither, don't know 37

Also asked of those who had heard or read about the summit: Do you think the Camp David agreements will or will not lead to a lasting peace between Israel and Egypt?

Will 31%
Will not 42
Can't say 27

Also asked of those who had heard or read about the summit: As a result of the Camp David summit has your opinion of President Carter changed?

Yes.................................36%
No..................................64

Asked of those who replied in the affirmative: Do you have a much more favorable opinion of him, a somewhat more favorable opinion of him, or a less favorable opinion of him?

Much more favorable..................14%
Somewhat more favorable 22
Less favorable .... *
Don't know .... *
                                    ___
                                    36%
*Less than 1%.

Note: The American public's first reaction to the Camp David summit is that President Jimmy Carter is very much responsible for Israel and

Egypt coming to a basic agreement on peace. In turn the president's popularity has increased by 11 percentage points since the convening of the historic conference.

These are among the major conclusions of a special Gallup Poll conducted Tuesday night.

1. President Jimmy Carter's personal popularity has improved dramatically. During the initial stages of the summit, Carter's popularity had risen slightly to 45% from 39% in August. After the announcement of the agreements the figure climbed to 56%.

2. Carter is given personal credit for making the summit a success. A 67% majority of those who have heard about the summit believe that the president played a "very important" role in getting Sadat and Begin to reach an agreement.

3. Public perceptions of Carter's efforts to bring about peace have also improved dramatically. A 42% plurality of those who have heard or read about the situation in the Middle East give Carter an "excellent" rating for his attempts to bring peace to the Middle East. This figure represents a significant increase from the 14% figure recorded while the summit was in progress. In comparison, 30% rate Sadat's efforts as "excellent" (an increase from 16%), while the comparable figure for Begin is 21% (up from 7%).

4. Despite the fact that Sadat is given a higher rating than Begin for his efforts in trying to come to an agreement, Israel, not Egypt, is perceived as having made more concessions at the summit. About one third of the public, 35%, believes Israel made the most concessions in order to come to the agreements reached at Camp David, while 28% think Egypt was the more conciliatory. Just days before, the picture was reversed, with the public believing Egypt was the party most willing to make gestures that would lead to an agreement.

5. The public is not convinced the agreements will lead to a lasting peace.

6. Carter's dramatic increase in popularity is buttressed by the finding that many Americans have changed their opinion of him directly as a result of the summit.

SEPTEMBER 21
PRESIDENTIAL CANDIDATES

Interviewing Date: 7/21–24/78
Survey #107-G

Between now and the time of the conventions in 1980 there will be more discussion about the qualifications of presidential candidates—their education, age, religion, race, and the like. If your party nominated a generally well-qualified man for president and he happened to be a Jew, would you vote for him?

Yes 82%
No 12
No opinion 6

By Sex
Male

Yes 80%
No 13
No opinion 7

Female

Yes 84%
No 11
No opinion 5

By Race
Whites

Yes 82%
No 12
No opinion 6

Nonwhites

Yes 81%
No 12
No opinion 7

By Education
College

Yes 91%
No 6
No opinion 3

High School

Yes 81%
No. 13
No opinion. 6

Grade School

Yes 68%
No. 22
No opinion. 10

By Region
East

Yes 87%
No. 8
No opinion. 5

Midwest

Yes 82%
No. 12
No opinion. 6

South

Yes 74%
No. 18
No opinion. 8

West

Yes 87%
No. 10
No opinion. 3

By Age
18–29 Years

Yes 82%
No. 12
No opinion. 6

30–49 Years

Yes 85%
No. 11
No opinion. 4

50 Years and Over

Yes 75%
No. 17
No opinion. 8

By Politics
Republicans

Yes 81%
No. 14
No opinion. 5

Democrats

Yes 82%
No. 12
No opinion. 6

Independents

Yes 84%
No. 11
No opinion. 5

By Religion
Protestants

Yes 78%
No. 15
No opinion. 7

Catholics

Yes 87%
No. 9
No opinion. 4

By Occupation
Professional and Business

Yes 91%
No. 7
No opinion. 2

Clerical and Sales

Yes 93%
No. 6
No opinion. 1

Manual Workers

Yes 81%
No 13
No opinion 6

Non-Labor Force

Yes 73%
No 19
No opinion 8

If your party nominated a generally well-qualified man for president and he happened to be a Catholic, would you vote for him?

Yes 91%
No 4
No opinion 5

By Sex
Male

Yes 91%
No 4
No opinion 5

Female

Yes 91%
No 5
No opinion 4

By Race
Whites

Yes 92%
No 4
No opinion 4

Nonwhites

Yes 89%
No 6
No opinion 5

By Education
College

Yes 97%
No 1
No opinion 2

High School

Yes 92%
No 3
Poor 5

Grade School

Yes 78%
No 13
No opinion 9

By Region
East

Yes 94%
No 3
No opinion 3

Midwest

Yes 91%
No 4
No opinion 5

South

Yes 83%
No 8
No opinion 9

West

Yes 98%
No 2
No opinion . . . . *

By Age
18–29 Years

Yes 95%
No 2
No opinion 3

30–49 Years

Yes 92%
No. 3
No opinion. 5

50 Years and Over

Yes 88%
No. 7
No opinion. 5

By Politics
Republicans

Yes 92%
No. 5
No opinion. 3

Democrats

Yes 92%
No. 4
No opinion. 4

Independents

Yes 90%
No. 5
No opinion. 5

By Religion
Protestants

Yes 88%
No. 7
No opinion. 5

Catholics

Yes 97%
No. 1
No opinion. 2

By Occupation
Professional and Business

Yes 97%
No. 2
No opinion. 1

Clerical and Sales

Yes 98%
No. 2
No opinion. . . . . *

Manual Workers

Yes 89%
No. 5
No opinion. 6

Non-Labor Force

Yes 86%
No. 8
No opinion. 6

*Less than 1%.

If your party nominated a generally well-qualified man for president and he happened to be an atheist, would you vote for him?

Yes 40%
No. 53
No opinion. 7

By Sex
Male

Yes 45%
No. 48
No opinion. 7

Female

Yes 35%
No. 58
No opinion. 7

By Race
Whites

Yes 41%
No. 53
No opinion. 6

Nonwhites

Yes 29%
No. 57
No opinion. 14

By Education
College

Yes 57%
No. 38
No opinion. 5

High School

Yes 37%
No. 55
No opinion. 8

Grade School

Yes 18%
No. 74
No opinion. 8

By Region
East

Yes 50%
No. 43
No opinion. 7

Midwest

Yes 36%
No. 57
No opinion. 7

South

Yes 26%
No. 67
No opinion. 7

West

Yes 50%
No. 44
No opinion. 6

By Age
18–29 Years

Yes 58%
No. 34
No opinion. 8

30–49 Years

Yes 44%
No. 52
No opinion. 4

50 Years and Over

Yes 23%
No. 69
No opinion. 8

By Politics
Republicans

Yes 33%
No. 61
No opinion. 6

Democrats

Yes 36%
No. 57
No opinion. 7

Independents

Yes 50%
No. 43
No opinion. 7

By Religion
Protestants

Yes 30%
No. 63
No opinion. 7

Catholics

Yes 47%
No. 46
No opinion. 7

By Occupation

Professional and Business

Yes 57%
No.................................... 37
No opinion........................... 6

Clerical and Sales

Yes 54%
No.................................... 40
No opinion........................... 6

Manual Workers

Yes 37%
No.................................... 56
No opinion........................... 7

Non-Labor Force

Yes 20%
No.................................... 73
No opinion........................... 7

If your party nominated a generally well-qualified man for president and he happened to be divorced, would you vote for him?

Yes 84%
No.................................... 9
No opinion........................... 7

By Sex

Male

Yes 83%
No.................................... 9
No opinion........................... 8

Female

Yes 85%
No.................................... 8
No opinion........................... 7

By Race

Whites

Yes 86%
No.................................... 7
No opinion........................... 7

Nonwhites

Yes 73%
No.................................... 21
No opinion........................... 6

By Education

College

Yes 92%
No.................................... 5
No opinion........................... 3

High School

Yes 84%
No.................................... 8
No opinion........................... 8

Grade School

Yes 72%
No.................................... 15
No opinion........................... 13

By Region

East

Yes 87%
No.................................... 8
No opinion........................... 5

Midwest

Yes 83%
No.................................... 10
No opinion........................... 7

South

Yes 77%
No.................................... 11
No opinion........................... 12

West

Yes 93%
No.................................... 4
No opinion........................... 3

By Age
18–29 Years

Yes 87%
No 7
No opinion 6

30–49 Years

Yes 86%
No 7
No opinion 7

50 Years and Over

Yes 81%
No 11
No opinion 8

By Politics
Republicans

Yes 86%
No 8
No opinion 6

Democrats

Yes 83%
No 9
No opinion 8

Independents

Yes 86%
No 8
No opinion 6

By Religion
Protestants

Yes 82%
No 11
No opinion 7

Catholics

Yes 86%
No 6
No opinion 8

By Occupation
Professional and Business

Yes 91%
No 5
No opinion 4

Clerical and Sales

Yes 93%
No 3
No opinion 4

Manual Workers

Yes 82%
No 10
No opinion 8

Non-Labor Force

Yes 79%
No 11
No opinion 10

If your party nominated a generally well-qualified man for president and he happened to be a homosexual, would you vote for him?

Yes 26%
No 66
No opinion 8

By Sex
Male

Yes 24%
No 68
No opinion 8

Female

Yes 28%
No 63
No opinion 9

By Race
Whites

Yes 26%
No 66
No opinion 8

Nonwhites

Yes 27%
No. 61
No opinion. 12

By Education
College

Yes 37%
No. 56
No opinion. 7

High School

Yes 25%
No. 66
No opinion. 9

Grade School

Yes 11%
No. 80
No opinion. 9

By Region
East

Yes 31%
No. 59
No opinion. 10

Midwest

Yes 25%
No. 67
No opinion. 8

South

Yes 19%
No. 73
No opinion. 8

West

Yes 30%
No. 63
No opinion. 7

By Age
18–29 Years

Yes 37%
No. 54
No opinion. 9

30–49 Years

Yes 31%
No. 61
No opinion. 8

50 Years and Over

Yes 13%
No. 78
No opinion. 9

By Politics
Republicans

Yes 21%
No. 73
No opinion. 6

Democrats

Yes 24%
No. 67
No opinion. 9

Independents

Yes 31%
No. 59
No opinion. 10

By Religion
Protestants

Yes 19%
No. 73
No opinion. 8

Catholics

Yes 32%
No. 59
No opinion. 9

By Occupation
Professional and Business

Yes 35%
No. 57
No opinion. 8

Clerical and Sales

Yes 34%
No. 60
No opinion. 6

Manual Workers

Yes 24%
No. 68
No opinion. 8

Non-Labor Force

Yes 15%
No. 76
No opinion. 9

If your party nominated a woman for president, would you vote for her if she were qualified for the job?

Yes 76%
No. 19
No opinion. 5

By Sex
Male

Yes 76%
No. 19
No opinion. 5

Female

Yes 77%
No. 18
No opinion. 5

By Race
Whites

Yes 76%
No. 19
No opinion. 5

Nonwhites

Yes 79%
No. 12
No opinion. 9

By Education
College

Yes 81%
No. 15
No opinion. 4

High School

Yes 78%
No. 18
No opinion. 4

Grade School

Yes 65%
No. 28
No opinion. 7

By Region
East

Yes 78%
No. 17
No opinion. 5

Midwest

Yes 76%
No. 19
No opinion. 5

South

Yes 73%
No. 21
No opinion. 6

West

Yes 80%
No. 18
No opinion. 2

By Age
18–29 Years

Yes 85%
No.................................. 10
No opinion.......................... 5

30–49 Years

Yes 80%
No.................................. 16
No opinion.......................... 4

50 Years and Over

Yes 67%
No.................................. 27
No opinion.......................... 6

By Politics
Republicans

Yes 72%
No.................................. 24
No opinion.......................... 4

Democrats

Yes 77%
No.................................. 19
No opinion.......................... 4

Independents

Yes 79%
No.................................. 16
No opinion.......................... 5

By Religion
Protestants

Yes 74%
No.................................. 21
No opinion.......................... 5

Catholics

Yes 78%
No.................................. 18
No opinion.......................... 4

By Occupation
Professional and Business

Yes 81%
No.................................. 16
No opinion.......................... 3

Clerical and Sales

Yes 80%
No.................................. 19
No opinion.......................... 1

Manual Workers

Yes 78%
No.................................. 16
No opinion.......................... 6

Non-Labor Force

Yes 65%
No.................................. 30
No opinion.......................... 5

Note: The climate for women, Blacks, Jews, and Catholics seeking the nation's political leadership roles has never been more favorable than it is today. One of the less-noted trends in United States society in recent decades has been the decline in prejudice toward persons of different races, religions, and backgrounds in terms of their running for the highest political office in the land—the presidency of the United States.

The current findings also show, however, that a majority of Americans would be opposed to an atheist or a homosexual president.

The most dramatic change has come about in terms of support for a woman for president. Since 1937 the percentage of Americans who say they would be willing to vote for a woman for president has increased from 31% to 76% in the latest nationwide survey.

Over this same forty-year period the proportion willing to vote for a Catholic for president has climbed 27 points, from 64% in 1937 to 91% today.

The percentage saying they would vote for a Jew was 46% in the 1937 survey and is 82% today.

As reported earlier, the percentage of people who would accept the presidential candidacy of a Black has doubled in just two decades. The first survey, in 1958, showed 38% willing to vote for a Black for president; the figure today is 77%.

A gain in tolerance—at least in terms of voting for presidential candidates—is also noted in the trend of willingness to vote for a divorced person for president. In 1963, 78% indicated a willingness to vote for a divorced person for president; today the figure is 84%.

One of the most interesing—and dramatic—changes has come about in terms of voting for an atheist for president. In 1958 only 18% said they would vote for such a candidate, but today the proportion is 40%. However, a majority, 53%, indicate they would not vote for an atheist.

Persons with a college background are less likely to object to voting for persons of different backgrounds, races, and religions than are persons with less than a college background.

In fact, the growing level of formal education in this country is presumably a key factor in the steady decline in prejudice toward persons of different backgrounds running for president. In 1937 only about 7% of the adult population had a college background; today the figure is more than three times as high.

SEPTEMBER 28
PRESIDENT CARTER

Interviewing Date: 9/14/78
Special Telephone Survey

Do you approve or disapprove of the way Jimmy Carter is handling his job as president?

Approve.............................56%
Disapprove 30
No opinion...........................14

Note: President Jimmy Carter's remarkable 17-point gain in popularity rating following the Camp David summit meeting represents the sharpest gain for a chief executive in four decades of Gallup Poll presidential popularity measurements.

Prior to the summit, 39% of the American people interviewed expressed approval of Carter's performance in office. Immediately following the summit, his figure stood at 56%, as determined by a Gallup survey conducted the day after the president's speech to Congress.

Sharp and dramatic gains in popularity for a chief executive are often recorded at the time of or following critical foreign policy events or decisions.

Carter's postsummit gain in popularity is virtually the same as the 16-point gain in approval for President Richard Nixon following the announcement of the Vietnam peace agreement in late January 1973.

In early January 1973, just prior to the peace agreement, 51% said they approved of Nixon's performance in office. Following the peace agreement, his rating shot up to 67%, Nixon's all-time high approval rating.

President Gerald Ford's stock with the American people showed a dramatic rise in a survey taken shortly after the *Mayaguez* incident in 1975, with his approval rating jumping from 40% in early May of that year to 51% in late May.

President John F. Kennedy made a 12-point gain after the resolution of the Cuban missile crisis in 1962.

One of President Dwight Eisenhower's largest gains in popularity came after his summit meeting with British, French, and Russian leaders in Geneva during the summer of 1955.

President Harry Truman's rating shot up 12 percentage points after the announcement of the Truman doctrine of aid to Turkey and Greece, as did President Franklin D. Roosevelt's in the wake of Pearl Harbor and the declaration of war on Japan.

The four decades of Gallup Poll measurements of presidential popularity show that these sudden gains are rarely sustained over a long period of time.

Ford's approval rating of 51% following the *Mayaguez* incident remained steady during June, but by early August it had declined to 45%.

Nixon's rating of 67% following the Vietnam peace agreement had declined to 54% in early April 1973, bottoming out at 27% in late October and early November, following the firing of Archibald Cox.

Kennedy sustained his high approval rating of 73% following the Cuban missile crisis for several weeks. In February 1963 his rating was still high, 70%, but by late May it was down to 64%.

Whether or not Carter will sustain his new high level of popularity will depend in considerable measure on further developments in the Middle East, the United States public's reaction to these developments, and whether or not a lasting peace is established.

At present, among respondents who think the agreement will lead to a lasting peace between Israel and Egypt, 49% reported an improved attitude toward Jimmy Carter. And among those who are not sure whether the agreement will lead to peace, 38% report a changed attitude. Among the pessimists with respect to the agreement, only 26% have a more favorable view of the president.

Carter's rating in the weeks ahead will also depend on how the public perceives his handling of the economy. At present he is not faring well in this respect. Recent Gallup surveys show 66% disapproving of his handling of inflation and 65% disapproving of his handling of the unemployment situation.

OCTOBER 1
REPUBLICAN PARTY VS. DEMOCRATIC PARTY

Interviewing Date: 9/8–11/78
Survey #111-G

Which political party—the Republican party or the Democratic party—do you think can do a better job of holding taxes down?

Democratic	31%
Republican	25
No difference	33
No opinion	11

By Politics
Republicans

Democratic	4%
Republican	64
No difference	24
No opinion	8

Democrats

Democratic	54%
Republican	9
No difference	28
No opinion	9

Independents

Democratic	15%
Republican	25
No difference	48
No opinion	12

Which political party—the Republican party or the Democratic party—can do a better job of reducing federal spending?

Democratic	30%
Republican	23
No difference	36
No opinion	11

By Politics
Republicans

Democratic	8%
Republican	58
No difference	25
No opinion	9

Democrats

Democratic	49%
Republican	11
No difference	32
No opinion	8

Independents

Democratic 18%
Republican 19
No difference 49
No opinion 14

Which political party—the Republican party or the Democratic party—do you think can do a better job of dealing with the problem of inflation?

Democratic 31%
Republican 23
No difference 35
No opinion 11

By Politics
Republicans

Democratic 6%
Republican 63
No difference 25
No opinion 6

Democrats

Democratic 55%
Republican 8
No difference 29
No opinion 8

Independents

Democratic 14%
Republican 21
No difference 51
No opinion 14

Which political party—the Republican party or the Democratic party—do you think can do a better job of dealing with the Soviet Union?

Democratic 29%
Republican 22
No difference 33
No opinion 16

By Politics
Republicans

Democratic 3%
Republican 61
No difference 25
No opinion 11

Democrats

Democratic 50%
Republican 9
No difference 28
No opinion 13

Independents

Democratic 15%
Republican 17
No difference 47
No opinion 21

Note: With fewer than six weeks remaining before election day, the Republican party has failed to convince voters that it is any better able than the rival Democratic party to handle taxation—a problem Republicans hoped to turn to their advantage.

In the latest Gallup Poll, just 25% of Americans say the GOP can do a better job of holding down taxes, while 31% name the Democratic party. Almost half the public, 44%, either sees no difference in the ability of the two major parties to handle this issue (33%) or is undecided (11%).

In fact, the GOP continues to suffer from a serious "issue gap." Not only do voters give the Democrats the benefit of the doubt on taxation, supposedly a Republican strong point, but they also credit the Democratic party with being better able to deal with three other critical questions—reducing federal spending, dealing with inflation, and handling relations with the Soviet Union.

With six in ten Americans naming inflation as the most important problem facing the nation, it would seem a particularly opportune time for the GOP to take advantage of this issue, but if present attitudes hold through election day this will not be the case.

Currently, 31% of Americans say the Democratic party is better able to handle the problem of inflation; only 23% give the nod to the Republicans. Another 35% see no difference between the parties, and 11% are undecided.

Another so-called Republican issue—reducing federal spending—is turning out to be nothing of the sort. On this question the Democrats hold a 30%–23% lead. Again, about half the public either perceive no difference in the abilities of the parties or are undecided on the issue.

If anything, the Republicans may be losing some ground on this issue. In a similar survey conducted in March there was virtually no difference in the percentages citing each of the two parties as best able to cut federal spending. At that time, 28% named the Democrats and 26% the Republicans.

Finally, the public also views the Democratic party as better able to handle relations with the Soviet Union—the one foreign policy issue that is virtually sure to persist during the coming years.

On this question the Democrats hold a 29%–22% lead, with 33% saying there is no difference between the two parties and 16% undecided.

This inability of the GOP to convince voters of its superior ability to deal with the nation's important problems is, no doubt, a major factor in Gallup Poll surveys showing that Republicans will gain few, if any, seats in the House this year.

Assuming voter intentions do not change dramatically during the closing weeks of the campaign, the political composition of the House of Representatives will likely remain much as it is today—about two-to-one Democratic.

The one bright spot for the GOP in the survey reported today is the fact that on all four of the issues tested, political independents—who account for about one-third of the electorate—are either evenly divided in their attitudes (as in the cases of taxation and inflation) or see the Republicans as better able to deal with the problem. Mitigating against this, however, is the fact that independents tend to vote less frequently in elections than do those affiliated with either the Democratic or Republican party.

OCTOBER 5
CONFIDENTIAL NEWS SOURCES

Interviewing Date: 8/18–21/78
Survey #110-G

Suppose a newspaper reporter obtains information for a news article he is writing from a person who asks that his name be withheld. Do you think that the reporter should or should not be required to reveal the name of this man if he is taken to court to testify about the information in his news article?

Should 23%
Should not 68
No opinion. 9

By Education
College

Should 18%
Should not 76
No opinion. 6

High School

Should 24%
Should not 67
No opinion. 9

Grade School

Should 28%
Should not 57
No opinion. 15

By Region
East

Should 25%
Should not 64
No opinion. 11

Midwest

Should 23%
Should not 70
No opinion.......................... 7

South

Should 24%
Should not 65
No opinion..........................11

West

Should 18%
Should not 75
No opinion.......................... 7

By Politics
Republicans

Should 22%
Should not 70
No opinion.......................... 8

Democrats

Should 24%
Should not 66
No opinion..........................10

Independents

Should 20%
Should not 72
No opinion.......................... 8

Note: A growing number of Americans believe a reporter should not be required to reveal confidential sources used in gathering information for a news report.

By a three-to-one margin—68%–23%—the public feels reporters should be able to preserve the anonymity of news sources who provide material used in stories. These figures represent a significant increase since 1972 in the percentage who believe reporters should be able to shield the identity of their news sources.

When the Gallup Poll first asked Americans about their views on this subject, in 1972, 57% supported the right of reporters to keep

sources confidential. One year later the figure had climbed to 62%.

The Supreme Court decided in 1972 that there are times when a reporter can be required to reveal information about sources. Since then there have been several cases involving the broad issue of confidentiality. The issue was most recently raised in the case of *New York Times* reporter Myron Farber and a series of stories he wrote leading to the indictment and murder trial of Dr. Mario Jascalevich.

Although each case is characterized by different sets of facts and circumstances, the survey results clearly point to increased public support for the right of reporters to protect news sources.

Support for the right of reporters to keep their sources confidential is widespread, with majorities in every demographic group holding the view that newsmen should not be forced to reveal this information. There are, however, significant differences of opinion on this question by education and geographic region.

The largest gains in support of the so-called "newsmen's privilege" in the past five years have occurred among Republicans (15 percentage points), westerners (13 points), and the college-educated (10 points)—all in excess of the nationwide change of 6 percentage points.

OCTOBER 8
PRESIDENT CARTER

Interviewing Date: 9/22–29/78
Special Telephone Survey

Do you approve or disapprove of the way Jimmy Carter is handling his job as president?

Approve.............................50%
Disapprove 37
No opinion..........................13

Note: President Jimmy Carter's popularity rating, which jumped a record 17 percentage points following the recent Camp David summit, has declined in the latest survey but nevertheless remains 11 points higher than his presummit rating.

The latest survey, based on interviewing conducted September 22–29, shows 50% of the public expressing approval of the president's performance in office, while 37% disapprove and 13% are undecided.

In a survey conducted the day following the president's speech to Congress on the Camp David agreements, 56% approved of the way Carter was handling his job, 30% disapproved, and 14% were undecided.

In the presummit survey, just 39% expressed approval, 36% disapproved, and 25% were undecided. The Camp David talks clearly drew many of the undecided into the approval column —at least temporarily.

Carter's rating in the weeks ahead will depend not only on further developments in the Middle East but also on public attiudes and concerns over the economy. For many months the American people have named the twin economic ills of high living costs and unemployment as the top problems facing the nation.

An examination of the four decades of Gallup Poll presidential popularity measurements prior to and following a dramatic popularity increase sheds light on a question now being debated by political observers: how long can Carter's new popularity level be sustained?

Of course, many factors are involved. Past history, however, indicates that when a president's rating climbs dramatically after a particular event, it ebbs to the level recorded prior to the event in about six months' time.

OCTOBER 12
MOST IMPORTANT PROBLEM

Interviewing Date: 9/8–11/78
Survey #111-G

What do you think is the most important problem facing this country today?

Inflation/high cost of living 59%
Unemployment 12

International problems/foreign policy 6
Energy situation 5
Crime and lawlessness 4
Moral decline/lack of religion 4
Dissatisfaction with government. 3
All others 20
Can't say 3
116%*

*Total adds to more than 100% due to multiple responses.

Asked of those who named a problem: Which political party do you think can do a better job of handling the problem you have just mentioned—the Republican party or the Democratic party?

Republican 20%
Democratic 34
No difference. 36
No opinion. 10

Those Who Cited Inflation as
the Most Important Problem

Republican 21%
Democratic 35
No difference. 36
No opinion. 8

Note: With election day less than one month away, the Republican party has yet to convince American voters that it is better qualified than the Democratic party to solve the nation's critical problems.

In the latest Gallup Poll, 34% of Americans say the Democrats can do a better job of dealing with the national problem they consider most important, while only 20% say the GOP is best qualified in this regard. If the views of those persons who say there is no difference between the two parties or who are as yet undecided are divided evenly between the Democrats and Republicans, the result is 57%–43% split in favor of the Democratic party.

Predictably, inflation continues to be the number one bane of most Americans. Nearly six persons in ten, 59%, rate inflation as the top problem facing the nation—five times as many as cite unemployment, the problem mentioned second most often (by 12%).

An additional finding that provides small comfort to GOP candidates and party strategists is one showing that even among those people who specifically name inflation as the top concern, the Democratic party holds a 35%–21% lead as the party best able to deal with this problem.

Today's survey results represent virtually no change from those of similar surveys taken since the beginning of the year—a situation that negates conventional political wisdom that a period of economic distress hurts the party in power.

OCTOBER 15
ECONOMIC SITUATION

Interviewing Date: 9/15–18/78
Survey #113-G

Do you think the economic situation in the United States during the next six months will get better or will get worse?

Better 22%
Worse 53
Same 18
No opinion 7

By Income
$20,000 and Over

Better 23%
Worse 54
Same 19
No opinion 4

$15,000–$19,999

Better 18%
Worse 63
Same 14
No opinion 5

$10,000–$14,999

Better 26%
Worse 50
Same 16
No opinion 8

$7,000–$9,999

Better 17%
Worse 56
Same 16
No opinion 11

$5,000–$6,999

Better 20%
Worse 48
Same 19
No opinion 13

$3,000–$4,999

Better 20%
Worse 48
Same 23
No opinion 9

Under $3,000

Better 27%
Worse 45
Same 22
No opinion 6

By Politics
Republicans

Better 16%
Worse 56
Same 20
No opinion 8

Democrats

Better 23%
Worse 51
Same 19
No opinion 7

Independents

Better 26%
Worse.................................. 53
Same................................... 14
No opinion........................... 7

By Occupation
Professional and Business

Better 22%
Worse.................................. 53
Same................................... 18
No opinion........................... 7

Clerical and Sales

Better 23%
Worse.................................. 57
Same................................... 14
No opinion........................... 6

Manual Workers

Better 23%
Worse.................................. 55
Same................................... 16
No opinion........................... 6

Non-Labor Force

Better 19%
Worse.................................. 50
Same................................... 21
No opinion........................... 10

Labor Union Families Only

Better 24%
Worse.................................. 54
Same................................... 15
No opinion........................... 7

In your opinion, which is most responsible for inflation—government, business, or labor?

Government 51%
Business.............................. 14
Labor 20
No opinion........................... 15

By Income
$20,000 and Over

Government 55%
Business.............................. 13
Labor 22
No opinion........................... 10

$15,000–$19,999

Government 54%
Business.............................. 16
Labor 18
No opinion........................... 12

$10,000–$14,999

Government 46%
Business.............................. 14
Labor 22
No opinion........................... 18

$7,000–$9,999

Government 49%
Business.............................. 13
Labor 18
No opinion........................... 20

$5,000–$6,999

Government 52%
Business.............................. 10
Labor 19
No opinion........................... 19

$3,000–$4,999

Government 48%
Business.............................. 14
Labor 14
No opinion........................... 24

Under $3,000

Government 37%
Business.............................. 21
Labor 19
No opinion........................... 23

By Politics
Republicans

Government 55%
Business........................... 7
Labor 26
No opinion........................ 12

Democrats

Government 50%
Business........................... 15
Labor 19
No opinion........................ 16

Independents

Government 50%
Business........................... 16
Labor 17
No opinion........................ 17

By Occupation
Professional and Business

Government 50%
Business........................... 16
Labor 21
No opinion........................ 13

Clerical and Sales

Government 49%
Business........................... 9
Labor 27
No opinion........................ 15

Manual Workers

Government 52%
Business........................... 16
Labor 16
No opinion........................ 16

Non-Labor Force

Government 51%
Business........................... 8
Labor 23
No opinion........................ 18

Labor Union Families Only

Government 54%
Business........................... 18
Labor 16
No opinion........................ 12

If a candidate for Congress ran on a platform calling for a reduction in the number of federal employees by 5% each year for the next four years, would you be inclined to vote for him or against him?

Vote for 58%
Vote against..................... 26
No opinion...................... 16

By Income
$20,000 and Over

Vote for 66%
Vote against..................... 24
No opinion...................... 10

$15,000–$19,999

Vote for 64%
Vote against..................... 27
No opinion...................... 9

$10,000–$14,999

Vote for 55%
Vote against..................... 26
No opinion...................... 19

$7,000–$9,999

Vote for 50%
Vote against..................... 29
No opinion...................... 21

$5,000–$6,999

Vote for 44%
Vote against..................... 34
No opinion...................... 22

$3,000–$4,999

Vote for 55%
Vote against. 19
No opinion. 26

Under $3,000

Vote for 52%
Vote against. 30
No opinion. 18

By Politics
Republicans

Vote for 69%
Vote against. 21
No opinion. 10

Democrats

Vote for 56%
Vote against. 27
No opinion. 17

Independents

Vote for 55%
Vote against. 28
No opinion. 17

By Occupation
Professional and Business

Vote for 62%
Vote against. 26
No opinion. 12

Clerical and Sales

Vote for 53%
Vote against. 31
No opinion. 16

Manual Workers

Vote for 55%
Vote against. 27
No opinion. 18

Non-Labor Force

Vote for 60%
Vote against. 23
No opinion. 17

Labor Union Families Only

Vote for 60%
Vote against. 27
No opinion. 13

In your opinion, which of the following do you think will be the biggest threat to the country in the future—big business, big labor, or big government?

Business. 19%
Labor 19
Government 47
Don't know 15

By Income
$20,000 and Over

Business. 15%
Labor 23
Government 51
Don't know 11

$15,000–$19,999

Business. 21%
Labor 16
Government 56
Don't know 7

$10,000–$14,999

Business. 25%
Labor 17
Government 41
Don't know 17

$7,000–$9,999

Business. 14%
Labor 18
Government 49
Don't know 19

$5,000–$6,999

Business.............................15%
Labor 20
Government 42
Don't know 23

$3,000–$4,999

Business.............................23%
Labor 19
Government 38
Don't know 20

Under $3,000

Business.............................28%
Labor 14
Government 37
Don't know 21

By Politics
Republicans

Business.............................12%
Labor 25
Government 52
Don't know 11

Democrats

Business.............................24%
Labor 16
Government 43
Don't know 17

Independents

Business.............................18%
Labor 18
Government 51
Don't know 13

By Occupation
Professional and Business

Business.............................18%
Labor 21
Government 50
Don't know 11

Clerical and Sales

Business.............................17%
Labor 17
Government 49
Don't know 17

Manual Workers

Business.............................21%
Labor 16
Government 48
Don't know 15

Non-Labor Force

Business.............................19%
Labor 23
Government 38
Don't know 20

Labor Union Families Only

Business.............................23%
Labor 12
Government 54
Don't know 11

Note: "Big government" will be on the minds of many voters when they cast their votes on November 7 for congressional candidates and on state referenda dealing with spending curbs inspired by California's Proposition 13.

Rank-and-file members of both the Republican and Democratic parties blame government for many of the nation's ills. Specifically, these findings emerge from the latest Gallup Poll: Government, not business or labor, is held most responsible for inflation; "big government" rather than business or labor poses the greatest threat to the nation's future; a majority of Americans say they would vote for, rather than against, a congressional candidate who called for a 5% reduction in the federal work force during each of the next four years.

The percentage of Americans currently citing government as the chief culprit in the inflationary spiral (51%) is the highest one found in surveys dating back nearly two decades.

At this time, six of every ten Americans name inflation as the number one problem facing the nation. This makes the fact that a majority blame the government for inflation particularly significant.

OCTOBER 19
DEMOCRATIC PRESIDENTIAL CANDIDATES

Interviewing Date: 9/22–25/78
Survey #112-G

Asked of Democrats and independents: Here is a list of people who have been mentioned as possible presidential candidates for the Democratic party in 1980. [Respondents were handed a card with nine names.] Which one would you like to see nominated as the Democratic candidate for president in 1980?

Choice of Democrats

Edward Kennedy	39%
Jimmy Carter	34
Edmund (Jerry) Brown, Jr.	8
Walter Mondale	4
Henry Jackson	3
George McGovern	2
Frank Church	1
Daniel (Pat) Moynihan	1
Morris Udall	1
Don't know	7

Choice of Southern Democrats

Edward Kennedy	35%
Jimmy Carter	41
Edmund (Jerry) Brown, Jr.	7
Walter Mondale	3
Henry Jackson	3
George McGovern	1
Frank Church	1
Daniel (Pat) Moynihan	1
Morris Udall	1
Don't know	7

Choice of Independents

Edward Kennedy	33%
Jimmy Carter	25
Edmund (Jerry) Brown, Jr.	13
Walter Mondale	3
Henry Jackson	4
George McGovern	6
Frank Church	1
Daniel (Pat) Moynihan	2
Morris Udall	3
Don't know	10

Note: Since the Camp David summit President Jimmy Carter has made substantial gains among Democrats as their choice for the party's 1980 presidential nomination.

In a presummit survey, conducted in July, Senator Edward Kennedy of Massachusetts held a 24 percentage point lead over Carter. In the latest survey this edge has been reduced to 5 percentage points.

Kennedy remains the top choice of Democrats across the nation today, winning 39% of their vote for the 1980 nomination, while Carter is the number one choice of 34%—a significant change since July when Kennedy's lead was 44%–20%.

The change since July has occurred outside the South as well as in the president's home region. In the states comprising the South, Carter now leads Kennedy 41%–35%, whereas in July he trailed the Massachusetts senator 44%–26%.

Outside the South Carter has narrowed the gap to 41%–30% in the latest survey—a gain for the president from the 44%–20% margin Kennedy enjoyed in July.

OCTOBER 22
PRESIDENTIAL TRIAL HEAT

Interviewing Date: 9/22–25/78
Survey #112-G

Asked of registered voters: Suppose the presidential election were being held today.

If President Jimmy Carter were the Democratic candidate and Gerald Ford were the Republican candidate, which would you like to see win? Those who named another person or who were undecided were asked: As of today, do you lean more to Carter, the Democrat, or to Ford, the Republican?

Carter.............................54%
Ford..............................40
Other 1
Undecided.........................5

Note: If a repeat of the 1976 presidential election were being held today, survey evidence indicates that President Jimmy Carter would defeat former President Gerald Ford by a substantially greater margin.

In the first test of Carter's strength against a possible Republican opponent since the Camp David summit, the president leads Ford by a 54%–40% margin. Before the summit, Carter and Ford were evenly matched—47% to 46%. Carter, it will be recalled, won a narrow 51%–49% win over Ford in the 1976 presidential election.

Despite his well-publicized troubles with the congressional Black caucus, Carter maintains a huge following among Black voters. Indications are that Carter would win more than 80% of the Black vote if the election were being held today.

OCTOBER 26
CONGRESSIONAL ELECTIONS

Interviewing Date: 9/15–18, 22–25/78
Survey #113-G, 112-G

How much thought have you given to the coming November elections—quite a lot, or only a little?

Quite a lot; some......................39%
Little; none..........................61

Note: One key indication of lower voter turnout this fall is seen in the proportion of Americans saying they have "a lot" or "some" interest in the coming elections compared to earlier congressional election years. In late September 1970, 49% expressed a lot or some interest in the coming elections. At the same time in 1974, the figure was 42%, while the current figure is 39%.

Another indication of lower voter turnout is seen in current figures on voter registration. There will be 155,492,000 people of voting age as of November, and current Gallup Poll data show that only 70% of those of voting age were registered to vote as of early October. This figure also falls below the percentage (72% registered) recorded at this time in 1974, the last congressional election year.

The level of voter turnout has important political implications, since those least likely to vote are downscale groups (lower income and educational levels) who tend to be more likely to vote Democratic. For example, if all persons voted, the nationwide vote for Congress would be about 62% for the Democrats and 38% for the Republicans.

However, when the race is based on those who are most likely to vote, the race is considerably closer. The latest Gallup Poll congressional figures show the Democrats leading, nationwide, 56%–44%.

In assessing the results on voter interest and registration, it is important to bear in mind that these refer to proportions of the voting population and not to actual number of voters. The number of those of voting age has increased, but the rate of voter participation will be down, at least on the basis of present indications. Therefore, even if there were a small decline in the percentage voting, the number of voters would probably increase. For example, if the same percentage of those of voting age voted this year as voted in 1974, the vote for congressmen would total about 57 million, an increase of four million votes. This would not represent any increase in the rate of voting for Congress, however.

OCTOBER 29
CONGRESSIONAL ELECTIONS

Interviewing Date: 9/15–18, 22–25/78
Survey #113-G, 112-G

Asked of registered voters: If the elections for Congress were being held today, which political party would you like to see win in this congressional district, the Democratic party or the Republican party? Those who were undecided were asked: As of today, do you lean more to the Democratic party or to the Republican party?

Democratic 48%
Republican. 37
Other 5
Undecided 10

Here is the two-way split of the vote with the vote for other candidates and the undecided portion allocated:

Democratic 56%
Republican. 44

Note: With the latest Gallup Poll findings showing the Democrats with a 56%–44% advantage in the national popular vote for the House of Representatives, the quarter-century domination of Congress by the Democratic party appears almost certain to continue after the November election.

Actually, the GOP has had control of Congress only four years since 1932. The extent to which the United States has become a one-party government is best illustrated by this example: if the United States were a parliamentary democracy such as Great Britain, a Republican would have occupied the White House only four of these thirty-six years. In view of the one-party domination of the legislature branch of government, political observers are speculating as to the causes for the GOP's failure to gain greater representation in Congress.

Although the GOP is currently trailing the Democratic party by a wide margin in the national popular vote for the House, this year should, in theory, be one of substantial gains for the GOP for these three reasons:

(1) President Jimmy Carter received a sharp popularity boost following the Camp David summit meeting, but his average popularity rating for the twenty months he has been in office is lower than that of most of his predecessors over a comparable period of time. In previous election years a low presidential rating usually has been accompanied by substantial congressional gains by the "out party."

(2) The "pocketbook" issue traditionally has been one that leads to more than normal gains by the party out of power in years when the nation's economic future is uncertain. Since the early years of the New Deal, Republicans have stood for cuts in government spending. But unfortunately for the GOP, as many voters now think the Democrats are likely to reduce government spending as the Republicans. Republicans do not score on the tax question, currently a GOP campaign issue, since many Americans credit the Democrats as being better able to hold down taxes.

(3) Finally—and what must be the greatest paradox of American politics—while the number of people who identify themselves with the Republican party has steadily declined in recent years, the number who identify themselves as conservatives (right-of-center) as opposed to liberals (left-of-center) has shown a steady increase.

The following table shows how the percentage of Americans identifying themselves as Republicans has declined while that of those who call themselves conservatives has, at the same time, increased:

Percentage of Americans Calling Themselves:

	Republicans	Conservatives
1978	20%	52%
1970	29	39
1953	37	32

The key problems facing the GOP are (1) a failure to shake its "fat-cat," pro-business image with many voters; and (2) failure to develop a strong basic policy position to attract voters.

The conclusion is based not only on many national Gallup Polls but on an intense in-depth survey in Gloucester County, New Jersey, by a team of Gallup Poll editors. Gloucester County is a remarkably good "barometer" county for the entire country, since the county presidential vote in elections of recent decades has closely paralleled the national popular vote.

OCTOBER 31
PRESIDENT CARTER

Interviewing Date: 9/29–10/23/78*
Special Telephone Survey

Do you approve or disapprove of the way Jimmy Carter is handling his job as president?

Approve............................50%
Disapprove 36
No opinion...........................14

Note: President Jimmy Carter has retained most of his Camp David popularity gains, with 50% in the latest survey saying they approve of his performance in office.

The latest approval rating represents a decline of 6 percentage points since a survey taken immediately following the Camp David summit when the president's rating hit 56% approval (a record 17-point jump), but is nevertheless 11 points above Carter's presummit rating. That approval figure was 39%, the president's low point to date.

Comparison of the president's current rating with those of other presidents at comparable points in time before midterm congressional elections shows Carter's rating to be higher than that of the incumbents in four of the last ten congressional election years, and lower in the other five.

Final Presidential Popularity Results
Prior to Midterm Vote for Congress

President Ford, October–November 1974

Approve............................44%
Disapprove 44
No opinion...........................12

President Nixon, October 1970

Approve............................58%
Disapprove 27
No opinion...........................15

President Johnson, October 1966

Approve............................44%
Disapprove 41
No opinion...........................15

President Kennedy, October 1962

Approve............................61%
Disapprove 24
No opinion...........................15

President Eisenhower, October 1958

Approve............................58%
Disapprove 25
No opinion...........................17

President Eisenhower, October 1954

Approve............................61%
Disapprove 26
No opinion...........................13

President Truman, October 1950

Approve............................39%
Disapprove 42
No opinion...........................19

President Truman, September 1946

Approve............................32%
Disapprove 53
No opinion...........................15

President Roosevelt, October 1942

Approve............................. 70%
Disapprove 19
No opinion........................... 11

*The latest results are based on continuous telephone interviewing between September 29 and October 23 with a total of 1,520 adults, eighteen years and older. The current results include an allowance for nontelephone households and an allowance for response differences between telephone and personal interviews.

NOVEMBER 6
CONGRESSIONAL ELECTIONS— FINAL SURVEY

Interviewing Date: 10/13–16, 27–30/78
Survey #114-G, 115-G

Asked of registered voters: If the elections for Congress were being held today, which political party would you like to see win in this congressional district, the Democratic party or the Republican party? Those who were undecided were asked: As of today, do you lean more to the Democratic party or to the Republican party?

Final Gallup Poll Report

Democratic 55%
Republican.......................... 45

Actual Election Result*

Democratic 54%
Republican.......................... 46

*Based on election data received from the secretaries of state of all fifty states.

Note: These final survey findings, reported on a two-party basis, are confined solely to House races. Since senatorial elections are not held in all states in any one election year, the House contests constitute the only nationwide test of party strength.

Congressional elections pose major problems in relating voter opinion to the election results. For example, to accurately anticipate the seat change in the election, a full-scale survey would have to be conducted in each of the 435 congressional districts in the nation. Thus, a nationwide sampling is substituted to produce an estimate of how the total popular vote cast for members of Congress divides between the two major parties. This provides a picture of party strength at the national level and, in fact, provides a truer measurement of party strength nationwide than does the distribution of House seats.

NOVEMBER 12
PRESIDENT CARTER

Interviewing Date: 10/6–30/78
Special Telephone Survey

Do you approve or disapprove of the way Jimmy Carter is handling his job as president?

Approve............................. 51%
Disapprove 35
No opinion........................... 14

Note: As the nation's voters went to the polls last Tuesday, President Jimmy Carter's popularity rating stood at 51% approval, just five points below his immediate postsummit rating.

Carter's postsummit rating of 56% represented a record 17-point jump in popularity and the president's highest score since last December.

The president has registered popularity gains in the latest survey among all major groups since his August low point of 39% approval, but his gains have been most pronounced among men, younger adults, persons living outside the South, and those with a college background.

The president's popularity profile is remarkable in that a higher proportion of the college segment—which includes a disproportionately high number of Republicans—say they approve of the president's performance in office. Approval ratings for the president's Democratic predecessors have been consistently lower among those with college training than among those with less formal education.

The following compares the latest results by groups with those from the August, pre-summit survey:

Percent Approval

	Aug. 4–7	Current*
By Sex		
Male	38%	53%
Female	40	49
By Race		
Whites	38%	50%
Nonwhites	48	58
By Education		
College	36%	54%
High school	40	49
Grade school	43	47
By Region		
South	44%	52%
Non-South	37	50
By Age		
18–29 years	43%	59%
30–49 years	44	54
50 years and over	32	42

*The results reported today are based on continuous daily telephone interviewing between October 6 and 30 with a total of 1,523 adults, eighteen years and older. The current findings include an allowance for nontelephone households and an allowance for response differences between telephone and personal interviews.

NOVEMBER 13
"CENTER PARTY"

Interviewing Date: 10/27–30/78
Survey #115-G

It has been suggested that the nation needs a new party—one that appeals to people who are middle-of-the-road in their political views. If there were such a party, then the Republicans would represent the people on the right—the conservatives; the Democrats would represent the people on the left—the liberals; and the new party would represent those in-between or in the middle. Do you think there is or is not a place for such a "center party" in the United States today?

Yes	41%
No	42
No opinion	17

By Sex
Male

Yes	42%
No	47
No opinion	11

Female

Yes	41%
No	37
No opinion	22

By Education
College

Yes	45%
No	47
No opinion	8

High School

Yes	44%
No	40
No opinion	16

Grade School

Yes 24%
No 38
No opinion 38

By Region
East

Yes 48%
No 37
No opinion 15

Midwest

Yes 40%
No 45
No opinion 15

South

Yes 29%
No 46
No opinion 25

West

Yes 51%
No 39
No opinion 10

By Age
18–29 Years

Yes 54%
No 32
No opinion 14

30–49 Years

Yes 39%
No 47
No opinion 14

50 Years and Over

Yes 33%
No 45
No opinion 22

By Politics
Republicans

Yes 39%
No 48
No opinion 13

Democrats

Yes 37%
No 45
No opinion 18

Independents

Yes 52%
No 34
No opinion 14

Note: A remarkable number of Americans favor major political realignments in the United States and would like to see the creation of a new "center party."

These views are recorded at a time when the Democratic party has just extended its control of both Houses of Congress for at least another two years, representing a half-century domination of the legislative branch of government.

As the question was posed in a new Gallup Poll conducted just prior to the elections, such a center party would appeal to people who are middle-of-the-road politically, while the Republican party would represent people who are right of center—the conservatives—and the Democratic party would represent people left of center—the liberals. A center party, as defined in the survey, should not be confused with third-party movements in America's past political history. Without exception these parties have represented the radical right or the radical left.

In the aftermath of the Democratic party's sweeping victory in the congressional races last Tuesday, political observers point out that the present two-party system exists largely in name only. Since 1932 the Republicans have held majorities in Congress only four years: 1946–48 and 1952–54. This half-century domination of the legislative branch of government by the Democratic party raises the question as to whether the nation is ready for a new party alignment. Some critics, in fact, say that we now have a four-party system: Democratic liberals, Democratic conservatives, Republican liberals, and Republican conservatives. And some cynics point out that we have a "one-and-a-half" party system, since approximately twice as many legislators in the nation are Democrats as Republicans.

The continuing decline in voter turnout—only slightly more than one-third of adults voted last Tuesday—is also a matter of great concern. Many feel this is due to the fact that the parties do not represent clear-cut ideological positions. Some of the nation's voters say, in effect, that "there's no difference between the parties; they both stand for the same things."

NOVEMBER 19
GOVERNMENT SPENDING

Interviewing Date: 10/27–30/78
Survey #115-G

Of every tax dollar that goes to the federal government in Washington, D.C., how many cents of each dollar would you say are wasted?

	Median Average
National	48¢

By Politics

Republicans	48¢
Democrats	49
Independents	48

And how many cents of each tax dollar that goes to the government of this state would you say are wasted?

	Median Average
National	32¢

By Politics

Republicans	31¢
Democrats	33
Independents	31

And how many cents of each tax dollar that goes to your local government would you say are wasted?

	Median Average
National	25¢

By Politics

Republicans	25¢
Democrats	24
Independents	25

Note: Much of the criticism of federal spending is directed not at the validity or purposes of these outlays but at what is perceived to be the waste of taxpayers' money.

In fact, the public judgment is that as much as half (48¢) of every tax dollar that goes to the federal government in Washington is wasted. This is a median average of all responses in a recently completed nationwide Gallup Poll.

In light of the public's views on the waste of tax dollars, it is not surprising that Americans are highly critical of federal spending per se.

In a survey reported this summer, an overwhelming 75% of the public said the federal government spends too much money. Just 5% said federal outlays were too small, and 11% felt spending was at about the right level.

As with views on the waste of tax dollar, criticism of government spending did not fall evenly on all levels of government. A 53% majority felt spending by their state government was too high. In the case of local government, only 38% held the same view. Of particular interest is the fact that for all three levels of government, the figures cited by Democrats are nearly identical to those offered by Republicans.

The same survey also showed that by a seven-to-one margin (81%–11%), the public favored amending the Constitution to require balancing the federal budget each year.

NOVEMBER 21
PRESIDENT CARTER

Interviewing Date: 10/20–11/13/78
Special Telephone Survey

Do you approve or disapprove of the way Jimmy Carter is handling his job as president?

Approve.............................52%
Disapprove 36
No opinion..........................12

Note: The elections for Congress and for state offices had no measurable effect on President Jimmy Carter's personal popularity.

The results reported today are based on continuous daily telephone interviewing between October 20 and November 13 with a total of 1,517 adults, eighteen years and older. The current findings include an allowance for non-telephone households and an allowance for response differences between telephone and personal interviews.

NOVEMBER 23
INTERFAITH MARRIAGES

Interviewing Date: 7/21–24/78
Survey #107-G

Do you approve or disapprove of marriage between Catholics and Protestants?

Approve.............................73%
Disapprove 13
No opinion..........................14

By Sex
Male

Approve.............................73%
Disapprove 11
No opinion..........................16

Female

Approve.............................73%
Disapprove 14
No opinion..........................13

By Education
College

Approve.............................82%
Disapprove 8
No opinion..........................10

High School

Approve.............................72%
Disapprove 13
No opinion..........................15

Grade School

Approve.............................57%
Disapprove 22
No opinion..........................21

By Religion
Protestants

Approve.............................68%
Disapprove 15
No opinion..........................17

Catholics

Approve.............................80%
Disapprove 11
No opinion.......................... 9

Do you approve or disapprove of marriage between Jews and non-Jews?

Approve.............................69%
Disapprove 14
No opinion..........................17

By Sex
Male

Approve.............................71%
Disapprove 11
No opinion..........................18

Female

Approve............................68%
Disapprove 16
No opinion......................... 16

By Education
College

Approve............................80%
Disapprove 10
No opinion......................... 10

High School

Approve............................69%
Disapprove 14
No opinion......................... 17

Grade School

Approve............................50%
Disapprove 20
No opinion......................... 30

By Religion*
Protestants

Approve............................64%
Disapprove 18
No opinion......................... 18

Catholics

Approve............................77%
Disapprove 7
No opinion......................... 16

*The small number of Jews in the sample does not warrant presentation of the results for Jews in percentages. However, among those who are included, opinion closely matches overall national opinion.

Note: One of the most interesting chapters in the social history of America has been the decline in prejudice toward persons of different religions, during recent decades. Further evidence that American society is becoming more tolerant can be seen in the trend of expressed attitudes on interfaith marriages during the last ten years.

Between 1968 and today the proportion of Americans who say they approve of marriages between Catholics and Protestants has increased from 63% to 73%. In the case of marriage between Jews and non-Jews, the percentage has risen from 59% in 1968 to 69% today.

NOVEMBER 26
THE MIDDLE EAST

Interviewing Date: 11/10–13/78
Survey #116-G

Have you heard or read about the situation in the Middle East?

Yes................................91%
No.................................. 9

Asked of those who replied in the affirmative: In the Middle East situation, are your sympathies more with Israel or more with the Arab nations?

Israel 39%
Arab nations 13
Neither............................. 30
No opinion.......................... 18

By Education
College

Israel 44%
Arab nations 16
Neither............................. 27
No opinion.......................... 13

High School

Israel 37%
Arab nations 13
Neither............................. 31
No opinion.......................... 19

Grade School

Israel 31%
Arab nations 5
Neither............................. 32
No opinion.......................... 32

Also asked of those who replied in the affirmative: Do you think Israel is or is not doing all it should to bring about peace in the Middle East?

Is.....................................27%
Is not..................................49
No opinion..............................24

By Education
College

Is.....................................27%
Is not..................................56
No opinion..............................17

High School

Is.....................................26%
Is not..................................51
No opinion..............................23

Grade School

Is.....................................26%
Is not..................................29
No opinion..............................45

Also asked of those who replied in the affirmative: Do you think Egypt is or is not doing all it should to bring about peace in the Middle East?

Is.....................................31%
Is not..................................44
No opinion..............................25

By Education
College

Is.....................................39%
Is not..................................42
No opinion..............................19

High School

Is.....................................28%
Is not..................................48
No opinion..............................24

Grade School

Is.....................................23%
Is not..................................30
No opinion..............................47

Note: While Egypt has gained some ground with the American people as the nation working for peace, basic sympathies have changed little over recent months. Israel continues to hold a wide advantage in the current survey; 39% sympathize with Israel while only 13% support the Arab nations.

While basic sympathies consistently have been on the side of Israel since the first measurement at the time of the Six-Day War (when a high of 56% sided with Israel and 4% with the Arab nations), the proportion who are divided or undecided in their loyalties has grown over the decade since that war.

NOVEMBER 30
URBAN PROBLEMS

Interviewing Date: 11/10–13/78
Survey #116-G

Asked of those who live in communities and cities of 2,500 and over: Suppose the mayor of this city appointed committees made up of average citizens to study local problems such as crime, housing, and public transportation—and to make recommendations. If you were asked, do you think you would be willing to serve on one of these voluntary committees without pay?

Yes....................................52%
No......................................42
Don't know 6

Asked of those who replied in the affirmative: This card lists various kinds of problems that might be studied by such voluntary committees. Which of these committees —if any—do you think you would be interested in serving on without pay?

Schools and education 22%
Senior citizen problems 21
Parks, playgrounds, sports/recreational
   facilities 19
Drug problems and rehabilitation 18
Activities for youth 18
Problems of the handicapped 17
Housing for the poor 16
Improving hospitals and health care 16
Problems of the poor 16
Unemployment problems 15
Dealing with crime 15
Courts and prison reform 13
Race relations 11
Air and water pollution 11
City beautification 10
Attracting new business/industry,
   keeping existing business/industry 10
Preservation of historic places and
   landmarks 9
Improving cultural opportunities 8
Noise pollution 7
Public transportation 7
Traffic control and parking 7
Sanitation, garbage, litter, etc. 7
Public libraries 6

Asked of those who live in communities and cities of 2,500 and over: Now, suppose there were voluntary committees, of the kind just described, in this neighborhood. These would be made up of neighborhood residents who would study problems and make recommendations to local officials. If you were asked, do you think you would be willing to serve on one of these committees without pay?

Yes 64%
No 28
Don't know 8

Asked of those who replied in the affirmative: This card lists various kinds of problems that might be studied by such voluntary committees. Which of these committees—if any—do you think you would be interested in serving on without pay?

Neighborhood crime, vandalism 28%
Neighborhood clean-up and
   beautification 22
Senior citizen problems 22
Neighborhood schools 22
Neighborhood youth activities 22
Neighborhood recreation, parks,
   playgrounds 17
Health care for neighborhood residents . . . 16
Neighborhood employment
   opportunities 13
Neighborhood housing problems 13
Establishment of neighborhood coopera-
   tives such as food stores, general
   merchandise, etc. 13
Neighborhood race relations 12
Preservation of old/historic buildings,
   landmarks 11
Air and water pollution 11
Neighborhood parking and traffic 9
Neighborhood noise control 9
Problems of neighborhood retail business,
   shops, stores 8
Public transportation 8

Note: A Gallup study completed recently for the National League of Cities reveals the existence of a vast resource of volunteer citizen energy that could be used in practical ways to alleviate urban problems.

The value of such voluntary efforts on the part of the nation's urban residents would be (1) as a low-cost option for providing some urban services—important now with the prospect of a reduction in urban funds—and (2) as an effective way to improve the social fabric of America's cities, as evidence to city government and the business community that residents believe their city has a future, and is therefore worth investing in.

Following are the key survey findings:

America's urban residents state that they would be willing to donate an average of nine hours per month to their city and their neighborhoods. Projected to the total population of the 125 million adults residing in nonrural areas, the hours available per month comes to the staggering total of approximately one billion.

About one-half (52%) of America's urban residents say they would be willing to serve without pay on city advisory committees to study problems facing their cities and to make recommendations.

Committees in which urban residents express interest include those that would deal with schools and education; senior citizen problems; activities for youth; problems of the handicapped, hospitals, and health care; air, water, and noise pollution; city beautification; attracting new business/industry; and preservation of historic places and landmarks.

About two in three (64%) express a willingness to serve on committees devoted to the specific problems facing their own neighborhoods. Most frequently mentioned are committees devoted to the following neighborhood problems: crime and vandalism; clean-up and beautification; schools; establishment of cooperatives such as food and general merchandise stores; and the problems of retail business, shops, and stores.

A still larger majority, seven in ten (69%), state they would be willing to engage in specific neighborhood activities, including assisting in the performance of some neighborhood social services.

Activities cited most often include serving on crime watch, working in child care center, helping in employment organization (matching jobs/part-time work with those who need employment), assisting in pick-up of trash and litter on streets and sidewalks, helping to fix up abandoned buildings in the neighborhood, helping to organize festivals and block parties, assisting in monitoring or checking store prices and customer policies, and working in cooperatives, such as food stores.

When the nation's urban residents were asked how much time they would be willing to donate to volunteer efforts at both the city and neighborhood level, the average number of hours is nine.

Although the number of hours Americans would be willing to contribute in public service is impressively high in virtually every population segment, it is not surprising that those willing to contribute the most time are the better educated, and particularly the retired.

When asked how they would distribute the nine hours between the city as a whole and their own neighborhood, urban residents allocate approximately three hours to the city and about twice this figure, six hours, to their own neighborhoods.

The reservoir of citizen talent is representative of virtually the entire urban population. Even those who are most pessimistic about the future of their city and their neighborhood—and those who say that they would move away given the opportunity—are as willing to volunteer their time as those who plan to remain and who are the most optimistic about their city and neighborhood's future.

DECEMBER 3
REPUBLICAN PRESIDENTIAL CANDIDATES

Interviewing Date: 6/16–19, 11/10–13/78
Survey #105-G, 116-G

Asked of Republicans: Suppose the choice for president in the Republican convention in 1980 narrows down to Gerald Ford and Ronald Reagan. Which one would you prefer to have the Republican convention select?

Ford 48%
Reagan 42
Undecided 10

By Sex
Male

Ford 51%
Reagan 42
Undecided 7

Female

Ford 46%
Reagan 43
Undecided 11

By Education

College

Ford	59%
Reagan	36
Undecided	5

High School

Ford	44%
Reagan	48
Undecided	8

Grade School

Ford	38%
Reagan	38
Undecided	24

By Region

East

Ford	48%
Reagan	41
Undecided	11

Midwest

Ford	51%
Reagan	39
Undecided	10

South

Ford	46%
Reagan	46
Undecided	8

West

Ford	45%
Reagan	47
Undecided	8

By Age

18–29 Years

Ford	53%
Reagan	37
Undecided	10

30–49 Years

Ford	50%
Reagan	46
Undecided	4

50 Years and Over

Ford	44%
Reagan	43
Undecided	13

Note: Traditionally, attention turns to the race for the presidential nomination after the midterm elections when strategists in both parties have had a chance to examine the returns and see which way the political winds are blowing.

Leaders of the Republican party were encouraged by the gains made in the November elections, when the GOP added to their list of governors and state legislators. At a meeting of GOP governors this last week, sentiment in favor of a moderate position was reported to prevail over support for more conservative policies.

This matches the sentiment expressed by Republicans across the nation in the latest survey. Ford's 48%–42% lead over Reagan closely parallels results recorded in a preelection survey and makes possible an examination of each man's strengths and weaknesses within the rank and file.

When the results of the last two surveys are combined and analyzed, the results reveal these significant differences among important groups within the Republican party:

Regionally, Ford leads Reagan in the Midwest, the area where many Republican gains were made in the election. Ford also leads in the East, while southern and western Republicans split their vote;

Ford commands greater strength among college-educated Republicans than does Reagan. Among those whose education ended at the high-school or grade-school level the results for the two men are even;

Young Republicans—those less than thirty years of age—prefer the former president, while among those thirty years and older, the vote is evenly divided between the two men;

Ford holds a clear lead over Reagan among men, whereas the vote of women is more closely divided.

DECEMBER 7
IDEAL FAMILY SIZE

Interviewing Date: 9/15–18/78
Survey #113-G

What do you think is the ideal number of children for a family to have?

One.................................	1%
Two	49
Three	23
Four	13
Five	2
Six or more	2
None...............................	2
No opinion.........................	8

Those Saying Four or More Children

By Sex

Male...............................	18%
Female.............................	16

By Education

College............................	9%
High school........................	18
Grade school.......................	29

By Age

18–29 years........................	15%
30–49 years........................	15
50 years and over	20

By Religion

Protestants........................	16%
Catholics	21

Note: Recent forecasts of a reduced rate of population growth in the United States during the next few decades may have to be revised.

One of the most important factors in projecting population trends are the public's views on the desirability of large families. Since 1936, the Gallup Poll has regularly charted these views.

At that time, 34% said that four or more children represented the ideal family size. The figures rose dramatically during the war years to a high of 49% in 1945, anticipating the "baby boom." As late as 1968, 41% of the public felt the model family would include four or more children. By 1971, however, the figure dropped to 23% and continued to decline steadily to 13% in 1977.

The 1977 figure was the lowest percentage favoring large families since the Gallup Poll began asking this question in 1936. Currently 17% say four or more is the ideal number of children for a family to have.

Following is the trend since 1936 in the proportion saying four or more is the ideal number of children:

Percent Saying Four or More Is Ideal Number of Children

1936...............................	34%
1941...............................	41
1945...............................	49
1947...............................	47
1953...............................	41
1957...............................	38
1960...............................	45
1963...............................	42
1966...............................	35
1968...............................	41
1971...............................	23
1973...............................	20
1974...............................	19
1977...............................	13
1978...............................	17

Significant differences emerge when the results are analyzed by major population groups. Those who have had only a grade-school education are far more likely than are the better educated to prefer larger families.

Attitudes of Roman Catholics on the question of family size have shown a marked change in the last decade. In 1968 a total of 50% of Catholics interviewed thought the ideal family consisted of four or more children. Only 21% hold that view today.

DECEMBER 10
ITEM VETO POWER

Interviewing Date: 11/10–13/78
Survey #116-G

At the present time, when Congress passes a bill, the president cannot veto parts of that bill, but must accept it in full or veto it. Do you think this should be changed so that the president can veto some items in a bill without vetoing the entire bill?

Yes 70%
No 19
No opinion 11

By Education
College

Yes 70%
No 23
No opinion 7

High School

Yes 73%
No 19
No opinion 8

Grade School

Yes 59%
No 10
No opinion 31

By Politics
Republicans

Yes 65%
No 27
No opinion 8

Democrats

Yes 71%
No 16
No opinion 13

Independents

Yes 72%
No 18
No opinion 10

Note: In this era of intensified public concern over federal spending, the American people send this message to the new Congress convening in January: give President Jimmy Carter the item veto power he seeks.

A record seven in ten persons (70%) in a just-completed Gallup survey favor giving a president this power—that is, permitting him to veto specific items in bills passed by Congress instead of having to veto or approve the entire bill as is the case at present.

Those who oppose the present system say that giving the president item veto power would stop "pork-barrel" legislation, which involves the inclusion of items to a bill that have the primary function of serving the political interests of certain members of Congress. Others contend that elimination of the expensive riders that are frequently tacked onto proposed bills will save millions of dollars.

The main argument offered by those in the current survey who favor the present system is that it gives the legislative branch more power by forcing a president to accept items (particularly in appropriation bills) that he might not otherwise accept.

Majorities in surveys going back more than three decades have favored changing the present rule. When the issue was first presented to the public in 1945, 57% voted in favor of allowing a chief executive to exercise item veto power.

Support for giving the president item veto power is found among all major population segments. Solid majorities of both Democrats and Republicans favor the change.

DECEMBER 14
"TEST-TUBE BABY" PROCEDURE

Interviewing Date: 8/4–7/78
Survey #108-G

Have you heard or read about the baby born in England from an egg fertilized outside her mother's body?

Yes 93%
No 7

Asked of those who replied in the affirmative: Just as you understand it, how was this done?

Egg was taken from the mother's body and
    fertilized with the father's sperm in a
    culture medium and then reimplanted
    in the mother's body 42%
Was fertilized in a laboratory 19
Incorrect answers 15
Don't know 24

Asked of the entire sample: Actually, what the doctor did was to remove an egg from one of the woman's ovaries and fertilize it in the laboratory with sperm from her husband. The embryo was then implanted in her uterus. The embryo grew inside the woman and was born like other babies. Some people oppose this kind of operation because they feel it is "not natural." Other people favor it because it would allow a husband and wife to have a child when otherwise it would be impossible. Which point of view comes closer to your own?

Favor operation 60%
Oppose operation 27
No opinion 13

By Sex
Male

Favor operation 59%
Oppose operation 26
No opinion 15

Female

Favor operation 61%
Oppose operation 29
No opinion 10

By Education
College

Favor operation 74%
Oppose operation 18
No opinion 8

High School

Favor operation 61%
Oppose operation 26
No opinion 13

Grade School

Favor operation 30%
Oppose operation 51
No opinion 19

By Region
East

Favor operation 62%
Oppose operation 29
No opinion 9

Midwest

Favor operation 56%
Oppose operation 27
No opinion 17

South

Favor operation 55%
Oppose operation 30
No opinion 15

West

Favor operation 70%
Oppose operation 22
No opinion 8

By Age
18–29 Years

Favor operation 71%
Oppose operation 21
No opinion. 8

30–49 Years

Favor operation 65%
Oppose operation 23
No opinion. 12

50 Years and Over

Favor operation 47%
Oppose operation 36
No opinion. 17

By Religion
Protestants

Favor operation 61%
Oppose operation 26
No opinion. 13

Catholics

Favor operation 56%
Oppose operation 32
No opinion. 12

*Also asked of the entire sample: Suppose
you were married and wanted to have a
child but were unable to do so. Do you think
you would or would not be willing to
undergo this procedure if it would enable
you to have a child?*

Yes, would. 53%
No, would not 36
Don't know 11

By Sex
Male

Yes, would. 54%
No, would not 33
Don't know 13

Female

Yes, would. 52%
No, would not 38
Don't know 10

By Education
College

Yes, would. 69%
No, would not 25
Don't know 6

High School

Yes, would. 53%
No, would not 35
Don't know 12

Grade School

Yes, would. 26%
No, would not 58
Don't know 16

By Region
East

Yes, would. 54%
No, would not 34
Don't know 12

Midwest

Yes, would. 49%
No, would not 39
Don't know 12

South

Yes, would. 51%
No, would not 38
Don't know 11

West

Yes, would. 63%
No, would not 31
Don't know 6

By Age

18-29 Years

Yes, would	64%
No, would not	28
Don't know	8

30-49 Years

Yes, would	57%
No, would not	34
Don't know	9

50 Years and Over

Yes, would	42%
No, would not	43
Don't know	15

By Religion

Protestants

Yes, would	53%
No, would not	37
Don't know	10

Catholics

Yes, would	50%
No, would not	39
Don't know	11

Note: If the federal government decides to fund research regarding vitro fertilization—the process of uniting a human sperm and egg outside a woman's body—the decision would, at the present time, meet with the approval of most Americans.

While the government is currently trying to decide whether this kind of research should be federally funded, the Gallup Poll, in a survey conducted after the birth of the successful "test-tube baby" last July, found the public favorably disposed toward this procedure.

Specifically, the survey found the following:

An extraordinary 93% had heard or read about the baby, a girl born in England;

Among those who had heard or read about the birth, understanding of this relatively complicated process was high;

By a two-to-one margin, the public approved of the procedure;

A majority of Americans said they would be willing to undergo this procedure if they were childless, wanted to have a child, and this would allow them to do so.

The birth of Louise Brown and the procedure by which she was conceived clearly fascinated many Americans. A huge segment of the public, 93%, either heard or read about the baby's birth. In no group of Americans did this simple recognition fall below 79%, and in some groups it reached as high as 98%.

The public's interest in the birth goes well beyond just knowing it happened. Of those who had heard or read about the birth, four in ten (42%) were also able to explain exactly what happened—that an egg was taken from the mother's body and fertilized with the father's sperm in a culture medium and then reimplanted in the mother's womb. Predictably, understanding of the operation is highest among the so-called upscale socioeconomic groups—that is, those in the upper educational and income brackets and those who work in either business or the professions.

Understanding of the procedure is clearly a key in the formation of attitudes toward it. For example, support for the operation is generally highest among those groups most likely to have heard or read about the procedure and who are best able to explain the procedure. Approval of the operation reaches 75% with these groups.

Generally, the same pattern of opinion obtains when people are asked whether they would be willing to undergo the procedure if they were unable to have a child, wanted one, and this procedure would allow them to conceive.

Interestingly, men and women have about the same views on each of these questions. Furthermore, despite the Roman Catholic church's labeling of vitro fertilization as "illicit," Catholics are favorably disposed toward the operation (56%) and half (50%) say they would use this method to conceive if they had to.

DECEMBER 17

CONGRESSIONAL PREFERENCES OF KEY VOTING GROUPS— AN ANALYSIS

Even with the change in the political party holding the presidency, the congressional preferences of key voting groups have changed remarkably little since 1970, as determined by a Gallup Poll analysis of November election survey data.

The 1970 congressional figures were used as a basis for comparison between the division of the national vote in that election was almost identical to the division of the vote in the latest election.

The major party division in the congressional vote in 1970 was 54.3% Democratic and 45.7% Republican. An estimate based on the latest available vote figures from the recent November elections indicates virtually the same division in the national vote on November 7: 54% Democratic and 46% Republican. The Gallup Poll's final preelection report of the division of the national popular vote for House candidates was 55% Democratic and 45% Republican.

In the recent election, nonwhites, despite their criticism of the present Democratic administration, voted as solidly Democratic as they did in the 1970 congressional elections. An estimated 83% of nonwhites in 1970 voted for Democratic candidates nationwide, compared to 84% in the latest election. In addition, Catholics—another traditionally Democratic group—voted as heavily for Democratic candidates this year as they did eight years ago: 62% this year and 63% in 1970.

Party loyalty also remains constant. For example, 85% of Democrats voted their party in the recent elections; 89% did so in 1970. Among Republicans, an estimated 90% voted their party; 93% did so in 1970. Today, as in 1970, independent voters are closely divided in their political choices for Congress.

Following is a comparison of the congressional vote by groups in the November elections with the vote in 1970, with the results given on the basis of the major party division:

Democratic (1978)....................55%
Republican (1978)....................45
Democratic (1970)....................54
Republican (1970)....................46

By Sex
Male

Democratic (1978)....................53%
Republican (1978)....................47
Democratic (1970)....................53
Republican (1970)....................47

Female

Democratic (1978)....................57%
Republican (1978)....................43
Democratic (1970)....................55
Republican (1970)....................45

By Race
Whites

Democratic (1978)....................52%
Republican (1978)....................48
Democratic (1970)....................52
Republican (1970)....................48

Nonwhites

Democratic (1978)....................84%
Republican (1978)....................16
Democratic (1970)....................83
Republican (1970)....................17

By Education
College

Democratic (1978)....................46%
Republican (1978)....................54
Democratic (1970)....................44
Republican (1970)....................56

High School

Democratic (1978)....................56%
Republican (1978)....................44
Democratic (1970)....................57
Republican (1970)....................43

Grade School

Democratic (1978)................... 70%
Republican (1978) 30
Democratic (1970)................... 60
Republican (1970) 40

By Age
18–29 Years

Democratic (1978)................... 58%
Republican (1978) 42
Democratic (1970)................... 61
Republican (1970) 39

30–49 Years

Democratic (1978)................... 54%
Republican (1978) 46
Democratic (1970)................... 55
Republican (1970) 45

50 Years and Over

Democratic (1978)................... 54%
Republican (1978) 46
Democratic (1970)................... 51
Republican (1970) 49

By Politics
Republicans

Democratic (1978)................... 10%
Republican (1978) 90
Democratic (1970)................... 7
Republican (1970) 93

Democrats

Democratic (1978)................... 85%
Republican (1978) 15
Democratic (1970)................... 89
Republican (1970) 11

Independents

Democratic (1978)................... 48%
Republican (1978) 52
Democratic (1970)................... 50
Republican (1970) 50

By Religion
Protestants

Democratic (1978)................... 50%
Republican (1978) 50
Democratic (1970)................... 48
Republican (1970) 52

Catholics

Democratic (1978)................... 62%
Republican (1978) 38
Democratic (1970)................... 63
Republican (1970) 37

DECEMBER 21
MOST ADMIRED MAN

Interviewing Date: 12/1–4/78
Survey #117-G

What man that you have heard or read about, living today in any part of the world, do you admire the most? Who is your second choice?

Following are the latest results, based on first and second choices combined:

Jimmy Carter
Pope John Paul II
Billy Graham
Anwar Sadat
Gerald Ford
Ronald Reagan
Edward Kennedy
Richard Nixon
Menachem Begin
Henry Kissinger

Note: Among those also receiving a high number of mentions are the following (in alphabetical order): Muhammad Ali, Bob Hope, Reverend Jesse Jackson, Vice President Walter Mondale, John Wayne, and United States Ambassador to the United Nations Andrew Young.

Survey respondents in these regular audits, which go back more than three decades, are asked to give their choices without the aid of a list of names. This procedure, while opening the field to all possible choices, tends to favor those who are in the news.

DECEMBER 24
MOST ADMIRED WOMAN

Interviewing Date: 12/1–4/78
Survey #117-G

Which woman that you have heard or read about, living today in any part of the world, do you admire the most? Who is your second choice?

Following are first and second choices combined:

Betty Ford
Rosalyn Carter
Golda Meir
Pat Nixon
Barbara Walters
Jacqueline Kennedy Onassis
Anita Bryant
Barbara Jordan }tied
Queen Elizabeth II
Shirley Chisholm
Indira Gandhi

Note: Receiving frequent mention but not included in the top ten are: Bella Abzug, Lillian Carter, Mamie Eisenhower, Rose Kennedy, and Coretta King.

DECEMBER 26
JONESTOWN TRAGEDY

Interviewing Date: 12/8–11/78
Survey #118-G

Have you heard or read about the mass suicides in Guyana among members of a cult called the People's Temple?

Yes 98%
No 2

By Education

	Yes
College	99%
High school	98
Grade school	96

Asked of those who replied in the affirmative: Why do you think people become involved in cults of this kind?

Need for leadership, a father figure	15%
Have unhappy lives, a feeling of hopelessness	13
Gullible	13
Need to have a sense of belonging, a sense of community.................	12
Searching for a deeper meaning to life, their lives are spiritually empty	12
They are mentally disturbed	11
A failure of churches—people are disillusioned with the churches	7
They are brainwashed	7
To escape from reality	7
Need for something to believe in.........	6
Insecurity............................	4
Homes have broken up/failed	4
Lack motivation, ambition, direction; have nothing better to do with their lives.............................	3
The devil, false prophets	3
Lack of education	3
They are confused.....................	2
Influenced by drug culture	2
Other reasons	2
No opinion...........................	12
	138%*

*Table adds to more than 100% due to multiple responses.

Note: The mass suicides and murders in Jonestown, Guyana, was the most widely followed event of 1978, with a remarkable 98% of Americans saying they had heard or read about this tragic occurrence. Few events, in fact, in the entire forty-three-year history of the Gallup Poll have been known to such a high proportion of the United States public. Similarly high recognition factors were recorded for the attack on Pearl Harbor in 1941 and the dropping of the atomic bombs on Hiroshima and Nagasaki in 1945. Even among persons in the latest survey who have had only a grade-school education, as many as 96% say they have heard or read about the deaths in Guyana of members of the People's Temple cult, led by Jim Jones.

For weeks in the aftermath of the grim developments on November 18, historians, religious figures, psychiatrists, and others have sought for motivations and have asked the questions: "How could this have happened?" and "Could it happen again?" Amid this speculation, the Gallup Poll sought to find what Americans think are the main reasons people become involved in cults of this kind.

DECEMBER 28
PRESIDENT CARTER

Interviewing Date: 12/1–4/78
Survey #117-G

Do you approve or disapprove of the way Jimmy Carter is handling his job as president?

Approve.............................50%
Disapprove 34
No opinion...........................16

By Education
College

Approve.............................49%
Disapprove 37
No opinion...........................14

High School

Approve.............................52%
Disapprove 32
No opinion...........................16

Grade School

Approve.............................49%
Disapprove 31
No opinion...........................20

Note: The year 1978 saw President Jimmy Carter's popularity dip to a low point of 39% in August but rise to a year-high of 56% following the Camp David summit meeting in September.

His August rating came at the end of an overall eight-month decline in approval—from 57% in December 1977 to 39%, reflecting growing concern over the economy and the president's leadership abilities.

Following the summit meeting, the president's popularity rating slipped back to the 50% level, where it has remained in subsequent surveys.

In the latest measurement—taken prior to the decision to establish diplomatic relations with the People's Republic of China—50% express approval, 34% disapprove, and 16% are undecided.

DECEMBER 31
CHURCH ATTENDANCE

Interviewing Date: Five various weeks during 1978
Various Surveys

Did you, yourself, happen to attend church or synagogue in the last seven days?

	Yes
National	41%

Note: Last year's rate of attendance was also 41%. Little change has occurred in recent years, although the trend reveals an overall gradual decline in attendance since 1958 when a peak in church attendance was recorded. That year 49% attended in a typical week.

Analysis of the 1978 figures shows attendance higher among Catholics than Protestants and among women than men. Adults eighteen to twenty-nine years old are less likely to attend than those thirty and over.

Index

A

Abortion, legal
  approval of circumstances allowing, 32-33
    in last three months of pregnancy, 33-36
    under any, certain, or no circumstance, 29-32
Abzug, Bella, as most admired woman, 275
Afterlife, belief in, 185
Age, respondents categorized by
  approval of Carter's handling of Middle East situation,
    59
  approval of Carter's handling of presidency, 19, 174,
    204
    before and after Camp David summit, 259
    intensity of, 107-8, 132
  approval of legal abortion under any, certain, or no
    circumstances, 31
  approval of making birth-control devices available to
    teenagers, 38
  approval of sex education courses in schools, 37
  approval of trade unions, 52
  approval of unmarried fifteen-year-old having legal
    abortion, 34-35
  attitude toward death penalty for convicted hijackers,
    114
  attitude toward death penalty for convicted murderers,
    111
  attitude toward death penalty for convicted rapists,
    113
  attitude toward death penalty for persons convicted of
    treason, 112
  attitude toward extramarital sex, 206
  attitude toward legalization of casino gambling, 194
  alcohol ever cause of trouble in your family, 195
  belief in afterlife, 185
  belief in angels, 185
  belief in astrology, 184
  belief in clairvoyance, 185
  belief in déjà-vu, 184
  belief in devils, 185

belief in ESP, 184
belief in existence of Loch Ness monster, 183
belief in ghosts, 183
belief in humanoids living on other planets in universe,
  163-64
belief in precognition, 184
belief in Sasquatch, 184
belief in witches, 184
believe "center party" needed, 260
Carter's policies in Middle East as favoring Israel,
  Egypt, or treating both sides equally fairly, 61
Carter's record to date on national problems, 179-80
Carter's record to date rated, 24
certainty of voting in November elections, 192
choice of Republican presidential candidate
  Ford vs. Reagan, 267
cigarette smoking in past week, 80
cigarette smoking per day, 81
congressional voting in 1970 and 1978, 274
desire to move away from city, 86
Egypt doing or not doing all it should toward peace in
  Middle East, 66, 227-28
expectations for 1978 as better or worse than 1977, 2
favor or oppose "test-tube baby" procedure, 271
firemen permitted to strike, 56
heard or read about Quebec independence issue, 186
ideal number of children, 268
involvement in Charismatic movement, 77
involvement in Eastern religions, 76
Israel doing all it should or not doing all it should
  toward peace in Middle East, 63-64, 226
knowledge of recent developments in Middle East, 57,
  225
less emphasis on money wanted, 188
less emphasis on working hard wanted, 190-91
more acceptance of marijuana usage wanted, 191
more acceptance of sexual freedom wanted, 189
more emphasis on self-expression wanted, 188
more emphasis on technological improvements
  wanted, 189
more emphasis on traditional family ties wanted, 190
more respect for authority wanted, 190
participation in Bible study groups, 77
participation in inner or spiritual healing practices, 78
participation in speaking in tongues, 77
peaceful year or troubled year in international relations expected for 1978, 12
plan to vote in congressional elections, 192
policemen permitted to strike, 55
presidential trial heats
  Carter vs. Ford, 144
  Carter vs. Reagan, 147-48
presidential trial heats of registered voters
  Ford vs. Brown, 151
  Kennedy vs. Ford, 166
  Kennedy vs. Reagan, 169-70
  Reagan vs. Brown, 154-55

Quebec independence favored or opposed, 187
reading magazines too much, too little, or about right amount of leisure time, 42-43
reading newspapers too much, too little, or about right amount of leisure time, 41-42
satisfaction with life in United States today, 74
saw something you thought was UFO, 161
support for Voter Initiative Amendment, 157
sympathies more with Israel or Arab nations in Middle East situation, 100, 225
teachers permitted to strike, 57
television viewing too much, too little, or about right amount of leisure time, 41
transcendental meditation practiced, 76
trust and confidence in Carter, 21, 176-77
UFOs believed real or imaginary, 162
United States sending arms and materiel to Arab nations wanted, 103
United States sending arms and materiel to Israel wanted, 101-12
use or abstention from alcoholic beverages, 196
visited gambling casino, 195
voting behavior if your party nominated qualified atheist for president, 237
voting behavior if your party nominated qualified Catholic for president, 235-36
voting behavior if your party nominated qualified divorced man for president, 239
voting behavior if your party nominated qualified homosexual man for president, 240
voting behavior if your party nominated qualified Jew for president, 234
voting behavior if your party nominated qualified woman for president, 242
willingness to undergo "test-tube baby" procedure, 272
yoga practiced, 76
Air quality, rated in cities by size, 116, 117, 118
Aircraft carriers, of United States, amount Panama Canal used by, 46-47
Airplane hijackers, attitude toward death penalty for, 113-14
Airplanes, ban on cigarette smoking on, smokers and nonsmokers on, 82
Alcoholic beverages
  ever caused trouble in your family, 195
  nonusers of
    attitude toward other people drinking, 197
    reasons for abstaining, 196
  parents' guidelines for children's use of, 197
  use or total abstention from, 196
  users of
    consider your pattern of alcohol use good model for your children, 197
    effects on you, 197-98
    reasons for drinking, 196
    rules or guidelines regarding your own use, 197

sometimes drink more than you think you should, 197
  see also Drinking problem
Alcoholics Anonymous, as choice for help with drinking problem, 195
Ali, Muhammad, as most admired man, 1, 274
Angels, belief in, 184-85
Arab nations
  sympathies with, or more with Israel in Middle East situation, 99-101, 225-26
  want United States to send arms and materiel to, 102-13
Armed forces, want equipped with neutron bomb, 181-82
Arms
  to Arab nations, 102-3
  to Israel, 101-2
  see also Neutron bomb
Astrology, belief in, 184
Atheist, as presidential candidate of your party, voting behavior and, 236-38
Atlantic City, New Jersey, personal interest in going to gamble in, 194
Authority, more respect for wanted, 189-90

B

Baker, Howard
  as choice for Republican presidential candidate, 140, 210
  vs. Ford, 140
  vs. Reagan, 140
  heard about, 139, 140, 210
Banks and banking, confidence in, 183
Begin, Menahem
  agreement with Sadat at Camp David summit importance of Carter's role in, 232
  as most admired man, 1, 274
  rating of efforts to bring peace to Middle East, 232
Beliefs, in paranormal phenomena, 183-86
Bible study groups, participation in, 77
Big business
  as biggest threat to country in future, 252-53
  confidence in, 182
Bigfoot see Sasquatch
Birth control
  approval of availability of devices for teenagers, 38-39
    approval of sex education courses in schools related to, 38
  as part of sex education courses
    approval of sex education related to, 38
Black people
  chances in this community of getting jobs they are qualified for vs. whites, 220-22
  coming to live in great numbers in your neighborhood, decision to move or stay by white people, 215-16

coming to live next door, decision to move or stay by white people, 214-15

treatment by Carter administration, 28

treatment in this community, 219-20

as unfairly treated by Carter administration, 205

see also Race, respondents categorized by

Blue-collar workers *see* Occupation, respondents categorized by

Broadcasting industry, antismoking messages increased by, 82

Brown, Edmund, Jr.

as choice for Democratic presidential candidate, 141, 254

vs. Carter, 142

vs. Kennedy, 141-42

in presidential trial heats of registered voters

vs. Ford, 150-53

vs. Reagan, 153-56

Bryant, Anita, as most admired woman, 275

Bush, George

as choice for Republican presidential candidate in 1980, 210

heard about, 210

Business

benefiting a lot, some, or not very much from tax cuts, 79

as benefiting most from any tax cuts, 78-79

responsibility for inflation, 250-51

see also Big business

Business people *see* Occupation, respondents categorized by

C

Califano, Joseph, antismoking proposals, 83

Camp David Summit meeting

believe agreements will or will not lead to lasting peace between Israel and Egypt, 232

effect on approval and disapproval of Carter's handling of presidency, 259

importance of Carter's role in getting Sadat and Begin to come to agreement at, 232

Israel vs. Egypt as country making most concessions at, 232

opinion of Carter changed by, 232

much more favorable, somewhat more favorable, less favorable, 232

Canada

Quebec Province separating from

in favor or opposed to, 186-87

heard or read about possibility of, 186

Canadians

likelihood of Quebec independence, 187

Quebec independence favored or opposed by, 187

on United States, Soviet Union, and China as increasing or decreasing in world power, 18

Capital punishment

for convicted airplane hijackers, 113-14

for convicted murderers, 110-11

attitudes toward from 1953 to 1978, 115

for convicted rapists, 112-13

for persons convicted of treason, 111-12

reasons for opposing or supporting, 114-15

Carter, Jimmy

amount of trust and confidence in, 20-22

approval of handling of domestic policy by, 27

approval of handling of foreign policy by, 27, 212

approval of handling of inflation by, 212

approval of handling of Marston affair by, 26

approval of handling of presidency by, 19-20, 43-44, 75, 87, 128-30, 173-75, 203-5, 212, 231-32, 243, 247-48, 262, 276

average, current, high and low points, 135

better or worse economic conditions in next six months expected by, 126

compared with other presidents, 26-27, 135, 243

compared with other presidents at midterm congressional elections, 257-58

compared with presummit survey, 259

expectations for prices and income for next twelve months by, 125

expectations related to, 28

handling of coal strike by, 119

intensity of, 26, 105-17, 131-35, 175, 212

Lance affair and, 29

rating of record to date by, 25

trust and confidence related to, 22

approval of Marston firing by, 26

arms sales in Middle East, 103

characteristics rated in 1977 and 1978, 211-12

as choice for Democratic presidential candidate, 141, 209, 254

vs. Brown, 142

vs. Kennedy, 141, 200

economic policies of, 212

efforts toward peace in Middle East rated, 232

energy policies of, 213

handling of coal strike by, 118-19

handling of domestic problems by, 212

handling of Middle East situation

approval or disapproval, 58-60, 213

as too much in favor of Israel, Egypt, or treating both sides equally fairly, 60-63

handling of relations with Soviet Union, 213

handling of unemployment problem, 213

importance of role in getting Sadat and Begin to come to agreement at Camp David, 232

as most admired man, 1, 274

most important achievement to date, 44

opinion of, changed by Camp David summit meeting, 232

popularity of, compared with share in 1976 presidential election, 93

Carter, Jimmy (*continued*)
  popularity in Midwest, 96
  in presidential trial heats
    vs. Ford, 142-46, 211, 254-55
    vs. Reagan, 146-49, 211
  rating of job done to date in dealing with nation's problems, 22-25
  record to date in dealing with nation's problems, 178-81
  State of the Union Message
    expectations for taxes after, 74
  tax cuts proposed by, expected benefits from, 79-80
  treatment of minority groups by, 28
  trust and confidence in, 28-29, 175-78, 181
    approval or disapproval of handling of presidency related to, 22
    rating of record to date by, 25
Carter, Lillian, as most admired woman, 275
Carter, Rosalyn, as most admired woman, 275
Carter administration
  groups unfairly treated by, 205-6
  and wage-price controls, 89
Casino gambling
  ever participated in, 194-95
  legalized in this state
    favored or opposed, 193-94
    increased crime rate expected, 194
    increased tourism expected, 194
    involvement of organized crime expected in, 194
    standard of living improved or not by, 194
  personally interested in going to Atlantic City for, 194
  personally interested in going to Las Vegas for, 194
Catholics
  approve or disapprove interfaith marriages between Protestants and, 262
  as presidential candidate of your party
    voting behavior and, 235-36
  as unfairly treated by Carter administration, 205
  see also Religious affiliation, respondents categorized by
"Center party," needed in United States today, 259-61
Charismatic movement, involvement in, 76-77
Children
  chance of being born deformed, approval of legal abortion in case of, 33
  ideal number for family to have, 268-69
  raising, as biggest personal problem, 202
  white persons' objections to sending to schools where a few of the children are Black, 216-17
  white persons' objections to sending to school where half of the children are Black, 217
  white persons' objections to sending to school where more than half of the children are Black, 217-18
China
  increasing or declining world power expected in 1978, 16-17
  status as world power
    people of NATO nations on, 18
    vs. Soviet Union and United States, 17

Chisholm, Shirley, as most admired woman, 275
Church, Frank
  as choice for Democratic presidential candidate, 209, 254
Church attendance
  attended church or synagogue in last seven days, 276
  attitude toward extramarital sex by, 207
  as choice for help with drinking problem, 195
  confidence in, 182
Cigarette smoking
  amount per day of smokers, 80-82
  antismoking messages on television and radio wanted increased related to, 82
  any in past week, 80
  attitude toward federal tax on cigarettes by, 82
  attitude toward increased expenditures on antismoking education by, 82
  banned on airplanes
    smokers and nonsmokers on, 82
  broadcasting industry should or should not increase messages against, 82
Cities
  desire to move away from
    reasons for, 86
    by size of city, 85-86
  desire to move from neighborhoods in,
    by population size, 84
  ratings for services, institutions, and facilities provided by, 115-18
  see also Urban problems; Urban residents
City council, rated in cities by size, 116, 117
City councilmen, rated in cities by size, 116, 117
Clairvoyance, belief in, 185
Clerical workers *see* Occupation, respondents categorized by
Climate, rated in cities by size, 116, 117, 118
Coal strike, Carter's handling of, 118-19
College educated *see* Educational level, respondents categorized by
College students, tax credits for parents vs. increased student loan programs, 120-21
Community size, respondents categorized by
  approval or disapproval of Carter's handling of presidency, 130
    intensity of, 133-34
  approval of legal abortion under any, certain, or no circumstances, 32
  approval of unmarried fifteen-year-old having legal abortion, 36
  expectations for 1978 as better or worse than 1977, 4
  presidential trial heats
    Carter vs. Ford, 145-46
    Carter vs. Reagan, 149
  presidential trial heat of registered voters
    Ford vs. Brown, 153
    Kennedy vs. Ford, 167-68
    Kennedy vs. Reagan, 171
  public services more efficient if taken over by private companies, 230-31

public services taken over by private companies wanted, 230

saw something you thought was UFO, 161

smallest amount needed by family of four to get along in this community, 94

smallest amount needed by your family to get along in this community, 94

UFOs believed real or imaginary, 162-63

weekly family expenditures on food, 97

Confidence

in American institutions, 182-83

in Carter, 20-22, 175-78, 181

lack of, as biggest personal problem, 202

Confidential news sources, reporter's right to, 246-47

Congress

bills passed by, item veto power by president wanted, 269

confidence in, 182

required by constitutional amendment to balance federal budget, 198

see also Congressional elections

Congressional elections

amount of thought given to coming, 255

certainty of voting in, 192-93

hypothetical

candidate calling for reduction in number of federal employees in, voting behavior and, 251-52

choice of Democratic or Republican party as winner of, 95, 98-99, 160-61, 191-92, 202, 228-29

choices of party in, compared with actual election result, 258

leaning more toward Democrats or Republicans, 95, 191-92, 202, 228-29

leaning more toward Democrats or Republicans in South and outside South, 229

party choices in 1970 compared with 1978, by key voting groups, 273-74

plan to vote in, 192

voter participation in, 96

Congressional representatives, knowledge of name of yours, 96-97

Connally, John

as choice for Republican presidential candidate in 1980, 140, 210

heard about, 139, 140, 210

Contraception *see* Birth control

Corporation executives, as unfairly treated by Carter administration, 205

Correctional facilities, rated in cities by size, 117

Cost of living *see* Inflation; Living costs

Counseling, as choice for help with drinking problem, 195

Courts, rated in cities by size, 117

Crime

increased if casino gambling is legalized in this state, 194

as most important national problem, 89, 158, 203

as reason for moving away from city, 86

victimized by, 114

Cronkite, Walter, as most admired man, 1

Cultural opportunities of cities, rated by size of city, 116, 117, 118

D

Death, pregnancy as threat of, approval of legal abortion for, 33

Death penalty *see* Capital punishment

Déjà-vu, belief in, 184

Democracy, in United States, satisfaction with, 172

Democratic presidential candidate

choice of Carter vs. Brown for, 142

choice of Kennedy for, 142

choice of Kennedy vs. Brown, 141-42

choice of Kennedy vs. Carter, 141

choices of Democrats and independents, 141, 254

Democrats *see* Democratic presidential candidate, choice of; Political affiliation, respondents categorized by

Devils, belief in, 185

Dissatisfaction *see* Satisfaction

Divorce, increased if casino gambling is legalized in this state, 194

Divorced man, as presidential candidate of your party, voting behavior and, 238-39

Divorced people *see* Marital status, respondents categorized by

Dole, Robert

as choice for Republican presidential candidate in 1980, 140, 210

heard about, 139, 140, 210

Domestic policy, Carter's handling of, 27

Drinking problem, you or someone else in family, choice of where or to whom you would turn for help, 195-96

see also Alcoholic beverages

Drug abuse, as most important national problem, 89, 203

E

East *see* Region, respondents categorized by

Eastern religions, involvement in, 76

Economy

better or worse in next six months, 125-27, 249-50

expectations for prices and income for next twelve months by, 125

Carter's handling of, 212

controlling inflation vs. cutting taxes, 74

expectations for income and price increases and decreases, 123-25

expectations for 1978 as year of prosperity or economic difficulty, 4-11

expectations for prices rising or falling in 1978 by, 5, 6-7

expectations for taxes rising or falling in 1978 by, 8

Economy (*continued*)
expectations for prices and income for next twelve
months
better or worse economic conditions expected in
next six months by, 127
as improving, staying same, or worsening
approval or disapproval of Carter's handling of
presidency related to, 130
political party that will do better job of keeping United
States prosperous, 202
tax cuts vs. balanced budget, 74, 122-23
taxes expected, 74
wage-price control reinstatement wanted, 87-89, 121-
22
see also Prices; Taxes
Education
antismoking, increased government spending wanted
on, 82
required course on drugs and alcohol use wanted, 198
yours, as preparation for life, satisfaction with, 172
yours, as preparation for work, satisfaction with, 172
see also Public schools; Sex education; Schools
Educational level, respondents categorized by
alcohol ever cause of trouble in your family, 195
approval of Carter's handling of Middle East situation,
58
approval of Carter's handling of presidency, 43-44,
87, 104, 128-29, 204, 276
before and after Camp David summit, 259
intensity of, 106-7, 131-32
approval of making birth-control devices available to
teenagers, 38
approval of marriages between Catholics and Protestants, 262
approval of marriages between Jews and non-Jews,
263
approval of Panama Canal treaties, 48, 49
by knowledge of treaties, 50
approval of sex education courses in schools, 37
approval of trade unions, 51
attitude toward confidential news sources, 246
attitude toward death penalty for convicted hijackers,
113-14
attitude toward death penalty for convicted murderers,
111
attitude toward death penalty for convicted rapists,
112-13
attitude toward death penalty for persons convicted of
treason, 112
attitude toward extramarital sex, 206
attitude toward legalization of casino gambling, 193-
94
attitude toward tax credits for parents of college
students vs. expanded student loan programs,
120
attitude toward wage-price controls reinstatement,
122-23
belief in humanoids living on other planets in universe,
163

belief oil is produced sufficiently by United States or
imports are necessary, 136
believe "center party" needed, 259-60
better or worse economic conditions in next six months
expected, 125
Black people
on chances in this community for getting jobs they
are qualified for vs. whites, 221
on treatment of Blacks in this community, 219
Black people's chances in this community for getting
jobs they are qualified for vs. whites, 221
Carter's policies in Middle East as favoring Israel,
Egypt, or treating both sides equally fairly, 60-61
Carter's popularity compared with share of 1976 vote,
93
Carter's record to date on national problems, 178-79
China increasing or declining as world power in 1978,
16
choice of Republican presidential candidate
Ford vs. Reagan, 267
cigarette smoking in past week, 80
cigarette smoking per day, 81
congressional voting in 1970 and 1978, 273
decision of white persons to move if Blacks came to
live in great numbers in your neighborhood, 215
decision of white persons to move if Blacks came to
live next door, 214-15
desire to move away from city, 86
Egypt doing or not doing all it should toward peace in
Middle East, 65, 227, 264
expectations for 1978 as better or worse than 1977, 1-
2
expectations for 1978 as year of prosperity or economic difficulty, 4
expectations for peace in Middle East, 68, 69
expectations for prices and income for next twelve
months, 124
expectations of rising or falling prices in 1978, 6
expectations of strikes and industrial disputes or
industrial peace in 1978, 9
expectations for taxes rising or falling in 1978, 7
favor or oppose "test-tube baby" procedure, 270
firemen permitted to strike, 55
full employment or rising unemployment expected in
1978, 10
heard or read about Jonestown tragedy, 275
heard or read about Panama Canal treaties debate, 45
heard or read about Quebec independence issue, 186
ideal number of children, 268
involvement in Charismatic movement, 76
involvement in Eastern religions, 76
Israel doing or not doing all it should toward peace in
Middle East, 63, 226, 264
Israeli withdrawal from Sinai Peninsula wanted, 67
item veto power for president wanted, 269
knowledge about Palestine Liberation Organization,
70
knowledge of amount of oil imported, 137
knowledge of name of representative in Congress from

your district, 97

knowledge of Panama Canal use by United States aircraft carriers and supertankers, 46

knowledge of recent developments in Middle East, 57, 225, 263

knowledge of rights of United States to defend Panama Canal after Panama takes control, 47

knowledge of year Panama Canal will be turned over to Republic of Panama according to treaties, 45

less emphasis on money wanted, 188

less emphasis on working hard wanted, 190

marriage between whites and nonwhites approved or disapproved, 218-19

more acceptance of marijuana usage wanted, 191

more acceptance of sexual freedom wanted, 188-89

more emphasis on self-expression wanted, 188

more emphasis on traditional family ties wanted, 190

more emphasis on technological improvements wanted, 189

more respect for authority wanted, 189-90

objections of white parents to sending children to school where a few of the children are Black, 216

objections of white parents to sending children to school where half of the children are Black, 217

objections of white parents to sending children to school where more than half of the children are Black, 218

Palestine Liberation Organization considered representative of majority of Palestinians, 70

participation in Bible study groups, 77

participation in inner or spiritual healing practices, 78

participation in speaking in tongues, 77

peaceful year or troubled year in international relations expected for 1978, 12

policemen permitted to strike, 54, 223

postal workers permitted to strike, 224

preferred plan for Palestinians, 71

presidential trial heats
　　Carter vs. Ford, 143
　　Carter vs. Reagan, 147

presidential trial heats of registered voters
　　Ford vs. Brown, 150
　　Kennedy vs. Ford, 165-66
　　Kennedy vs. Reagan, 169
　　Reagan vs. Brown, 154

Quebec independence favored or opposed, 186

rationing vs. taxation on gasoline to decrease consumption preferred, 138, 139

reading magazines too much, too little, or about right amount of leisure time, 42

reading newspapers too much, too little, or about right amount of leisure time, 41

satisfaction with life in United States today, 74

saw something you thought was UFO, 161

seriousness of energy situation in United States, 135-36

Soviet Union increasing or declining as world power in 1978, 15

strikes by public employees permitted or not, 223, 224

support for Voter Initiative Amendment, 157

sympathies more with Israel or Arab nations in Middle East situation, 100, 225

teachers permitted to strike, 56, 224

television viewing too much, too little, or about right amount of leisure time, 40

transcendental meditation practiced, 76

treatment of Black people in this community, 220

trust and confidence in Carter, 176

UFOs believed real or imaginary, 162

use or abstention from alcoholic beverages, 196

United States increasing or declining as world power in 1978, 14

United States sending arms and materiel to Arab nations wanted, 102

United States sending arms and materiel to Israel wanted, 101

visited gambling casino, 195

voting behavior if your party nominated qualified atheist for president, 237

voting behavior if your party nominated qualified Catholic for president, 235

voting behavior if your party nominated qualified divorced man for president, 238

voting behavior if your party nominated qualified homosexual man for president, 250

voting behavior if your party nominated qualified Jew for president, 233-34

voting behavior if your party nominated qualified woman for president, 241

wage-price controls wanted, 88, 121, 207-8

willingness to undergo "test-tube baby" procedure, 271

willingness to vote for Black presidential candidate of your party, 214

yoga practiced, 75

Educational services, rated in cities, 116, 117, 118

Egypt
　　vs. Israel as country making most concessions at Camp David summit meeting, 232
　　see also Middle East

Eisenhower, Dwight
　　popularity after fifteen months in office, compared with Carter, 135
　　popularity prior to midterm vote for Congress, 257

Eisenhower, Mamie, as most admired woman, 275

Elections see Congressional elections; Presidential elections; Presidential trial heats; Voter Initiative Amendment

Elizabeth II, Queen, as most admired woman, 275

Employment, full, or rising unemployment expected in 1978, 10-11

Energy situation
　　Carter's handling of, 213
　　as most important achievement, 44
　　enough oil produced in United States or imports necessary, 136-37, 138-39
　　knowledge of percent of oil used in United States presently imported, 137, 138

Energy situation (*continued*)
    as most important national problem, 89, 203
    as most important political problem, 158
        political party best for handling, 90, 158-59
    rationing gasoline vs. gasoline tax preferred to reduce
        consumption of oil and gas, 137-38, 139
    seriousness of, 135-36, 138-39
        belief oil is produced sufficiently in United States or
            imports are necessary related to, 137, 138-39
Environment, rated in cities by size, 116, 117, 118
Equal Rights Amendment
    extension of time limit for states to ratify wanted, 201
    favored or opposed, 201
    heard or read about, 201
ERA *see* Equal Rights Amendment
ESP, belief in, 184
Extramarital sex, as always wrong, almost always
    wrong, wrong only sometimes, not wrong at all,
    206-7
Extraterrestrial humanoids, existence of, 163-64

F

Family (ies)
    alcohol ever been cause of trouble in, 195
    break-ups and divorce if casino gambling is legalized in
        this state, 194
    budget
        smallest amount needed to get along in this com-
            munity, 93-95
    of college students
        tax credits for, vs. expanded student loan programs,
            120-21
    labor union affiliation *see* Union affiliation, families
        categorized by
    maintaining harmony in, as biggest personal problem,
        202
    more emphasis on traditional ties wanted, 190
    size of *see* Household size
    weekly expenditures on food, 97-98
    yours, smallest amount needed to get along in this
        community, 94
    see also Family life; Family size
Family life, satisfaction with, 172
Family size
    ideal, 268-69
        percent saying four or more is ideal from 1936 to
            1978, 268
Farmers, as unfairly treated by Carter administration,
    205
Federal budget
    balanced, vs. tax cuts
        attitude toward reinstatment of wage-price controls
            by, 122
    see also Government spending
Federal employees

candidate for Congress calling for reduction in number
    of, voting behavior and, 251-52
Females *see* Sex, respondents categorized by
Fetus, stage of pregnancy when it becomes human being,
    by religion, 36
Finances
    amount of cents wasted from tax dollars to federal,
        state, and local government, 261-62
    as biggest personal problem, 201
    per capita weekly food expenditures, 1975-1978, 98
    tax credits for parents of college students vs. increased
        student loan programs, 120-21
    weekly family expenditures on food, 97-98
Firemen
    permitted or not permitted to strike, 55-56
    rated in cities by size, 116, 117, 118
Food
    per capita expenditures on, 1975-1978, 98
    weekly family expenditures on, 97-98
Ford, Betty, as most admired woman, 275
Ford, Gerald
    as choice for Republican presidential candidate in
        1980, 140, 210
        vs. Baker, 140
        vs. Reagan, 140, 200, 266-67
    heard about, 139, 210
    as most admired man, 1, 274
    popularity after fifteen months in office, compared
        with Carter, 135
    popularity prior to midterm vote for Congress, 257
    in presidential trial heats
        vs. Carter, 142-46, 211, 254-55
    in presidential trial heats of registered voters
        vs. Brown, 150-53
        vs. Kennedy, 165-68, 210
Foreign policy
    approval of Carter's handling of, 27, 212
    want arms and materiel sent to Israel, 101-2
    see also International relations
French people, on United States, Soviet Union, and
    China as increasing or decreasing in world power,
    18
Friends, as choice for help with drinking problem, 196

G

Gambling *see* Casino gambling
Garbage collection *see* Public services
Gasoline
    approval of rationing of
        seriousness of energy situation related to, 136, 139
        vs. taxing to decrease consumption, 137-38, 139
Gasoline tax, attitude toward, seriousness of energy
    situation related to, 136, 139
Gandhi, Indira, as most admired woman, 275
Ghosts, belief in, 183

Government
  big, as biggest threat to country in future, 252-53
  Carter's restoration of faith in, as his most important achievement, 44
  dissatisfaction with, as most important national problem, 89, 158, 203
  employees see Federal employees
  reinstatement of wage-price controls wanted by, 87-89
  responsibility for inflation, 250-51
  student loan program expansion vs. tax credits for parents of college students, 120-21
Government spending
  amount of cents wasted from each tax dollar, 261, 262
  balancing budget vs. cutting taxes, 74
  constitutional amendment requiring Congress to balance federal budget each year wanted, 198
  as most important national problem, 89
  political party best for reducing, 244-45
  too much, too little, or about right, 198-99
Grade-school educated see Educational level, respondents categorized by
Graham, Billy, as most admired man, 1, 274
Great Britain
  attitudes toward trade unions in, 54
  rating of United States, Soviet Union, and China as increasing or decreasing in world power in, 18
Guyana, mass suicides in see Jonestown tragedy

H

Healing see Inner or spiritual healing
Health
  as biggest personal problem, 201
  damaged by pregnancy, approval of legal abortion for, 33
  satisfaction with yours, 172
Health services, rated in cities, 116, 117, 118
High-income people
  as benefiting a lot, some, or not very much from any tax cuts, 79
  as benefiting most from any tax cuts, 78-79
High-school educated see Educational level, respondents categorized by
Highway system, rated in cities by size, 116, 117, 118
Hijackers see Airplane hijackers
Holocaust (television series)
  any programs seen, 171
  number of programs seen, 171-72
Homosexual man, as presidential candidate of your party, voting behavior and, 239-41
Hope, Bob, as most admired man, 1, 274
Hospital, as choice for help with drinking problem, 196
Household size, respondents categorized by
  per capita weekly food expenditures, 1975-1978, 98

smallest amount needed by your family to get along in this community, 94
weekly expenditures on food, 97
Housing, satisfaction with yours, 172
Human relations
  alcohol ever cause of trouble in your family, 195
  satisfaction with yours, 172
Human rights, Carter's stand on, as most important achievement, 44
Humphrey, Hubert, as most admired man, 1

I

Incest, pregnancy resulting from, approval of legal abortion for, 33
Income
  expectations for next twelve months vs. prices, 123-25
  low, high, middle, businesses, and people like yourself group believed benefiting most from tax cuts, 78-79
  smallest amount needed by family of four to get along in this community, 94
  smallest amount needed by your family to get along in this community, 94
  yours, satisfaction with, 172
Income, respondents categorized by
  approval of Carter's handling of Middle East situation, 59
  approval of Carter's handling of presidency, 104-5
    intensity of, 108-9, 132
  approval of legal abortion under any, certain, or no circumstances, 31
  approval of making birth-control devices available to teenagers, 39
  approval of sex education courses in schools, 37
  approval of trade unions, 52
  approval of unmarried fifteen-year-old having legal abortion, 35
  attitude toward tax credits for parents of college students vs. expanded student loan programs, 120
  attitude toward wage-price controls reinstatement, 123
  belief in humanoids living on other planets in universe, 164
  better or worse economic conditions in next six months expected, 126
  big business, big labor, or big government as biggest threat to country in future, 252-53
  Carter's policies in Middle East as favoring Israel, Egypt, or treating both sides equally fairly, 61-62
  Egypt doing or not doing all it should toward peace in Middle East, 66
  expectations for better or worse economic situation in next six months, 249
  expectations for 1978 as better or worse than 1977, 2-3

Income (*continued*)
expectations for 1978 as year of prosperity or economic difficulty, 5
expectations for prices and income for next twelve months, 124
expectations of rising or falling prices in 1978, 6
expectations of strikes and industrial disputes or industrial peace in 1978, 9
expectations for taxes rising or falling in 1978, 7-8
full employment or rising unemployment expected in 1978, 10-11
full employment or rising unemployment expected in 1978, 10-11
income group believed benefiting most from any tax cuts, 78-79
Israel doing or not doing all it should toward peace in Middle East, 64
knowledge of recent developments in Middle East, 58
peaceful year or troubled year in international relations expected for 1978, 13
presidential trial heats
Carter vs. Ford, 144
Carter vs. Reagan, 148
presidential trial heats of registered voters
Ford vs. Brown, 151-52
Kennedy vs. Ford, 166-67
Kennedy vs. Reagan, 170
Reagan vs. Brown, 155
responsibility of government, business, or labor for inflation, 250
smallest amount needed by family of four to get along in this community, 94
voting behavior for congressional candidate calling for reduction in number of federal employees, 251-52
wage-price controls wanted, 88, 121-22, 208
Independents
choices for Democratic and Republican presidential candidates *see* Democratic presidential candidates; Republican presidential candidates
knowledge of Republican presidential candidates, 139-40
see also Political affiliation, respondents categorized by
Industry, relations with labor *see* Labor relations
Inflation
balancing budget vs. tax cuts, 74, 122-23
Carter's handling of, 212
expectations for next twelve months for income and prices, 123-25
as most important national problem, 89, 158, 203
political party best for handling, 90, 158-59
political party best for dealing with, 245
responsibility of government, business, or labor for, 250-51
Inner or spiritual healing, participation in, 77-78
Institutions, confidence in, 182-83
Interfaith marriages

between Catholics and Protestants approved or disapproved, 262
between Jews and non-Jews approved or disapproved, 262-63
International relations
American power increasing or declining in 1978, 14-15
as Carter's most important achievement, 44
China's power increasing or decreasing in 1978, 16-17
as most important national problem, 89, 158, 203
peaceful year or international discord expected in 1978, 11-14
Americans compared with other nationalities, 13-14
Soviet power increasing or declining in 1978, 15-16
Soviet Union, United States, and China rated as world powers, 17
by Americans compared with other nationalities, 17-18
see also Middle East
Interracial marriages, between whites and nonwhites, 218-19
Israel
vs. Egypt as country making most concessions at Camp David summit meeting, 232
sympathies with or more with Arab nations in Middle East situation, 99-101, 225-26
want United States to send arms and materiel to, 101-2
withdrawal from Sinai Peninsula wanted or not wanted, 67-68
see also Middle East
Item veto power, wanted or not wanted for president, 269

J

Jackson, Henry, as choice for Democratic presidential candidate, 141, 209, 254
Jackson, Jesse, as most admired man, 1, 274
Jails *see* Correctional facilities
Jew(s)
approve or disapprove interfaith marriages between non-Jews and, 262-63
as presidential candidate of your party, voting behavior and, 233-35
as unfairly treated by Carter administration, 205
Job problems, as biggest personal problem, 201
John Paul II, Pope, as most admired man, 274
Johnson, Lyndon
popularity after fifteen months in office, compared with Carter, 135
popularity prior to midterm vote for Congress, 257
Jonestown tragedy
heard or read about, 275-76
reasons why people become involved in cults of this kind, 275
Jordan, Barbara, as most admired woman, 275

Jordan, Vernon, 28
Justice system, rated in cities by size, 117

K

Kennedy, Edward (Ted)
  as choice for Democratic presidential candidate, 141, 142, 209, 254
    vs. Brown, 141-42
    vs. Carter, 141, 200
  as most admired man, 1, 274
  in presidential trial heat of registered voters
    vs. Ford, 165-68, 210
    vs. Reagan, 168-71, 211
Kennedy, John F.
  popularity after fifteen months in office, compared with Carter, 135
  popularity prior to midterm vote for Congress, 257
Kennedy, Rose, as most admired woman, 275
King, Coretta, as most admired woman, 275
Kissinger, Henry, as most admired man, 1, 274
Knowledge
  of amount of oil imported, 137, 138
  of debate over Panama Canal treaties, 44-45
  heard or read about increase in Social Security taxes, 79
  heard or read about Jonestown tragedy, 275, 276
  heard or read about neutron bomb, 181
  heard or read about Palestine Liberation Organization, 70
  heard or read about Quebec independence issue, 186
  heard or read about "test-tube baby" procedure, 270
  heard or read about UFOs, 161
  heard of Republican presidential candidates, 139-40
  of how neutron bomb works, 181
  of name of representative in Congress from your district, 96-97
  of Panama Canal treaties
    amount of use by biggest United States aircraft carriers and supertankers, 46-47
    approval or disapproval of treaties by, 48-50
    rights of United States to defend against attacks after Panama takes control, 47-48
  of Republican presidential candidates, 210
  of recent developments in Middle East, 57-59, 99, 119, 225, 263
    approval of Carter's handling of situation by, 58-60
    expectations for peaceful settlement of differences by, 68-70
  of year Panama Canal will be turned over to Republic of Panama according to treaties, 45-46

L

Labor, responsibility for inflation, 250-51
Labor relations

expectations of strikes and industrial disputes or industrial peace in 1978, 8-10
  Americans compared with other nationalities, 11
Labor union affiliation, families categorized by
  approval of Carter's handling of presidency, 130, 175
  approval of trade unions, 53
  attitude toward wage-price control reinstatement, 122
  better or worse economic conditions in next six months expected, 126
  big business, big labor, big government as biggest threat to country in future, 253
  Carter's record to date on national problems, 180-81
  economy better or worse in next six months, 250
  firemen permitted to strike, 56, 223
  full employment or rising unemployment expected in 1978, 11
  policemen permitted to strike, 55, 223
  postal workers permitted to strike, 224
  presidential trial heats
    Carter vs. Ford, 146
    Carter vs. Reagan, 149
  presidential trial heat of registered voters
    Ford vs. Brown, 153
    Kennedy vs. Ford, 168
    Kennedy vs. Reagan, 171
    Reagan vs. Brown, 156
  responsibility of government, business, or labor, 251
  sanitation workers permitted to strike, 223
  strikes and industrial disputes or industrial peace expected, 10
  teachers permitted to strike, 57
  trust and confidence in Carter, 178
  voting behavior for congressional candidate calling for reduction in number of federal employees, 252
  wage-price controls wanted, 208
Labor unions
  approval or disapproval of, 51-54
    Americans compared with British on, 54
  big, as biggest threat to country in future, 252-53
  confidence in, 182
  members of, as unfairly treated by Carter administration, 205
  see also Union affiliation, families categorized by
Lance, Bert, controversy over, approval of Carter's handling of presidency and, 25, 29
Las Vegas, Nevada, interest in visiting to gamble in casino, 194
Laws
  abortion see Abortion
  on casino gambling see Casino gambling
  passed by Congress, item veto power by president wanted, 269
Leisure activities
  reading magazines too much, too little, or about right amount, 42-43
  reading newspapers too much, too little, or about right amount, 41-42
  religious disciplines and movements, 75-78

Leisure activities (*continued*)
  satisfaction with yours, 172
  television viewing too much, too little, or about right
    amount, 40-41
  willingness to spend time improving neighborhoods,
    84
Lewis, Jerry, as most admired man, 1
Life, satisfaction with yours, 172
Life after death *see* Afterlife
Liquor *see* Alcoholic beverages
Living costs
  smallest amount needed by family of four to get along
    in this community, 93-95
  weekly family expenditures on food, 97-98
Living standards, yours, satisfaction with, 172
Local governments
  amount of cents wasted from tax dollars to, 261, 262
  spending too much, too little, or about right amount,
    199
Loch Ness monster, belief in existence of, 183
Love life, as biggest personal problem, 202
Low-income people
  as benefiting a lot, some, or not very much from any tax
    cuts, 79
  as benefiting most from any tax cuts, 78-79

M

McGovern, George, as choice for Democratic presidential candidate in 1980, 209, 254
Magazine reading, too much, too little, or about right
  amount of leisure time, 42-43
Males *see* Sex, respondents categorized by
Manual workers *see* Occupation, respondents categorized by
Marijuana use, more acceptance of wanted, 191
Marital status, respondents categorized by
  alcohol ever cause of trouble in your family, 195
  approval of legal abortion under any, certain, or no
    circumstances, 29
  approval of unmarried fifteen-year-old having legal
    abortion, 33-34
  use or abstention from alcoholic beverages, 196
Marriage *see* Interfaith marriages; Interracial marriages
Marston, David, Carter's firing of, approval of Carter's
  handling of presidency and, 25-26
Mass media *see* Broadcasting industry; Magazines;
  Newspapers; Radio; Television
Mayor, rated in cities by size, 116, 117, 118
Meir, Golda, as most admired woman, 275
Mental health, endangered by pregnancy, approval of
  legal abortion for, 33
Middle East
  approval of Carter's handling of situation in, 58-60,
    213
  Carter's handling of situation in
    as favoring Israel, Egypt, or treating both sides
      equally fairly, 60-63

knowledge of Palestine Liberation Organization, 70
knowledge of recent developments in, 57-58, 99, 119,
  225, 263
likelihood of peace in, by knowledge of recent developments, 68-70
peace in
  attitude toward Israeli withdrawal from Sinai Pe-
    ninsula, 67-68
  Egypt doing or not doing all it should toward, 65-67,
    227-28, 264
  Israel doing or not doing all it should toward, 63-65,
    226-27, 264
  sympathies more with Israel or Arab nations, 99-101,
    225-26
talks on
  as Carter's most important achievement, 44
want United States to supply arms and materiel to
  Arab nations, 102-3
want United States to supply arms and materiel to
  Israel, 101-2
see also Camp David summit meeting; Egypt; Israel;
  Palestine Liberation Organization; Palestinians
Middle-income people
  as benefiting a lot, some, not very much from any tax
    cuts, 79
  as benefiting most from any tax cuts, 78-79
Midwest
  Carter's popularity in, 96
  choice of Republican or Democrat in hypothetical
    congressional elections, 95
  see also Region, respondents categorized by
Military aid *see* Arms
Military establishment, confidence in, 182
Minority groups, Carter's treatment of people like
  yourself, 28
Mondale, Walter
  as choice for Democratic presidential candidate, 141,
    209, 254
  as most admired man, 1, 274
Money, less emphasis wanted on, 188
Moral decline, as most important national problem, 89,
  158, 203
Most admired man, 1, 274-75
Most admired woman, 275
Moynihan, Daniel (Pat)
  as choice for Democratic presidential candidate, 209,
    254
Municipal government, rated in cities by size, 116, 117,
  118
Murderers
  capital punishment for, 110-11
  attitudes toward from 1953 to 1978, 115

N

Nader, Ralph, as most admired man, 1
Names
  of congressional representative from your district,

knowledge of, 96-97
of Republican presidential candidates, recognition of, 141
National problems
alcohol use as, 197
Carter's handling of, 22-25, 212
Carter's record to date in handling as excellent, good, fair, or poor, 178-81
most important, 89-90, 158-60, 202-3
NATO nations *see* Canada, France, Great Britain, West Germany
Neighborhood
Black people coming in large number to live in, decision to move or stay by white people, 215-16
desire to move from, 83, 84
satisfaction with yours, 172
Neutron bomb
armed forces and allies equipped with, 181-82
chief military advantage of, 181
heard or read about, 181
"Newsmen's privilege," support for, 246-47
Newspaper reading, spending too much, too little, or about right amount of leisure time on, 41-42
Newspapers, right to confidential news sources, 246-47
Nixon, Pat, as most admired woman, 275
Nixon, Richard
as most admired man, 1, 274
popularity after fifteen months in office, compared with Carter, 135
Noise level, rated in cities by size, 116, 117, 118
Non-labor force *see* Occupation, respondents categorized by
Nonwhites *see* Race, respondents categorized by

O

Occupation, respondents categorized by
approval of Carter's handling of Middle East situation, 60
approval of Carter's handling of presidency, 174-75
intensity of, 109-10, 133
approval of legal abortion under any, certain, or no circumstances, 32
approval of trade unions, 53
approval of unmarried fifteen-year-old having legal abortion, 35-36
attitude toward reinstatement of wage-price controls, 122
big business, big labor, or big government as biggest threat to country in future, 253
Carter's policies in Middle East as favoring Israel, Egypt, or treating both sides equally fairly, 62-63
Carter's popularity compared with share of 1976 vote, 93
Carter's record to date on national problems, 180
cigarette smoking in past week, 80
cigarette smoking per day, 81-82
economy better or worse in next six months by, 250

Egypt doing or not doing all it should toward peace in Middle East, 67, 228
expectations for 1978 as better or worse than 1977, 3
full employment or rising unemployment expected in 1978, 11
Israel doing or not doing all it should toward peace in Middle East, 65, 226
knowledge of recent developments in Middle East, 58, 225
presidential trial heats
Carter vs. Ford, 145
Carter vs. Reagan, 149
presidential trial heats of registered voters
Ford vs. Brown, 152
Kennedy vs. Ford, 167
Kennedy vs. Reagan, 170-71
Reagan vs. Brown, 156
responsibility of government, business, or labor for inflation, 251
smallest amount needed by family of four to get along in this community, 94
smallest amount needed by your family to get along in this community, 94
strikes and industrial disputes or industrial peace expected in 1978, 9-10
sympathies more with Israel or Arab nations in Middle East situation, 226
trust and confidence in Carter, 177
voting behavior for congressional candidate calling for reduction in number of federal employees, 252
voting behavior if your party nominated qualified atheist for president, 238
voting behavior if your party nominated qualified Catholic for president, 236
voting behavior if your party nominated qualified divorced man for president, 239
voting behavior if your party nominated qualified homosexual man for president, 241
voting behavior if your party nominated qualified Jew for president, 234-35
voting behavior if your party nominated qualified woman for president, 242
wage-price controls wanted, 88-89, 122
Oil
imports, knowledge of amount, 137, 138
production sufficient in United States, or imports required, 136-37, 138-39
Old age, as biggest personal problem, 202
Onassis, Jacqueline Kennedy, as most admired woman, 275
Organized crime, expected involvement in legalized casino gambling, 194
Organized religion, confidence in, 182

P

Palestine Liberation Organization (PLO)
heard or read about, 70

Palestine Liberation Organization (PLO) (*continued*)
preferred plan for future of Palestinians by, 71-72
as representative of point of view of majority of Palestinians, 70-71
Palestinians
Palestine Liberation Organization as representing point of view of majority of, 70-71
preferred plan for future of, 71-72, 119-20
Panama Canal
amount used by largest United States aircraft carriers and supertankers, 46-47
approval or disapproval of treaties on
by extent of knowledge on treaties, 49-50
people who had not heard or read about debate on, 48-49
people who heard or read about debate on, 48
heard or read about debate over treaties on, 44-45
knowledge of rights of United States to defend against attacks after Panama takes control, 47-48
knowledge of treaties in dispute, 44-51
knowledge of year canal will be turned over to Panama by terms of treaties
people hearing or reading about debate over treaties on, 45-46
Paranormal phenomena, belief in, 183-86
Parents
of college students, attitude toward tax credits vs. expanded student loan programs, 120
guidelines regarding use of alcoholic beverages by your children, 197
white
any objection to sending your children to school where a few of the children are Black, 216-17
any objection to sending your children to school where half of the children are Black, 217
any objection to sending your children to school where more than half of the children are Black, 217-18
Parking facilities, rated in cities by size, 116, 117, 118
Parks and playgrounds, rated in cities by size, 116, 117, 118
Paul VI, Pope, as most admired man, 1
Peace
Carter's efforts toward as his most important achievement, 44
expectations for 1978 as peaceful year or troubled year for international relations, 11-14
in Middle East
attitude toward Israeli withdrawal from Sinai Peninsula, 67-68
Egypt doing or not doing all it should toward, 65-67, 227-28, 264
Israel doing or not doing all it should toward, 63-65, 226-27, 264
likelihood of, by knowledge of recent developments, 68-70

rating of Carter's efforts to bring, 232
political party most likely to keep United States out of World War III, 202
People, most admired *see* Most admired man; Most admired woman
People like yourself
as benefiting a lot, some, or not very much from any tax cuts, 79
as benefiting most from any tax cuts, 78-79
living on other planets in universe, 163-64
as unfairly treated by Carter administration, 205
People's Temple *see* Jonestown tragedy
Personal problem
biggest in your own life, 201-2
none, 202
Physicians, as choice for help with drinking problem, 195
Planets, people like ourselves living on, 163-64
PLO *see* Palestine Liberation Organization
Police
permitted or not permitted to strike, 54-55
rated in cities, 116, 117, 118
Political affiliation, respondents categorized by
amount of cents wasted from tax dollars to federal, state, and local governments, 261-62
approval of Carter's handling of Middle East situation, 59-60
approval of Carter's handling of presidency, 20, 44, 129, 204-5
intensity of, 133
approval of trade unions, 52
approval of Panama Canal treaties, 48, 49
by knowledge of treaties, 50
attitude toward confidential news sources, 247
attitude toward death penalty for convicted hijackers, 114
attitude toward death penalty for convicted murderers, 111
attitude toward death penalty for convicted rapists, 113
attitude toward death penalty for persons convicted of treason, 112
believe "center party" needed, 260
big business, big labor, or big government as biggest threat to country in future, 253
Carter's policies in Middle East as favoring Israel, Egypt, or treating both sides equally fairly, 62
Carter's record to date on national problems, 180
Carter's record to date rated, 24
China increasing or declining as world power in 1978, 16-17
congressional voting in 1970 and 1978, 274
constitutional amendment requiring Congress to balance federal budget wanted, 198
economy better or worse in next six months by, 249-50
Egypt doing or not doing all it should toward peace in Middle East, 66-67

expectations for 1978 as better or worse than 1977, 3
expectations for peace in Middle East, 69, 70
federal government spending too much, too little or about right amount, 199
heard or read about Palestine Liberation Organization, 70
heard or read about Panama Canal treaties debate, 45
Israel doing or not doing all it should toward peace in Middle East, 64
Israeli withdrawal from Sinai Peninsula wanted, 68
item veto power for president wanted, 269
knowledge of Panama Canal use by United States aircraft carriers and supertankers, 46-47
knowledge of recent developments in Middle East, 58
knowledge about Republican presidential candidates by, 139-40
knowledge of rights of United States to defend Panama Canal after Panama takes control, 47-48
knowledge of year Panama Canal will be turned over to Republic of Panama according to treaties, 45-46
local government spending too much, too little, or about right amount, 199
Palestine Liberation Organization as representing point of view of majority of Palestinians, 71
peaceful year or troubled year in international relations expected for 1978, 13
percentage of Americans calling themselves Republicans and Conservatives, 256
political party best for dealing with inflation, 245
political party best for dealing with Soviet Union, 245
political party best for holding taxes down, 244
political party best for reducing federal spending, 244-45
preferred plan for Palestinians, 72
presidential trial heats
    Carter vs. Ford, 145
    Carter vs. Reagan, 148
presidential trial heats of registered voters
    Ford vs. Brown, 152
    Kennedy vs. Ford, 167
    Kennedy vs. Reagan, 170
    Reagan vs. Brown, 155-56
responsibility of government, business, or labor for inflation, 251
Soviet Union increasing or declining as world power in 1978, 15-16
state government spending too much, too little, or about right amount, 199
support for Voter Initiative Amendment, 157
sympathies more with Israel or Arab nations in Middle East situation, 100
trust and confidence in Carter, 21-22, 177
United States increasing or declining as world power in 1978, 14-15
United States sending arms and materiel to Arab

nations wanted, 103
United States sending arms and materiel to Israel wanted, 102
voting behavior for congressional candidate calling for reduction in number of federal employees, 252
voting behavior if your party nominated qualified atheist for president, 237
voting behavior if your party nominated qualified Catholic for president, 236
voting behavior if your party nominated qualified divorced man for president, 239
voting behavior if your party nominated qualified homosexual man for president, 240
voting behavior if your party nominated qualified Jew for president, 234
voting behavior if your party nominated a qualified woman for president, 242
wage-price controls wanted, 208
Political party
    best for dealing with inflation, 245
    best for dealing with Soviet Union, 245
    best for handling inflation, unemployment, and energy problems, 89-90
    best for handling most important national problems, 158-59, 203
    best for holding taxes down, 244
    best for keeping country prosperous, 202
    best for reducing federal spending, 199, 244-45
    best for solving problems, midwestern voters on, 96
    "center party" needed, 259-61
    Democratic vs. Republican
        in hypothetical congressional elections, 95, 98-99
    most likely to keep United States out of World War III, 202
    supported in congressional elections of 1970 and 1978, 273-74
    undecided voters leaning more toward in hypothetical congressional election, 95, 191-92, 202, 228-29
    yours
        nominating Black man for president, willingness to vote for him 214
Political views, self-ratings, 231
Politicians
    city councilmen, rated in cities by size, 116, 117
    representative in Congress from your district, knowledge of name of, 96-97
Popularity see Most admired man; Most admired woman
Postal workers, permitted to strike or not, 224
Poverty, as most important national problem, 89
Power see World powers
Precognition, belief in, 184
Pregnancy, point at which fetus becomes human being, by religion, 36
see also Abortion
Presidential candidates see Democratic presidential candidates; Republican presidential candidates

Presidential elections
  of 1976, Carter vs. Ford in, 146
  of 1976, Carter's share of vote in
    Carter's current popularity compared with, 93
  voters in, call for national referendum by *see* Voter
    Initiative Amendment
  willingness to vote for atheist candidate of your party,
    236-38
  willingness to vote for Black candidate of your party,
    214
  willingness to vote for Catholic candidate of your
    party, 235-36
  willingness to vote for divorced candidate of your
    party, 238-39
  willingness to vote for homosexual candidate of your
    party, 239-41
  willingness to vote for Jewish candidate of your party,
    233-35
  willingness to vote for woman candidate of your party,
    241-42
  see also Presidential trial heats
Presidential trial heats
  Carter vs. Ford, 142-46, 211, 254-55
  Carter vs. Reagan, 146-49, 211
  of registered voters
    Ford vs. Brown, 150-53
    Kennedy vs. Ford, 165-68, 210
    Kennedy vs. Reagan, 168-71, 211
    Reagan vs. Brown, 153-56
Presidents
  comparative popularity after fifteen months in office,
    135
  item veto power wanted for, 269
  popularity prior to midterm vote for Congress, 257-58
Price controls *see* Wage-price controls
Prices
  expectations of next twelve months vs. income, 123-
    25
  rising or falling in 1978
    Americans compared to other nationalities on, 11
    by expectations for prosperous or economically
      difficult year, 5, 6-7
Problems *see* National problems; Personal problems;
    Urban problems
Procrastination, as biggest personal problem, 202
Professionals *see* Occupation, respondents categorized
    by
Protestants, approve or disapprove interfaith marriages
    between Catholics and, 262
  see also Religious affiliation, respondents categorized
    by
Public employees *see* Strikes, permitted for public
    employees; Uniformed services
Public schools, confidence in, 182
Public services
  more efficient if taken over by private companies, 230-
    31

want taken over by private companies, 230

Q

Quebec independence
  favored or opposed, 186-87
  heard or read about, 186

R

Race, respondents categorized by
  alcohol ever cause of trouble in your family, 195
  approval of Carter's handling of Middle East situation,
    58
  approval of Carter's handling of presidency, 19, 43,
    87, 92-93, 104, 128, 173, 203-4
    before and after Camp David summit, 259
    intensity of, 105-6, 131
  approval of trade unions, 51
  approval of legal abortion under any, certain, or no
    circumstances, 30
  approval of Panama Canal treaties, 48, 49
    by knowledge of treaties, 50
  approval of unmarried fifteen-year-old having legal
    abortion, 34
  attitude toward death penalty for convicted hijackers,
    113
  attitude toward death penalty for convicted murderers,
    111
  attitude toward death penalty for convicted rapists,
    112
  attitude toward death penalty for persons convicted of
    treason, 111-12
  Black people's chances in this community for getting
    jobs they are qualified for vs. whites, 221
  Carter's popularity compared with share of 1976 vote,
    93
  Carter's policies in Middle East as favoring Israel,
    Egypt, or treating both sides equally fairly, 60
  Carter's record to date on national problems, 178
  Carter's record to date rated, 22
  Carter's treatment of Blacks, 28
  cigarette smoking in past week, 80
  cigarette smoking per day, 81
  congressional voting in 1970 and 1978, 273
  desire to move away from city, 86
  Egypt doing or not doing all it should toward peace in
    Middle East, 65
  expectations for 1978 as better or worse than 1977, 1
  expectations for 1978 as year of prosperity or eco-
    nomic difficulty, 4
  expectations of rising or falling prices in 1978, 6
  expectations of strikes and industrial disputes or
    industrial peace in 1978, 8-9
  expectations for taxes rising or falling in 1978, 7
  firemen permitted to strike, 55

full employment or rising unemployment expected in 1978, 10

heard or read about Panama Canal treaties debate, 45

Israel doing or not doing all it should toward peace in Middle East, 63

knowledge of name of representative in Congress from your district, 96-97

knowledge of Panama Canal use by United States aircraft carriers and supertankers, 46

knowledge of recent developments in Middle East, 57

knowledge of rights of United States to defend Panama Canal against attacks after Panama takes control, 47

knowledge of year Panama Canal will be turned over to Republic of Panama according to treaties, 45

marriage between whites and nonwhites approved or disapproved, 218

policemen permitted to strike, 54

political party best for solving most important national problem, 159

presidential trial heats
    Carter vs. Ford, 143
    Carter vs. Reagan, 146-47

presidential trial heat of registered voters
    Kennedy vs. Ford, 165
    Kennedy vs. Reagan, 168-69
    Reagan vs. Brown, 153-54

reading magazines too much, too little, or about right amount of leisure time, 42

reading newspapers too much, too little, or about right amount of leisure time, 41

satisfaction, 222

satisfaction with life in United States today, 74

sympathies more with Israel or Arab nations in Middle East situation, 99

teachers permitted to strike, 56

television viewing too much, too little, or about right amount of leisure time, 40

treatment of Black people in this community, 219-20

trust and confidence in Carter, 20-21, 175-76

United States sending arms and materiel to Arab nations wanted, 102

United States sending arms and materiel to Israel wanted, 101

use or abstention from alcoholic beverages, 196

voting behavior if your party nominated qualified atheist for president, 236-37

voting behavior if your party nominated qualified Catholic for president, 235

voting behavior if your party nominated qualified divorced man for president, 238

voting behavior if your party nominated qualified homosexual man for president, 239-40

voting behavior if your party nominated qualified Jew for president, 233

voting behavior if your party nominated qualified woman for president, 241

Race relations
    any objection to sending your children to school where a few of the children are Black, 216-17
    any objection to sending your children to school where half of the children are Black, 217
    any objection to sending your children to school where more than half of the children are Black, 217-18
    approve or disapprove of marriage between whites and nonwhites, 218-19
    Black people on treatment of Blacks in this community, 219-20
    chances of Black people in your community getting jobs for which they are qualified vs. whites, 220-22
    decision by whites to stay or move if Blacks came to live in large numbers in your neighborhood, 215-16
    decision by whites to stay or move if Blacks came to live next door, 214-15
    as most important national problem, 89, 203
    willingness to vote for well-qualified Black man for president, 214

Radio, antismoking messages on, increase wanted in number of, 82

Rape
    death penalty for, 112-13
    pregnancy as result of, approval of legal abortion for, 33

Reading
    magazines
        too much, too little, or about right amount of leisure time, 42-43
    newspapers
        amount of time spent on, 41-42
    see also Knowledge

Reagan, Ronald
    as choice for Republican presidential candidate in 1980, 140, 210
        vs. Baker, 140
        vs. Ford, 140, 200, 266-67
    heard about, 139, 210
    as most admired man, 1, 274
    in presidential trial heats, vs. Carter, 146-49, 211
    in presidential trial heats of registered voters
        vs. Brown, 153-56
        vs. Kennedy, 168-71, 211

Recreation see Leisure activities

Recreational facilities, rated in cities by size, 116, 117, 118

Referendums, states authorizing, 158
    see also Voter Initiative Amendment

Region, respondents categorized by
    alcohol ever cause of trouble in your family, 195
    approval of Carter's handling of Middle East situation, 58-59
    approval of Carter's handling of presidency, 19, 44, 75, 87, 103-4, 129, 173-74, 204

Region (*continued*)
    before and after Camp David summit, 259
    intensity of, 107
    approval of legal abortion under any, certain, or no circumstances, 30-31
    approval of unmarried fifteen-year-old having legal abortion, 34
    attitude toward confidential news sources, 246-47
    attitude toward wage-price controls reinstated, 123
    belief in humanoids living on other planets in universe, 163
    belief oil is produced sufficiently in United States or imports are necessary, 136-37
    believe "center party" needed, 260
    better or worse economic conditions in next six months expected, 125-26
    Black people
        on chances in this community for getting jobs they are qualified for vs. whites, 221
        on treatment of Blacks in this community, 220
    Black people's chances in this community for getting jobs they are qualified for vs. whites, 221-22
    Carter's handling of coal strike by, 118-19
    Carter's policies in Middle East as favoring Israel, Egypt, or treating both sides equally fairly, 61
    Carter's popularity compared with share of 1976 vote, 93
    Carter's record to date on national problems, 179
    Carter's record to date rated, 23-24
    China increasing or declining as world power in 1978, 16
    choice of Republican presidential candidate
        Ford vs. Reagan, 267
    choice of winning party in hypothetical congressional elections, 98-99
    decision of white persons to move if Blacks came to live in great numbers in neighborhood, 215-16
    decision of white persons to move if Blacks came to live next door, 215
    desire to move away from city, 86
    Egypt doing or not doing all it should toward peace in Middle East, 65-66, 227
    expectations for 1978 as better or worse than 1977, 2
    expectations for peace in Middle East by, 68, 69
    expectations for prices and income for next twelve months, 124
    favor or oppose "test-tube baby" procedure, 270
    firemen permitted to strike, 55-56
    heard or read about Palestine Liberation Organization, 70
    heard or read about Quebec independence issue, 186
    involvement in Charismatic Movement, 77
    involvement in Eastern religions, 76
    Israel doing or not doing all it should toward peace in Middle East, 63, 226
    Israeli withdrawal from Sinai Peninsula wanted, 67-68
    knowledge of name of representative in Congress from your district, 97

knowledge of recent developments in Middle East, 57, 225
leaning more toward Republican or Democratic party in hypothetical congressional elections, 229
marriage between whites and nonwhites approved or disapproved, 219
objections of white parents to sending children to school where a few of the children are Black, 216-17
objections of white parents to sending children to school where more than half of the children are Black, 217-18
Palestine Liberation Organization as representing point of view of majority of Palestinians, 70-71
participation in Bible study groups, 77
participation in inner or spiritual healing practices, 78
participation in speaking in tongues, 77
peaceful year or troubled year in international relations expected for 1978, 12
policemen permitted to strike, 54-55
political party best for solving most important national problem, 159
preferred plan for Palestinians, 71-72
presidential trial heats
    Carter vs. Ford, 143-44
    Carter vs. Reagan, 147
presidential trial heats of registered voters
    Ford vs. Brown, 151
    Kennedy vs. Ford, 166
    Kennedy vs. Reagan, 169
    Reagan vs. Brown, 154
Quebec independence favored or opposed, 187
saw something you thought was UFO, 161
seriousness of energy situation in United States, 136
smallest amount needed by family of four to get along in this community, 94
smallest amount needed by your family to get along in this community, 94
Soviet Union increasing or declining as world power in 1978, 15
support for Voter Initiative Amendment, 157
sympathies more with Israel or Arab nations in Middle East situation, 100, 225
teachers permitted to strike, 56-57
transcendental meditation practiced, 76
treatment of Black people in this community, 220
trust and confidence in Carter, 21, 176
UFOs believed real or imaginary, 162
United States increasing or declining as world power in 1978, 14
United States sending arms and materiel to Arab nations wanted, 102-3
United States sending arms and materiel to Israel wanted, 101
use or abstention from alcoholic beverages, 196
voting behavior if your party nominated qualified atheist for president, 237
voting behavior if your party nominated qualified Catholic for president, 235

voting behavior if your party nominated qualified divorced man for president, 238

voting behavior if your party nominated qualified homosexual man for president, 240

voting behavior if your party nominated qualified Jew for president, 234

voting behavior if your party nominated qualified woman for president, 241

wage-price controls wanted, 88, 121, 208

weekly family expenditures on food, 97

willingness to undergo "test-tube baby" procedure, 271

willingness to vote for Black presidential candidate of your party, 214

yoga practiced, 75

Registered voters

midwestern

most important issues for, 96

presidential trial heats

Ford vs. Brown, 150-53

Kennedy vs. Ford, 165-68

Kennedy vs. Reagan, 168-71

Reagan vs. Brown, 153-56

self-rating of political views by, 231

Relative, as choice for help with drinking problem, 195

Religion

attended church or synagogue in last seven days, 276

as choice for help with drinking problem, 195

organized see Organized religion

transcendental meditation practiced, 76

see also Church; Religious affiliation, respondents categorized by

Religious affiliation, respondents categorized by

approval of Carter's handling of Middle East situation, 60

approval of Carter's handling of presidency, 20, 44, 105, 130, 174, 205

intensity of, 133

approval of legal abortion under any, certain, or no circumstances, 32

approval of making birth-control devices available to teenagers, 39

approval of marriages between Catholics and Protestants, 262

approval of marriages between Jews and non-Jews, 263

approval of sex education courses in schools, 38

approval of trade unions, 53

approval of unmarried fifteen-year-old having legal abortion, 35

attitude toward extramarital sex, 207

attitude toward legalization of casino gambling, 194

belief in humanoids living on other planets in universe, 164

Carter's record to date on national problems, 180

Carter's record to date rated, 24

Carter's policies in Middle East as favoring Israel, Egypt, or treating both sides equally fairly, 62

congressional voting in 1970 and 1978, 274

Egypt doing or not doing all it should toward peace in Middle East, 67

expectations for 1978 as better or worse than 1977, 3

expectations for peace in Middle East by, 69, 70

favor or oppose "test-tube baby" procedure, 271

heard or read about Palestine Liberation Organization, 70

ideal number of children, 268

involved in Charismatic movement, 77

involved in Eastern religions, 76

Israel doing or not doing all it should toward peace in Middle East, 64

Israeli withdrawal from Sinai Peninsula wanted, 68

knowledge of recent developments in Middle East, 58

Palestine Liberation Organization as representing point of view of majority of Palestinians, 71

participation in Bible study groups, 77

participation in inner or spiritual healing practices, 78

participation in speaking in tongues, 77

preferred plan for Palestinians, 72

presidential trial heats

Carter vs. Ford, 145

Carter vs. Reagan, 148-49

Kennedy vs. Ford, 167

Kennedy vs. Reagan, 170

Reagan vs. Brown, 156

stage of pregnancy when fetus becomes human being, 36

sympathies more with Israel or Arab nations in Middle East situation, 100-1

trust and confidence in Carter, 22

United States sending arms and materiel to Arab nations wanted, 103

United States sending arms and materiel to Israel wanted, 102

voting behavior if your party nominated qualified atheist for president, 237

voting behavior if your party nominated qualified Catholic for president, 236

voting behavior if your party nominated qualified divorced man for president, 239

voting behavior if your party nominated qualified homosexual man for president, 240

voting behavior if your party nominated qualified Jew for president, 234

voting behavior if your party nominated qualified woman for president, 242

willingness to undergo "test-tube baby" procedure, 272

yoga practiced, 76

Religious disciplines and movements, involvement in, 75-78

Relocation, desired by city residents, 85-86

Reproduction see "Test-tube baby" procedure

Republic of Panama see Panama Canal

Republican party

presidential candidates

heard about, 210

see also Political affiliation, respondents categorized

Republican party (*continued*)
  by; Republican presidential candidates
Republican presidential candidates
  choice of Ford vs. Reagan, 140, 200, 266-67
  choice of Ford vs. Baker, 140
  choice of Reagan vs. Baker, 140
  choices for 1980, 140
  heard about, 139-40
  name recognition, 141
Republicans
  knowledge of Republican presidential candidates, 139
  see also Political affiliation, respondents categorized
    by
Respect for authority, more wanted, 189-90
Retirement, as biggest personal problem, 202
Richardson, Elliot
  as choice for Republican presidential candidate in
    1980, 140, 210
  heard about, 139, 140, 210
Roosevelt, Franklin D., popularity prior to midterm
    votes for Congress, 258
Roberts, Oral, as most admired man, 1
Rockefeller, Nelson, as most admired man, 1
Rural residents *see* Community size, respondents cate-
    gorized by

S

Sadat, Anwar
  agreement with Begin at Camp David summit
    importance of Carter's role in, 232
  as most admired man, 1, 274
  rating of efforts to bring peace to Middle East, 232
Salespeople *see* Occupation, respondents categorized by
Sanitation workers, permitted to strike or not, 223
Sanitation services, rated in cities by size, 116, 117, 118
Sasquatch, belief in, 183-84
Satisfaction
  with life in nation today, 73-74
    Blacks vs. whites, 222
  ratings for, 172
    Americans compared with other nationalities, 172
Schools
  approval of courses on sex education in, 37-38
  where a few of the children are Black
    white parents' objections to sending children to,
      216-17
  where half of the children are Black
    white parents' objections to sending children to, 217
  where more than half of the children are Black
    white parents' objections to sending children to,
      217-18
Self-expression, more emphasis wanted on, 188
Senior citizens, as unfairly treated by Carter admin-
    istration, 205
Separated people *see* Marital status, respondents cate-
    gorized by

Sevareid, Eric, as most admired man, 1
Sex, respondents categorized by
  alcohol ever cause of trouble in your family, 195
  approval of Carter's handling of Middle East situation,
    58
  approval of Carter's handling of presidency, 128, 173,
    203
    before and after Camp David summit, 259
    intensity of, 105, 131
  approval of legal abortion under any, certain, or no
    circumstances, 29
  approval of marriages between Catholics and Prot-
    estants, 262
  approval of marriages between Jews and non-Jews,
    262-63
  approval of Panama Canal treaties, 48, 49
    by knowledge of treaties, 49
  approval of trade unions, 51
  approval of unmarried fifteen-year-old having legal
    abortion, 33
  attitude toward death penalty, 114
  attitude toward death penalty for convicted hijackers,
    113
  attitude toward death penalty for convicted murderers,
    110-11
  attitude toward death penalty for convicted rapists,
    112
  attitude toward death penalty for persons convicted of
    treason, 111
  attitude toward extramarital sex, 206
  belief in afterlife, 185
  belief in angels, 184
  belief in astrology, 184
  belief in clairvoyance, 185
  belief in déjà-vu, 184
  belief in devils, 185
  belief in ESP, 184
  belief in existence of Loch Ness monster, 183
  belief in ghosts, 183
  belief in humanoids living on other planets in universe,
    163
  belief in precognition, 184
  belief in Sasquatch, 183
  belief in witches, 184
  believe "center party" needed, 259
  Black males and females
    treatment of Black people in this community, 219-
      20
  Black people
    on chances in this community for getting jobs they
      are qualified for vs. whites, 221
  Carter's policies in Middle East as favoring Israel,
    Egypt, or treating both sides equally fairly, 60
  Carter's record to date on national problems, 178
  choice of Republican presidential candidate
    Ford vs. Reagan, 266
  cigarette smoking in past week by, 80
  cigarette smoking per day, 80-81
  congressional voting in 1970 and 1978, 273

Eastern religions practiced, 76

Egypt doing or not doing all it should toward peace in Middle East, 65

expectations for 1978 as better or worse than 1977, 1

extension of time limit wanted for ratification of Equal Rights Amendment, 201

favor or oppose Equal Rights Amendment, 201

favor or oppose "test-tube baby" procedure, 270

heard or read about Panama Canal treaties debate, 45

heard or read about Quebec independence issue, 186

ideal number of children, 268

involved in Charismatic movement, 76

marriage between whites and nonwhites approved or disapproved, 218

Israel doing or not doing all it should toward peace in Middle East, 63

knowledge of name of representative in Congress from your district, 96

knowledge of Panama Canal use by United States aircraft carriers and supertankers, 46

knowledge of recent developments in Middle East by, 57

knowledge of rights of United States to defend Panama Canal against attacks after Panama takes control, 47

knowledge of year Panama Canal will be turned over to Republic of Panama according to treaties, 45

participation in Bible study groups, 77

participation in inner or spiritual healing practices, 77

participation in speaking in tongues, 77

peaceful year or troubled year in international relations expected for 1978, 12

presidential trial heats
    Carter vs. Reagan, 146
    Carter vs. Ford, 143

presidential trial heats of registered voters
    Ford vs. Brown, 150-53
    Kennedy vs. Ford, 165
    Kennedy vs. Reagan, 168
    Reagan vs. Brown, 153

Quebec independence favored or opposed, 186

reading magazines too much, too little, or about right amount of leisure time, 42

reading newspapers too much, too little, or about right amount of leisure time, 41

satisfaction with life in United States today, 74

saw something you thought was UFO, 161

sympathies more with Israel or Arab nations in Middle East situation, 99

television viewing too much, too little, or about right amount of leisure time, 40

transcendental meditation practiced, 76

trust and confidence in Carter, 175

UFOs believed real or imaginary, 162

United States supplying arms and materiel to Arab nations wanted, 102

United States supplying arms and materiel to Israel wanted, 101

use or abstention from alcoholic beverages, 196

voting behavior if your party nominated qualified atheist for president, 236

voting behavior if your party nominated qualified Catholic for president, 235

voting behavior if your party nominated qualified divorced man for president, 238

voting behavior if your party nominated qualified homosexual man for president, 239

voting behavior if your party nominated qualified Jew for president, 233

voting behavior if your party nominated qualified woman for president, 241

wage-price controls wanted, 207

willingness to undergo "test-tube baby" procedure, 271

yoga practiced, 75

Sex education
  approval of schools giving courses in, 37-38
    approval of making birth-control devices available to teenagers related to, 39
    birth-control information as part of, 38

Sexual freedom, more acceptance wanted of, 188-89

Sexual relations
  attitude toward birth-control devices made available for teenagers, 38-39
  extramarital, attitudes toward, 206-7

Small business, as unfairly treated by Carter administration, 205

Shipping, amount Panama Canal used by United States aircraft carriers and supertankers, 46-47

Sinai Peninsula, Israeli withdrawal wanted or not wanted from, 67-68

Single people see Marital status, respondents categorized by

Size of household see Household size, respondents categorized by

Skilled workers see Occupation, respondents categorized by

Smoking see Cigarette smoking

Social changes, in future, welcome and unwelcome, 187-91

Social class see Business; High-income people; Low-income people; Middle-income people

Social Security taxes
  increase in
    heard or read about, 79
    proposed tax cut as more or less than or same as increase, 79-80

South see Region, respondents categorized by

Southern Democrats
  choice of Democratic presidential candidate by, 254
  see also Political affiliation, respondents categorized by

Soviet Union
  Carter's handling of relations with, 213
  increasing or declining world power expected in 1978, 15-16
  political party best for dealing with, 245
  status as world power

Soviet Union (*continued*)
    vs. China and United States, 17
    people of NATO nations on, 18
Speaking in tongues, participation in, 77
Spiritual healing *see* Inner or spiritual healing
Standard of living, improved by legalization of casino
    gambling in this state, 194
State government
    amount of cents wasted from tax dollars to, 261, 262
    spending too much money, too little, or about right
        amount, 199
Street cleaning *see* Public services
Strikes
    expected in 1978, 8-10
    permitted by public employees
        firemen, 55-56, 223
        policemen, 54-55, 223-24
        postal workers, 224
        sanitation workers, 223
        teachers, 56-57, 223-24
    see also Coal strike
Students *see* College students
Suburbs, desire to move away from, 84, 85-86
Supreme Court, confidence in, 183

T

Tax cuts
    vs. balancing federal budget, 74
    income groups benefiting most from, 78-79
    as more, less, or about same amount as Social Security
        tax increase, 79-80
Taxes
    on cigarettes, attitudes of smokers and nonsmokers
        toward increases in, 82
    credits for parents of college students vs. expansion of
        student loan programs, 120-21
    expected increases in, before and after Carter's State
        of the Union message, 74
    political party best for holding down, 244
    rising or falling in 1978, 7-8
        Americans compared with other nationalities, 11
    see also Social Security taxes; Tax cuts
Teachers, permitted or not permitted to strike, 56-57
Technological advancements, more emphasis wanted
    on, 189
Teenagers, approval of birth-control devices made
    available to, 38-39
Television
    antismoking messages on
        increase wanted in number of, 82
    confidence in, 183
    Holocaust series on
        any programs seen, 171
        number of programs seen, 171-72
    spending too much, too little, or about right amount of
        leisure time on, 40-41

"Test-tube baby" procedure
    favored or opposed, 270-71
    heard or read about, 270
    understanding of method used, 270
    willingness to undergo, 271-72
Thompson, James
    as choice for Republican presidential candidate in
        1980, 210
    heard about, 210
Time *see* Leisure activities
Tourism, increased by casino gambling legalized in this
    state, 194
Trade unions *see* Labor unions
Traffic, rated in cities by size, 116, 117, 118
Transcendental meditation, practiced, 76
Transportation, rated in cities by size, 116, 117, 118
Treason, death penalty for, 111-12
Treaties, on Panama Canal *see* Panama Canal
Truman, Harry, popularity prior to midterm votes for
    Congress, 257
Trust *see* Confidence

U

Udall, Morris
    as choice for Democratic presidential candidate, 141,
        209, 254
UFOs
    believe real or imaginary, 161-63
    ever seen anything you though was a UFO, 161
    heard or read about, 161
    people who saw something they thought was
        belief in humanoids living on other planets in uni-
            verse by, 164
        believed real or imaginary, 163
Unemployed, as unfairly treated by Carter adminis-
    tration, 205
Unemployment
    as biggest personal problem, 201
    Carter's handling of, 213
    expected increase in 1978 in, 10-11
    as most important national problem, 89, 158, 203
        political party best for handling, 90, 158-59
    reduction of, as Carter's most important achievement,
        44
    rising or falling in 1978
        Americans compared with other nationalities, 11
Uniformed services
    ratings of opinions on, 116, 117, 118
    see also Firemen; Postal workers; Sanitation workers;
        Policemen
Unions *see* Labor unions
United States
    amount Panama Canal used by biggest aircraft car-
        riers and supertankers of, 46-47
    approval or disapproval of equipping armed forces and
        allies with neutron bomb, 181-82

biggest threat in future as big business, big labor, or big government, 252-53

as increasing or declining world power in 1978, 14-15

institutions, confidence in, 182-83

as place to live, satisfaction with, 172

right to defend Panama Canal after Panama takes control, 47-48

satisfaction or dissatisfaction with life in, 73-74

satisfaction with way democracy is working in, 172

should or should not send arms to Arab nations, 102-3

should or should not send arms to Israel, 102-3

status as world power

vs. China and Soviet Union, 17

people of NATO nations on, 18

United States Constitution, amendments to

Equal Rights Amendment

extension of time limit for states to ratify wanted, 201

favor or oppose by sex, 201

heard or read about, 201

requiring Congress to balance federal budget, 198

Voter Initiative Amendment, support for, 157-58

United States Department of Health, Education, and Welfare, expenditures on antismoking education, increases in, 82, 83

Unskilled workers see Occupation, respondents categorized by

Urban problems

committees to study and make recommendations on

choice of those willing to serve on without pay, 264-66

Urban residents, willingness to spend time improving neighborhood, 84-85

V

Values, changes in, welcome and unwelcome, 187-91

Veto power see Item veto power

Voluntary organizations

membership in, 191

to study local urban problems

choice of those willing to serve on without pay, 264-66

willingness to serve without pay, 264-66

Voter Initiative Amendment, in favor or opposed to, 157-58

Voter participation, in off-year elections, 96

see also Voting behavior

Voters see Registered voters; Voting behavior

Voting behavior

certainty of voting in November elections, 192-93

if congressional candidate calls for reduction in number of federal employees, 251-52

in congressional elections, 1970 compared with 1978, 273-74

if your party nominated a qualified atheist for president, 236-38

if your party nominated a qualified Catholic for president, 235-36

if your party nominated a qualified divorced man for president, 238-39

if your party nominated a qualified homosexual man for president, 239-41

if your party nominated a qualified Jew for president, 233-35

if your party nominated a qualified woman for president, 241-42

plan to vote in elections this November, 192

willingness to vote for Black presidential candidate of your party, 214

W

Wage-price controls

approval of

better or worse economic conditions in next six months expected by, 126-27

reinstatement wanted, 87-89, 121-22, 207-9

by expectations for prices and income for next twelve months, 125

Walters, Barbara, as most admired woman, 275

Wayne, John, as most admired man, 1, 274

Weapons see Arms; Neutron bomb

Welfare recipients, as unfairly treated by Carter administration, 205

West see Region, respondents categorized by

West Germans, on United States, Soviet Union, and China as increasing or decreasing in world power, 18

White-collar workers see Occupation, respondents categorized by

White people

any children now in grade school or high school, 216

decision to move or stay if Black people came in large numbers to your neighborhood, 215-16

decision to move or stay if Black people came to live next door, 214-15

see also Race, respondents categorized by

Widowed people see Marital status, respondents categorized by

Witches, belief in, 184

Woman (women)

nominated for president by your party, voting behavior and, 241-42

as unfairly treated by Carter administration, 205

see also Sex, respondents categorized by

Work, less emphasis on wanted, 190

Workers see Occupation, respondents categorized by

World powers

ratings for United States, Soviet Union, and China as, 17

Americans compared with other nationalities, 17-18

status of China as, in 1978, 16-17

World powers (*continued*)
    status of Soviet Union as, in 1978, 15-16
    status of United States as, in 1978, 14-15

XYZ

Yoga, practice, 75-76
Young, Andrew, as most admired man, 1, 274